A Southern Boy in Blue

A Southern Boy in Blue

The Memoir of
MARCUS WOODCOCK
9th Kentucky Infantry
(U.S.A.)

Edited by
Kenneth W. Noe

Voices of the Civil War
Frank L. Byrne, Series Editor

THE UNIVERSITY OF TENNESSEE PRESS
KNOXVILLE

The Voices of the Civil War series makes available a variety of primary source materials that illuminate issues on the battlefield, the homefront, and the western front, as well as other apsects of this historic era. The series contextualizes the personal accounts within the framework of the latest scholarship and expands established knowledge by offering new perspectives, new materials, and new voices.

Library of Congress Cataloging-in-Publication Data

Woodcock, Marcus, b. 1842.
    A southern boy in blue : the memoir of Marcus Woodcock, 9th Kentucky Infantry (U.S.A.) / edited by Kenneth W. Noe. — 1st ed.
        p.   cm. — (Voices of the Civil War series)
    Includes bibliographical references and index.
    ISBN 0-87049-921-1 (cloth : alk. paper)
    1. Woodcock, Marcus, b. 1842. 2. United States. Army. Kentucky Infantry Regiment, 9th (1861–1864) 3. United States—History—Civil War, 1861–1865—Personal narratives. 4. Tennessee—History—Civil War, 1861–1865. 5. Soldiers—Tennessee—Biography. I. Noe, Kenneth W., 1957–   . II. Title. III. Series.
E509.5 9th.W66 1996
973.7'469—dc20   95-32485
                                                  CIP

Contents

Illustrations

Figures

Map

Foreword

In its second year, the Voices of the Civil War Series again offers the words of witnesses on both sides in the national epic. As its title suggests, *A Southern Boy in Blue* contains the reminiscences of a Middle Tennessee Unionist, William Marcus Woodcock, who fought in the 9th Kentucky Infantry (U.S.A.). He was an inhabitant of a district where divisions among neighbors over national issues made civil war so immediate that he sometimes was afraid to visit home because of the risk of guerrilla attack. A strength of Woodcock's narrative is its revelation of how the war moved him away from a conservative position on social change. Apparently to his surprise, he found that, in arguing with comrades over the use of black soldiers and the re-election of Abraham Lincoln, he came to favor both these measures. Indeed, he converted himself to Radical Republicanism.

As Kenneth W. Noe, who has skillfully edited the Woodcock manuscript, indicates, it is based firmly on contemporary diaries. Thus it conveys a good sense of the confused first rallying of troops which drew Woodcock into the military. Beginning as an enlisted man, he soon became an effective officer. Despite his limited education, he wrote well about his experiences. While telling his own story, he presents a credible history of the service of his regiment. Especially useful are his descriptions of its involvement in the battles of Perryville and Murfreesboro. In the latter battle, his unit fought mainly other Tennesseans and Kentuckians. His truly excellent account of Chickamauga conveys vividly a sense of the confusion of that finally indecisive episode of butchery. While his treatment of the battles of Chattanooga is limited because sickness kept Woodcock in the rear, it nonetheless is mostly accurate. More informative is his treatment of the regiment's share in the expedition to Knoxville, with his thoughts on Unionism in that vicinity. While the battle pieces are rich in both facts and spirit, so too are the accounts of everyday army life.

Many readers are likely to be especially attracted to (and occasionally shocked by) Woodcock's observations about wartime civilian life in Tennessee. Although he viewed with an unromantic eye some of the families with whom he came in contact, he recognized that the civilians' situations often were made grimmer by the soldiers' depredations. Especially instructive are the specific examples that he gives of the extreme hardships of wartime travel.

While Woodcock's account is valuable on its own, readers might find it helpful to compare his version of the fighting in Tennessee with that of the Confederate Robert T. Coles in the companion volume of this series.

Frank L. Byrne
Kent State University

Acknowledgments

During the two-plus years I spent in the company of Marcus Woodcock, I ran up enormous intellectual debts. Many people played a role in getting this memoir into print. For them, it was a labor of love— one of many years' duration. In contrast, I sometimes have felt like Woodcock's adjutant, John Shepherd, the "newcomer" who showed up out of nowhere to assume the rank that others believed they deserved. The big difference is that Shepherd had a hard time winning the regiment's trust, while all, from the outset, greeted my participation with support and good cheer.

I especially want to thank Woodcock's descendants, who worked tirelessly to see this manuscript published. All deserve gratitude, but particularly I want to thank his grandchildren, Mary Elizabeth Cain, Martha Teschan, Clarence C. Woodcock, Jr., and Wilson W. Woodcock, Jr.; his grandniece, Betty Margaret Thomas; and his great-grandsons, Ed Arning, Bill Woodcock, and John Woodcock. All of them enthusiastically shared their time, memories, and effort, not to mention the wealth of material their ancestor left behind. Biographers usually grow to like or dislike their subject; it was impossible not to become attached to Woodcock, given the splendid qualities characteristic of the members of his family.

Two other people deserve special thanks. In 1989, Leslie and Helen Holland discovered a photocopy of the original manuscript that Ed Arning recently had deposited at the Stone's River National Battlefield Park. Leslie Holland is a descendant of both the 9th Kentucky's James P. Durham and John M. Holland. Bravely, the

Hollands volunteered to take on the onerous task of transcribing. They labored relentlessly for several months, Leslie carefully deciphering Woodcock's tight and increasingly small handwriting while Helen, a retired legal secretary, typed away. The result, which I term the Holland Typescript, quickly became the major source for those interested in the 9th Kentucky. Without the Hollands' labor and Helen's disks, graciously given to me without question, this project would have taken months longer to complete.

As time passed, the circle of Marcus Woodcock's modern "friends" grew even wider. Doug Cubbison, a fine Civil War writer, gave the Holland Typescript a preliminary reading and made several useful editorial suggestions, most of which I have incorporated here. Randy East, like Woodcock a native of Macon County, Tennessee, made available to me his collection of 9th Kentucky Infantry photographs. Geoff Michael, historian of the modern 9th Kentucky Volunteer Infantry living history unit (a group founded on the basis of the Holland Typescript, thanks to Bill and Ada Woodcock) also could not have been more supportive. The results of his extensive research, published in the unit's newsletter, the *Journal Junior*, have been most helpful, as the notes here indicate. Finally, Albert Castel and Stuart Seely Sprague laid aside their own work to review some of my editing, correct errors, and make good suggestions.

Several archivists and librarians have been helpful in uncovering information on the 9th Kentucky. I particularly want to thank Walter Bowman, formerly of the Kentucky Department of Military Affairs; Marie Concannon of the Missouri State Historical Society; Patricia M. Hodges of the Kentucky Library, Western Kentucky University; and Jim Prichard of the Kentucky Department for Libraries and Archives.

At West Georgia College, my colleague Ben Kennedy helped provide the assistance of three excellent graduate assistants, Vicki Anderson, Teresa Leslie, and especially Michael Fitch, who helped in matching some of the original manuscript to the Holland Typescript. Vedat Gunay translated the Hollands' disks into a format my computer could read. At the Ingram Library, Nancy Farmer cheerfully acquired many items through Interlibrary Loan, while Joanne Artz and John McPhearson granted me special *Official Records* privileges. Tom Beggs supplied photographs of several of the older portraits that grace this volume.

At the University of Tennessee Press, Meredith Morris-Babb took an early interest in this manuscript and, much to my delight, persuaded me that I really did want to take on another project. Jennifer M. Siler, taking over the series in midstream, provided constant support. Frank Byrne's comments, as well as those of an anonymous reader, were helpful indeed.

Finally, I must thank my family. My son Jesse walked several battlefields with me, often helpfully dramatizing the Federals in mid-charge. At other times, he let me bang away on the computer when I know he would have preferred that I play with him. He is a good son for a historian to have. Meanwhile, my wife Nancy has put up with the same battlefield campaigns, my occasional solo forays into Tennessee, and innumerable mealtime references to Marcus Woodcock and the 9th Kentucky. As the northern-born daughter of Missouri German Unionists, she has taken perhaps a little too much pleasure in watching her Virginia-born husband approach the war from what she calls "the right side." Nonetheless, it is to Nancy and Jesse that I dedicate my small contribution.

Editor's Introduction

While the American Civil War popularly has been depicted as a conflict between "North and South," in fact the situation was much more complex. To be sure, every student of the war knows that a few of the leading personalities of the conflict—generals such as Josiah Gorgas, Bushrod Johnson, John C. Pemberton, and George H. Thomas—fought against the sections of their birth. Such complications extended even to the White House, as Mary Todd Lincoln's brother-in-law, Ben Hardin Helm, donned Confederate gray. These men were not rare exceptions, as once was assumed, however. Indeed, Richard Nelson Current recently asserted that the Confederate states furnished perhaps 100,000 white soldiers to the Union during the conflict, roughly 10 percent of the Confederacy's available manpower. Nearly half of "Lincoln's Loyalists," 42,000 Federals, were Tennesseans. Most hailed from the eastern part of the state, but not all. One of these southern "boys in blue," as Union soldiers invariably were called at the time, was a young Middle Tennessean named William Marcus Woodcock, whose remarkable soldier's memoir, previously unpublished, stands as one of the few testaments of southern Unionism outside of East Tennessee and West Virginia.[1]

Marcus Woodcock was a native of Macon County, Tennessee, an area located just along the Kentucky border in the Middle Tennessee highlands. The first Woodcocks had moved from the southern piedmont of Virginia to what was then Smith County, Tennessee, around 1807. The young man's ancestors, Mark and William Woodcock, served under Andrew Jackson at New Orleans. When Mark

Woodcock settled along Long Creek in 1826, he erroneously believed he was putting down stakes in Kentucky. Despite the error, the area was attractive enough that many of his relatives followed. In 1837, five Woodcocks signed a petition calling for the creation of Macon County out of Smith. By the time of Fort Sumter, the Woodcocks were an established and respected Macon family, although not numbered among the county's landholding or slaveowning elite. Marcus Woodcock's father, Wiley Woodcock, was both a solid yeoman farmer and a self-educated doctor, one of nine physicians in the county. He seems to have moved in and out of the slaveholding class.[2]

Born in September 1842, Marcus was the eldest of Wiley and Harriet Woodcock's eleven children. He attended two neighborhood schools and at age sixteen taught at one, the Enon Free School. Following that brief and apparently unremarkable teaching experience, Woodcock enrolled in a private academy operated just a few miles to the north in Gamaliel, Kentucky, by teacher and Unionist L. M. Lankford. Crossing the state line to continue his education was hardly an unusual course for a Macon Countian to follow. In fact, the more rugged northern half of Woodcock's county and the southern section of Monroe County, Kentucky, comprised a single rural neighborhood, inhabiting land drained by tributaries of the Barren River and further linked by an important road running to Tompkinsville, Monroe County's seat. The state line, in other words, meant relatively little before the war. Taken as a whole, this community was relatively poor economically and was dominated by yeomen owning small tracts of land. Several slaveowners lived in the more accessible sections of both counties, but slavery became less common as the landscape became hillier. Politically, both counties tended to support Whigs, although the Woodcocks apparently were Democrats. The Macon-Monroe community was strongly Unionist as Civil War approached. As Stephen V. Ash succinctly put it, Woodcock's neighborhood had more in common with Unionist East Tennessee than with the Middle Tennessee heartland or the Kentucky Bluegrass.[3]

The border could not be ignored, however, as the onset of war in 1861 pushed Kentucky and Tennessee in opposite directions, cleaving the Macon-Monroe community. Although Tennesseans had rejected calling a secession convention in January 1861, Gov.

William Marcus Woodcock, c. 1864. Courtesy of the Woodcock family.

Isham Harris managed to bring the state into the Confederacy after Fort Sumter and Lincoln's call for volunteers. Ironically, the same events pushed some fence-sitters, including Woodcock and his neighbors, into the opposite Unionist camp. Confederate authorities acted quickly to squelch growing Unionist sentiments in places such as Macon County, one of the four Middle Tennessee counties still openly loyal to the Union. The military established three training camps in Macon, and eventually many of her men served in several Confederate units.[4]

Meanwhile, for the people of Monroe County, Kentucky, natives as well as refugee Tennesseans, the story was quite different. With a pro-Confederate governor, a largely Unionist legislature, two rival state armies, and a frightened populace, Kentucky initially opted for neutrality. As the summer of 1861 passed, however, Unionism clearly began to gain in strength. While states' righters increasingly slipped into Tennessee to join the Confederate army, the Unionist Home Guards began to drill openly, and ultimately the Lincoln administration created Federal camps of instruction. In Gamaliel, Woodcock and other pro-Union Tennesseans joined Kentucky's Home Guards. Whether Kentucky would have remained neutral even without a violation is open to debate. At any rate, after Confederate forces crossed into the state in September, neutrality collapsed. Most Kentuckians cast their lot with the Union. Monroe Countians, including 129 Tennesseans from Macon County, joined a new Federal infantry regiment being formed there, the 9th Kentucky. Nineteen-year-old Marcus Woodcock was one of them. His company's records described him in September 1861 as five feet and eleven inches tall, with a fair complexion, gray eyes, and light hair that apparently darkened during the conflict. He was, by his own admission, innocent of the realities of war.[5]

For the next three years, Woodcock served in his "brave 9th Kentucky," rising from the rank of private to that of first lieutenant. A near-fatal case of the measles kept him out of the Battle of Shiloh, the regiment's baptism of fire, but by December 1864, he had, by his own reckoning, seen more than enough action, having fought in some of the war's fiercest engagements. As described wonderfully in the memoir that follows, he marched and countermarched in the Corinth and Perryville campaigns, fought bravely at Stone's

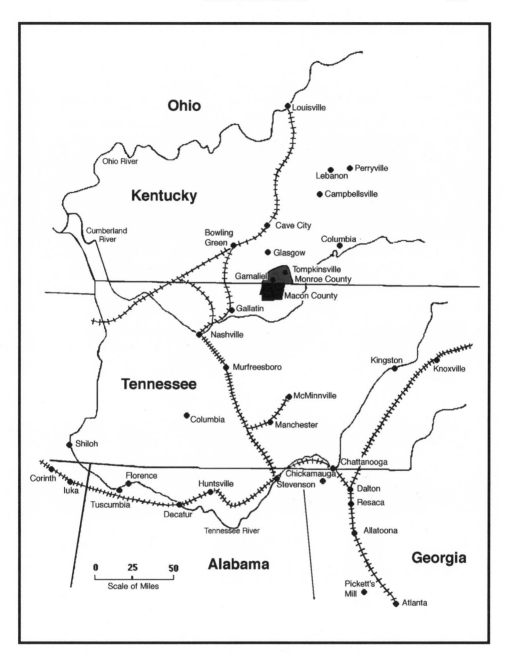

Marcus Woodcock's Civil War.

River, broke and ran with his regiment at Chickamauga only to take part in the dramatic stand atop Snodgrass Hill, watched his soldier friends sweep up Missionary Ridge, marched from Chattanooga to Atlanta with William Tecumseh Sherman, and pursued John Bell Hood after the latter had abandoned Georgia's Gate City. By December 1864, he was a veteran, with a scar on his leg to prove it. His war ended then; like most of the regiment's survivors, he chose to muster out rather than re-enlist. For many of the others, the decision to go home reflected a lack of enthusiasm for a Union war aim added in mid-war, the abolition of slavery, and for the black soldiers who came with emancipation. While emancipation was unpopular with most Upper South Unionists, it found a supporter in Woodcock, however. Indeed, his wartime experience, coupled with his already great ambition, had transformed the young southern Democrat into an increasingly vocal Radical Republican and had launched him into a new postwar career, politics.

Woodcock returned home to Macon County only to run for election to the Tennessee House of Representatives, something he had contemplated for at least a year. Reconstruction began in Tennessee well before Appomattox. Loyal Tennesseans, largely in uniform, met in January 1865 to craft a new state constitution. The "January Convention" authorized elections in the following March, with Confederate sympathizers denied the ballot. As a result, "Parson" William G. Brownlow, the state's foremost Radical Unionist, became governor, and Marcus Woodcock, greatly assisted on the campaign trail by his father, went to Nashville as a legislator. The so-called "Brownlow Assembly" soon began to divide into factions styled "Radicals" and "Conservatives." The former supported Brownlow and his plan to disenfranchise and punish "traitors." The latter, increasingly identified with United States President Andrew Johnson, favored allowing ex-Rebels to vote. While hardly a leader on the floor, Woodcock proved to be a safe Radical vote, although he sometimes criticized the government's spending habits. To him, Reconstruction was merely another phase in the war to preserve the Union; Conservatives were "Copperheads," "Traitors," and "Unwhipped Rebels." Notably, he backed Brownlow's revised Franchise Act, voted in favor of the Fourteenth Amendment, and supported extending the vote to Tennessee's freedmen. These stands did not hurt him at home, for Macon County re-elected him in 1867. He also was moving up in the party, attending the Republican National Convention in 1868, serving as an elector for Ulysses S. Grant, and later witnessing Grant's inauguration. It all came crashing to an end soon after, however. In August 1869, a coalition of Conservatives and moderate Republicans swept to victory, in effect ending Reconstruction in the state. Woodcock once again found himself a private citizen, although eventually he would run for election to the legislature in 1888.[6]

The immediate postwar years also were busy ones for Woodcock outside the legislature. Often depressed and worried about his future, Woodcock feverishly explored many career paths. He enrolled in a local business college to study bookkeeping and at night read extensively in literature, mathematics, and political science, augmenting knowledge acquired earlier through his passion for history. He secured a position with the Internal Revenue Service as a claims agent for Macon County. From June until October 1866, he clerked in Washington, first in the Patent Office and then the Pension Bureau, but then, apparently for political reasons, he was fired.[7]

In March 1865, just after he arrived in Nashville, he also began "transcribing my Journal while in the U.S Service." Woodcock originally intended that "My Soldier's Experience," as he called it, would cover his entire career, but the manuscript, really only a first draft, ends just after his May 1864 wound at Pickett's Mill, near Dallas, Georgia. Importantly, the work turned out to be more than a mere transcription. The author greatly expanded upon material in his six surviving wartime journals, which in fact are rather sketchy. Woodcock's journals suggest that he feverishly wrote most of the narrative from March until mid-April, when the legislative session finally began. Internal evidence within the memoir corroborates the journal entries. For example, the material in chapter 6 clearly was penned after John Wilkes Booth's murder of the "lamented Lincoln," yet a chapter later, Woodcock prays pessimistically for the ongoing war to end. It is only in chapter 10 that Woodcock discusses the "late war" in past tense. That reference, plus a noticeable change in Woodcock's hand, suggests that perhaps the post–Missionary Ridge material was written later in the year. All that is certain, however, is that in July 1865, back home in Macon County after the end of the legislative session, he began revising, writing a slightly expanded and ultimately abandoned second draft that extended only into the Corinth campaign. "Fact is," he lamented, "I have too many irons in the fire to do any good at any."[8]

In his introduction, Woodcock claims that he wrote at the behest of his "soldier friends" and of his "own inclination." It does seem possible, of course, considering his political activities and aspirations, that the memoir originally was intended to function, at least in part, as a sort of campaign autobiography, describing to his political "friends" his service to the Union and illustrating his conversion to Radical Republicanism. It is worth noting, however, that Woodcock, in his journals, never mentioned discussing his writing with anyone, even his patron, the Unionist politician A. J. Clements. It is entirely possible, then, that he wrote only for himself and his friends among the Federal soldiers encamped around Nashville. These he visited frequently, nostalgically looking back to a period when his life had had more purpose and less loneliness and confusion.

Whatever the reason, Woodcock wrote with an honesty not usually associated with politicians, describing in some detail both his frailties and events hardly calculated to gain a young politician renown. He seemingly could not help telling the truth, especially about himself. Considering the speed with which he wrote, he also displayed a marvelous eye and ear for detail and a wry sense of humor, which add immeasurably to the volume's usefulness and readability.[9]

No matter why Woodcock sat down to write so soon after his discharge, the modern reader should be thankful that he did. Woodcock's memoir is significant, not only because it is one of a handful of such works written by southern Unionists in uniform but also because it is one of a very few soldier memoirs written by anyone at all in the 1860s. As Gerald Linderman has noted, most Civil War memoirs were written after 1880. By then, he argues, the writer veterans had learned what their civilian audience wanted to read, and that was a flag-waving narrative full of glory rather than bloody reality. In Linderman's words, the soldiers had "surrendered the war they had fought to the war civilian society insisted they had fought." One might suggest a visual analogy in the contrast between the stark, even sickening after-battle photographs of Matthew Brady and the bright but unrealistic popular prints of the

William Marcus Woodcock, c. 1868.
Courtesy of the Woodcock family.

1880s, which claimed to demonstrate what a battle had been like, complete with flowing banners and generals on horseback leading bloodless charges.

Woodcock's memoir surrendered nothing. Much like the photographs, his work is fresh and vivid, full of immediacy, blunt honesty, and sometimes the adrenaline surge of battle. Such qualities are not always present in manuscripts written decades after the conflict. Reading the section on Stones River, for example, where the author's

Ellen Waters Woodcock, c. 1868.
Courtesy of the Woodcock family.

dashes substitute for periods, one almost can feel Woodcock's heart
pounding again as he puts pen to paper; his sorrow is palpable as
he mourns the loss of his closest friend. Also evident in the memoir
as a result of timing is the mild *Frontideologie*—that nostalgia for camp
coupled with a sense of alienation and even anger toward noncomba-
tants—so common among veterans just after Appomattox. As Stuart
McConnell notes, it had ebbed away into tamed niceties by the
1880s; it is fresh here. Conversely, one does not find the name

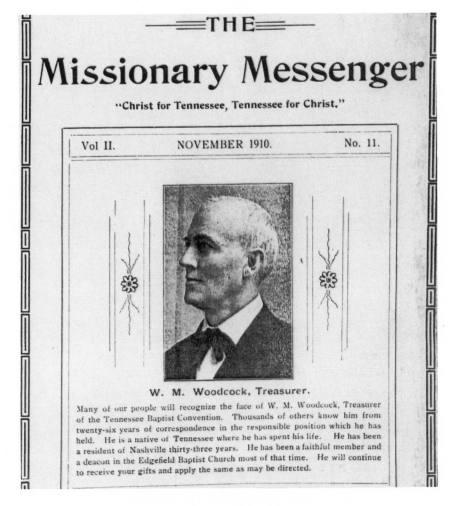

=THE=
Missionary Messenger
"Christ for Tennessee, Tennessee for Christ."

| Vol II. | NOVEMBER 1910. | No. 11. |

W. M. Woodcock, Treasurer.

Many of our people will recognize the face of W. M. Woodcock, Treasurer of the Tennessee Baptist Convention. Thousands of others know him from twenty-six years of correspondence in the responsible position which he has held. He is a native of Tennessee where he has spent his life. He has been a resident of Nashville thirty-three years. He has been a faithful member and a deacon in the Edgefield Baptist Church most of that time. He will continue to receive your gifts and apply the same as may be directed.

William Marcus Woodcock, 1910.
Courtesy of the Woodcock family.

calling, blame placing, and political grandstanding that often mars similar works, especially those written by the generals. Taken as a whole, these qualities make the memoir all but unique and, in consequence, very important.[10]

While he wrote, changes were taking place in his personal life. As a freshman representative, Woodcock roomed with Wilson L. Waters, a prominent Wilson County farmer, merchant, and legislator. According to family tradition, Waters at once determined to make the promising young veteran his son-in-law. Having persuaded Woodcock to give up alcohol (a soldierly habit that included downing a shot of whiskey every morning), Waters introduced his daughter Ellen to Woodcock. Woodcock was eager to marry, and the two were wed in January 1868. The couple eventually had eight children, although only three survived him.[11]

After leaving the legislature, the couple moved to Watertown, Tennessee, Ellen's home. Woodcock lived there for five years, excepting a few weeks in 1871, when he worked in Nashville as business manager of the *Nashville Gazette*, a Republican weekly. More profitably, Woodcock began riding to nearby Lebanon, Tennessee, to attend Cumberland University's law school, thus fulfilling his great desire for a college education. The couple relocated to Lebanon in 1874. After Marcus's graduation the following year, they moved back to Nashville. Woodcock worked for several hardware firms and then, in 1880, went to work as U.S. Collector of the Internal Revenue for the Fifth District of Tennessee. With another son-in-law of Waters, Eugene Priest, Woodcock, in his four years as collector, gained a reputation as a decided enemy of moonshiners. When he left the position in 1884, almost certainly due to the election of Democratic President Grover Cleveland, the title stayed with him. As "Collector" commonly was abbreviated "Col.," many people in Nashville, including nieces, nephews, and grandchildren, began erroneously to call Woodcock "Colonel," a practice the former first lieutenant apparently did nothing to correct.[12]

In his later years, Woodcock held various positions as an executive in Nashville's iron and steel industry. His real work, however, increasingly involved serving God. As a soldier, his faith hardly had been exceptional. Indeed, except for a few stock references to the Supreme Being and some scattered references to church services, Woodcock, in his memoir, hardly mentioned religion at all. In the years following the war, however, his faith grew. In 1870, he agreed to serve as a Baptist Sunday School superintendent, which he later called the beginning of his new life. He continued to rise in the church until, in 1885, he assumed the role of treasurer of the Tennessee Baptist Convention and also of the Baptist State Mission Board. In these positions, he became one of the most recognizable and beloved Baptists in the state.

Sadly, Woodcock's important position within the church also put him on the road to staggering financial difficulties and mental anguish. In an ill-advised moment, he loaned twelve hundred dollars in State Mission funds to a friend. When the friend died insolvent and his collateral proved to be worthless, a stunned Woodcock felt it his duty to repay the debt out of his own pocket. He began to take in boarders to raise extra money. Blaming himself for the strain on his wife and especially for the inability to educate his children as he wished, Woodcock nearly buckled. Guilt and depression overwhelmed him for the rest of his life. His faith helped him cope, but so did a renewed interest in his Civil War service. In September 1911, Woodcock returned to Chickamauga to stand once again next to the Brotherton House and on Snodgrass Hill.[13]

Marcus Woodcock died following surgery in February 1914, at the age of seventy-two. His obituary noted that he was "universally loved by the . . . Baptists of Nashville. . . . He was simple, unassuming, but true, genuine, sincere, courageous. There was one remarkable fact about him. He nearly always talked at prayer-meeting, but no one ever got tired of hearing him talk. . . . His way of presenting a matter was original and unique."

How many of his mourners could have known that the same sincerity, courage, and truth could be found in the remarkable, already dusty Civil War memoir written almost forty-nine years earlier? Honest and immediate, representing as it does the often-ignored experience of southern Unionists who donned blue coats, Marcus Woodcock's memoir stands as a lasting monument to a young southern boy in blue who put his life on the line to help save the Union.[14]

Woodcock wrote his untitled memoirs in pen on 359 sheets of common, unlined stationery eight by twelve inches in size. In editing the text for publication, I compared a photocopy of the original manuscript with a computer printout of the Holland Typescript, in order to create a computer-readable version of the manuscript exactly as written by Woodcock. That process mainly involved reinserting errors and inconsistencies in capitalization, punctuation, and spelling that had been corrected or modernized in the Holland Typescript, and changing a few words erroneously transcribed. All blanks appeared in the original as well. The end result is a text that duplicates Woodcock's original draft. In a few cases where clarity demanded the insertion of a word, period, or parentheses, I indicated my additions by placing them within brackets. The reader also will find in brackets several given names of individuals whom Woodcock mentioned only by surname; this seemed the least obtrusive way of identifying them within the text. Finally, I divided the manuscript into eleven chapters of roughly equal length. Woodcock initially created short chapters himself, but as the manuscript progressed, he ceased. I have indicated in notes where his untitled chapters began and ended.

The notes in general are intended to amplify, correct, or explain as succinctly as possible, without interfering with the narrative. This is Marcus Woodcock's book, not mine. Thus, in editing the manuscript, I have tried to follow Gary W. Gallagher's admonition "not to impose the type of pedantic scholarly apparatus that sometimes overpowers" works of this kind.[15] At times, I am sure enthusiasm has overtaken good sense, but on the whole I hope that I have succeeded. I must confess that just a few names and events baffled me, and I have left these unnoted.

The Memoir of
MARCUS WOODCOCK
9th Kentucky Infantry
(U.S.A.)

Author's Introduction

In consequence of the solicitation of my soldier friends and also my own inclination, I have determined to present to you *my experience as a soldier.*

The fact that many of my friends have desired me to do this is by no means the only reason why I have at last consented to do so nor would I have consented to do so under any consideration but for the fact that while giving incidents relating to myself I intend to make as conspicuous as possible the daring deeds of my comrades in arms, and this work is designed for a memorial of the brave and patriotic soldiers that composed the noble Regiment in which I fortunately cast my lot, more than it is for any other purpose, though I can't hope to do justice &c.

My readers must pardon me for not giving them an official History of the Regiment for I not only think that that would be in a great measure uninteresting, but it would at the same time place many facts before the public that were better forgotten.

It would also be nearly if not entirely an impossibility to give a complete official History of the Regiment for a great many of the important papers, especially General and special Orders, have been lost; thus only a partial official history could be given and then many would feel disappointed.

I desire while making this as interesting as I can to the reader, to add here to a simple narrative and illustration of facts.

As I underwent many disadvantages at the beginning of the war, or rather early after I first inlisted in the service, my narrative of that period will pretty generally be coupled with matters of but little interest.

I also had the misfortune to lose all papers, the most important being my diary which I had with much perseverance and under many disadvantages kept complete previous to the twentieth day of August 1862.

I was so disheartened by this misfortune that for many months subsequent to this period I gave but little attention to the keeping of a diary and thus another impediment is presented to my cherished scheme.

This work will comprise an account of all that an eye-witness could see and *feel* of the skirmishing incidental to the capture of Corinth Mississippi; The Battle of Stone River, Chickamauga, Mission Ridge, and the campaign into Georgia in 1864, till May 27th when the Author was slightly wounded [in the] Battle of New Hope Church [and so] was not to be with the Regiment again till the 26th day of July when the history again commences and goes on to the Battle of Lovejoy's Station, which was the closing scene, and finally till the Regiment is mustered out of the Service December 15th, 1864.[1]

I do not aspire to any right of patronage at all, but I have always found the *un*official account of a battle or any incident much more interesting than the formal and precise official Report.

The *un*official is free. He is at liberty to give all the colorings of the remarkable incidents that may have occurred that he thinks appropriate, and due to the hero[,] without doing injustice to any one.

Without the fear of exciting the envy of anyone, he can justly applaud some hero who has won laurels never to be published except by the casual observer who happens to note the facts.

Many of the private soldiers that have leaped a ditch or scaled a parapet and turn[ed] from thence the hated insignia of his enemy and in bearing it away received his death warrant whose gallantry would have been lost to history but for the history of it given by some humble comrade in arms.

A private soldier receives his only reward for valor in the esteem of his fellow soldiers, beyond that his deeds are never narrated except he through his own bravery and the combination of the gifts of Providence is enabled to perform some feat of such wonderful daring and attended with so much danger that it is a mystery to the wisest of even the *double stars* how he could have escaped with life.

I shall ask leave to dedicate this to the officers and soldiers of the 9th Ky Infantry U.S.A. without making a single exception, for I came away from the service, and separated from the afore-mentioned persons without a single feeling of animosity for any member of the Regiment.

I do not claim for myself the right of being called Phenomanon in the line of even-tempered persons but I do claim to have gotten along as smoothly with the members of our Regiment as any officer or soldier in it.

I also claim to have had as few if not fewer difficulties than anyone and I *know* I possessed as warm feelings of admiration, love or respect for the Regiment as any one, and also I acknowledge that I had cause for this feeling.

The 9th Kentucky Infantry has in my humble estimation received less from the pens of the historian according to its merits than any Regiment that has ever enlisted in the U.S. Service. We never had but one News-Reporter in our immediate company and that for only a few weeks while in Kentucky attending to the "Bragg raid" and despite the current solicitation of a few of us, the boys hooted him out and that seemed to bring the wrath of the News Reporter down on us in such a manner as to never have mentioned us since in connection with any battle except that of Mission Ridge, and then they could not well help it.[2]

I have always in a measure favored the News Reporter accompanying our armies, for were it not for him, much that is important and interesting would be forever lost to history.

I must ask you to pardon the errors of an illiterate man, and not to accept this as an intended display of powers to secure popular favour (for in that respect the work will condemn itself) nor as a history of myself for the same purpose (for I have done nothing *great*), but a simple narration of facts because others wanted me to do so, and because *I wanted to do so myself*. Please take the work for what it is worth with the distinct understanding that I ask no favours nor attempt to excuse any deficiencies but simply submit my work to the generous but critical public.

I am, &c.

Chapter 1

I Would Enlist in the U.S. Armies

In the five months following Fort Sumter, a deeply divided Kentucky walked an increasingly treacherous tightrope of neutrality. While growing numbers of states' righters from Simon Bolivar Buckner's Kentucky State Guard slipped across the border into Tennessee to enter Confederate camps, the Unionist Home Guards armed themselves and drilled openly in support of their native son in the White House. In August, after Unionists swept the state's elections, Naval Lt. William Nelson baldly opened Camp Dick Robinson in Garrard County as a Federal recruitment station. Neutrality could not last much longer. Finally, on September 4, Confederate troops under the orders of Maj. Gen. Leonidas Polk occupied Columbus. Brig. Gen. U. S. Grant followed suit by taking Paducah. On September 18, the largely Unionist state legislature ordered all Confederates out of Kentucky. Immediately, Buckner struck across the border from Middle Tennessee into Western Kentucky, occupying Bowling Green and establishing several Confederate camps in the vicinity of the Green River, including one at Cave City.

For nineteen-year-old student Marcus Woodcock, a member of the Monroe County Home Guards, the war that already had come to his parents' Tennessee home now was at the front door of his schoolhouse. In the days that followed Buckner's incursion, the Home Guards sprang to action. Out of their nucleus would grow the Army of the Cumberland.[1]

It was on a beautiful Thursday evening on the 19th day of September 1861 that I was at a beautiful spot in Monroe County, Kentucky known as Gamaliel. I was then a student in the common branches of an English education and was a member of a school that was then being taught at the place by Mr. L. M. Lankford. I was enjoying all the pleasures that a poor boy of an humble country school could aspire to.

Our teacher was a man of excellent qualifications, intellectual and moral.—Had received a rather extensive Education in the face of great pecuniary embarassments.—Had felt the sting of poverty, and was consequently one that could sympathize with those that needed sympathy.

The students, in general, were of that superior class of back-woods rusticity that is rarely found in such numbers in such a small collection.

They were plain without courseness, frank without forwardness, reserved without self-importance, intelligent without the great advantages of an Education, polite without a knowledge of the great system of etiquette, and in fact possessed every vestige that would have to facilitate the happiness of such a community.

It was just at the announcement of the ever-rejuvenating word, giving a few moments for play and rest and known among us as "recess" that a young gentleman rode up and alighted among us, and after a few moments of general conversation among the students, challenged the teacher or any member of the school to a debate on a certain "query" that had been exciting some interest in the neighborhood for a considerable time past. After giving everyone an opportunity, I accepted the challenge and designated that night as the time for the discussion to take place. He accepted it as agreeable to his preparations.

Early after supper we were in view of the school-house again and both of us felt rather disappointed to see such a large collection of people for we felt that the people were attaching more importance to the matter than ever *we* had, for we had only intended it as a source of a little amusement.

When we arrived upon the ground we found that all were in the greatest whirl of excitement from the rumor of an approaching body of rebels. The old men had assembled, to devise means of defense and the younger ones were present to act on the dictation of the older. A message had also arrived that there were a supply of muskets at or near Cave City for the Home Guards of Monroe County, and the Gamaliel Company was required to furnish 20 men.[2]

After some deliberation, it was finally agreed that the assembly should break up till the next morning when we would all meet at the parade ground and the detail from the company would be made.

We were separated into different squads and ordered to stand picket in the neighborhood till daylight, and there on Barren River on this clear moonlit night, where the Stars and Stripes had been dear to all till such a recent date, where within the last six months the trump of the warrior had sounded through the land calling men from the various pursuits of a peacable and happy life to go to the tented field and there shed the blood of their fathers, brothers, or sons either for or against the Union, I did my first "picket duty." Ah how bitterly I have since realized the dream of which that was not even a preface. That beautiful night I sat in a comfortable position in a shaded part, and had such a view of the ground we were guarding that we (there were two others) could carry on a conversation in the usual tones without the fear of being heard. Often have I thought of that night when since I have when going to the picket line had to use every precaution to prevent being shot by the wary enemy, or when posted in the dark forest I could not see nor hear the noiseless sentry on the next "beat," when I had to use every precaution lest an enemy should steal around me in the darkness and carry me off to be reported the next morning missing as a deserter. On the cold (and dreary) nights that I have had to face my beat and use my powers of exertion in every imaginable way that would keep up a sufficient temperature of heat in my system to prevent me from freezing! But the worst of all nights is when a thunder storm arises and fills the soldier with the triple dread of being thoroughly drenched with the cold rain, struck dead by the dangerous element, or the possibility of the wind tearing away a branch from some monarch of the forest and thereby losing his neck or some of his limbs. Oh, ye brave soldier, you will never be repaid for your troubles except in the knowledge that through your exertions your country is preserve[d].

We left our post at daylight and repaired to our respective "stopping places" to refresh ourselves with a few minutes repose, a good breakfast, and then repair to the parade ground.

I was there in due time and found a very large crowd assembled and ready to furnish the required number of men to go to Cave City after the arms before referred to. Somehow I felt a desire to undertake the job and proposed to accompany the expedition if any person would furnish me a horse; this was quickly closed in with by a gentleman that asked me to go in his place, but I repented it for instead of a horse he had there a little mule that seemed scarcely large enough to be *weaned* but for aught I knew was as old as Methuselah, and had the very spirit looking from his eye that fully justified the phrase "as stubborn as a mule."

At 12 M. [noon] we were in Tompkinsville and there found the people strung to the highest pitch of excitement.

W. J. Hinson[3] Major of Home Guards was using every effort to preserve order and insure a successful defence of the town in case of an attack.

There were a great many armed men in the place and squads were continually coming in, and all seemed to be in anxious expectation of an attack at any moment.

I think it was about 2 P.M. that we sat out on the road for Cave City, leaving Glasgow to the left and I think we traveled at least 60 miles and arrived at Woodland Station near Cave C——— just a few minutes before day break the next morning.

The rebels had I believe in the day previous established a camp of instruction at this place and there were some hundreds reported to be lying up in camp not above one-fourth of a mile from where the guns were concealed.[4]

Our party was originally composed of 60 men representatives of three companies, but our number had become augmented by recruits on the road to around one hundred, yet with this small force and our great inexperience we did not choose to throw ourselves on the offensive or hazard a battle unless compelled to. We found our guns in a straw stack and each of them had been loaded and capped by the person who had charge of them, he suspecting that it would be impossible for us to get them away without a skirmish with the rebel recruits.

We could begin to see a faint gleam of the approaching daylight as we mounted our horses and rode off.

Since that time I have served for three years and two months and 19 days as a soldier in the United States service, but I have never since that time been so completely worn out and exhausted as I was on this expedition. About noon I and my mule, that was harder to drive than the rebels at Stone River and which caused me to have to get up a system of incessant kicks and thrusts with my bayonet to keep "in position" had gotten some miles behind the main body and I think that the whole party was scattered along 5 miles of the road, for everyone had concluded that we were past all danger, when on ascending a hill in the road, and looking ahead I saw in the distance that all were coming to a halt at a given point and appeared to be rather confused about something.

I hastened forward and found that by some means someone had learned that a body of rebels were posted on the road some miles ahead to intercept our approach, and that our party was making active preparations for a fight: ten rounds of cartridges all we had, were being issued to each man, the powder and lead was being divided out among those that were best mounted. The older ones were instructing "we" boys in regard to how to use our muskets of which many of us had never even seen a single one and indeed it was a general state of combined consternation and determination. As for myself, I felt "sorta any way" and was so near dead with fatigue that I could scarcely be brought to comprehend the true state of circumstances till we were again on the way.

We then traveled about 5 miles at "common time" using great caution, having a select body under Captain Lankford thrown forward as an advance guard, but we finally concluded that there was no danger and again struck out at every man in his own time.

A little while before sundown the other two companies broke off in another direction leaving us alone but we still struggled manfully on, my mule acquitting himself with great credit and on that very trip establishing the honor of that noble order of Beings that has since rendered so much valuable service to the armies of Uncle Sam. We passed the house of Mr. Rankin about 10 P.M. and aroused him from his slumbers by giving three times three rousing cheers for Freedom and Nationality and by way of Supplement, three cheers for "Woodcock and his mule." I was very grateful for this evidence of their consideration for us, but I was so fatigued that I could or rather did not return our thanks for this appreciation of our actions, and mule was suffering so greatly from wounds inflicted by spur and our bayonet, and by girth of the saddle from the absence of a crupper that I don't think he even heard himself named in connection, at any rate, he said nothing. I arrived at my boarding house about midnight and never in my life I think have I been so greatly fatigued. This was Saturday night and I had been in the saddle ever since about 10 o'clock A.M. Friday except the time required for ourselves and horses to eat a "bite" (usually 15 minutes and three times on the trip). Had rode about 130 miles over a rough country at least half the distance in the night, and had not been accustomed to hardship of any kind for a considerable period. I could eat nothing but was soon in bed, and in, or rather beyond the land of dreams where I remained til old "Sol" had been gazing for two hours upon the next day, seeing what it might bring forth.

I partially awakened myself and bathed my temples in water for a considerable time, but it had no effect only to make more perceptible to my feeling the effects of recent exertions.

I ate a scanty breakfast and hastened home to beg forgiveness of my parents for "going" without permission. Mother shed more tears of joy than she did when I in last December returned from the three years service. Father simply said in his blunt way "you did right."

I never have in my life at any other time felt such a great degree of absence of mind as I did through the whole of this day. It is impossible to analyze my feelings. I threw myself on bed and tried to sleep but for some unaccountable reason could not. I walked, ran, took a few turns on a gymnasium but felt nothing as to effect, and I have since thought that I was not properly awakened through the whole day. I ate but little for dinner, and that did not refresh me in the least.

I returned to Gamaliel that evening to attend a meeting to propose plans for the future and found that most of the raiders had got pretty well straightened up again and were by resting another night ready for another trip. I could not vouch so much for myself yet. The result of the meeting was an agreement that twenty of the Gamaliel Home Guard should attend the general "drill school" at *Indian Creek Meeting House* superintended by Major Dunn of the Home Guards and I agreed to represent one of the Company. Accordingly, on the next day much improved I filled a haversack, *pro tem* with Baked fowl, Corn Bread, and a few sweetmeats and "in state" repaired to the "camp of instruction" to be initiated into the mysteries of the military tactics, and thus be prepared (as I had already determined) to become a "soldier boy" when I should find another recruiting officer. I arrived in time for the "afternoon drill." The company was just being formed and such was my foolish ardor that notwithstanding I had ridden 15 miles during the day, I laid aside my equipage and stepped into ranks.

That night I was detailed to "stand picket" for two hours, the post being about one mile from the parade ground and no Reserve, but I simply had to stand my 2 hours and then return to the camps (And) that night—for the first—I enjoyed a pretty good sample of a soldier's bed, which was nothing more or less than a bunk upon which I stretched myself and by the assistance of one blanket, obtained about 1 hour of rather unsettled sleep, and next morning I had a pretty fair sample of soldier's breakfast by toasting a piece of bread and eating it with a bit of cold, cooked fowl, and no coffee.

All went on smoothly to day and towards evening we were making such rapid advances toward a knowledge of the science that to all appearances we bade for soon to vie with the most thoroughly experienced veterans of the Regular Army in perfection of movement and promptness to obey commands.

We were considerably edified this morning by the announcement that a courier had just arrived bearing a dispatch that Nashville was in possession of Federal troops. We gave three rousing cheers, but I was at the time very much perplexed in my mind as to where the Federal troops had been keeping themselves recently that had made this brilliant achievement.[5]

I stood my round on picket again that night, or at least had nearly completed my time when here came the corporal to tell us that the rebels had burned Burksville, robbed New Albany, killed several citizens and were playing trumps generally, and were now threatening the "city of Tompkinsville" and would most assuredly attack it soon and we were desired to go there immediately.

A Call was made for volunteers and I immediately stepped forward after nearly every other member of the Company had done so and we were then ordered to get ready and that we would march as far as Gamaliel on that night, and on to Tompkinsville next day. I had sent my horse home on the day previous and there I was ten miles from home, worn out with constant fatigue, and the excitement that had held me up all the time now began to abate and consequently I felt the hardships of this night were the greatest I had ever endured.

I arrived at home just at daylight, completely exhausted and more out of spirits than at any time previous. Nevertheless I was asleep the minute I got in bed, first admonishing my mother to let me sleep but one hour and to have my breakfast ready when I was awakened. Oh, that sweet nap!

I have a thousand times since when on the march on dark and stormy nights reverted to that beautiful sound when all nature seemed to be bound by a spell of silence as I footsore and weary approached that spot dear alike to all, Home. I have never been more solemnly impressed with the idea of the frailty of human nature or the greatness of a Supreme Being than when I was crossing the fields on that beautiful but apparently exceedingly lonely morning towards my father's house. My mind reverted back to better days—Days when the trump of the warrior and the clangor of arms had never been heard by scarcely any of the present generation,—days when the people instead of being on the alert to prevent surprise by some wary and perhaps unscrupulous enemy, were following the pursuit of a peaceful life,—days when we were enjoying all the blessings of a Republican Government, the right of suffrage being extended to all honest men, the advancement of education becoming more popular everywhere, the people becoming every day more able to prove to the world the greatness, glory, and justice of self-government,—and days when we were called by all nations "The Star of the world."

I then turned to the present; alas, what a contrast! How we were accustomed every day to see the preparation for the bloody practice of *war*, Brother against Brother, and Father against Son, Oh what a war! and also one in which both parties were of the same nation, the same ancestors, and which ancestors had the clearest fighting record that ever went on the pages of history, and in course I anticipated, if the war was not averted, bloody work, and I have since *realized it*—yea, I have since seen the descendants of the noble heroes of '76 marshalled in battle array against each other, on the stirip mountains of Kentucky, the fertile fields of Tennessee, the offensive swamps of Mississippi and the barren pine forests of

Georgia, and oh, they did such bloody work; but pardon this digression of my story and I will resume.

I was aroused from my slumber a little after sunrise and ate the last breakfast that I ate as a citizen before entering upon the dangerous and difficult duties of a soldier. O God! had I known what was in store for me, I could not have endured the thought of it; for a citizen's idea of soldiering is that it is ten-fold more dangerous and difficult to follow than it really is, and that man cannot endure such a great amount of fatigue and destitution as he really can, at least that was my opinion at the present date of my story.

I have a vivid recollection of that sunny morning, when old Sol seemed to come forth in all his glory as if to mock me in my intentions, for Gentle Reader you must understand that I had determined to enlist in a company of volunteers that Capt Hinson was recruiting for the service of the State of Kentucky to be annexed to a Regiment that was to be commanded by Col. B. C. Grider of Bowling Green Ky.

With a heavy heart, and a mind filled with doubt and perplexities, and my physical system almost prostrated under the immense exertions it had recently been called upon to make, and nevertheless with a feeling of consciousness that I was doing my Duty, I secretly invoking the mercy of a Divine Providence, mounted my horse and set out to meet my friends at Gamaliel to go on from there to the defense of Tompkinsville.

As I rode along I meditated deeply upon the question am I risking too much when I enter the army? Am I going to cast my fortunes with the party that are striving to maintain the true principle[s] of Self Government and National Sovereignty? Am I enlisting in the cause of the aggrieved or the aggressor? And am I able to undergo the trials, hardships, privations, and dangers attendant upon the soldier's career? [A]nd am I able in every way to discharge the duties of a soldier? The three first questions were easily answered to my not over-comprehensive mind, and the last only time could solve.

Notwithstanding, I was young, I had many reasons for wishing to stay out of the Army besides the natural one of dread. I had many connections that it would almost rend my heart to break off. My schoolmates, the most choice body of young persons with whom I was ever acquainted, were so connected with me by the strongest ties of almost filial affection that I could not keep back a burning tear when I thought of parting with them; as I passed the school-house on the Friday morning previous, I had stopped in to see them, but few were there, and those [who] were seemed to have come together more for mutual consolation than for study. All looked as solemn as if they were attending a funeral procession, and as I shook hands with them and told them that I hoped to be back, "all right" among them on the next Monday, they all seemed to have apprehensions of doubt and one of them stated that she had a presentiment that I would never be among them again as a student;

I affected to not notice the remark, but nevertheless it impressed me deeply and the *presentiment* has to this date been fulfilled.

Also, I was just beginning to improve my Education in a man-ner that would be of service to me,—was just getting my mind in train for study and had begun to advance into the mysteries of Science with a speed and ease truly encouraging to myself, and had arrived at an age when to obtain an Education no time must be lost, and when three years lost entirely from study would prove fatal to all such hopes. But I must cease to make such extravagant digressions and resume my story.

I found the Country in the greatest state of excitement imag-inable,—A general state of alarm and even terror seemed to pervade with a large portion of the community. Women were in tears as they looked at their sturdy husbands or tender sons disappear in the distance going to the defense of Tompkinsville. At this remote date it seems almost fiction that such a state of things could have existed when there was really such little immediate cause. Yes there was a cause for the aged wife or mother, and the tender sister looked at their beloved husbands, sons or brothers, and knew from the signs of the times, that if not then they soon would be torn from their loving embraces to go to the tented field and share the dangers of a soldier. Oh ye incarnate fiends, political demagogues of the South, why were ye not content to fill your pockets with Northern Gold without using every exertion to bring about this most disastrous war, which has been by the Justice of Almighty God rendered a curse to the south? But here I am away from my narration again[.]

I arrived at Gamaliel about 9 A.M. and found the company generally ready to move, and we accordingly set out and arrived in

Tompkinsville about 11 1/2 A.M. and there found that the excitement had gotten a few degrees below the boiling point again. If I recollect right an expedition or scout had been sent out in the direction of Burksville, and returned reporting the coast all clear and that the cause of the whole alarm was the robbing of a few stores in New Albany by a squad of Rebel Cavalry. I cant make Statements as to any other person's feeling at this time, but I felt "kind, o, sold." Yet, we resolved to make the best of it we could and as a retaliatory measure resolved to go to Glasgow and chastise the rebels stationed there i,e, if they attempted resistance, and if they did not to disarm them, and make a general tour through the country to convince the people of our ability and determination to maintain our character as Home Guards and the safety of the citizens of the County. A portion of us were serving as Infantry and another portion as Cavalry. We were formed in order, the infantry in advance, the music accompanying them under the "Star spangled Banner" playing the National tune, Yankee Doodle, and the scene was to our then inexperienced citizens indeed imposing. The Infantry were ordered to march steadily forward on the Glasgow Road in charge of a subordinate while the Cavalry halted to give them a start. At this juncture a council of war was called composed of the Company officers to arrange a plan for the *campaign*. After a consultation of about 5 minutes they decided that the campaign was given up for the present, and that we would all return to our homes. A courier was immediately sent forward to order the Infantry to turn back and we were soon returning into Tompkinsville. Captain Lankford proposed that we should have the band to play Boneparte's Retreat and I believe it was played though I am not certain. I think no one heard the proposition but myself and Lieut. Hayes.[6]

We stopped in town and remained there till after supper, but in the meantime, Capt Hinson's Company of recruits was paraded through the streets with "martial music and flying colors" to give others an opportunity to enlist. Several gay fellows stepped into lines and took the step, and finally I in defiance of urgent remonstration of my best friends, stepped into line from which, strung the path of honor, there is no stepping back.

I enrolled my name and then learned that the Company was being made up for three years instead of two; but I did not care for that for I felt very confident that the war would terminate ere six months, and moreover that I could not indure the fatigue of camp life for even *two* years and would ere that time be dead or discharged for disability.

The Union people were very much stirred up that evening ere the general signs of the times, and were getting pretty confident that this section of the country could easily defend itself against all roving bands of thieves and guerillas, from whom they anticipated all the trouble. I procured a *furlough* for two days and directly after dark I in company with the Gamaliel Home Guards, set out for home, but it was now true I could not call that spot that was endeared to me by the strongest ties of infancy and childhood by the sweet and endearing name of home, without shedding a tear at the thought that I had now for the first time permanently withdrew from its kind protection to go out in the cold world among a body of strangers and liable to meet with new persons at every turn, and even to be thrown in company of probably bad proclivities where I had never been before; but I thought I would make my way through the strife as well as anyone, and consequently felt rather indifferent about it as there were so many thousands that were at this time in the commitment of the very same act.

I arrived in the neighborhood of Gamaliel and rested for the night, and on the next day posted for home, not with that light heart and firm tread that I approached in December 1865[7] but with a heart filled with anxious misgivings and a step faltering as if in obedience to the throes of my heart. Now, do not conclude from this that the least thought of having committed an error had ever entered my mind; on the contrary, I felt that I had done what every loyal citizen of the United States should do. Ever since the fall of Fort Sumpter I had resolved that if ever I had an opportunity, I would enlist in the U.S. Armies. Immediately after arriving at home I posted a messenger to A. J. Hibits, (blacksmith) with an order for the usual home manufactured Bowie-knife, without which a soldier's equipment was then considered very imperfect, and then devoted the rest of the day to writing letters, arranging my earthly good[s], (Books) and making such a final disposition of my limited business as I judged most proper.

I was in a continued whirl of excitement during the whole evening, continually walking back and forth over the floor around the yard and through the fields.

A little while after dark the messenger whom I had dispatched to the blacksmith's returned and brought with him a most formidable looking species of Bowie Knife manufactured from an old horseshoe rasp, and now the object was to go to the grindstone and put it in the proper state for service, which we managed to effect to a certain extent after several hours of incessant labor; and then a scabbard was to be made, but that was soon executed out of a piece of thin soleleather, and a belt prepared from one of father's finest kips, and I was pronounced ready at least to maintain my ground against at least two of the "secesh," felt pretty confident myself as long as "Secesh" would keep out of the way.

Next morning I was ready and did start back in accordance with the terms of my furlough, and never a knight felt greater self importance, when riding forth with his retinue of retainers, girt with crimson sash and gilded sword than did I as I rode forth that morning accompanied by "Tom" and girt with my western belt and homespun Bervil.

Saw many friends on the way each of whom had a kind word of parting, and a gentle admonition to "be careful" and "be sure to write", &c. All of which I hurried away from, and at 12 M, found myself at Camp Lyons, two miles from Tompkinsville on ——— road, and arrived just as the company was sitting down to dinner. I dismounted on the instant and there for the first time in my life did I take a real soldier's dinner, and I feasted as though it had been at the best of tables, and the truth of it, is I was about as thoroughly initiated as anyone present, and needed no inaugural ceremonies to enable me to do full justice to a soldier's hard fare; but ah none of us were ere initiated! Ere twelve months rolled over our heads we felt for days in succession the gnawing of hunger—had been compelled to live on a rather inferior article of hard bread and bacon and coffee issued as 1/2 rations and which did not serve to keep us from feeling at all times a degree of hunger.

Having lost my journal for all this period I may make some error in committing this to paper, and if I do, it must be excused as unavoidable. We remained here I think till the Monday following and whiled away the time, as soldiers usually do: i.e. Eating, drinking, walking, running, jumping, and sometimes drilling, &c. We got up a system of debates for night amusement which would probably have proven beneficial to us all had we remained there long enough to advance in it. On Sunday evening we either received orders, or the Capt thought it was best for us to go to Camp Anderson and we accordingly made preparations to leave on the next day.[8] It must be remembered that during this interval I had announced myself as a candidate for the, supposed to exist, office of third lieutenant, as none of the military in our Country had learned yet that there was no longer such office in the U.S. Army. When I enlisted in the Company, I was acquainted with but one of its numbers, viz., J. I. Tooley, and consequently the chances were considerably against me when I came to consider that the opposing candidate was well acquainted with almost everyone. I was very confident in my own mind that I had the strongest claims on the position; but nevertheless was willing to leave it to the decision of the Company. On the next morning the sun rose clear and beautiful, as if to encourage me in the first march I was ever to make with a military Company. The citizens of the surrounding vicinity began to turn out early after sunrise to see us take our final leave of Camp Lyons and surrender the distinction of being the whole force of a military post.

We had a fine party to witness our final leave-taking and some solemn looking ones in the assembly, for not one was there, but what was related to some of the Company that was going to war.

At the urgent request of the citizens, we agreed to delay our time of starting till after they could furnish us with an early dinner, and it proved to be a sumptuous repast indeed. We had milk, butter, potatoes, roasting ears, baked and boiled meats, fowls, do[ugh], pies, cakes, "Corn pones" and in fact anything that suits us Country-bred *gentlemen*. Dinner being over and the usual supplementaries disposed of we were ordered to gird on our baggage and arms and accoutrements and fall into line. It should have been previously stated that each of us was armed with a Home Guard musket or Minnie Rifle. Then there was hurrying and bustling around, parents, children, brothers, sisters and friends taking for what they all knew this last farewell. But these preliminaries were soon adjusted and more reported, to the Capt Hinson as ready for the march. And then to the tune of Yankee Doodle we stepped lightly away and were soon out of view.

We passed through Tompkinsville and there stopped a moment to transfer our baggage from our shoulders to a wagon that was going to accompany us; and again we were on the road, and arrived at Camp Anderson about one hour before sunset; were met on the parade ground by a company who gave us three cheers, and escorted us into camp in truly military style. Oh! but I was so tired. This was the first time I had ever visited a really military camp. Here the soldier did his own cooking, made his own bed, did his own eating and sleeping, drilled from four to six hours per day, and took his regular turn at "Camp Guard" and "picket", and in fact did all.

Military rules were strictly adhered to so far as the experience of the officers extended, a strict Camp Guard was kept continually posted, and it would have been as safe to have broke from a Rebel prison as to have attempted to violate its rules.

After resting a few moments, I concluded to satisfy my curiosity by taking a stroll over the camps and making a general survey of the premises to see how I liked the prospects. And as a result I was not very favorably impressed with the arrangement; but I will not pretend to here enumerate my objections, as I suppose almost everyone whom these pages will reach has seen the encampment when in its greatest glory. After awhile my friend B. M. Fishburn[9] came around and invited me to take supper, and I tell you it was a treat; consisting of a large kettle full of green beans which had been cooked and off the fire a sufficient time to enable one to eat them from the kettle, and cornbread. I ate heartily. About this time a subordinate of some description *bawled out* "O yes! Oh yes! Oh yes!!! all that belong to Capt Roark's Company[10] parade here and form a line." Soon the other sub's of that Company, and of all the other companies were "*bawling*" the same expression just given at the tops of their voices, only they named other Captains, viz., Martin, Mulligan, Fraim, Hinson, and others.[11] The companies were, after a considerable time, formed and each Captain taking the ground that best suited him, all stood at "attention."

Maj Dixon addressed the Battalion from his horse, informing them that there was a rumor abroad, but did not say to what effect, that the men must all go over to Mr. J. Y. Fraim's residence[12] and procure *three* rounds of cartridges each, and that the men must sleep on their arms that night, and that extreme vigilance must be kept up by the camp Guard, and that if through the night an alarm should be raised that the Companies must be immediately formed and placed in Battle array.

For my part, I did not feel very apprehensive and was so weary with my evening's tramp that it did not take me a great while after laying down to fall into a most profound slumber, from which I did not awake till about sunrise on the next day, when to my chagrin I learned there had been a general alarm on the night previous, caused by one Tolliver Moore (since Capt. Co. E 9th Ky. V.I.)[13] discharging his gun at what he supposed to be an enemy, but which proved to be a *cow*. The general report was that great excitement pervaded the whole encampment, that there was a considerable degree of alacrity evinced in forming the companies, and that there was noise enough to make an Elephant deaf, and the great wonder was I did not wake. I did not attempt to explain away my drowsiness and consequently there was but little said about the matter. Well, after breakfast we (The Hinson Company) were marched out for organization, or to elect the Captains, Lieutenants and Sergeants. Captain W. J. Hinson was unanimously chosen as Captain and a William G. Bryan[14] as First Lieutenant, and A. W. Smith after a sharp contest as Second Lieutenant. Philip H. Emmurt was elected Third Lieutenant defeating me by an overwhelming majority. Thus I was defeated and so *badly*, too, made it rather hard to bear, but having at least enough moral courage to work my way with, and a character free from blemish I endured it pretty well for it was clear the simple reason of personal acquaintance had defeated me. Nevertheless, I cheerfully acquiesced and proceeded to vote for the other fellows. Sergeant 1st, 2nd, 3rd, 4th, 5th being according to the election the following persons respectively Silas Clarke, Isaac Hix, William B. Roddy, Andrew J. Carter and Benjamin Thompson. After the Company broke ranks, Captain Hinson touched me to walk aside and informed me that I should be appointed *first Corporal. Now wasn't that cheering?* I accepted the office and was from that day forth "an officer in the U.S. Army." hum!

I next obtained a special leave of absence for four days and set out for home going via. Gamaliel to pay a last visit to my old school-mates.—, But alas! I found that splendid school of 60 students reduced to 30 and they all looked so dejected and sorrowful that it caused me such grief to be in their company and hear them deplore the awful condition of affairs.

I remained with them but a little while, took a final leave of them and sat out for home, arriving there all safe in life and limb. But no object seemed as of old, as I passed enclosures and noted particular spots where I had been want to amuse myself in my childhood days. I found in them fresh fuel for my already over-depressed mind.

But enough of that. I had arrived at home not a free man, but, and I was proud of the name, a soldier. I have always, from my earliest infancy, cherished an ardent feeling of love and admiration for my country. Have read books that only tended to increase the intensity of that feeling, viz., Life and correspondences of Geo. Washington, History of the Revolutionary war, Daring deeds of American Heroes, Frost's History of the United States, American Generals, &c., &c. And now I felt that I was but doing justice to myself, to my country, to my forefathers, and to future generations. Now I did not possess an extraordinarily great amount of courage or desire to fight, but I *did* to some extent cherish a desire to obtain with my own arms a right to distinction while I should be defending my Country's rights. These hopes had been in a measure, seemingly rendered hopeless by my defeat in seeking office, yet I still hoped, for I knew I would at least *do my duty* and this I had resolved to do at all hazards.

I remained closely at home during the few days of my furlough, spending my time in making a final disposition of affairs and of sauntering about, striving to reassure myself that I was satisfied with the great change my own act had so recently effected in my affairs. The day came for me to return to camp; when I started, mother admonished me to be sure and return again soon; I promised, with real sincerity that I would be back in two weeks; but alas! The shortsightedness and precipitation of human nature is continually involving him in error, and as an evidence of this assertion, I did not see my mother again till the 17th day of February, 1862.

I returned to camp on Saturday, as I recollect, about noon, and found that the most of my Company had gone home on a short furlough but their time was up that evening, and prompt to obey orders night found them all back again and ready for duty, and on this night I took my first round and stood my first tour as a sentinel of the Camp Guard. Now this is one part of a soldier's duty that I am very decidedly unable to perform on important occasions, viz., standing guard on a dark night at a post of danger when I can be guided in my actions only by the sense of hearing; for I was unfortunately born deaf in my right ear, and am utterly unable to distinguish the direction of a sound, even at the distance of ten feet. Yet I have always stood my turn without having ever gotten into difficulties on that account. On the next day "Sunday" I went to Church at Indian Creek and on my way back to Camp took dinner with Mr. William Neal and late in the afternoon returned to camp.

Monday was a rainy, disagreeable day, yet we all stood our time at drilling and such other duties as devolved upon us, in the forenoon, for in the afternoon we were pretty much puzzled by the knowledge that all the commanding officers were in secret council on some matter of importance. Late in the evening, the subject of their deliberations was disclosed by the order to be ready to move on tomorrow morning. Everyone was filled with wonder and running over with conjectures as to which way we would move, and what we would move for, and "what does the whole thing mean anyhow[.]"[15]

That night one of our Company was taken sick with Measles, which was the first sick man in our Company, and who afterwards proved to be a brave and efficient soldier, viz., Isaac Maines.

Next morning Tuesday Oct. 8th We all got under way and traveled in the direction of Ray's Cross Roads (?)[16] and marched to that point distance about twenty miles and I tell you it tried our powers of endurance to a great extent. As for myself I held up wonderfully and in the afternoon I relieved some of the most weary for several minutes at a time by carrying their guns, &c. Now I began to think myself a real whetzel for travelling. Our supper was already prepared for us at the X roads and we ate a hearty supper, then went to the wagons and took out our blankets and began to look around for some place to sleep. I found a bunk about one fourth of a mile from the supper table in the residence of a Mr.

Rush, or rather on the floor of the piazza, for he had already taken as many on the inside as he could comfortably stow away. I went to sleep to dream of better days, and awoke at the usual hour next morning. We got an early breakfast and off again at quick time marching that day about twenty miles and stopped that night at the house of a Mr. [Willis] Grissom.[17] Supper was again ready for us, and after eating our Company was marched to a neighboring church about one fourth of a mile away, which we had to ourselves for the night. After we had gotten the room properly warmed by kindling fires in the stoves, Capt Hinson called on us to give attention to a few remarks he was about to offer. He then proceeded to deliver a sensible and well composed speech, in which he reminded us of the responsibilities we had assumed in becoming soldiers of the Federal Army; the dangers we would have to risk to be of service to our country, and to sustain our reputation as soldiers; the toil, fatigue and mental suffering we would necessarily encounter, and in short that soldiering was not a holiday frolic but a succession of stern realities. He then admonished us to stand by him, and by each other like true patriots and brave men, and assured us that if we did so, we would never repent the day that we became soldiers, regardless of what we might have to risk or undergo.

After Captain Hinson had closed his remarks, Mr. M[ontraville] Waddle[18] offered a short and appropriate address which was well received and we then retired to rest, or rather lay down on the seats we had occupied during the speaking exercises.

Early on the following day we had gotten our breakfast and were again on the road. This was the hardest day's march we had yet made and I think it must have been 25 miles. We passed through the town of Columbia Addair Co. about sunset, and were there informed that we would have to go about 5 miles further yet to reach *the supplies*. Then there was the first unanimous outburst of disapprobation that I ever heard from the Regiment. All were worn out nearly, and had hoped to stop at Columbia; but thinking we were going to get something good we bowed our heads like the rebels at Chickamauga and dashed onward and in another hour were at our camp.

The supper that had been ordered for us here was served in a quantity and quality that was truly offensive, outrageous, disgustingly mean.

The beef was not warmed through; the bread was not there but a kind of raw material was substituted instead, and then to make the whole thing more unacceptable, the remains of the beeves were (as if on purpose) strewn all around the tables. I took a piece of raw beef and one of flour dough and sat down in the darkness to make my meal, and when I had done justice to the fullest extent of my abilities to this repast I was struck with a loathsome sense of disgust to find myself sitting on a (excuse the expression) beef's paunch. The boys were all mad and as they did not know who to vent their malice upon, they "kicked up a row" arming themselves and according to reports, came very near having a bloody time of it.

I can make no positive statements in regard to the matter myself, for in the first place I never mingle in such Scenes, and secondarily I had gone off to seek a good place to sleep; and on that night I took my first night's rest in the forest.

During the night we had a small shower of rain which was rather disagreeable to we fellows that had in all probability never lain *outside* a single night like this in our lives.

We were up on daybreak to learn that no breakfast had been prepared for us. This was pretty severe to us, but I suppose it could not be helped, but I tell you it went very hard with *me* and I suppose with the balance to march all that day, 16 miles without any breakfast. However, after standing around for an hour or two as if to ascertain that matters were precisely as had been represented, we again started.

Late in the evening we approached Campbellsville, and were apprised of the fact by being met by an immense throng of citizens for so small a place who welcomed us to their really loyal town by lusty cheers, cordial congratulations, and hearty shaking of the hands. And as we entered the town, were met by a band of music and escorted by the citizens through the most prosperous part of the *city* to the Public Square and then there was a feast indeed prepared for us. We had "Corn-pone", common biscuit, bakers bread, a variety of vegetables, meats of all kinds, coffee and tea, and in fact the supper was not wanting in anything that was substantive and refreshing to *we* descendants of the backwoods.

This kind of reception by the citizens of Campbellsville and the citizens of the vicinity made an impression of an enduring character upon the minds of our Regiment.

We had now arrived at our destination without knowing it however, and such a march we had made, as is well worthy of the notice of other pens than mine. When we left Camp Anderson we were about six hundred strong, and we always marched in two ranks on account of its narrow roads and consequently were a pretty long line. Everywhere along the march we received tributes to our *imposing* appearance and advanced into the neighborhood by the cheers of its multitudes, the waving handkerchiefs and patriotic speeches of the ladies and look of *wonderment* of the rebel or unsophisticated.

One day I got a little behind the troop which was an uncommon thing for anyone, and I saw a *contraband*[19] by the roadside eagerly gazing back from the way I had come. When I came up to him he said "Massa, how far back are the cannons?" We would throw off our hats and give three cheers to every demonstration of respect towards us, and our band of music, composed of a few home-made drums and reed fifes would strike up on some of the National airs and thus a great deal of the fatigue of our march was in a measure compensated for.

We were under the command of Colonel J. R. Duncan of the Home Guards, and Major —––— (I again forget his name) was the acting commisary, and a considerable amount of the boys spite was vented on him the evening last mentioned before arriving at Campbellsville, or in other words the evening we arrived at "hungry run."

We were quartered in the Campbellsville Court House and after "early candle lighting," a large number of citizens being assembled Mr. Joseph Chandler addressed the assembly upon the present state of national affairs; the advent of ourselves into the town, and our purpose; the prospects of the Union; Condition of Tennessee Refugees, &c., &c. after his sensible and appreciable discourse, Mr. A J Clements, was called on and made a few appropriate remark[s],[20] also Capt. Martin of our Regiment and Mr. M. Waddle of our Company offered a few remarks, by solicitation.

I did not enjoy a very good night's rest in consequence of having to lie on the brick floor and not having a sufficiency of blankets (one) to keep me out of absorbing distance of the bricks.

Next morning a party of ninety men were called for to go to Lebanon after the arms and Equipment for the Regiment. Our

Company was required to furnish fifteen of them and I was one of the number, and the whole detail was placed under the command of Capt Martin. As Lebanon was "twenty miles away" we started early and arrived at that place about 3 P.M. and there for the first time I saw Col. B. C. Grider, and I liked his appearance pretty well, of course.

The fare that we received here was also very good, and on that night we drew, each man one woolen blanket. Slept to night on the brick floor of the depot, standing guard, or rather acting corporal two hours.

Next morning after breakfast, there was a general over hauling of military stores and we were all supplied with Haversacks and canteens, and subsequently, with guns and accouterments, in order to be ready to guard the train loaded with our stores down to Campbellsville.

At three o'clock in the afternoon we started out in two squads, one in advance and one in the rear of the train. The train, whew! *Nineteen wagons* and all loaded with ordinance and Ordinance stores, Camp and Garrison Equippage, and some provisions & *enormous* indeed; surely we would need no more supplies in a whole month. A correct idea of the great amount that a few hundred men will soon consume, never having once entered our minds.

Col. Grider rode along and gave us a gentle admonition that if attacked we must not "flicker" and a few words of general information.[21] We arrived in Campbellsville some hours after dark, having met the Regiment some miles out to give us three cheers for our success.

By this time I was almost completely worn out having marched six days in succession and not having enjoyed a good night's rest in the whole time, in consequence of cool weather, scarcity of blankets and being unaccustomed to sleeping on hard floors, but I was destined to become adapted to all these inconveniences and to make preparations for them, and I tell you I have fulfilled my destiny in that respect to the fullest meaning of the word.

I found that the soldiers were again preparing to do their own cooking "and living." And as I knew very little in the culinary line I generally let someone invite me to his table, and I managed to get an invite whenever I wanted it, and consequently I had plenty to eat of the quality.

Chapter 2

An Attack of Measles

Disease, not battle, was the great killer in the Civil War. Twice as many soldiers died of illness as succumbed to enemy bullets. This was particularly true during the war's first year, as armies largely made up of rural youths, lacking previous exposure to contagious diseases, joined together in crowded, dirty, and unsanitary camps. Woodcock's regiment, soon to be mustered as the 9th Kentucky Infantry (U.S.A.), was no exception. Between November 1861 and June 1862, 92 members of the regiment died of fever, pneumonia, and measles, most of them while at Camp Boyle in Columbia, Kentucky. They constituted 36 percent of the regiment's entire death toll of 252; many fewer—only 57—actually died as a result of combat. In addition, 30 percent of the soldiers, on average, spent time on the sick list. Woodcock was one; he nearly died of measles in Columbia. Ironically, his near-fatal illness may have saved his life, for, while he was recovering, the 9th Kentucky received a bloody baptism of fire at Shiloh.[1]

About the 14th or 15th days of the month, all the recruits received regular government arms and turned over the Home Guard guns and accouterments.[2] Also we had under-clothing, camp and Garrison Equippage issued to us. I did not know how to get my knapsack "into shape" and put it on, and was not well enough skilled in the accomplishments of harness making to accomplish it after much study on the subject. But some *Yankee* solved the mystery and we were soon, as some of the boys laconically expressed it, "geared up" and they were kicking, jumping, running and plunging to prove that they would be difficult to break to the harness. They at last got calm and joked and laughed over the subject—little dreaming that they would have to wear these equippages or their equivalent for three whole years. For no one expressed the least intimation that we would have to be in the service longer than four months, or six at most, and that we would all get home to plant crops the next spring. If I could have been made to believe at this time that I would have to serve three years in the Army, and *that* at the dark and difficult "front," I don't think my moral courage would have sustained me for one hour. And it is real truth that the greater number of our Regiment had thoughts that the war would end ere our time was out till about the time of the battle of Stone River. They (the home seekers) would be continually speculatory about the prospects of peace; but this very suddenly ceased in the winter of '62 and '63 and turned to that of when our term of service would expire. Some thought that we would get our furlough time (40 days per year by U.S. Army Regulations) thrown in, or in other words that we would get out of the Service 120 days previous to the expiration of three years from date of first enlistment; others that we would get out at the date of enlistment without our furlough; while others still argued that we would be mustered out according to muster-in in the State Service; and a *few* argued that we would not get out till the 26th day of November, 1864, three years from date of muster-in to the U.S. Service; but I must not anticipate.

About the 16th we started for Columbia having in the meantime drawn one month's pay (13.00), and marched out 12 miles to one Mr. Grissom's, and camped for the night in his lot. Just after we had gone into camp some of the boys accidentally threw down a stack of muskets and one of them discharged itself, one of the shots taking effect in the thigh of Theo. Lewis, a private of Capt. [Isaac] Dickinson's Company (afterwards Co. G),[3] several shots going through his knapsack. The wound, if I recollect right, was not very severe.

That night I was detailed to stand my turn at Camp Guard as a private, and being informed that my relief would go on at just two hours before daylight, I retired to rest. Was waked up at the usual time and posted without any instructions, and consequently, as I felt very stupid I sat down by the side of a tree and gave way to the ruminations of my mind.

Silas Clark and Walter M. Clark, c. 1863.
Courtesy of Melba Keith and Randy G. East.

I was soon dreaming, dreaming of quite a different state of being.
I was in fairy land, in a garden of most beautiful flowers and nice
streams traversing their way among the stems of varigated plants.
In the middle of the garden was a beautiful harbor containing a sofa
of almost unimaginable luxury. I was reclining on this sofa indulg-
ing a sleepy doze which was like balm to my weary limbs and sleepy
eyes. I was though still a soldier, but not a poor private soldier of
an obscure Volunteer Company, but such a soldier as I have read
of flourishing in the chivalrous days of the knight-errants. I was
dressed in a splendid oriental costume, a plume of gaudy feathers
streaming from my helmet, a coat of mail protected my body. A
lady of surpassing beauty and lovliness approached and kneeling
before me implored my protection from the insults of some rude
suitor. I was just bidding her to rise and giving her assurances of
my protection when my mother approached and placed her hand
upon my head, and blessed me as her darling son. And next my
sister made her appearance, and after salutation suddenly pointed
at some approaching objects a short distance away. I suddenly sprang
to my feet seizing my spear at the same moment, only to find that
I was approached by Corporal W. M. Clarke with a relief and that
instead of the mighty spear I was firmly grasping my musket, and
instead of the rich Oriental Costume I was clothed in the humble
garb of a Tennessee farmer. *The Corporal had caught me asleep upon
my post* and the penalty is *death*. But the Corporal, being a fellow
of great magnanimity of character and a kind and humorous [one]
withal simply remarked "Now I guess you will give me chestnuts"
and I don't think he ever related the circumstances to any living
mortal till some two years subsequent I related [them] to a story-
telling squad myself. On that day we continued our journey to
Columbia arriving about late in the evening and camping in the
various vacant houses. I think we remained there on the next day
again and until the next morning. That night, however, I slept in
the office of a lawyer whose name I have forgotten—Capt Hinson
and a few others of the Company being also of the party. A member
of the Kentucky Legislature talked with us an hour or two, making
himself very agreeable and interesting to our party, and then left us
to ourselves. On the next morning we were aroused early with the
information that our troops at Greensburgh were threatened by the

approach of a rebel army, and that our assistance was required at that place.

There was a slight rain falling and had been for a greater part of the previous day and night, and consequently the roads could at best be in a sad plight for traveling. But we were on the road early and as the rain soon ceased falling the march was not so disagreeable. We went about fifteen miles on the Campbellsville Pike, and then turned off to the left in the direction of Greensburg and marched till near sunset and which could not have been less than ten miles from the Pike and then we struck the Campbellsville and Greensburg road. There a sight met our eyes that we were not prepared for, viz. the Greensburg troops were falling back to Campbellsville and were going in a totally perfect specimen of a "hasty retreat." Ah but our boys were mad in earnest, and they would with a much greater degree of cheerfulness follow Col. Grider to Greensburg than they did to Campbellsville, which place we went to that night, making our whole day's march something very nearly to 35 miles. At any rate, that was the estimate of a citizen of Campbellsville. Our boys jested with the Greensburg troops so severe concerning the affair that a kind of hardness or antipathy of feeling was sprung up that remained a long time though the private soldiers were not to blame as probably the Regimental officers, for all our boys can testify to the subsequent patriotic roles of one regiment of these, viz. 13th Kentucky Infantry, at the Battle of Shiloh, or Pittsburg Landing, April 7th, 1862.[4]

We turned up on the Campbellsville Road and now that we were relieved of the excitement incidental to the prospect of a battle, we began to feel very much fatigue and many of the Regiment did not get into town that night. As for myself, I with great difficulty managed to arrive there and there found a very substantial supper prepared for me.

In consequence of having left our blankets, by orders, at Columbia, I did not rest very well tonight and most of the boys were considerably inconvenienced from the same fact.

We remained at Campbellsville a few days doing little of consequence but loafing around and nothing of interest occurring: Unless we should remark that a detachment of the Greensburg cavalry that had been in that direction on a scout came dashing into town one day in the greatest haste, and evincing great alarm some without hats, and the ominous appearance of a few riderless horses along with them. They had run upon a squad of Rebels some miles out, and getting defeated had galloped back, losing some of their party, but I now disremember who, or how many.

It was about this time that a new incident was provided for the Calendar list (if the date had not been lost) by the arrival of one of that famous rebel organizations known as "Bull Pups." I gazed upon him with more eager curiosity than I did upon first seeing the Elephant, or other wild animals.[5] He was a nice looking man and well dressed, and exceedingly well mannered. Had been captured by one Miller Hayes of Monroe County Kentucky. Col. Grider took possession of his splendid charger and rode him till after the Battle of Shiloh, but I have forgotten what disposition was finally made of him. I wrote the name of Miller Hayes in my journal as one of the Heroes of the war, so much importance did I attach to this little incident, and indeed the greatest importance was attached to incidents of the most trivial (if warlike) nature, not detracting any from the praise due Mr. Hayes, for in capturing this Bull Pup heavily armed as he was, he (Hayes) did more than almost any other citizen in the same circumstances would have done.

We remained at Campbellsville a few more days and then took up our line of march for Columbia. We got there all right without accident in life or limb and in a few days commenced setting up tents and preparing for soldiering in reality, sleeping in unoccupied houses about town in the meantime, drilling considerably and learning but little except how to eat badly cooked provisions. Our rations consisted principally in flour and beef, with sometimes a few potatoes or cabbages, and as scarcely any of us had any knowledge or experience in the art of cooking, it was necessarily served very badly and soon began to produce disease among us, aided by our being unaccustomed to the exposure and the appearance of measles in our Camp.

It was at this time that "hard times" set in to have his turn at our poor fellows. Every day sent new patients to the hospitals and the duty list was getting materially decreased. About this time I saw the first battalion drills and something like an appearance of real military order began to spring up among us. A vigilant Camp Guard was kept posted at all times which it was death to violate; the regular calls were all observed. Grand Rounds were made every night, dress parade a thing of every day occurrence, and all rules coming down pretty heavily.

Recruits were also coming in in great numbers and the prospect was that we would soon have a full Regiment: and it is a significant fact that our Regiment would have been filled with picked men young, able bodied, and healthy. But all were accepted that applied; old crippled, infirm, &c. and the consequence was that many of them never did any real service. On the 3rd day of November I did my first regular day's work at the Kitchen, and it fell to my lot to work dough, and you must remember that it was flour dough. I think it was as disagreeable a day's work as I did in that year. The rain fell continually from morning till night, and I was thoroughly drenched. And when night came I had such a bad opinion of my darlings (although I did the best I could) that I could not eat that I had cooked; and went over to town and bought a chicken and some biscuits from "Old Pete" and made a splendid supper on them. I then went to a room occupied by some others of our company, and taking off my clothes, hung them up around the stove and by midnight had them dried and then spread my blankets and commenced negotiations with old Morephus [Morpheus], asking a few hours sleep, which was kindly granted.

Slept soundly till a late hour the next morning and then repaired to camp and to other duties besides that of cooking, but feeling very badly in regard to bodily health, yet I had been with the measles for several days and was not to be surprised if I took it at any moment. Notwithstanding, my feeling of general dibility continued[.] I still kept about but not able for duty, and spent my time in laying around and eating scarcely anything and suffering considerably till the 6th. That was a fine day, and everything had gone off smoothly, and I and several others of the Company had gone over to town to sleep.

We took a room on the Southwest side of the Public Square, upstairs. [A]nd had kindled a fire in the stove, and getting the room heated to a comfortable degree had all commenced the evening amusement of telling stories of history and tradition, and singing pieces of war and Religion, when a citizen hastened upstairs and informed us that rebel soldiers were in the suburbs of town and that we had better hasten away or we might be captured. Giving full confidence to the validity of the information, we all hastened downstairs and double-quicked it to the camp and there we found the Regiment in line of battle "*steadily* waiting the approach of the enemy."

Soon after we came upon the ground and ere we had time to gird on our armor the Regiment was dismissed and the alarm proven to be false.

I never did ascertain the true cause of the alarm, but I think it was the efforts of a drunken teamster[6] attempting to drive over a picket sentinel; and refusing to obey the command to halt was as a matter of course fired upon by the soldier; and reader, the report of a musket in those days of general demoralization was enough to set a whole county to moving i.e. if any man ever *heard* the report of the gun without *seeing* the gun.

I soon returned to town and lay down upon my hard bed, from which I was destined to arise as an invalid, for I awoke a little after midnight, and was suffering from acute pains in my limbs and dull aching sensation in my head. An early examination by Dr. A. J. Clements pronounced me to be suffering from an attack of measles and I was immediately placed on the sick list.

I had no appetite for anything to eat, but thinking that I *should* eat something, I went over to the residence of that honest, clever, and *loyal* citizen, Judge Wheat and called for some cornbread baked in a peculiar style; it was served on short notice and just as I had ordered it, free of charge, and on occasions after that, in the same town I paid other citizens for the small amount of one teacup full of milk and mush. Now I do not claim that a citizen is under obligation to furnish the soldier anything he may ask for, but I do think that when a soldier is prostrate upon a bed of sickness, far from home and friends with no mother to prepare his cordials or smooth his pillow, no sister to give him kind words of encouragement, and point him to Him who rules all nature, and without whose notice, not even a sparrow falls to the ground, or to speak to him of happy days when he will again be hale and stout and ready to participate in the amusements of or business of life; In this case I think the citizen, if he can do so without sacrificing more than the worth of a cup of milk and mush, should render the soldier some assistance. The value of the article is of no importance to the soldier, but when you *give* it to him, it makes him know that you sympathize with him in his sufferings and I tell you, openly evinced sympathy on the part of the citizen for the sick soldier is one of the greatest balms that can be administered.

But what a depraved creature man is! for it is a significant fact that while I lay in the hospital at Columbia, (17) days I never once, as I now recollect, saw a citizen of Columbia within its walls, and I am positive there was not a single lady in there. Oh woman! Would that my pen had the powers of Byron's Shakespears's or Milton's that I might here pay a tribute to you who *are women*. Would you soothe the soldier when he is prostrated on the bed of sickness, racked with acute pain and scorched with burning fevers? Would you make his path easy when he is about to "shuffle off this mortal coil" and go into regions of Eternity, and would you prepare him for this great transition? Would you make many a weary moment, while on the Convalescent couch, be to him as dreams of bliss? Then go to the hospitals.—Your *presence* alone will do him good, be with him in the first stroke of disease; in the awful hand of Death or in the doubtful state of convalescence. But let us resume.

I ate a few morsels of my bread and then returned to the room where I had slept the night before and which was to be converted into a hospital and spread my blanket upon the floor and thereon stretched my aching body, an invalid among strangers; no opportunity of communicating with friends at home, by mail or otherwise, unaccustomed to sickness and a stranger to the treatment I would in all probability receive, and as yet no nurse appointed for my room.

Now, my patient reader, this was enough to depress stouter minds than mine, enough to prostrate more healthy physical frames than mine and consequently it must not be wondered at that I became slightly depressed in spirit and awfully weakened in body. The sick list increased with such fearful rapidity that ere night the room was filled with patients, all cases of measles. I think there were about 15 in the room and it not more than 20 feet square, and we lay till the third day ere we even got straw to put under our blankets.

We finally got this very desirable article though and then by sleeping two together (for we had only one blanket each) we could keep tolerably warm, but I cant say comfortable for that is impossible with two sick persons lying in the same bed. The stench was horrible from the fact that the beds were simply a continuation of the straw pile[d] around the room, and that we lay with our heads close to the wall and our bodies close to and parallell with each other we could not have the advantages of spittoons which if ever needed, are in cases of measles, and consequently were subjected to the necessity of spitting against the wall. This was not washed more than twice in a week. Our diet was of a very inferior quality for sick persons, but I do not now recollect the Bill of fare.

Now I am not making this story of our hospital experience as a complaint against the Government or the Officers of our Regiment, but simply to show that the privations endured by the troops that came out under the first call were in a measure unknown to those of a subsequent date.

At that time we did not enjoy the benefits of that great institution known as the U.S. Sanitary Commission,[7] were 40 miles from Rail Road transportation, not a Government wagon had yet come into the possession of the Regiment, and as a matter of necessity no comforts could be provided for the sick only as obtained from the surrounding country, and I tell you that was a very limited quantity.

The Medical Department was rather badly served and I never could account for it unless it was on account of the bad health of our chief Surgeon J. R. Duncan.[8]

I never saw him but three times while confined to my room and then he was just making tours of inspection. I never took a dose of medicine while in that room, ere my father came except cough drops, and Dover's powders, for the prescription invariably consisted of Blue Mass Calomel, Quinine, or all combined, and as I had been bred in the Physo-Medical faith these mercurial prescriptions were truly alarming to me; but the M.D.'s were kind enough to allow me my own judgment in the matter, and that always dictated to me to let the mercury alone.[9]

I think I had been in the hospital about four days when the measles began to "break out." But it only appeared on the surface to a very small extent and soon "went in" leaving me in a bad condition. I would have sent for my father but the refugees that were continually coming and going reported him to be in very bad health, so as not to be able to ride, therefore I urged everyone to tell him that I was improving and would soon be well. Finally, the great amount of cold I had taken fell on my lungs and I was rendered unable to speak above a faint whisper.

Yet on the morning after I found myself in this condition I penned a letter to my father informing him that I was still in bad health, but *no worse* and would probably soon be about again.

I kept in good spirits nearly all the time, and was confident that I would get well, yet everyone that saw me at this time said that *it looked like a gone case with me*, and I *now* think that I would not have recovered had it not been for the kind and diligent attentions of the nurses, and two of them in particular, viz. B. H. Waddle and Samuel Steel both of my company. Steel provided for my comfort by stirring my *straw*, cooking my tea, roasting apples, warming my blankets, and in numerous ways contributed to my comfort with a magnamity and generosity of heart that is as a general thing a stranger to hospital nurses. Waddle could go to the citizens and by dent of perseverance in the face of their rebel proclivities, could procure such articles as milk, milk-and-mush, butter, pickles (to drive out the abominable measle taste), canned fruit and various vegetables, which other persons delegated by me on the same mission had signally failed in and it was this that kept me alive, for I loathed the regular foods furnished by the hospital cooks with such an intensity that I verily believe I would have starved to death in the sight of plenty of it. The rash in my mouth was so bad that I could not swallow anything that had to be chewed, and thus my reason for preferring milk and mush to any other diet. About 9 o clock at night of the third day after writing the last-mentioned letter, I was startled by a seemingly somewhat familiar voice inquiring for me in the room, but it was impossible for me to recognize it. The person came to where I was laying in the corner of the room and asked after my health, &c., and then if I did not yet recognize him. I coolly told him I did not, and asked the nurse to bring the candle, when lo! it was father. Gentle Reader, I have all through my life had reasons to be thankful to Him who rules all and have many times enjoyed His benevolence to such an extent as to make me truly happy, but never in my life was I so filled with thankfulness to Almighty God, and as transported with the most estatic joy as I was on that night when I saw father in my room; in that little dark room where I had passed the darkest and most doubtful period of my life.

I rose in valor of strength according to my own estimation about 50 percent in an exceedingly short space of time. Father had come all the way from home that day, a distance of about 60 miles and seemed to not be much wearier by it either although it was the first time he had been on horseback for four weeks on account of ill health. He could now tell me all about my brother Thomas' arrest and imprisonment by the Rebel Colonel Head, and of his subsequent trial and release, all of which I heard of soon after it happened (Nov 1st & 5th), and which had caused me a deal of trouble and into mental Suffering.[10]

After administering some stimulating teas, and leaving directions for me to take more, Father for want of room in the hospital to lie down went to a Hotel and remained all night. On the next morning he went to that kind, generous, and caring old lady, viz. the widow [Mary] Epperson[11] and engaged a room for him and myself till I should get well, having already procured a permit from the surgeon, J. R. Duncan, to remove me to a private house. But the weather was so inclement during the day that it was thought inadvisable to remove me, and I had to remain till after dark when the wind growing calm, and the air becoming warmer I was transferred to Mrs. Eppersons, and once more was blessed with the privilege of laying on a good bed. Though I was first careful to put on a new change of underclothing which my father had procured for me that day, and which was the first change of clothes I had had in three weeks. That was a delicious night's rest indeed and had it not been for my very bad cough, it would have been one of uninterruption. I then remained here just one week and during the time ("Nov 26th") was mustered into the U.S. Service. Also I drew a full suit of Government clothing, and notwithstanding my weakness, I persisted in the purpose of immediately donning them to see how they became me. I was very well satisfied with my appearance with the exception of the leanness of my face, and thought that when it got "filled out" I would be the most perfect personification of a hero.

But I must not engross your attention altogether with myself but give at least a passing notice to the other equally suffering and deserving boys of the Regiment. Disease had by this time thrown scores of them into the hospitals, and deaths were becoming matters of not infrequent occurrence. Friends were daily arriving from home, but that was often the cause for fresh trouble instead of pleasure; for each one of them brought fresh news of some depredation committed by the rebels in our county. The draft had been made in Tennessee and a large number upon whom it fell were leaving the country and coming to Columbia: thus was our condition rendered deplorable in more senses than one.[12]

The boys that had been all the time healthy had not the greatest reason in the world for not wanting to change their condition, for the weather had been remarkably rainy all the time and they were encamped on ground of such a nature that the water was not quickly absorbed, and so level that it could not be "ditched off," and as a consequence they had a perfect swamp at all times. Our force, in the meanwhile, had been considerably increased by the arrival of the 19th O.V.I. and 59th O.V.I., 13th and 21st Ky V.I., and soon afterwards by a battery of artillery of what Regiment I do not know.[13] We were therefore a pretty formidable party and any attempt to *oust* us must, to be successful, have been made by at least a respectable party. Also, the 5th Ky Cavalry was being organized here and was pretty well filled, but about this time they had become slightly dissatisfied with the general movement of affairs, and the prospect that they would have trouble in their camps now seemed very strong; And at a subsequent date a large number of them did leave without leave but did not remain away very long.[14]

On saturday the 30th day of November I and father left Columbia to go to the country to the residence of Mr. J. R. Akin, he having agreed to board me awhile.

We went out 4 miles into the country and in consequence of my great weakness stopped at the residence of a widow woman named Scott to stay all night.[15]

Had good fare and some real living specimens of the Kettle Creek folks to call after supper for another supper, 6 of them and a jolly crowd, going to Columbia to inlist in the Army.

Paid our bill and started next morning to Mr. Akin's yet five miles away, and arrived there about noon and was favorably impressed from the beginning with the kindness of Mrs Akin, who immediately took charge of me and said that she knew that she could cure me right away.

On this day I began to find myself able to speak in a slightly audible voice but with great effort and I improved very fast in my speech from that time forward and soon could talk as well as ever.

I improved in health very slowly from this time forward, notwithstanding I had every care and attention that the inventiveness of a very kind and intelligent lady could bestow on me, and such physicianness [as] my father could do.

After some days I began to walk about a little and then my father, and brother, who had come up some days since concluded to go home and leave me with the Akin family.

There was no lack of a sufficiency of young people in the neighborhood, and they all used every effort to make me comfortable and seemed to vie with each other in bestowing favors upon me. I shall ever revert with grateful remembrance to the pleasant hours I spent in the society of these generous, magnanimous, and intelligent young people. Some of them were to see me almost every day, and of evenings they would get up quiet amusements of such a nature that I could participate and thus they made the long hours of weakness and affliction roll away very smoothly. One day I was sitting in the door tugging away at a large piece of molasses Candy and enjoying the sport very much, when very much to my surprise, father made his appearance at the door with a "shelaly" in his hand and making gestures as though he intended to give me a little gentle admonition for some offense unknown to me. I could see from the old fellows countenance that he was not very mad and consequently I did not break. After comparing notes it seems that he had been about as equally surprised as myself, for a report had reached him to the effect that I was dangerously low and not expected to survive but a few days.

I *believed it was false* as soon as I heard it—but nevertheless I kept my tongue still. He had no news of great interest to speak to me about only that "Woolford's Cavalry"[16] had broken open the Macon County Jail and taken therefrom all the arms the rebels had collected from the county and stowed away there. There was great alarm among the rebels lest the indomitable Woolford should do more mischief, but he was never heard from again in that quarter. The deed had been accomplished just a few nights previous and not by Woolford, but by the yeomanry of Macon and Monroe Counties. The whole affair promised to go off very nicely and did for the time being, but it would have been a fact of great significance if there had been no *traitors* in the party. At any rate, the whole thing and many of the men's names were soon after divulged and Col. Bennett, with his Cavalry Regiment of rebels[17] came up to Lafayette and arrested every Union [man] in Macon County nearly, accused all of being participators, and had some of them tried and condemned to die by hanging, but they were spared through the intervention of some influential persons on condition that they would bring back a certain number of the arms. I think this was the terms but not positive. My father and brother were arrested also but both proved clearly to the Colonel's mind that they were not concerned in the affair. At the time of his arrest (This was subsequent to the visit I have just spoken of made to me by my father) my father was suffering with a very severe and torturing sore known as a Carbuncle, and had not been able to walk for some days, in consequence of the pain it gave him. Notwithstanding all this, the *brutes* that came to arrest him compelled him to go to Lafayette on horseback, a distance of twelve miles, starting at about 10 o clock A.M.

And the commander of this squad of rather *indifferent brutes* had the audacity to insult my father by speaking lightly of his sufferings, and also by making some *slang* remarks concerning myself and of the fact of my being a soldier in what he termed the Lincoln army, saying that I had "gone to Abraham's bosom."

This band also took my father's Rifle, but Col. B. had magnaminity enough to return it. Those were days when the rebels ruled with a heavy hand in our devoted little County (Macon). There was an enrolling officer for the County and sub-enrolling officers for the sub-districts, and these sub-enrolling officers assumed more importance and authority by the favors of their offices than Jeff Davis did in his. They were a brave set of gentlemen also; for evidence of this assertion I can state that the one for our district made it conveninent to come to Father's house after his gun, when he was certain that he had been some days up at Columbia with me. But thanks to the wise precaution of Black Ben,[18] the gun was resting quietly beneath a straw stack and could not be found.

The rebels were crowing everywhere, and felt confident that ere another twelve-month had lapsed the Independence of the Southern

Confederacy would be peaceably acknowledged and we Tennessee-ans that had enlisted in the Federal Army, together with all our natural kinsfolk that were Union in sentiment would be forced to seek an asylum north of Mason and Dixon's line.

If I ever were to be caught by the rebel authorities I was to be tried as a deserter, for at the first draft *two months after I had been in the Federal* Army, I was drafted. Such is Southern Chivalry, Southern Equity and Southern "rights."

But such a doom was not destined for me, and I have since shaken hands with the very *gentlemen* that were then so desirous to take me, and now "of all men they are the most miserable."

But I am degressing too far and will resume.

Father did not remain but a few days this time and accordingly set out for home. On the night of the same day he left I was violently attacked with gravel,[19] and then I suffered the most acute and distressing misery it has ever been my lot to undergo, and had it not have been for the knowledge of old Mrs. Akin in such affairs it might have resulted worse than it did. She subjected me to a series of bathings for about an hour and then completely enveloped me in hot rocks. I was to some extent rendered easy, but by no means entirely so. On the next evening I concluded to take an emetic, much against the opinion of Mrs. Akin who was a decided enemy to lobelia[20] in any form; but I took it, and not knowing how to administer it in my weak state, it proved a very serious looking affair and we all became alarmed. Now for the first time I became thoroughly disheartened *and gave up to die* and of all the miserable men on the earth it is one that is under a defection of spirits to an excessive degree. I believed that I was a going to die and still was not sick enough to *want to die* and consequently was in a most miserable condition. Sometimes I fancied that my heart ceased to beat for several minutes in succession, and every half hour in the day I could put my hand to my left breast to ascertain if my heart was still moving. But according to the wisdom of a just God I didn't die but was a long time getting a proper start towards improvement again.

By some means or other, father got an inkling of the fresh attack and here he came again on the wings of speed but did not arrive till the crisis had passed and Dr. [U. L.] Taylor[21] had pronounced me in a condition to get well, but I was yet suffering considerably, and such continual sickness tended to depress my spirits and make me inclined to be peevish and whindling.

In a few days father went home again and I was again improving to some extent and wanting to eat everything that I could think of and did not have. About this time I received a letter from Capt Bryan stating that there was yet a great amount of sickness in the camp, that five of the Company had died and many more were very low. This did not tend to reassure me any for I had begun to intertain thoughts of going back to Camp for it seemed that I could not get well out in this country.

But Mr. and Mrs Akin prevailed with me to stay till about the 16th day of January when I vowed I must go to the camp, and old Mr. Akin fixed up and carried me out. I had no particular desire to go to Camp, for I was far from being well yet, but I simply wanted to change water and diet, &c. to see if that would not start my physical system on the road to health and strength once more. I had now been sick over two months, and with the best care that could be given. I would not be well enough for duty many days short of a month; but I went to the Camp and reported to Capt Bryan for duty, and was marked immediately on the sick list.

I was pleased with the new position on which the camp had been pitched since I went to the hospital in November. It was placed on an elevated, rolling piece of ground in an open field but so near a thick wood that it was no trouble to keep a sufficient quantity. The camps were also well laid off, and had we been experienced then as we afterwards were, many a poor fellow would now be alive and well and a comfort to his friends and relatives that is gone from the earth to try the awfulness of Eternity. The men slept on piles of straw, *laid on the ground* and not changed more than once in every two weeks. Since[,] that experience has taught us that it is better to lay on a pile of sticks than on straw thrown on the ground, when in regular camp.

I never saw a bed in the whole camp that was raised from the ground, except Maj. Hinson's. The tents were also very badly ditched, the trenches in many instances being barely sufficient to keep water from running under the straw, and not deep enough to have the best effect upon the moisture of the earth inside the tent. A considerable improvement had been made in the cooking line since I left the camp. The Companies were now divided off into messes of 15 men each and each mess allowed two cooks who cooked, one each day alternately. A Corporal was put in charge of each mess, and was responsible for its good behavior, soldierly deportment, cleanliness, &c. and indeed considering the length of time they had been soldiering, the boys were doing right well, and were rapidly advancing into the mysteries of the soldier's duties; at least they thought so; but alas for human shortsightedness, how badly they were mistaken!

A great many were yet sick in the hospitals, and a considerable number had been returned to duty, but of these a very few were able to even take care of themselves.

On the next evening after I arrived in Camp, a general order came for all who were able to walk to fall into line and be marched to the creek and there everyone must take off his clothing and plunge into the stream; no matter if he had only been out of the hospital one day. Now this did not suit me very well, but never the less, I was always remarkable for obeying orders, and I accordingly "fell in" and went to the river but was scarcely able to get there, and then I took off my upper garments and washed the upper part of my body, but did not plunge in, mind you, but the Captain excused me on account of *protracted* illness. I never could vouch for the wisdom of this act, for while it might have been beneficial to the larger portion and would be to all if regularly adhered to it resulted fatally in a few instances.

Company and Battalion drills were now kept up with great regularity, 2 hours in the morning and two in the evening respectively. The troops were advancing in the science with great alacrity, and promised soon to be efficient for any service.

Religious ceremonies were held every Sunday by parson [James C.] Rush of the Methodist or Baptist Church,[22] and whose residence was Munfordville. After a few Sundays some of the boys got tired of listening to the (to them) uninteresting services, and in all probability they may have cherished a personal dislike for the parson also. At any rate on the first Sunday after I arrived, a goodly number considered they would stay at home and do their own preaching for their own special benefit, and as a consequence when the services were over I looked accidentally toward the guard-house and saw about 50 men "marking time" at common, quick, and double-quick time "first one and then t'other", rendering the affair rather amusing.

Several men had also deserted by this time, and a general dissatisfaction had seized upon all because we were not allowed to go back to our own immediate country. We could not see the propriety of laying inactive a whole winter at an unimportant point when the rights of our own personal firesides were being every day desecrated and this being arranged by some brutal outrage of rebel partisans.

In consequence of my feeble health and the inadequate comforts our (privates) tents afforded us, Maj Hinson, as kind hearted a man as ever was[,] invited me to share his tent and bed and as he had a stove, plank floor, table, plenty of straw and other conveniences, I gladly accepted the invitation and in this manner things rolled on smoothly for nearly a month, and during this month I think I received but one direct communication from home and that was in the form of pies, custards, cakes, and sweetmeats of various descriptions, sent by the kindness of Mrs. William Holland, Sen[ior]. This was about the 9th day of February and in consequence of an order to take charge of a mess that had no non-comissioned officer I was necessarily compelled to move my sleeping from the Major's tent to Mess No. 3 (?) and suffered so much with cold on the first night that in the next day my cough was much worse and by the morning of the 12th I could perceive that I was again growing weaker and my health gradually failing.

I think it was on the 12th that the joyful news came, "Orders," "Have two days rations cooked and be ready to march out tomorrow morning." Whoopee! Immediately there was a thousand tongues speculating over the good news, and the only cause of trouble was, *they did not [know] which of the two places they were going to, Tompkinsville or Scottsville*, it being a fact that would not admit of doubt that they were going to one of the two places. That was indeed a busy evening of preparation. Rations were drawn, divided and given to the men, Cooks were flying around ordering this one to bring water, that one to bring wood and a third to do something else. All was in a confused hurry of getting things ready for packing, &c. As for myself I took only a partial interest in the proceedings for it was decided that I could not go with the Regiment and consequently I could only feel pleased to see the others going. That night I could sleep very little in consequence of the violent fits of coughing that seized me every time I attempted to lay down.

On the next morning everything was astir long ere daylight, and by sunrise the tents had been struck and packed, cooking vessels collected, and everything stowed carefully away in the wagons, and the men fully equipped were in line and ready to move off! which they soon did leaving myself and a score of Convalescents to gaze with longing eyes after the beautiful lines of blue as they made their disappearance over the distant hills, going in the direction of the "Sunny South" where treason reigns supreme.

Oh how I wished to go with them and never let the Regiment march a single mile without I were along at my post, and ready to do my duty, and by this time it began to look to me as if I were not a going to pay Uncle Sam for the expenses I would help to incur.

With tearful eyes I finally saw the Regiment go out of view, and then with a heavy heart I turned my course toward the hospital to report. I was ordered to do the best I could in common with the others till some hospital tents could be erected and prepared for our reception. I went to Mrs Epperson's to get my dinner, and of supper I took nothing and went over to the tents before referred to and found them to be very comfortable considering there was no fire. Had a very pleasant night's rest and on awaking and turning out next morning was surprised to find a frozen snow on the ground.

This began to look bad again, for we had no stove, no stout persons to help us get wood and had to walk near one-half of a mile to the *hospital* to obtain our meals, but were not able to do that this morning, for coming out of the close tents we were soon very cold and now hastened on to get to the fire. When I got into the hospital I was most sincerely confused by some person asking me if *I had seen my father* yet. Good thought I, and said is he here, and received an affirmative answer to the effect that he had been searching the hospitals early that morning for me. I guessed where he was stopping at, and pushing aside a dish of beef soup, thickened with corn meal I started in search of him and soon found him, and back we went to his boarding house (Mr. Page's) and I again got a good breakfast.

Father said he had come to take me home this time, and when

I reminded him of military authority and the order to grant no more furloughs, he simply said that I should go home and ordered me to be ready to march early on tomorrow morning. After I had done my breakfast he said let us go to the Doctor's office.

We went to the door and that magnanimous, kind-hearted—generous—easy-tempered old fellow known as Dr. Thos. R. W. Jeffray would not even let us come into his room although the morning was very chilly. And years after this event when I was a *comissioned officer*, this same magnanimous, kind-hearted, generous, easy-tempered old fellow known as Dr. Thos. R. W. Jeffray would speak of my severe illness at Columbia and dwell largely on his genurosity in letting me come home. And I really believe that if the affair had been entirely in Dr. Jeffray's charge that my bones would to day be rotting beneath the soil of Addair County Kentucky.

Father simply remarked that this was as good as he expected, but that he simply did it out of respect for the *old fools* shoulder straps, and that he would next try Brig. Gen. Boyle,[23] who is at any rate a *perfect gentleman*. I stepped into a store to warm myself and wait the result of the interview with the General, and soon saw Father coming back with an expression on his face that indicated perfect success, and which proved to be the case.

I then returned to Mrs Page's residence and father to the country to make a search for Uncle Nathan Woodcock, who had been left sick by a road working party, and he ascertained that Uncle Nathan had started to the Regiment on the same morning it marched and was ere thus undoubtedly with it.

On Thursday the 15th day of February I sat out for home in company with my father. We traveled that day about 20 miles, stopping at night with a gentleman by the name of Bragg,[24] 5 miles from Edmonton, but on the *old Columbia Road*. Riding on horseback seemed to agree with me, and though it is irregular, it is true that riding all day seemed to strengthen instead of wearying me, at any rate, I felt a considerable *percent* better in health and strength at the end of my journey than when I sat out in the morning. We were well fed and lodged and kindly treated by Mr. and Mrs. Bragg during our stay, but were off again next morning, and on that day went as far as the residence of Rev. L. A. Smithwick, a firm and fearless Union man, and one for whom I had great respect and esteem. He had formerly been my teacher and is also an ordained minister of the Missionary Baptist Church. We got there about 10 o'clock P.M., and I called upon Mrs Smithwick for some Egg-bread in the preparation of which article she was, in my humble opinion unsurpassed. Supper was soon forth coming and as quickly dispatched, and then I was into bed and asleep, but my cough was so very violent that I could not rest well.

Feb. 17th. Next morning I was off again and by 12 o'clock P.M. Oh, joy! I was home. Now it may appear simple to you, reader, that I should feel any great pleasure in arriving at home when I had been absent only 4 months and one-half and during all that time except a few days had been within 60 miles of home, and at no time over eighty.

But you must recollect that I had been kept at home or near about there all my life, and previous to the date connected with the beginning of this narrative, *I had never been thirty miles from home.* Neither had I ever been permanently absent from home for more than two weeks in succession. And you must also recollect that during this last trial I had much to render home dear to me and to teach me what it was worth. But if you are a soldier no explanation is necessary. My disease had about the first of this month (February 1862[)] assumed a most malignant form of that almost incurable disease, *Chronic diarrhea,* and that accounts for me being able to ride so far on horseback, while in such low state of health.

I was so reduced in flesh that mother positively asserted "that if she had met me at a time and place entirely unexpected, *she would not have recognized me.*["]

It was several days ere I began to recuperate, either in strength or flesh, for the disease had become so deeply impregnated through my system that it was a matter of great difficulty to work it out.

Old friends were in to see me every day and I got almost worn out relating to them all the incidents connected with the history of the Regiment that I could think of, also giving a full detail of how a man could get naturalized to cooking—how funny he must undoubtedly look, and how awkward—how did I like to sleep in a tent; what did we have to eat, and was it good; how did I like soldiering, &c. Finally my health had so far returned that I began to ride about a little and this caused me to improve finely, and I was soon fattening equal to a Berkshire with a plenty of stile slop. I remained at home till the 27th day of April following, but nothing of interest occurred to me during the whole term that would pay to include in this work, except that on the 18th April I had started to the Regiment via Nashville and when I arrived nearly to Gallatin here learned that I could not go to my Regiment by that route, but that I would have to go to Louisville and there take a steamer to Pittsburg Landing. The Reader undoubtedly knows that during this time the memorable, bloody, but indecisive Battle of Pittsburg Landing had been fought, which resulted in a glorious victory to our armies. But in all probability that reader dont know that the 9th Ky was in this Battle and that they lost many men in killed and wounded.[25]

When I heard of this Battle, my nerves were strung to the highest pitch of enthusiasm by the praise that was alloted by all to the "brave 9th Ky".

My only *regret* was that I was not there myself. Now I do not make any pretensions to valor or claim that I am anything to be placed in the line of heroes, but it is a significant fact that when a Regiment has its first battle all those that are *necessarily* away, and have never seen a fight, as a general thing sincerely regret that they were not there! And the feeling will last to the very battle field. And I think, or rather know, that the first battle a man participates in causes less fear than any subsequent one. He has no idea of battle. He may have read the most powerful efforts of the best Historians to make a perfect description of a battle, yet he never has one correct idea of the confusion, noise, tumult and excitement incidental to a battle *till he has been in the midst of one.*

I had been in a tumult to get away ever since the news of this battle came to hand, and having failed in my first attempt had resolved to be certain about the matter ere I sat out again. On Sunday the 27th day of April I went to Gamaliel to church and there learned that our Regimental Sutlers, Harling & Ray, were going to start to the Regiment on the next morning. I immediately resolved to meet them at the Depot at Cave city and have their company on the route.

I saw a good many of my former school-mates to day, and many warm recollections of former days flitted through my mind, as I grasped their proffered hands and listened to their candid greetings and witnessed their manifestations of pleasure.

Oh how I regretted inwardly that I could not stay away all the time, but I put a good face on the matter, spoke lightly of the fact that I was to leave home and happiness for the scene of strife and blood tomorrow, and assumed the appearance of one who was enjoying himself finely, or, in other words, regarded nothing and was simply *glad that I was a soldier.*

Some painful remembrances also cause me to revert occasionally to that day, but I am forgetting all that I can.

I returned home in the evening with a kind of mingled feeling of joy and sorrow. For Gentle reader, I was very anxious to see the boys of my company, and consequently was glad that I would soon have the opportunity. But alas! for this pleasure I must sacrifice a greater;—must change the pleasant fireside for the cheerless camp—must give up old associations for the society of strangers—must leave parents, brothers and sisters, and all that was dear by blood probably never more to be with them—must now prepare to endure the ten-fold hardships, trials, dangers and disease attendant upon a soldier's career.

Chapter 3

❦

Between the River and Corinth

After the Battle of Shiloh, Maj. Gen. Henry Halleck arrived from St. Louis to take personal command of the three Federal armies in the area, Maj. Gen. Don Carlos Buell's Army of the Ohio, Grant's Army of the Tennessee, and Maj. Gen. John Pope's Army of the Mississippi. Halleck's target was the vital railroad center of Corinth, Mississippi, occupied by Gen. P. G. T. Beauregard's Confederate Army of the Mississippi after Shiloh and reinforced by Maj. Gen. Earl Van Dorn's Army of the West. On April 29, Halleck began to inch forward toward the city, entrenching nearly every night to avoid any Shiloh-like surprises. It was slow going, and a month passed before Halleck's force of 110,000—including Marcus Woodcock, now healthy and recently returned—crossed the twenty miles to Corinth's outskirts. A huge battle seemed imminent, but on the night of May 29, Beauregard quietly evacuated the city and retreated south to Tupelo.

After the fall of Corinth, Halleck determined first to solidify the Union's hold on Tennessee. He divided his force and gave Buell the important job of taking the city of Chattanooga, a major step toward Lincoln's cherished goal of liberating Unionist East Tennessee. Buell's Chattanooga campaign went badly from the first, however. Guerrillas constantly cut the Memphis and Charleston Railroad, the Army of the Ohio's lifeline, as Buell slowly moved eastward across northern Alabama. Further in the rear, raids by Confederate cavalrymen Nathan Bedford Forrest and John Hunt Morgan cut Buell off from his main base at Louisville. Much to Lincoln's chagrin, the advance stalled. More important, by late July Buell's failure had given the Confederacy new hope of regaining Tennessee and Kentucky.[1]

Monday, April 28th I started again for the army in company with my fellow-soldier John M. Holland,[2] and we were attended by two other Gentlemen who were going with us to Cave City to bring our horses back.[3] By hard or rather steady riding, we got to Cave City that night and in the meanwhile had stopped near two hours at Glasgow. There we met up with Maj Hinson who was on his way home from the army, having resigned in consequence of a difficulty between himself and Col. B. C. Grider. This was a source of much trouble to me, for Maj. Hinson was one of my most particular friends, and had shown me many little favors without which I would have been inconvenienced in body and in mind.[4]

After giving me all the particulars incident to his resignation he remarked "but do not think that, because I cannot agree with Col. Grider that he is not a worthy man, on the contrary, he is one of the bravest and most efficient Regimental Commanders in our Division."

At Cave city we stopped with the family of Mr. C. Roberts and found his wife to be a lady of great intellectual worth and merit, and moreover that she was loyal as was also her husband and during the occupation of the place by the rebels in the preceding winter they had left home, and had returned at the appearance of our troops to find their house almost completely divested of everything that had been left in it, and it was well furnished. Their once beautiful yard had been torn up by rebel cavalry flower beds and everything pertaining to beauty and usefulness destroyed.[5]

On our offering next morning to pay for lodging, &c. our kind hostess informed us that she could accept no remuneration from any Federal Soldier, for so small a consideration as a night's lodging. [A]ccordingly after returning her our most earnest thanks for her kindness we took our leave to repair to the Rail Road nearby and wait the approach of the up train from Nashville for Louisville. During the intervening time, we amused ourselves by examining the Depot, freight boxes, ruins of a large hotel burned by the rebels, and such other objects of interest as presented themselves to us.

At 1:30 the Engineer's whistle announced the approach of the train, the down train having passed some minutes before, thus we hustled our baggage in an inconceivable degree of haste and made preparations for getting on the train, as soon as it should arrive. We were also rather apprehensive as to whether we would be permitted to get on the train, for neither of us had any written authority for being away from our regiment except the duplicate certificate of Dr. J. R. Duncan. We had both gone home by *verbal* permission from Gen. Boyle which in these days of inexperience was considered sufficient.

We were doubtful as to whether the civil conductor would transport us without pay, and whether the military conductor would *pass* us. When the train stopped we made a hasty compromise with the Lieutenant in charge of prisoners and he told us to mix with the guard which he commanded and take off our knapsacks and that we would not be noticed. The deception was perfectly successful and unmolested we both took our *first Rail Road ride*, for it was a fact that neither of us had ever mounted a R.R. train till on that the 29th day of April, 1862. Arrived at Louisville in the evening on time and then after eluding the patrol guard at the depot by telling them we had furloughs, and they not being vigilant enough to demand them to be produced.

Then we took our pack and went to *Maj. Flint's*[6] hd Quarters to receive further instructions, and my friend Holland went into *Maj. Flint's* office to attend to our business in that quarter while I was attempting to make satisfactory terms with the hack-driver with whom I was about to have some trouble in consequence of his refusal to accept for pay, my Tennessee money, and in consequence of my having none of any other kind except $0.30 in specie. We finally made a conclusion of the matter by my throwing him the specie and starting off after Holland who was calling to me to hurry, as Maj. Flint had informed him that there was a boat then at the wharf loading with soldiers and would start almost immediately. Accordingly, we hastened to the wharf and onto the boat where we found several of our Regiment on board who had been on furlough like ourselves and were now returning to their Command. They pretty quickly satisfied our eager curiosity by showing us all over the boat and by telling us that we would have hard bread, bacon, and coffee for fare, would have to sleep on deck, and moreover that the boat would not leave that place till the next day; which last assertion rather pleased us for we had a natural desire to see a little more of Louisville. I was never so completely mystified in my life as I was on coming up from the supper room and finding that dark had come on, the many thousand lights of the city and boats at the wharf, all in a confused commotion on every side of me almost made me think I was in fairy land. Never had I before, nor ever have I since enjoyed a scene after dark so much as I did that. And amid all this grandeur my mind, after considering all, would naturally revert to itself and to myself.

What was I? Amid all this mess of animated and inanimated matter representing every quality and trade in America, or probably in the world. What was I? A poor private soldier of a Volunteer Regiment, who can boast of nothing but a desire to succeed in life and that with such correctness that there will surely be some re-ward. The natural feeling of insignificance and worthlessness seized upon me and after a long spell of abstractedness I fell asleep.

On the next morning at about ten o'clock *April the 30th* we left Louisville and started down the beautiful and at this time very large Ohio. And arrived at Pittsburg Landing late in the afternoon, *May the 2nd.*

If it were necessary I would give a complete list of incidents that occurred on the passage, but as there was nothing of great interest. I will in the main forbear. The number of Steamers we saw going and returning was astonishing, the great amount of stores that were required for the Army and the fact that it had to all go by Steamer, and the present favorable condition of the River rendered the large number of Steamers very easily accounted for.

I formed the acquaintance of a musician of the 77th P.V.I.[7] on the passage, and was very much pleased with the conversation, which was principally in regard to the difference of Northern and South-ern states as regarded the Educating of the youths of the country.

During the day the men would amuse themselves by shooting at ducks and other wild fowls that they might happen to see on the river.

There was a good band on the boat, and after everything would get calm at night it would strike up in some of the National Tunes that sounded delightful in the swiftly passing air. Our fare was not the best, yet we did very well on it, and as to sleeping we got very cold every night so that we would occasionally be necessitated to get up and go to the stove in the fore part of the boat. Taking all into consideration, and that this was our first boat ride, and that we were only entitled to *soldiers fare*, I think we had not much room to grumble, and I have done much worse boating since then that was by a big sight, but for the present I was well pleased with my trip.

On the morning of the 3rd day of May we were transferred to another boat and ran up the river to *Hamburg* where we were put ashore to find our respective commands without any guide, there being two or three hundred carried up there.

Roads led off in any direction almost, and all of them were filled with wagons, coming and going from and to the various departments of the army, but it seemed that none of them belonged to our Department. The Reader must not be surprised that it was a difficult matter to find the locality of any particular Corps for there was at this time the largest army by far that was ever mustered in the West encamped between the River and Corinth. As we moved away from the River accidentally striking the right road we at ever[y] turn saw new evidence of the recent proximity of large bodies of troops. Dead horses and mules; broken Cracker boxes; old clothing; torn blankets; remains of arms, such as gun barrells, broken stocks, bent bayonets, fractured locks, worthless Cartridge boxes, and occasionally the ugly mark of a rude cannon ball that had impolitely torn a rough path through some monarch of the forest. All these seemed to portend something not very pleasant at the front, or at least that a few days since it would not have been very pleasant to have been about the place just described. We found water in very small quantities and a very inferior article, generally a small muddy stream that scarcely ran and as warm as could be under the hot sun of a clear May day.

As we advanced we began to hear an occasional boom at the front, which only served to stimulate our inexperienced ideas of fighting, and caused us to summon new resolution to reach the Regiment that night, but up to 4 o. clock   we had not obtained any certain clue to its whereabouts. [N]otwithstanding, we had inquired at Gen Rosseau's Hd Qrs.[8] During the whole evening we had encountered large bodies of troops moving towards the front and all the indications were that some important movement was going on.

About sundown by accident we stumbled upon the advance of our Division just as it was going into camp, and after waiting in anxious suspense for a half an hour our Regiment came up and then we had (of course) a hearty shaking of hands and exchange of greetings of welcome.

I found the boys much healthier and in much better spirits than I expected after such bad times down in that land of swamps and rebels. As an evidence of the good spirits of the troops, and the general characteristic of our going upon anything firing just before we got into camp, the Brigade in our advance had gone into camp and a rabbit jumping up in their midst they took after him from all quarters; no matter which way the poor rabbit turned his course, he was met by some careful sentinel that was too punctual to obey orders to let anyone pass him.

After a sharp chase and as unearthly loud yelling as human beings could be expected to get up for about one minute, the poor rabbit was taken and immediately the chase was ended, the yelling ceased, and everyone resumed his particular occupation about the mess, either to do some part toward supper or to assist in putting up the tent. We were in camp by dark, camping in "columns of Companies", and after supper and a *long* conversation with the boys about affairs at home, I retired to rest on a *real soldier's bed*. I will not attempt to describe the course of my thoughts during that night, for I slept but very little, what with my thoughts, but they were confined in too great a measure to myself. The *Corporalcy* had been taken from me in my absence and given to another person, in consequence of the impression with the Captain that I would not be able for service any more. Now the office is by no means one worth caring for, but then the idea of reduction went against my feelings. I also mentally surveyed the many new phases that soldiering was appearing in to me and comparing them to my idea of my own physical strength the result of the deliberations was not very satisfactory. To complete the unsettled state of my mind, towards day the rain began to fall in torrents and I had to be continually shifting positions to keep "in the dry." Next morning (to my eye) everything looked desolate indeed: For being restless I was stirring as early as objects could be discerned at any distance, and before any other person was awake. The rain had put out all the fires, tent flies were drooping over the poles, as if they were chilled. Cooking vessels of various descriptions were scattered around (for the boys had not yet got to stealing from each other) the rain was still falling in a sufficient quantity to wet a person very soon who should expose himself to it, and really I felt dejection of spirits in the fullest meaning of the term. After a little the *Reville* was blown and I was surprised to see the wonderful alacrity with which the boys sprung from their blankets, and hastened on their clothing, and dashing out of the tent, fell into line to answer to their names at the Roll Call. After this much to my astonishment fires were soon blazing in all directions and preparations were going on for breakfast with, as much regularity as is sometimes seen about households of no mean pretensions.

I here found that I was acquainted with a very limited number of the members of the Regiment, and knew hardly any of the officers at all, and a certain spirit of indiference that I unpretendingly say, I imbibed prevents me from seeking their (the officers) acquaintance. I could not endure that restraint and discipline that compels the private to stand in the attitude of *attention*, till the officer has time to speak with him, and then probably to receive only a cold no to his petition, or a sharp order to get out.

"We hold these truths to be self-evident that all men are created equal," &c. but this is a great principle of Republicanism usually departed from by the petty officers of the U.S. Volunteer Army at the time of which we are speaking.

Capt Bryan was sick and had been left back with the wagons on the evening before, but was expected to come up on that day. He was a man whom I doted on till the day of his death, and now had a small present that I had brought him all the way from home. Yet it is a fact that during the last 8 or 9 months of his life he evinced evidences of a permanent dislike for me, though I never could ascertain the cause; and indeed never endeavored to. Our Company was at this time commanded by Rufus Somerby, a first Lieut though I believe he never was commissioned in our Company.[9] He was a fine looking young man of considerable military knowledge, good intellect, and a tolerable education. Lieut [Warmer] Underwood, who was really first Lieutenant had been wounded at the Battle of Pittsburg Landing and had gone home on furlough.[10] A. W. Smith who was 2nd Lieut. had resigned, and Sergt. Silas Clarke promoted to fill vacancy thereby occasioned. Benjamin Thompson, Vice-Clarke, Benjamin M. Johnson, vice-Thomson—Considerable change in the "Non-commish" since I had been gone[.]

May the 4th 1862 was a rainy, cheerless day and I was compelled to keep within doors a greater part of the time to keep from getting wet. I was rather unwell in consequence of the great amount of cold I caught on my way, and the generally discouraging aspect of things made me truly miserable. About 12 o'clock I was detailed on the fatigue-duty list to go and help clean off a neighboring thicket for the purpose of establishing our camp there. About two o clock P.M. a shower of rain coming up putting an end to our operation and we retired to our camp. But I had not been long in a resting position till Sergt Hix came around and detailed me to go on camp guard. I dont think that any human being in a state of good health and at personal liberty ever passed a more miserable day than I did on this.

First, I was reduced from a corporalcy, second was compelled to go on fatigue duty, and thirdly was detailed to do guard duty, shockingly disrespectful thought I! But our non-commissioned officers had a way of *breaking* fellows right at the beginning, and I was not to expect to be excluded from the general rule. So I went on guard. Lieut A. J. Pipkin[11] was officer of the guard, but I have forgotten the officer of the day. I was on the third relief, and my Corporal was Proffit of Co. G. (? Slaughter[)].[12] Oh, but the rain did pour down on us that night! and me, poor boy, had to stay out in it all the time. The second time that my relief was to go on, the Corporal nor Sergt. could find me nowhere and consequently my post was left vacant during that tour. After daylight, one of them discovered me asleep just a few feet from the fire but on "tother side of a tree" and, of course, as I was not on immediate duty when I fell asleep no censure was in store for me. On that morning after breakfast I drew my first installment of "Greenbacks" from one of Uncle Sam's Paymasters.[13] *I received $55.00, or $3.00 over 4 months wages*, the same that all the others had recieved, consequently this cleared up any blame that could have been attached to my protracted absence.

I felt pretty grand as I thrust both hands deep into my pockets and crushed the rattling paper in my pocket, for reader, I will frankly tell you that I had never possessed so much money before in my life that I could call my own.

On that day about noon the rain ceased falling and old Sol occasionally peeped through the clouds to cheer and dry us, and immediately the Regiment commenced pulling up stakes and preparing to move to the place where I had worked on yesterday, and by the time I got off guard, which was nearly sunset, every thing was permanently transferred to the new camp. As I was being relieved, I noticed my friend Holland that was just coming in the new guard. He also had been reduced from the corporalcy for the same reason as myself, and as we passed each other, we smiled recognition so much as to say, "pretty hard, but nevertheless will bear it."

I retired to sleep in the tent and you may be sure I rested finely on a pile of leaves I had brought in for the purpose, though that was against the rules, and it would have been nothing to wonder at if I had rested well upon the ground, for I really had not had a good night's rest since the one at *Cave City*. For I got very cold on the boat every night, so that I could not sleep long without going to the fire, and had been prevented from sleep as already related both nights after arriving with the Regiment. The next morning the sun rose clear and beautiful as if to mock the lonliness of my mind, for my most cherished hopes had been disappointed, and are very low. I saw some occurrence to remind me of my failures.

I was vain, and I tell you I suffered for my vanity. I think I made a full atonement though. I will not say in what way my vanity caused me trouble as I would be making myself probably an object of ridicule. But enough of this and I will resume. Just after sunrise, the Regiment was formed on the parade ground and some orders of, I have forgotten what import read and Commissions presented to some that had been recently promoted. Soon after this I was detailed by the Colonel to accompany an ambulance back to Hamburg that was to carry Lieut. B. O. Rodes, Co. K. who had been very violently taken on the night of the 4th with Cholera-Morbus, and whom the M.D.'s now thought proper should go to the rear. I was detailed in consequence of the teamster (L. D. Massey,) not knowing the road. The roads were in such a sad plight that we had a disagreeable drive, yet we arrived at Hamburg in due season and depositing the Lieutenant in a Steamer, that was chartered by the U.S. Sanitary Commission we set out to return. At a little stream not far from the river which was like all southern streams, *narrow*, deep and muddy, and made passable by a kind of floating bridge, one of the horses fell through and we had a considerable amount of trouble, but finally extricated him, and got on our way again without any injury, mentally or physically, except that I had been compelled to make the humiliating confession that I did not know how to gear a horse for an ambulance.

As we returned through Hamburg we bought some cakes and after eating as many as we wanted, sold the remainder for what we gave for the whole, which was the only thing I bought while in the Army and sold for gain (speck).

On the next day (I think it was) we pulled up stakes and moved toward the front, for the reader must recollect that every day we could hear cannons booming from each wing of the Army, foretelling the grave continuation of movements that finally compelled the enemy to evacuate his stronghold, Corinth, Miss., which was now about 15 miles in our advance. An order had been received to cause the men to leave their knapsacks with the wagons, and to carry only their haversack, canteen, and blanket, besides guns and accouterments, and the indications were that active operations would immediately commence.

We moved some five or six miles that day out on what is known as Pea Ridge, and went into camp without seeing any more indications of the enemy than when we started, although I expected to jump them every minute.[14]

About a half an hour after sunset someone of a Regiment near by accidently shot himself in the hand and made a most unearthly noise, which affected my nerves powerfully, and I then came to the conclusion that it would be a difficult matter for me to stay at my post in battle. A few evenings afterward, and after our tents had come up, we were all at once ordered to be ready to march immediately with our haversacks, canteens, blankets and two days' rations.

We were soon "underway" travelling over a road that had been corduroyed[15] the greater portion of the route; and was then in consequence of the darkness of the night very troublesome to travel over. The course was rather to the left of Corinth and we went about 6 or 7 miles and then formed in line of Battle, stacked arms, and lay down to sleep.

We remained there till near sundown of the next day, and then formed and moved back to our encampment.

These little marches wearied me very much and I scarcely now can conceive how I mustered resolution to put a good face upon matters as I did when I was suffering to such extent from mental and physical sickness and fatigue.

On the next evening I was put on camp Guard with Lieut. Clark as Officer of the Guard. The night was clear and beautiful the moon giving his light to greater portions of the night, and I also had a good nap between reliefs and therefore upon the whole I fared much better than when I stood on that rainy night.

We remained at this place several days and here our former Sutlers, Ray & Harling came up with us to make settlement, and by them I sent home $40.00.

The Reader must not expect me to give any particulars of or even a notice of the movements of the Army in general, for our Division, commanded by Brig. Gen. T. L. Crittenden[16] had up to this date been continually kept in the back-ground, consequently I could relate nothing gathered from personal observation and would have to resort to the productions of other writers, which I deem unfair in a certain manner. It would be unfair to transcribe the history of this Campaign from the production of some other person, and therefore I, to do justice, would have to hunt all the official documents and correspondents' letters which would in this limited work cause more trouble than it would benefit anyone after such publications as have already been *made*.

The weather during our stay was remarkably fine, and was getting very warm,—water was of an inferior quality and in limited quantities, Rations were hard tack, and bacon, sugar and coffee without any vegetable food at all, only as we would occasionally gather a mess of "greens" composed of every description of plant almost that the country afforded. But the feasts were delightful. The troops had cut away the underbrush for hundreds of yards in every direction, and thus we could plunge into the deep recess of the green timber and roam for hours, unmindful of the occasional crash of the cannon at the distant front. At last the order came to move, this time carrying everything, and leaving our camp about 8 or 9 o clock in the morning.[17] We marched on over mudholes, corduroyed roads, and occasionally a firm spot of ground till about noon when we filed off to the left of the road and soon into line according to command "on the right to file into line" at right angles with the road, and in a place where the undergrowth was exceedingly heavy, and the taller trees were rather scarce, yet enough to answer the purposes of shade which we were beginning to need very much, and this day was exceedingly hot. In the afternoon we cut away all the underbrush and swept up and burned the leaves, and by the appearance of night had a very nice camp; but no water except by going about 3/4 of a mile and then waiting your turn at a very much crowded well.

On the next day *we dug several wells* on a low spot of ground near the camp and then procured a supply of tolerable water. While we remained at this place, we performed all the usual role of a soldier in camp, viz. camp guarding, camp policing, Company and Battalion drilling, &c. But we were getting much nearer the front, and the now very frequent booming of the cannon was becoming very distinct and it seemed that another move would put us very near the rebel line.

The drilling was very irksome to me, for mentally I was well acquainted with the whole principal of all drills that had been taught in our Rgt, but the thing of putting it into practice and getting able to execute the commands with the necessary promptness to ensure efficiency and the approbation from inspectors was a part that I almost loathed the performance of, not that I thought it unnecessary, but simply from a feeling of indolence! but you must understand that I was not one of the class that are always asking "to be excused from drill to day."

One day the Regiment was sent out on picket, but did not have to go very far, and we were all allotted our respective positions, and had gotten things arranged tolerably conducive to our comfort, when at 2 P.M. we were suddenly relieved, and ordered to go to camp and get ready to move immediately. Soon we were back to the camp and on the march leaving knapsacks and tents, &c. Marched about 4 miles when about sundown as we came to the summit of a small eminence, a most grand and striking sight was presented to our view.

The fields were uninterrupted and cleared of any obstruction to vision for nearly one mile and a half, and on this ground our whole division and a portion of Pope's[18] was preparing to go into camp. Bodies of Infantry were marching and countermarching, suddenly wheeling into line, into column, into platoon, section and almost any evolution of the tactics could have been witnessed that evening.

Batteries of Artillery were galloping across the fields, General officers, and staffs were moving steadily among the whole and the scene altogether was one the equal of which is rarely witnessed. Just as the scene came into our view, we were ordered "by Company into line" and immediately afterwards "Companies forward to a line," which threw us into line of battle, in the hurry of the moment, my first impression was that we could see the enemy in the distant part of the opening, and hence so much activity by our troops in the fore ground, and the fact of us being ordered into line of battle tended not a little to increase this impression, but I should never have mentioned this fact had I not heard several others say that for a moment their impressions were just the same.

This was in view of the village of Farmington and here we were destined to stop. [W]e went into Camp between sundown and dark and had strict orders to lie close to our guns and be ready for an alarm at any moment. After a night of disturbed slumber, we awoke upon the beauties of another beautiful day. Every thing remained as calm as if no enemy had been near and the booming of the cannon now seemed to be as far off as when I first heard them.

This morning I saw Gen Pope and staff.

The General at a distance is a splendid looking man and this evening was splendidly mounted, and *according to his reports*, he did some fine work among the rebels. On that evening I was detailed with a large *fatigue party* to go out and assist in working on some fortifications, nearly a mile to the front, and from the works about one and one-half miles farther on I saw the first skirmish line that was really fighting that I had ever seen in my life, and also the first shells I had ever seen burst in the air, and the first cannons I had ever seen fired.

In fact, I saw a very animating skirmish out in advance between our men and the "secesh," and really to look at that distance I could not see anything about it that was so very distasteful, for I saw no one seem to get hurt, and I saw a brilliant charge made by our line and I saw the secesh fall back and this of course all looked very nice.

We continued working away at our breastwork till sometime after dark when through some misunderstanding the men all threw down their picks and spades to return to camp. We had worked very negligently all the evening. Considerable confusion was raised by this act of the mens, and the officers could not be heard above the general clamoring as they attempted to restore order, till at last some officer that was about, and I think a General, suddenly whipped out his sword and threatened to whip off the first man's head that uttered a word. All stopped as if in astonishment at his impudence when he seized his opportunity and said that the rebels were near and that such loud noise would betray us, and after this[,] order was preserved [and] we were soon relieved and sent to camp.

We camped that night on the same spot as on the night previous and on the next day moved back about one mile and the wagons having come up we put up tents and were again regularly encamped. And we remained at this place for several days again. In the meantime, the weather had become very warm and the water was very indifferent, which was a source of inconvenience to us. The drills were regularly attended to both Company and Battalion. We (Co. B) were much pleased with our Lieut (Somerby) who seemed to understand his business. Our Battalion drills, were generally under the supervision of Lieut. Col. Geo. H. Cram[19] and Maj. J. H. Grider.[20] Vice Roark, accused;[21] and Hinson resigned; respectively. The Lieut. Col. showed great judgment in training raw troops, but according to our undisciplined minds he was a degree too harsh in his orders, commands, &c.; but I will speak of him more fully hereafter *as an officer and a gentleman.* The Major was a man of no great military acquirements, and in fact I think he was not cut out for a military man, yet he was the soul of courage and presence of mind in danger.

He was at this time the idol of the Regiment, treating all with kindness and respect, he was beloved by all.

I think it was about the 24th or 25th of May[22] that our Regiment was sent on picket about 4 miles in advance of the camp and in two miles of Corinth and that I did my first picket fighting or fighting of any kind. Our Company in consequence of having Enfield Rifles, which no Companies except ours and "A," as flanking Companies had ever been armed with,[23] was thrown forward on the left to a house that formerly was a dwelling but was now used to shelter cotton of which it contained a large amount. The position was evidently one of danger, so far as regarded the enemy's sharpshooters, but was safe in case of a charge from the fact of the many fences about the house that formed the yard and garden, and also hedges, and a plum orchard that was almost impassable.

It was at this point that I hiard the first ball whistle from a rebel gun.—It was here that I first saw the ground torn up about my feet by a leaden agent, it was here that I learned to promptly fall on the ground on its approach of a certain object that foretold it's coming, about the one hundred and fiftieth part of a semi-second ere its arrival, and it was here that I first pointed my rifle at a human being and used effort to make my aim so true that it would drive a ball through his brain. Seriously thought of it is an *awful* thought, and one year previous to this time it would have made me shudder to even see a man through the sights of an empty Rifle, but now it was enough for me to know that the man was dressed in gray and that he was trying to get a shot at some of our boys even to my left, and so I fired away. I cannot state whether I "winged" him or not, for the morning was very damp and heavy, and ere the smoke of my gun cleared away the rebel for some cause had changed position. I would have been very much pleased to know that my first shot had killed one of my country's enemies.

During the day *Ben H. Waddle* was posted at a small apple tree which was by no means sufficiently large to protect his body. He had not been at his post a sufficient length of time to become by any means in the slightest degree domesticated when he accidentally attracted the notice of two secesh sharpshooters who seem inclined to contest his right of living and they, both, Ben and the "secesh" put into shooting with all haste. The rebs out-shot *Ben* in a style that was truly dangerous to be the object of, but Ben returned their fire with much spirit and after a term he turned and said, "God! I have killed one of them!["] And the evidence of this fact was very conclusive from the fact that the secesh fire slackened considerably. After a time I was called upon to relieve *Waddle* and with many misgivings and thoughts of danger I crouched along till I reached him, he then remarked "*Woodcock*, I am very glad you have come, but am very sorry for you." But it seemed that the other rebel had also decamped, for not a single shot was fired while I occupied the post.

At night we were posted two together at posts about 15 yards apart and had to remain there without relief during the whole night, with orders to be on the alert at all times and in no case to go to sleep. I was posted with my friend, that worthy soldier *James M[adison]. Crabtree*,[24] and tediously did the hours roll away. Finally I and Madison concluded to sleep awhile. I sat down and leaned against the tree *facing to the rear*, and was soon in the land of dreams while *Madison* standing directly in front or rather over me kept a look-out till he thought I had slept long enough to entitle him to a short nap and then he aroused me. Thus we relieved each other by turns till day-light. I don't think I ever, at any other time, experienced such extreme anxiety, when there was such little danger, as I did in the first half of the night, for it was very dark, and I being from my inexperience naturally apprehensive, also from a natural deficiency unable to discern the direction of sounds, consequently every time any of the sentries on the post to the right or left made a noise I immediately supposed it to be a rebel trying to steal a march (on me of course). I was inwardly very much exasperated at the carelessness exhibited by my friend, who having been at the Battle of Pittsburg Landing, and all the incidents connected with the operations against Corinth, and in fact with the Regiment every day since its organization, had become accustomed to such work. And to add to my perplexity, we could at all times hear the secesh talking, laughing, &c. on a hill about 400 yards in our advance, and we could hear occasional noises, at their skirmish line in our immediate front and not more than 200 yards away at the bottom of a slight depression from us and in a heavy thicket where it was impossible to discover any of them at all in daylight by the most vigilant watchfulness.

After midnight the moon rose, and there when I could bring my ocular powers into service I thought I was much safer. Just at day light according to orders we all fell back to the house and remained there some minutes when the usual number were again thrown forward to the line. And it was about one hour of the sunrise this morning that I shot at my first secesh which has been referred to.

On the morning previous past as our Company went on post a skirmish line moved forward through a field of rye on our left and brought on a small skirmish, but on the whole the affair was conducted rather awkwardly and we were not much edified by the opportunity of seeing the engagement.

At the expiration of our 24 hours we returned to camp and then I sat down to write a letter home and to tell father I had been in a skirmish and had *"shot at a secesh"*, and in fact I was a real tip-top, up and down, thorough bred soldier.

In fact, I greatly delighted in the pop shooting carried on out at the skirmish line, for while there was no real danger by a little care, there was occasionally an opportunity to pop away at a rebel, and thus the thing was just exciting enough to keep us from tiring.

Our Camp at this place (Farmington) was one that gave us many opportunities for observation, and of becoming acquainted with the general machinery of campaigning and noting many facts which we had not the opportunity of again for many months. Here I saw the first regular Magazine that I ever saw.—It was built while we were at this place.—Also an observatory, or long pole ran up some twenty feet above the top of a tall tree to look from into Corinth. We had a regular News Dept. to which we could go and procure any kind of *novel* we wished and the latest *papers* from the East and West. Sutlers abounded on every side. No nourishment that it was possible to transport from the North but what was there. And money in profusion, and when I say money, you must not understand me simply to mean "Green Backs." Nay, but the regular "yaller boys" were jingling in every man's pocket. Persons that were going hence were glad of the opportunity to give gold for the green-backs we had. We also made a considerable advancement in the art of drilling at this place. Sickness was becoming very general.— *Mumps* was loose among us, and that most fatal disease "Chronic diarrhea," which I judge almost incurable in the army. And it was while at this place that our Regiment received its first pair of colors, Battle Flag with the word "Shiloh" inscribed on it beside the name of the Regt.

The weather gradually grew warmer till it had become almost intolerable; and we at length carried the branches of green trees and sat up around the tents to protect us from the rays of the sun. We procured water from some gums that were sunk in the earth,[25] and had plenty of Army rations and consequently lived tolerably well.

In four days from the time we came off, we were again sent on picket and the companies posted as originally or at least Co. B was, but this time there was very little shooting, and I did not see a single rebel at a reasonable distance while out and consequently did not shoot. Petty flags of truce were matters of frequent occurrence, conversations between the pickets of the two armies occasional, and from the general signs of the times it was evident that affairs were on the eve of a great change.

The boys of the right wing were during the evening very much annoyed by the vigilant attention given them by a rebel sharpshooter, who was mounted upon a tree a great distance off, and whose gun threw balls with a force and speed truly remarkable.

Several of the boys gave him their whole attention for several hours, and at last by a regular volley succeeded in bringing him down, or at least they thought so. Again we returned to Camp without getting anyone injured, and again assumed the usual *routine* of duties devolving upon us. On the 29th[26] we again moved out toward the front, and were formed in line of battle along near the rear of the picket line. The whole army seemed to be stirring, Generals and staffs were galloping around; orderlies bearing the dispatches were flying from point to point; Aides-de-camp were prancing to and fro. The Ambulance Corps was all out with their yellow rags,[27] and, what caused me to feel uneasy, the inevitable "stretcher" which is a bier for carrying wounded off the field. Cannons were booming very frequently along different parts of the line as far as we could hear to the right and left. The skirmishing in our immediate front was very severe, and men were *occasionally* getting hurt. Our Brigade Battery in our immediate front which was playing vigorously was occasionally answered by the secesh artillery and which answers came fearfully near us.

But night came in without disclosing to us any incident of great interest and with the appearance of night the firing generally ceased, and with the usual prospect of rest we returned to sleep, but I was detailed to act as sergt. of the guard and there had my first talk with a secesh all to myself. And as I found him not very interesting I soon delivered the necessary orders to the Cprl. of the stock guard and retired to rest and slept till near daylight. This was a day of great moment to America. Two of the largest armies that ever were marshaled in the Western Continent were here arrayed (as we thought the rebels were arrayed) to make history for the benefit and curiosity of the world, many loving wives; who had sent their husbands willingly yet reluctantly to the battlefield to contend for the cause they deemed just, would ere night be bereaved.—The next letter instead of containing words of love and encouragement, and an admonishment to "pray for me" and signed by "your affectionate Husband," after having been filled from beginning to end of probably two sheets closely written—Instead of all this the next letter would be a few unfeeling business-like lines written by the Captain, Colonel, or some comrade of my *dead* husband.

Sisters, whose love for their brothers amounted almost to idolatry, are little dreaming this morning that those whom they love so dear are in such great danger.—Little do they think that his cheek is now turning pale, his lips compressed, and his eyes flashing fire as he hears the order to prepare for battle.

Parents, and especially Mothers; you whose love for offspring is so great that you can hardly get your consent to sacrifice the Company of your dear child to the performance of any duty. Mothers pray; for this morning your son is expecting to lay aside his auxiliaries for comfort and through the whole of this day to use only the weapon of death. Horrible! that your boy, who was so fair and tender, so chicken-hearted, and so kind to everything that needed his attention; Horrible! that he will today engage in the strife of blood and will be unceasing in his efforts to slay his fellow man— and doubly horrible, he may get terribly mangled, probably killed by the rude thrust of an enemy's bayonet or the irresistible crash of a cannon shot.

Gentle maiden, you that have given your *dear sweethearts*, probably betrothed, to the service of this country, weep not, but rather do you *pray also*—Pray that the special object of your mind may on that day make himself a record on the scroll of fame and gain a station among the list of heroes that will make you doubly proud to receive him in arms of love when he returns battle-scarred and war worn from the tented field, bringing assurances that he has done his whole duty.

All was in a busy, hurried state of preparation—men in the ranks were placing money and other articles of value in the hands of those who had been so fortunate as to be excused at "sick call" and were now going to the rear.—occasionally an ambulance or caisson rolled swiftly along the road, aids and orderlies were flying in every direction giving the orders and dispatches of "the General"—field officers, and occasionally subordinates could be seen on the summit of the nearest elevation, striving anxiously to catch some object in view, as if by that they could foretell the "events of the day." The rumor through the lines was that the whole artillery of our army (supposed by the common class of us to be six hundred pieces) would be discharged that morning so nearly as possible at one moment as a signal for the grand attack, and now the occasional boom of the cannon only serves to remind us that the awful moment is drawing near. Soon an awful succession of explosions similar to the bursting of shells is heard in the direction of Corinth, but which we supposed to be in Grant's Division of the army,[28] and that it was the opening scene of the day's work; but after a few moments the sound died away without seeming to get any nearer, and again all was quiet—even the skirmishing seemed to be growing less severe, and the firing of the cannon much less frequent.—By this time the Sun had crawled almost unawares a considerable distance above the horizon,—old officers began to think it pretty late in the day to begin the battle;—little knots of the *knowing* ones could be seen gathered about and speculating upon the perplexing appearance of affairs, and the seeming mystery connected to the operations of the day,—as yet no one had hazarded the expression, or even thought that the rebels were evacuating, for reader, that was at a time when the rebels had as yet choosed to give battle at every important point before retiring. An orderly was seen to dash up to Brigade Hd Qrs.— another almost in the same moment came to Regimental Hd Qrs. The rebels were evacuating, or rather had evacuated, Corinth, and our Cavalry were now ordered to the pursuit.

The news was received with as much suprise as would have been a snowstorm on this sunny morning—the incredulous would not give it a moments consideration, but just simply said it was unreasonable—the *knowing* ones said they *knowed* it yesterday, and scores of them said "didn't I tell you so?"

But we soon had every confirmation of the report by the arrival of numerous orderlies, stragglers, and hospitalmen, each of whom had been in Corinth, and had brought one or more specimen[s] of the rebel camp. One would suppose that the relief of the army from the anxiety peculiar to the expectations of a battle produced great joy and satisfaction among the troops this morning: such was only partially the case. We had all anxiously expected that we would just make a final "smash up" of the rebel Army at this place and thus bring about a speedy termination to the war; but we thought their army was pretty generally demoralized anyhow, and that it would never be arrayed again in formidable opposition to a single Division of our irresistible troops, and I really believed that the war would end within another six months.

Soon after receiving the news of the evacuation, the line of battle was broken up and our Brigade was moved some distance back to a good shade and encamped—Then the Cavalry began to pass in long dusty columns, going toward Corinth with the intention of picking up those of the Rebels who were too *sore-footed* to keep within the protection of their main lines. We were compelled to remain here all day and not be allowed to see the prize for which we had *fought* till other portions of the Army had occupied it and destroyed many of the objects that claimed attraction.

I am again puzzled to know how long we remained at this place ere we were marched into Corinth, (whether one or two days) but I think that on the next morning we were marched out and carried through the almost impregnable, *abbatis* and various forts, lunettes[29] and breastworks of every description, flanked by dead mules, old clothing, provision boxes and barrels of every description, and occasionally a dead rebel, till we entered the town. In the appearance of the village we were all invariably deceived, for we had expected to see a town of considerable size and wealth, judging from the important position it held in regard to railroads (two of the most important railroads of the South crossing each other at this point). But instead of a rich and populous inland town, we found it to be (or probably in its best days had been) but little more than an ordnary Railroad station. The houses were all in a dismantled and wretched condition; many of them bore marks of the cannon balls of our artillery; others had been burned to the ground, and one spot that had been occupied by the magazine presented abundant evidence of the real origin of the explosion we had heard the morning previous by the numerous fragments of shells that were scattered around, and cannon balls and arms of various descriptions (rendered useless by burning) that were among the ruins. Among other matters of interest there was a matter of a hundred bushels of dried beans lying in a heap in the street, on fire—a few hundred citizen wagons that the rebels had *stolen* because they had nothing else to do were also *parked* on one square of the town, but it is not worth your attention for me to attempt to describe the general ruin and devastation that presented itself on every hand in this ill fated little rail-road station.

We marched through town and about a half mile beyond between the South Mobile, and West Charleston Railroads, and encamped on the site of the recent rebel encampment. The relics left here by the rebels were, in the general, so different from those always·to be found afterwards in hastily evacuated camps that a good description of the encampment would repay the perusal by anyone, but my feeble pen shall not aspire to do justice to this extensive encampment—to its numerous beef barrels, old tents, mess conveniences, temporary wells, &c., I could say nothing of interest,—to its famous Bowie knives, which were scattered promiscuously over the grounds by the thousand, and with which *one rebel* was going to whip *five Yankees* I will add no comment.[30]—to its numerous old-shotguns, sporting rifles, *war guns* of Southern invention, and old flint lock muskets marked 1776 you need no introduction. It seemed that the rebels had surely shed the *old skin* and were either retreating in a new one or *none at all*.

We remained here on picket twenty four hours and then returned to camp (near Farmington).

I have forgotten how many days we remained at this point, but it could not have been more than three or four, when we again set off on the march, leaving wagons and knapsacks behind, and marched out, leaving Corinth to the right, but going in a Southerly direction—marched several miles, and encamped for the night in a little field that had been planted with corn. Next day we moved a few miles farther in the same direction and (about noon) turned off to the left of the road and encamped in a shady spot and again remained all night.—Weather very warm and water scarce and inferior. Next day we moved a few miles farther, which brought us in the neighborhood of Booneville, and which I suppose made about twenty-five miles we had marched in the three days, and again we encamped on the right of the road.

Next day we did not move, and early in the morning a detail was made to stand guard at Gen. Crittenden's Hd Qrs that day (the *famous* organization known as *Provost Marshall's Guards* had not been organized at this time). In the evening Gen Crittenden issued an order to be ready to march on the following morning in an easterly direction along the line of the Memphis and Charleston RR? and next morning we were tramping very early going over a portion of our last days march and turning off to the right—we passed through a little village on the railroad known as Ravenna. On this or the succeeding day, we passed through Jacinto—(Shire Town of Tishimingo County) which was neither a neat nor interesting little town, and the only prominent feature of art in it was a very tall flag pole from which only a few days since had streamed in all its beauty, "the (*anti*) glorious Stars and bars" of the (so called) brilliant, wonderful, and *chivalric* Southern "Conthieveracy." The few squalid, miserable, and thievish-looking persons that showed themselves at their doors gave one look at our Regiment colors, and another at their naked flag pole, and then turned away as if they could not help it. After a few days of pretty heavy marching during which time Lewis Underwood of our Company arrived at the Regiment, and Lieut. Somerby was transferred to Co. K, and promoted to Captain, we arrived at that little town rendered famous by a battle being fought there at a subsequent date in which our troops were successfully led by the gallant but unfortunate General Rosecrans—viz *Iuka*.[31]

We remained at this point a few days, being paid two month's wages in the time by Maj. Martin. Lieut. Underwood also resigned in consequence of an appointment as Cadet in the U.S. Military Academy at West Point. I suppose that those of my readers who have never seen this country would like for me to give a general description of this country as I saw it, but that is almost wholly out of my power, for the memoranda that I preserved extended with considerable trouble while in this country, and in which I was very careful to note all matters of local interest is lost, and consequently as I did not attempt to tax my memory with the preservation of them I cannot now scarcely recollect anything. My only impression in regard to the general topography of the country is that after leaving the swamps of Corinth and vicinity we had found the country invariably covered with heavy pines, the other timber being generally scrubby and altogether presenting a barren appearance. The soil was generally sandy, especially after leaving Jacinto, and did not appear to be very productive, though the inferiority of the crops might have been imputed to the fact that there had been a heavy conscript laid on the citizens of this country after the planting of the crops. Springs of water were very scarce, but occasionally there could be found magnificent ones both in the quality of the water, and the quantity afforded, and this was especially the case at Iuka. The wagons, which we had left at Farmington came up at this place bringing tents, cooking vessels, knapsacks, &c.

The weather was now growing so warm that we had no use for the heavy army overcoats, and roundabouts[32] we drew the previous winter at Columbia. They were accordingly turned over at this point to the Quartermasters and were never afterwards heard from. (I left my overcoat at home), which was the cause of much discontent among the boys at the approach of winter again and they had to *draw* and be *charged* for new overcoats.

We left this place I suppose about the fourteenth day of June and marched toward *Tuscumbia, Alabama*, passing through the latter place on the seventeenth of the month and camping three miles beyond on the banks of the Tennessee River, near Florence.

I was attacked with a severe headache the day after leaving Iuka and on the day we arrived at the river I was not able to march and therefore had to be hauled in a wagon, for the ambulances were already filled with persons whom the hot weather and heavy marching had disabled. The troops seemed very much worn when we arrived at this point, but we had not the slightest idea when or where we would stop. My ideas of our destination were about as correct as those of the probable end of the war—"fact is," I had *no idea* about it and had questioned familiar shoulder straps for some point to base my opinions in vain, and had necessarily come to the conclusion that it would pay me about as highly not to bother my brains upon the subject. It is true that we occasionally receive newspapers but they contained not even a hint officially as to our probable destination, and the opinions of the Correspondents were already vanished ere we would have received the paper containing their letters.

A considerable change was made in the Non-commissioned officers while at this place. Sergt. W. B. Roddy had been appointed *first Sergeant* vice B. Thompson who had requested the Captain to

William B. Roddy, c. 1865.
Courtesy of Vernon Roddy and Randy G. East.

put another man in his place on account of his general ill health. All the other Sergeants were reduced to ranks and the places filled by other members of the Company, as I always thought, just to satisfy some whim of the Captain. I and my friend Holland were reinstated in our offices of first and second Corporal, respectively, to fill the vacancies occasioned by the promotions required to make Sergeants.

Preparations were made for crossing the river, and the second day after we arrived at this place an order came for all who were not able to make a long and heavy march to be sent to the rear. I fell among that number and about noon, the 19th day of June I was sent to Tuscumbia and lodged in the barracks at the "fair ground." Be patient reader and dont come to the conclusion that I remained in hospital nearly all the time I was a soldier for you will very soon begin to learn that such was not the case, and it was nearly two years from this time ere I was again placed on the sick list. At this time

I was not really *sick* and only needed a few days rest to enable me to be ready to discharge the duties connected with a long campaign. My headache was caused by over-marching and drinking bad water to an excess; and in four days from the time I reached the barracks I was abundantly able for duty but could not get to go to the Regiment. The trains were running regularly to Decatur, and connecting with the Nashville trains, but I did not know anything about where the Division had gone, and never heard from it from the 19th day of June till about the 6th day of July, or I should have attempted to have gone to it much sooner than I did.

Tuscumbia *was* a beautiful little village and the country in the immediate vicinity has its many attractions being very productive also. The town is famous for the many large springs in its suburbs which afford the best of water.

The barracks contained a great many sick and deaths were very frequent. After I had been there a few days, a large number of the "wellest" were removed to some tents that had been pitched near the barracks, and were laid off in Companies and placed under the command of numerous Sergeants who were giving us the usual trouble to be experienced in Convalescent Camps by coming around continually to make details for every imaginable *duty* that an M.D. who has nothing else to [do] can think of.

At one time an attempt was made to establish a Camp Guard to surround the hospital and camp—I think it took the Sergt. Major at least two hours to get his detail reported and formed; then we went through the *ceremonies* of *Guard Mounting*, and the first relief was placed on the line and the second and third reliefs permitted to go to their *quarters* till they would be required. When the bugle was blown for the second relief, not one-fifth of the number answered to the call. The Corporal went over camp in search of his men, but there were not a sufficient number of men in the whole camp of the two reliefs to make one—they had gone to the spring which was outside the guard line on the opposite side of a creek and had not returned. After several attempts about half the posts were occupied by a second relief—after it had been on post near an hour *somebody* concluded that a *mistake* had been made and the whole thing was broken up and that ended guard duty during my stay at this place.

My messmates were generally very interesting fellows—three of the 39th Ind. Infantry, and three of the 19th O.V. Infantry besides A. J. Carter of my Company. We had quite an interesting time during our stay here, considering it was a convalescent camp.

The citizens of the country seemed desirous either to add to our comfort, or to possess some of our "greenbacks," for every day they brought us fresh supplies of fruits and berries, also fresh meats cooked and uncooked, and anything that the country afforded, for which they demanded very moderate prices compared with what we had to pay for such articles at a subsequent date.

On the 4th of July we had a political sermon by a chaplain of some Ohio Regiment, a national salute at the proper time of day and at sundown we went up to town and saw that the officers and soldiers of Gen Thomas' Division were celebrating in a high style. A stand had been erected for the occasion in one of the principal streets, and from this we heard some able and eloquent speeches by several of the officers which was being responded to in a *stirring* manner by the cheers and shouts of the numerous soldiers. All the Regimental flags of the Division were gathered near the stand; rockets were flying up from several batteries, while loud buzzes announced their upward flight, and in fact everything that could be done by the soldiers to commemorate the importance of Independence day was done, but not a single demonstration was made by the citizens of the town—no flags floated from the housetops, nor was a single window illuminated.

During my stay here, a newspaper was started by some former attachees to the *Louisville Journal*, under the title of *Louisville Journal Junior*. I dont recollect how long the paper flourished, nor what was its title but know that my mess had many a hearty laugh at the idea of soldiers getting up a paper in a *foreign* office.

About the 5th day of July an examination of all the convalescents was made by the Surgeon, and a squad of us were marked for the front and immediately ordered to be ready—were marched to the railroad depot and kept sitting in the sun during the whole day, and then marched back to the camp.

On the 6th, *another examination* was made and almost every member of the Camp pronounced able to go to the front, and this time we started—Left Tuscumbia early in the afternoon on a very heavily laden freight train, which we had to assist the locomotive in taking past the *up-grades* by "main force." After riding and *pushing* alternately for about three hours, we found ourselves about 20 miles from Tuscumbia at a little station.—the engine out order and compelled to go back to Iuka for repairs and we were compelled to remain there till we could get away.[33] There were about 300 men on the train but not more than twenty had arms, therefore we naturally felt very apprehensive to be left thus out on a railroad in an enemy's country—far from any considerable body of our troops.

Several citizens lived near the spot and all seemed to be friendly disposed, and treated us very kindly, coming out among us and conversing very freely on the condition of affairs.

We remained here three days living on the two days rations with which we started from Tuscumbia,—yet fared very well, for we managed to procure some little *delicacies* from the country. The evening of the third day of our stay here the citizens came in and told us that there was a body of rebel Cavalry in the neighborhood and that they supposed them to be intending to attempt to capture us, and in reality they expected them to come on us ere sundown. They envinced so much concern for us, and had all along treated us so kindly that we believed them to be representing the state of affairs in a truthful light. We accordingly marshalled our forces and divided into as many squads as there were cars and each squad taking a car we were soon making some progress in the direction of Courtland, and as the route was principally level or *down-grade* we made the trip in about three hours, arriving safely at Courtland about sundown or a little later.

It will be a matter of curiosity to the reader why we had to lay three days on railroad without being able to get on a passing train, but it is a fact that not a single train passed us during the three days that we remained at the station[.] The bridge had been burned some distance in advance between us and Decatur (the evening we left Tuscumbia) and therefore no more trains could be expected till they were repaired. I dont think our forces did repair that road very soon again; at any rate there was no indication of such a purpose at the time I left the road.[34]

We found two companies of the Tenth Ky Inftry at the bridge near Courtland under command of Capt Davidson who were stationed there as guards.[35] We still had no rations—there were none on the train except a few days' supply for Captain D———'s command, therefore we were reduced to the nesessity of subsisting on Roasting ears, of which we could now procure a tolerably mature article, and fruits and berries. Remained here most day (July 9th) vainly hoping that a train would come along and carry us on at least to the end of the road where the first bridge was burned; but no train came and early next morning (July 10th) I and four others of my regiment concluded that we would attempt to walk to Decatur which was now about "20 miles away." We set out very early but on account of the weakness of some of the party we travelled necessarily very slow, and had only completed eight miles about 2 o'clock in the afternoon which brought us to the first of the burned bridges and at which two more companies of the Tenth Ky Infantry were stationed; and as if to irritate us for our sore feet and tired limbs just as we sat down in the edge of the camp, a train came up, but it could not go beyond this point. Several boys whom we had left back at Courtland were on this train, but when they saw the burned bridge and heard the engine whistle for backing they stuck to the train and urged us to get on and go back with them. We did not choose to go back, thinking that it was about as safe walking to the front as riding to the rear; for this train brought news that about sundown on the evening we left the station where the locomotive left us, a body of rebel cavalry under the notorious Roddy[36] had charged in and captured the station and a few of our party who were too lazy to come with us—had burned the depot, woodyard and about twenty cotton bales, and burned a small trestle-work, and cut the telegraph wire.

So we remained here all night, these companies being kind enough to furnish us rations which added to some fish bought on the route made us a very plentiful supper. Next morning (July 11th) we again set out for Decatur, and as the weather was very warm, and much of the road lay in long lines, and some of our party were very weak, we did not get to Decatur till very late in the afternoon.

Sergt. J[oseph] Meader of Co. C[37] and one of our party here procured one days rations for us and then we crossed the river in the steam ferry Tennessee, which had enough black paint and port holes to give her the appearance of a most formidable "ironsides", "but she wasn't big enough."[38] Across the river, we walked up to the *Junction*, which I believe is about three miles from the river,[39] and about sundown a train came down the road from Nashville took us on board, and we were whirling away over the country in the direction of Huntsville, at which place we arrived a little while after dark, and immediately taking shelter under the boughs of a spreading oak we were soon in the "Land of Nod."

Early next morning we were up and took a pleasant walk about this beautiful little town to view its many reputed attractions and were much pleased with it's general appearance. It is true that we saw no wonderful curiosity—of nature or art; but the nicely laid off streets—the large lots—the splendid residences —the beautiful yards and gardens—its large pure spring, and in fact everything about Huntsville goes to prove that before the war it was undoubtedly one of the most beautiful and pleasant little towns in the Southern States.

A little while after sunrise we again got on a train and were soon jolting along through a principally uncultivated country in the direction of Stevenson—rode on top of the cars, and as the day was very warm we were anything but comfortable. Arrived at Stevenson about noon and found that to be from all appearances a very important post,[40] but like most other southern towns, that have an advantageous situation—remarkably shabby. A train load of troops was just leaving for Murfreesboro which was reported to have been captured the day previous with all its garrison. We could get no transportation beyond this point—neither could we procure any rations, but were informed that our Division was camped somewhere near the mouth of Battle Creek on the Tennessee River, and about fifteen miles from this place. We started again pretty soon and traveled about 8 miles that evening, procuring our supper about sundown from an old soldier of the Seminole war,[41] when, night coming on, we turned aside into the bushes, spread our blankets, and went to sleep—were afraid to travel the road after dark on account of rumors of guerillas.

We were up and traveling early next morning (July 13th) and about noon arrived within the camp of the Division and of course soon found our Regiment which had arrived only the day previous and was clearing the bushes from the camping ground.

The boys had made a very lengthy, wearisome, hot, dusty and

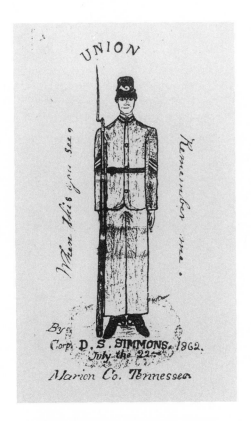

Self portrait of D. S. Simmons, 1862.
Courtesy of Billy Simmons.

generally disagreeable march since I had left them, and presented visible proofs of the hardships they had undergone. They had also at the last draw been reduced to half rations and of course the thought of this did not serve in the least to rest their wearied limbs, and to increase the enjoyment of the repose they were now promised from long and heavy marches.

Upon the whole they looked rather gloomy and cheerless and went *moping* about more like inmates of a Convalescent camp than of a regimental camp.

The camp was being established in a beautiful grove, which after all the underbrush and *trash* were cleared off proved to be a very pleasant one. The water was procured from springs almost a mile off but in a sufficient quantity and of a very superior quality.

The citizens of the surrounding country occasionally brought in fruit and vegetables, but it was in very small quantities compared with the wants of the army.

Duties came very regularly on us during our stay here in the performance of all kinds of Camp duties, picket, &c. We were called up and into line on the parade ground a little while before daybreak, and kept standing one hour; then followed breakfast and *fatigue call*, next guard mounting and then The Company drill occupied about two hours in the forenoon; then came the non-commissioned officers' drill which lasted one hour.

In the evening came battalion drill, which also lasted two hours,— Went on picket every four days by Brigades.

The principal source of amusement to the boys was the nice bathing place at the mouth of the creek, across which a floating bridge was laid—from this place we could very distinctly see and even *converse* with the rebels on the opposite bank of the river, and there was many a hearty laugh ringing across the quiet waters of the Tennessee, occasioned by the comic speeches of some sedate Yankee, or the tart replies of some specimen of Southern Chivalry.

Our boys would frequently swim across the river and converse with them a few moments and then return unmolested. One of these fellows was detained and made prisoner in consequence of some new rebel order—as the rebs carried him over the bank he hollowed back to his comrades, "Just take care of my clothes."

Toward the close of our stay here our company concluded to have some amusement in a new style—by a general understanding, each mess sent a representative to a Convention that was convened under the shade of a spreading oak within the *municipality* of the second mess, and this Convention saw proper to select another man from the Company who was to officiate at once as Speaker and Clerk.

This Convention proceeded to frame a Constitution and Code for the government of "B County," and as the Convention was omnipotent there was no election for its adoption, but a proclamation from the Chairman of the Convention at once placed the Constitution and Laws in full force. Next followed the election of the officers—The Constitution allowed us to elect all the officers peculiar to a County, and a Circuit Court Judge and Attorney General.

The members of the Convention established some laws that

were very contrary to the spirit of most Republican Governments, and among the rest there were some very severe and extensive *retrospective* laws, but still the boys said *let's support the Administration* and all vowed a strict obedience to the officers who should be elected. The election for the various officers proved to be an exciting contest, but went off without any blood being shed.

Soon after the new government got in motion, the Magistrate Courts were overflowing with business, and the "appeals to the Circuit Court" soon ran up a long list in the Clerk's "docket book?["]

Then at the first Session of the Circuit Court we had the beginning of a series of amusements that helped very much to wile away the *hungry* hours of the long evenings after Battalion Drill.

The Attorney General was an able and *tricky* lawyer who could so completely construe any part of our laws or Constitution to suit his purposes that he rarely failed to succeed in condemning a culprit, and his wit brought labored speeches from his opponents who were assailing his wit and *trickery* more than the evidence against their clients.

Sometimes he (the Attorney) would bring a charge of the most felonious character against some person and the evidence would be so conclusive in proof of the defendants guilt (who sometimes happened to be *really* guilty) that I have known disinterested persons to prevail with him to withdraw his suit lest some trouble should be produced. Yet, we never had any difficulties to arise from any of the testimonies, pleadings or decisions.

But our government was as shortlived as it was *glorious*. When we had to evacuate that place, the public *archives* were placed in my possession and I had the misfortune to lose the whole concern.

Our rations were very short during the whole of our stay here, and if it had not been for some amusement to keep us cheerful, we would undoubtedly have become in a measure despondent.

It is with great dissatisfaction that I pass over many interesting incidents of our stay at this place, but from the fact that my Journal was lost, I am compelled to, for want of confidence in my memory, to give an accurate account of them.

Col. Grider obtained a leave of absence of twenty days and went home. Lieutenants [Daniel] Stout, Co. E.; [William] Gregory, Co. D., and [Smith] Pipkin Co. H resigned.[42] Lieut. Rodes (Co. K.)

sent back sick during the siege of Corinth, returned to his Company, and Ben M. Johnson was promoted to Second Lieutenant of our Company, vice Silus Clark promoted to First Lieutenant during our stay at this place.

Also about the first of August we commenced to erect a fort on a commanding piece of ground just below the mouth of Battle Creek and had it pretty nearly completed when we left—It was styled Fort McCook in honor of the Commander of the troops at this point.[43]

Chapter 4

※※※

In the Direction of Perryville

When Gen. Braxton Bragg replaced Beauregard as commander of the Confederate Army of Mississippi—soon to be renamed the Army of Tennessee—his mind was very much on his cavalry. During Buell's march across Alabama, Forrest and Morgan had shown how raids on communications could immobilize an entire army. Bragg now followed suit, but on a grander scale. Moving his army from Mississippi to Chattanooga via a circuitous railroad route 776 miles long, Bragg intended to move into Middle Tennessee and even into Kentucky, threaten Buell's supply line, and force Buell to follow him. Bragg then could fight on ground of his choosing. He expected to see an outpouring of Confederate patriotic sentiment in Kentucky that would produce enlistments to swell the ranks of his army.

The invasion began on August 14, when Maj. Gen. Edmund Kirby Smith left Knoxville with twenty-one thousand men and headed for Cumberland Gap and the Kentucky Bluegrass beyond. Bragg crossed the Tennessee River a week later. Confused at first, Buell first fell back to Nashville to secure that city from Bragg, then raced across western Kentucky to Louisville, dogging Bragg's heels. Ultimately, on October 8, the two main armies, parched by the hot sun and desperate for water, met at Perryville. It was a confusing if bloody affair, as Buell got less than half of his army into action. For Woodcock, idle at Perryville along with the rest of Crittenden's corps, the return to Kentucky ended in frustration. At least the pursuit of the fleeing Bragg briefly brought the 9th Kentucky back to their homes.[1]

With this chapter, Woodcock begins to write directly from his surviving journals, occasionally even copying passages word for word. As a result, the memoir now takes on the style of a diary.

Aug. 19th (first day accounted for in my journal) we went out on picket, up Battle Creek some distance at the foot of the mountain. Rumor through the camp in the afternoon that the Rebels had made a fresh inroad on our communication line and several of the boys immediately charged upon a field of corn near by and secured a good supply of roasting ears.

Aug. 20th, we returned to Camp and soon heard reports going about the camp to the effect that we were going to move in a very short time. There seemed to be a general *stir* about head quarters, and the common duties and amusements of the men were all suspended.—During the afternoon these reports received confirmation, and about 6 o'clock P.M. we were ordered to "strike tents, pack up and be ready to move immediately.["]

This was gotten through with the usual confusion after being in camp so long, but we were ordered to be very noiseless in our operations. At 7 o'clock P.M. we were called into line and marched up the river to the mouth of Battle Creek which we crossed on the before-mentioned floating bridge, which had now been covered over with green corn and sand to prevent the noise of our crossing disturbing the quiet slumbers of the Rebels on the opposite bank of the river. Then we marched up the river and off the left on the road to Jasper making one of the most disagreeable imaginable of a dry moonshining night. The road was every where filled with large stones, and most of the way shaded by heavy timber and consequently the walking was very tedious and irksome. We arrived at Jasper a little while after midnight having travelled near ten miles.

Aug 22nd sunrise this morning found us scattered over the cornfields and orchards adjacent Jasper in search of anything nourishing to the inner man, such as roasting ears, peaches, apples, &c. Jasper is a very gloomy looking prospect for a town, and especially a County Seat; the buildings are mostly brick, but generally in a state of dilapidation. About 11 o'clock A.M. our whole force composed of Crittenden's and McCook's Divisions, left Jasper and marched off in a northeasterly direction on [Gizzard] Road[2] and traveled till about 1 o'clock P.M. our regiment being in the advance. We then halted and went into camp and the remainder of the day was principally consumed in passing the long supply trains to the front. One circumstance occurred after our halt and as it was the first of the kind I was ever witnessed I think it deserves special mention—*It was the shameful pillaging of a house within the precincts of the camp.* A bunch of *straggling vagabonds*, after having taken everything the yard and garden afforded went into the house and searched through the whole house, carrying off anything they could find that suited them. Despite the entreaties of a tender little girl they bursted bureaus containing clothing, table ware, and anything they had no use for, and carried off the contents—tore down ladies ward robes and carried off any and all that suited them, and what they could not carry off, they destroyed.

It was the first and I think the most blamable piece of robbery I ever saw committed—and the greatest cause for dissatisfaction I ever had with our Guards was the attention I necessarily give to carelessness they generally exhibited in regard to this certain class of *thieves* who had crept into blue uniform, and were serving as soldiers, but who were daily committing deeds that would *disgrace* the humblest convict in "Sing Sing." There seemed to be a charm about them as soon as they turned out to stealing, and when provosts would charge upon a body of offenders, *they* were sure to escape.

Aug. 22nd Our Regiment on picket to day, but late in the evening were relieved and ordered to get ready to move at once—At 7 o'clock P.M. we started back on the road we had come, and turning to the right near Jasper marched toward Battle Creek and encamped nearly opposite to our former picket ground—night was very dark and road rough, some rain falling, therefore, we of course had disagreeable marching. I can not now see what all this marching and countermarching meant, "for a large body of Rebels were in Jasper in the forepart of the night on which we arrived and again on last night."

Sat. Aug 23rd went about three miles up Battle Creek and again encamped in a very nice bunch of trees and sent our wagons on a foraging expedition to procure roasting ears, &c. We were yet on very short *half rations*—were in an enemy's country—heard various rumors and constructions in regard to the passage of and nature of the "Confiscation Bill"—therefore we could not be expected to suffer from want when surrounded by plenty.[3]

Sun. Aug 24th Set out early and climbed Cumberland Mountain, reaching the summit about 2 o'clock P.M. and marched till several hours after dark—in order I suppose to reach water for we found scarcely any at all after arriving on the mountain till we got into camp. A large number of the boys gave out and were left behind being overcome by the excessive heat and fatigue, and scarcity of water. The right wing of our Regiment with the Colonel strayed from the main road in the darkness of the night and it was a considerable time after we arrived in camp till they came in. During the night, after all had become quiet, an alarm was created in some portion of the camp by some loose horses running through the lines and the men raising a yell to frighten them away.—immediately the whole camp was up and hollering, and all in our part of the camp not knowing the cause of the disturbance a general panic seized upon all parties.—many supposed that a body of rebel cavalry had charged into the camp and therefore broke to the gunstacks and took position, some who were awake from the beginning and knew the real cause of the alarm got behind trees and some of them even climbed trees to avoid being run over; I think two or three climbed a very thorny tree of some description near which I posted myself to avoid the expected trampling, but within the space of two minutes, the excitement had entirely subsided and all returned to their blankets.

Monday Aug. 25th. Marched early, and began to descend the mountain about 10 o'clock A.M. and by noon had reached its base in a rich and beautiful country, known I believe as Sweden's Cove. We now were compelled entirely upon *foraging* for subsistence, for the wagons had left us on the 23rd with scarcely a day's rations in our haversacks. But the country was very productive and was now loaded with a heavy crop of corn, and some of the finest peach orchards I ever beheld; and on such rations as this we were now mainly living—if hogs had been plenty, we would have fared better, but stock of all kinds seemed to be very scarce.

Tu Aug. 26th. the wagons came up and six days half rations were issued to us, but as we had not yet become accustomed to living on short rations, much *forage* was still consumed, and as a consequence, many of the boys began to complain of diarrhea. We remained in camp Wednesday sweeping and cleaning off our camp as though it was intended for us to remain there several days.

Thursday. Aug. 28th—were roused up at 3 o'clock A.M. and ordered to be ready to march at daylight. At daylight an order countermanding the other was received, and we took another nap. At noon heard a rumor that the enemy had opened upon Fort McCook with several batteries of artillery, and that our troops, left there, had evacuated the fort and were now coming up with us. I have forgotten what troops were left there but I think it was only a regiment of infantry and a battery of artillery to divert the rebels from our real purpose.

Friday. Aug. 29th. our regiment went on picket about three miles from camp, but was called in about 3 o'clock P.M. and ordered to be ready to march immediately. The march soon began, our regiment acting as rear guard—marched in a North Westerly direction, passing through Pelham, a little village about three miles from our camp, and going six miles beyond to a stream which I learned was named Fishing Creek, where we encamped. The roads were very dry and dusty and therefore marching was very disagreeable.

Sat. Aug 30th Marched about three miles to a little village named Hillsboro where we took the McMinnville Road. Passed a beautiful little lake at the head of the creek before-mentioned and encamped about a mile from town between the McMinnville and Nashville roads. We now had no idea as to the purposes of our Commander (McCook) and knew as little about the whereabouts of the rest of the Army as if they never had existance. I did not see a newspaper for weeks, and had not received a letter from home in such a great while that I almost despaired of hearing from them again at all. The men almost ceased to speculate upon the prospects, and I think there was greater ignorance of the state of affairs among the men at that time than I ever knew at any other time.

Sun. Aug 31 Marched to Manchester, the County Seat of Coffee County, a distance of 7 miles. A considerable shower of rain fell during the evening which was very disagreeable for we had not been accustomed to camping without our tents but the boys remedied the defect by stretching their blankets something after the fashion of the famous Dobia tent which had not been invented.[4] Thus a new novelty was created in the formation of a camp that elicited much remark.

Mon. Sept. 1 marched on the Pike 13 miles in the direction of Murfreesboro and encamped about noon on [Garrison Ford] Creek, just beyond a little hamlet known as Beech Grove. The road passes through a rough hilly country but it was in a high state of cultivation,—our march was principally along a deep narrow valley which presented many beautiful scenes of nature. A very hard rain fell in the morning, but the almost baking sun soon dried the earth again. Next day we marched 14 miles in the direction of Murfreesboro and encamped on a little creek just three miles to town. After we had gotten into camp and were all lying around in the shades, a large and fat frightened hog ran over our Orderly who was asleep and (the boys said) hurt him seriously. This anger of our Company and Co. "G" was aroused to the highest pitch upon seeing such an indignity offered to a United States officer, and they immediately gave chase to the offender; and after running him almost under Col. Beatty's tent (Brigade Commander)[5] they came up with and killed this specimen of the grunting race.

He was considered too heavy to carry away and a *council of subsistence* decided that he should be immediately dressed and cooked in retaliation for the injury inflicted on our Sergeant.

We marched through Murfreesboro on the morning of the third and halted about three miles beyond on the Lebanon pike till about 4 o'clock P.M. when we again took up the march and went across a branch of Stone's River seven miles from Murfreesboro on the above-named road and encamped, making our day's march about 11 miles. This evening I began to feel rather unwell again, and when we got into camp very sick and could eat nothing.

Sept. 4th (the twentieth anniversary of my birth day) and 5th we remained in Camp and enjoyed the good water and fine forage the country afforded. About this time creditable reports were in the camp that served to discourage us very much. The *Grand Army of the Potomac* had been reduced to the extremity of acting on the defensive, and were reported to be in full retreat for Washington City—the rebels were making threatening demonstrations on Baltimore.[6] And Bragg was reported to be attempting to *flank* Gen Buell and our army and capture Louisville and Cencennatti. Many little skirmishes were spoken of in which the rebels were reported victors, and affairs in general wore a very bad face. The troops seemed to be very much discouraged, and began to feel a considerable lack of confidence in the Commanders. We were receiving no newspapers or mails and consequently had no means of judging how nearly all these reports might be true; but the short rations that we were continually receiving served to confirm our fears that the Government must for some cause or other be very much straightened.

Sat. Sept 6, marched early in the direction of Nashville, and went to within four miles of that place, (whole days march 27 miles). This was an exceedingly warm and dusty day and the great distance marched, together with the scarcity of the water rendered it very disagreeable and fatiguing, and I dont think there were fifty men with the Colonel when he arrived in camp. I was so unwell in the morning as to be unable to march and by order of the Surgeon was placed in Ambulance and was hauled the whole day. The Regiment arrived in Camp by 3 o'clock P.M. but a large number of the boys did not get in till that night or the next morning. A heavy mail, but of rather ancient date, was here received from the north, but not a letter from my part of the country. The rail road all along from Nashville to Louisville, and no trains were running at all, therefore, we received but little news of interest. We expected that we would get plenty of rations here, as we had believed all the time that there was plenty at Nashville, but in this we were again mistaken.

Sun. Sept. 7. We marched at 3 P.M. and arrived in Nashville just as the last wagon of the preceding Division was going on the bridge (an evidence of the ability of Gen Buell to march a large Army) and consequently were detained in the City but a few moments but passed on over the bridge and then marched five miles up the Gallatin road and encamped. We were now becoming very much perplexed as to what was next in store for us, for I had all along believed that we would surely not go north of Cumberland river, but it now seemed as if we were going to leave Nashville and the whole of *my state* to the mercy of the rebels. We had collected all the livestock (cattle and sheep) that could be found on our march—the whole Army was going northward—the rebels were in our front and on our right flank—Nashville was garrisoned by a very small force who would be compelled to succumb if attacked by any considerable force— really a generally [*i.e.,* general] contemplation of the state of affairs left me in a situation bordering very closely on hypochondria.

Mon. Sept. 8th, marched 5 or 6 miles and encamped on the rail road not far from Lebanon Junction where the road crossed a creek. The wagons again came to us this evening and we were ordered to procure anything from our knapsacks that we would be likely to stand in need of very soon for "the probability is that you will not see your knapsacks again for a long time."

It should have been stated ere this that our knapsacks had been hauled for us ever since leaving Battle Creek on account of the hard marching and the *scarcity of anything else wherewith to load the wagons.*

As we did not march very far on this day the boys were not very tired, and after supper (about sunset) they had secured the services for the evening of the celebrated vocal and instrumental musician [Benjamin] Mayhew of the Eleventh Kentucky Infantry,[7] and had just commenced a series of amusements which promised great recreation,—when an order came for Co's A and B to prepare to go on picket—the musicians struck out on one verse of: "hang up the fiddle and put away the bow," and the boys immediately proceeded to obey orders.

We went five or six miles to stand picket, and were posted at a little town known as Goodrichville (?)[8]

On the 9th we marched on the Franklin (Ky) Pike to Lyra Springs, and the next day to Mitchellsville, the *ancient* site of Camp Trousdall, which was a large camp of instruction the rebels established at this place in the spring of 1861[.]

Thur. Sept. 11th. Marched through Franklin Ky and encamped about 6 miles beyond at a large spring which runs through the bottom of a sink hole.

We now began to meet with some evidences of respect to our army by the citizens, they flocking in large numbers to the road to see us pass and bearing numerous national flags. Many of our Regiment met with acquaintances in Franklin, and several of them ventured a few miles out into the country to take dinner with their friends.

Our rations still continued to be found in very small quantities, and we were now reduced to the necessity of *gritting* corn to procure bread as it had become too hard to use as roasting ears.

Friday, Sept. 12th. several of the boys of our Regiment were missing this morning, and a citizen of the neighborhood (Rev. Nimrod Davis) with whom a large number of the Regiment was acquainted, came into camp very early and confirmed the suspicion that they were captured by the rebel cavalry. Two of them had been captured at his residence the day previous and in the fray a lady had discharged one of the boy's muskets at the rebels and had now fled with the old gentleman to our camp for safety.

Companies G, K & I of our Regiment and as many companies from the other regiments of the Brigade were immediately ordered to be ready to go a scouting. They were loaded into covered wagons and sent to where the rebel cavalry was last heard from, as a foraging expedition, but failed to attract the attention of any of the rebels. Soon after this detachment started John Smith of Co. D (one of boy's captured at Davis' residence) came into camp, having escaped from the rebels a few hours previous, but not till after he had been paroled—he reported the enemy to be at least one thousand strong and not more than two miles distant.[9] The seven companies of our Regiment that were left in camp were immediately ordered to be ready to march and *fight*. We set out about 10 o'clock & accompanied by about 80 men of the Second Kentucky Cavalry, the whole being under command of Col. [Buckner] Board of the latter regiment,[10] and marched up the pike to Woodburn and then turning off into the country to the right we began to skin our eyes for the enemy. We marched three or four miles when we came on a squad of negroes who informed us that a rebel company was on picket about one-half a mile ahead at the house of Mrs. Bunch or rather in an adjoining lot, and that they were making preparations for "big dinner" on the provisions taken from the premises.[11] We were immediately ordered to "double quick" and so devoted were the rebels to the preparations for this dinner that we got within two hundred yards of them before they perceived us.—then in an instant we were thrown into "line of battle" and ordered to *Charge the fence and rebels— double quick—march*, which we obeyed in a spirited style, firing a volley as we went which killed one (*a negro, clothed armed and equipped in Confederate* custom)[12] and frightened the rest so terribly that they mounted their horses and left in *splendid style*, but some of them didn't wait for their horses, but went off through a field of corn.

In their haste, they left several shot-guns, carbines, rifles, sabres, bacon hams, and about one bushel of corn-bread.—we did not stop to take any of these articles but kept on in the direction of the frightened rebels—soon came on their main body, a whole brigade, stationed on an elevated piece of ground behind a high fence near the residence of Mr. ———— an old acquaintance of the Colonel.

We exchanged a few shots with them and then charged them notwithstanding they were all on their horses, our cavalry charging through the lane on our left in the most gallant style, as we advanced to the charge, they gave us a parting volley and fled. We charged across a lot about 150 yards wide and when we came to their position they in large numbers were about 150 yards farther on and endeavoring to make their way through a thicket, but the bushes were so thick that it was with great difficulty that they could make their way, and till they did we had the fairest opportunity desirable of just literally slaughtering them, but the Colonel mistaking them for our cavalry which we had lost in the great cloud of dust peremptorily ordered us not to fire, and thus rendered the whole expedition ineffectual. As the last of them entered the thicket, he turned and discharged his carbine at us as if to defy us. *Somebody made an inexcusable blunder.* In the last affair we captured two of the enemy, and they said we had killed and wounded several—also captured several horses. We halted and formed after the last charge and concluding that we could hold Cavalry a good race much farther we turned and started to camp, after performing a few evolutions for the benefit of the enemy whom we could now see in a field away to our right. Our Regiment lost only one man wounded (Andrew J. Moss of our Co) and it was a slight gunshot in the side of the head. The Second Ky lost a Sergt killed in the last charge—returned to camp ere nightfall.

Sat. Sept. 13. Marched toward Bowling Green Ky and encamped at Cave Spring, 3 miles to Bowling Green. Remained in Camp at this place during the 14th and on this day many *refugees* from our country came into camp giving doleful account of the passage of Braggs Army through Macon, & Jackson Counties Tennessee, and Monroe County Ky but by this time we had become accustomed to such reports and they did not affect us only to serve to increase our anxiety to meet the rebels at an early day and contend for their right to thus desolate our fields. To day an Uncle of mine (Smith Woodcock) who had met us at Franklin, started for home.

It was with much difficulty that I managed to pen a cheerful letter to my parents, for I could not feel cheerful in the least and had not a single encouraging item to speak of—could tell him no good news from any part of our army—could not tell him that I was

getting plenty to eat and enjoying myself well; and finally I concluded that it would not be safe for Uncle to carry a letter and
accordingly did not send it.

Mon. Sept. 15. Received news that Munfordville was taken yesterday by the rebels, together with its garrison of 2500 men under
command of Col. Wilder. To take a casual glance at affairs at this
period it seemed as if the rebels were *really* getting *ahead* of us. Col.
Wilder and his valiant little garrison had defended M———ville
with a valor that would have acquitted and distinguished the arms
of any troops, and the news of the Rebel attack on them was received within our lines a sufficient length of time ere their surrender
for some of us to have been marched to their relief, but we just *fooled
along* and did not get there soon enough.[13]

The 16th we went through Bowling Green, crossed Barren river
on a Pontoon bridge and encamped a few hundred yards further on;
and on the 17th we marched in the direction of Bells Tavern, our
advance guard skirmishing with and driving the enemy continually,
taking also a few prisoners.

Thurs. Sept. 18th. Marched to Cave City and went into camp—
skirmishers brought in about one hundred rebel prisoners, among
them several officers—again bad news of the capture of Munfordville and garrison but that it was done at a later date than was before
represented. We got into camp here very late and could find no
water except that in the *reservoir*, which had probably been in there
for a month as the water-works were not in operation.

Fri. Sept. 19th we were greeted early this morning by the painful
yet welcome appearance of about 4500 U.S. troops coming into
lines from the direction of Munfordville without arms or accouterments or anything of the kind. They were the troops that had
composed the recent garrison at Munfordville, and it sorely pained
my heart to see this fine body of troops thus lost to our service, for
a considerable time at least, through the tardiness of our movements. The[y] seemed [?] at the fact of having been compelled to
lower their flag to their enemies and many of them as they came
into our lines were so enraged at the seeming carelessness of our
troops in marching to their aid that they could not suppress frequent expressions of indignation—They had made a desparate resistance and only surrendered when longer resistance was worse than

useless—Remained in camp at this place during this day and the next hearing very favorable rumors in regard to the numbers and disposition of our troops to the north and east of the rebel army, which, if they had been true, would have inevitably resulted in the complete capture of the rebel Army.

Sun. Sept. 21st. "rebels all gone and we are ordered in pursuit—it is very discouraging to be always getting up with them and then not being allowed the privilege of fighting them a little!" We marched this evening to Green river and waded it at Munfordville, and then went about one mile further and encamped, it being very late in the night ere we halted. On the 22nd we marched about 10 or 12 miles on the Louisville road, and on the 23rd we passed through Elizabethtown about sunset and marched 9 miles further making this days march at least 26 miles. We were very much fatigued and worn out when we arrived at Elizabethtown, and had hoped that we would get to camp near that place for the night, but as I have already stated, we had to march 9 miles further; but the dread of the march and the soreness of our feet and weariness of limbs were almost forgotten, amid the many tokens of sympathy and respect evinced by the numerous, unanimously beautiful and loyal ladies of the town—the stars and stripes were floating from every window, and through the beautiful floatings we could see numerous black eyes and rosy cheeks looking on us with evident feelings of pleasure and approbation, and making numerous little speeches of encouragement to us to follow the ruthless enemy and subjugate or *exterminate* him.

As we passed a lovely group standing on a corner one of them made a remark that clearly evinced wit and patriotism in the superlative degree, and which called forth a cheer from all who heard it (I have forgotten what the remark was). One man of our company of a very ardent and excitable temperament could not suppress his feelings, and losing all command over his tongue and selection of language, he bawled out "bully for you"—the first word of the expression and the accompanying knowledge of the person's partiality for ladies raised such a peal of laughter among our animated troops that I dont think the lady hiard the remark, and I hope she did not, for it would have given a serious offense where the very opposite was intended.

Wednesday Sept. 24, Marched to West Point at the mouth of

Salt River and encamped during the heat of the day. A member of our regiment died by the roadside today of overheat[14]—drew a considerable quantity of flour after we got into camp and for want of baking vessels, some of us were laying large pieces of dough on piles of coals, while others would roll it around a stick and hold it near the fire, but in different ways we managed to cook about the best meal we had since leaving Battle Creek.

But such straits as we had been reduced to for the proper kind of food, and the consequent excesses in eating too great quantities of *trash*, together with the hard marching, excessive heat, and scarcity and inferiority of water[15] had told of their effects in our ranks. We left Battle Creek with more than six hundred able-bodied men in our Regiment and now were reduced by the above named causes to less than three hundred, and a large number were afflicted with camp diseases to such an extent that they could scarcely keep along with us. I had, for a wonder, been able to keep with the company all the time by being hauled one day and was at this time actually gaining in health and strength—About sunset we crossed the river and marched three miles on the bank of the river and encamped[.]

Thur. Sept. 25, Marched to within eight miles of Louisville, and then turned square to the left again and marched to the river and about two miles along its bank, "up stream," and then went into camp—had put out a Camp Guard to keep the boys from straying off to the numerous and plentiful orchards of the vicinity, and had eaten our supper and in general lay down to sleep when, at 8 o'clock P.M. we were aroused from our early slumbers and to Louisville that night; arriving at the latter place just as the town clocks were pealing the still hour of midnight.

Fri. Sept. 26th remained in camp in the suburbs of Louisville (near the cemetery) during the day, largely *but individually* enjoying the hospitality of many of its citizens who seemed to think that much was due to "Buell's men" for the preservation of the city from capture by Bragg's army. It seemed that they had been very fearful that we would not get there in time to effect that object, and they had only partial confidence in the troops that were defending the place as they were mostly new, and hardly at all disciplined. It was very easy to discern between the soldiers of our army and the garrison of Louisville, by the dirty and ragged clothing and rusty guns of the former, and the shining uniform and polished arms of the latter.[16] The Provost Guards were quickly subdued after the approach of daylight by some of our (probably too "fust") boys and we had full liberty to roam over the city during the whole day, when and where we pleased, and the effects of this began to be plainly visible by now in the numerous "turning up" of canteens by almost everybody; the numerous whoops and huzzas, and jovial speeches and comical remarks, and staggering forms of our boys all told but too plainly that ardent spirits had in a measure got the better of martial spirit, and was waging a fearful war with good order and military discipline. Many a soldier was on that day considerably intoxicated that was never known before or since to be in the least affected by any intoxicating drink—Regular teetotalers even succumbed to the attack of the fire water, giving way at the first shock, but returning to the attack with determination to *exterminate* the vile enemy that was well worthy a nobler cause—they fought hard for a considerable time, but were finally left weltering in their gore (vomit), completely subdued.

Sat. Sept. 27 marched through the southern edge of the city and out about 3 miles southeast of the same and again encamped—considerable rain fell today and as it was very cool, the want of our tents proved very disagreeable, but all this inconvenience was more than compensated for by the receipt of full rations of all kinds of army fare.

We were also gratified today by the appearance of Ex. Major Hinson in Camp for whom almost every man in the regiment cherished a warm friendship. Since leaving the regiment he had been compelled to live almost entirely on the scout, and compelled to be at all times on his guard except when within our lines—he had run many narrow risks and had many hair-breadth escapes from the guerillas. Subsequently to this he served over a year as Captain in the Twelfth Kentucky Infantry, and was afterwards promoted Colonel of the First Tennessee Mounted Infantry, and was on his way to assist in recruiting this regiment when the brave but unfortunate man was killed by a squad of guerillas in Macon County Tennessee.

The 28th and 29th presented nothing of interest—our regiment went on picket on the former and came back on the latter day.

Tu. Sept. 30th remained in camp, drawing a little clothing, but not by any means enough to fill the demand, as we could not hear anything of our knapsacks in which almost all of us had full suits of clothing, drawn just before leaving Battle Creek.

We also drew a supply of tin vessels of various sizes and shapes that were to answer all the purposes of cooking, and which we would have to carry about our persons on the march. The boys grumbled very much at the idea of having to carry their cooking vessels, but a few days experience proved to them that it caused scarcely any more fatigue (from the lightness of the vessels) and was far more convenient than any other arrangement on a long and heavy march.

If a sufficient number of wagons to haul "any and everything" *do* accompany an army it is always necessarily several hours after the troops arrive in camp till the wagons come up, and thus they are frequently kept till very late in the night without their supper, and a warm dinner is out of the question.

When the soldier carries his coffee-pot and frying pan about his person, one hour at noon is sufficient to enable to cook and eat his dinner; and when he goes into camp at night he will have his supper served and eaten, and be sleeping soundly long ere the wagons would have arrived into camp.

Wed Oct 1st, marched back through the edge of the city and took the Bardstown pike, and marched 12 1/2 miles ere night, and encamped in a nice grassy lot on the left of the road—Our advance skirmishers had a severe fight with the enemy this evening at the creek 4 miles in advance of our camp. Our regiment went on picket tonight.

Thurs. Oct. 2nd. our Regiment in advance,[17] we moved on till we came in sight of our cavalry skirmishing with the enemy across the creek—were immediately marched near the summit of an elevation that gave artillery complete command over the point where the road crosses the creek, and halted and lay down, when a section of artillery coming up, poured a few shells among the rebels who immediately fell back out of our view. Our Brigade (the 11th commanded by Col. Samuel Beatty) immediately advanced and crossed the creek, and went about a half a mile further when we discovered the enemy about three fourths of a mile ahead near Mt. Washington. A line of battle was formed by the Brigade and a battery coming up again poured the shells into the rebels and the town at a furious rate. Without returning the fire the rebels again fled. We then marched up near town and encamped for the night having marched about 5 miles. The citizens said that the force opposed to us numbered about six hundred, cavalry, and that they had two pieces of artillery.

Fri. Oct. 3rd. received four months' pay by Paymaster, Maj. Hazelton. Also about this time Gen Crittenden was promoted to the command of a Gran[d] Division, and Brig. Gen. H. P. Van Cleve (Commander of 14th Brig. of our Division) was placed in command of our Division.[18] In the evening we marched across Salt River and encamped.

Sat. Oct. 4th. Marched up the Lebanon Road to Fairfield then turning to the right we went to within one mile of Bardstown where we had expected to find the rebels in full, and rather desired than dreaded to give them a fight, hoping it would in some way terminate the long and heavy marches we were almost daily being compelled to make; but we learned that the last of the Rebels had left Bardstown just as our advance came in sight.

We encamped there all night and were much amused at the manner in which the 79th Ind Infantry came into line to encamp. They were a perfectly raw regiment, and had a strict disciplinarian for their Commander[19] and the required precision, promptness and celerity of movement caused much disorder and confusion among his undrilled troops.

Sun. Oct. 5th. passed through Bardstown, and went about 2 1/2 miles on the Springfield Road, then turning to the left we marched across the country to another road, and then went "zig zagging" about the remainder of the day, encamping that night at a little hamlet on Buck Fork, the name of which I have forgotten (9 miles)[.][20]

Mon. Oct. 6 Marched to Springfield, a distance of twelve miles— Gen. Rosseau had a severe skirmish with the enemy at this place this morning "and we are getting our army in so many places that I am looking on every side of me for rebels, skirmishing is a matter of hourly occurrence with different portions of the army, and I think we will surely catch the Rebels somewhere in these parts and give them a good whipping."

Tu. Oct. 7th. marching in a direction leading rather to the right of Danville, having to leave the main road on account of water, and encamped that night on Rolling Fork—8 miles to Perryville, and two miles to Haysville. The greatest scarcity of water prevailed on this and the preceding day that I had ever known, and nearly all we could obtain at all was from stagnated ponds, and as the weather was very dry and warm we suffered very much. The only water we obtained here was from the creek, which was only a succession of filthy ponds, the stream being so low that it did not run.

Wed. Oct. 8 our Division was marching early in the direction of Perryville, and about 10 o'clock A.M. the cannon began to roar in front. We then marched about three miles in "quick time" which brought us very nearly to Perryville—were then formed in line of battle on the left of the road, and advanced a short distance into the timber and halted and remained there the whole evening within hearing of that dreadful and sanguinary *Battle of Perryville.* We could hear the cannons "peal upon peal" and at times the sound of distinct volleys of musketry was lost in one continual roaring sound of the discharges of these awful instruments of death. Our Gallant General Crittenden chafed under the restraint that prevented him from leading us to assistance of the brave and impetuous McCook and the chivalric men under his command who were now contending for the mastery against the greater portion of the rebel army, but *"Somebody blundered"?*[21] (The censure of the failure of our army to almost completely annihilate the rebels in this memorable battle has been divided by public sentiment between General's Buell and McCook—one part censuring McCook for his impetuousity, while the other censures Buell for his tardiness[)].[22] I never read the official reports of either of the Generals in regard to the above named battle, nor did I ever see their statements before the "Courts of Inquiry,"[23] nor do I even know that they made any statements before such courts in regard to this battle, and consequently could not be expected to know much about the true merits of the case, but I, of course have my opinions. It is possible that McCook might have acted too rashly or in violation of orders by attacking the enemy at the time he did; and if such was the case he is very censurable, for thereby he might have frustrated some design of the Commanding General, which would probably have resulted more decisively.[24] But after McCook had attacked the enemy and had drawn them into one of the bloodiest battles of the war,[25] and was being compelled to make almost superhuman exertions to save his Grand Division from total annihilation by the vastly outnumbering enemy, and had drawn the attention of the whole rebel army to his force, it does seem that the Commanding General should have sent *troops* enough to make the battle at least a fair one, and not punish troops on account of the disobedience of their commander,—also, when McCook had engaged the attention of the whole rebel army, it seems that something might have been effected by bringing the wings of our Army to bear upon the flanks of the enemy. Let the case be viewed as it may we are forced to the conclusion already arrived at, that *somebody blundered.* We were kept in line the whole evening, and not even allowed to send a detail for water till near dark, and as it had to go near two miles it was near two hours after dark ere we received the first canteen of water since filling at camp in the morning. After shifting positions a little we retired to rest that night almost wholly unconscious of the terrible slaughter that had been carried on so near us. At dark everything was perfectly quiet.

Thur. Oct. 9th. 7 o'clock A.M. the first cannon is just fired away to the left, and we are ordered to fall into line. Our Division advanced very slowly and cautiously in a direction leading rather to the right of Perryville and soon our Company and a Company of the 79th Ind were deployed as skirmishers in advance of the Brigade and placed under command of Col. Fred. Kneffler.

We advanced in this manner about 2 or 3 miles, very cautiously, without seeing anything to shoot at though—halted every few hundred yards for a considerable time—finally we struck the road that we had left on the day previous just before forming the line of battle. We came on it just to the right of town, then marched "as skirmishers by the left flank" into town, but found the place already occupied by our troops—then marched half a mile beyond town and encamped near the scene of the preceding day's battle ground.

Immediately we were all strolling over the battle field. The first point of interest I came to was where a rebel battery had been stationed during the engagement—near thirty were laying dead, nearly all being horribly mangled by cannonshot, and as it the first sight of the kind that I had ever seen, turned me very sick for a few moments, but I soon got the better of my feelings and went further; but it is useless for me to attempt to describe this bloody field— in some places the dead could be found lying almost in columns, sometimes U.S. and C.S. being piled promiscuously together— again we would find them thickly scattered over earth that bore marks of furious charges and counter-charges, and all seemed to have been fought over by both parties, for the dead of both armies could be found almost anywhere either were laying.

Narry a fierce remark did I hear that evening by the soldiers who were viewing the field—the fact of their having been kept from assisting their friends when they were being slaughtered in such heaps seemed to cause their very blood to boil with indignation.— that our friends should there within our hearing be compelled to stand up and contend for life against such a vastly superior force while so many thousands of us were so near, and laying idle, was enough to cause the uninformed soldier to give vent to exclamations of anger and disapprobation.

Fri. Oct. 10th. Marched about three miles on the Harrodsburg road, then turning to the left on a dirt road that led to the Danville and Harrodsburg road we marched about two miles when our Brigade had to march back to the pike and remain there a few hours to protect our train which was being threatened by a body of rebel cavalry. We remained here till near dark then marched on the same road as before about two miles,—then turned back a half a mile, then forward again, and we kept stumbling and butting our heads against various objects, and among wagons, logs, fences, stumps, gullies, and every other obstacle to progress that is commonly met with on a dark rainy night till about 9 o'clock when we got into camp.

Sat. Oct. 11th aroused early and were eating breakfast when we heard a sharp firing commence at the picket line. We gave it but little attention at first, and continued unconcernedly to eat our breakfast, but presently it began to come nearer so rapidly that we were ordered to "fall into line, quick," and be ready for the rebels. Just then one of our cannon ran up near the line, and by firing one shot into the advancing rebels, restored good order and caused the rebels to scamper away like so many frightened sheep. It was altogether one of the most impudent acts on the part of the rebels that

I ever heard of, I dont suppose the rebel force consisted of more than a small scout, and they were within three hundred yards of the main lines of our division.

After we had completed our breakfast we were moved about one mile across the fields in the direction of Danville, and deployed in line [of] battle and kept there the whole day, which was so cool from the recent rain and cloudy weather that we found it necessary to build fires for comfort. Also to day we received the first news of the bloody battle at Corinth Miss. between our troops under Gen. Rosecrans and the rebels.[26]

Sun. Oct. 12th Marched 8 or 9 miles across roads and through fields, three columns of our troops moving parallel to each other frequently being visible at the same time. When we arrived in about 4 miles of Camp Dick Robinson[27] we halted, formed in line of battle and remained till near night—seeing no sign of the Rebels in the meantime, we then fell back near one mile and encamped— Had a real feast tonight on *pumpkins* gathered from a field near by and cooked. Also for the first time after entering Ky we were ordered to not burn any rails, although we were encamped in the midst of a large farm.

Mon. Oct. 13th, marched nearly to Danville, then turning to the left our Brigade went about two miles in the direction of Dick's River on picket, and remained all night; and on the 14th we turned back and marched through Danville and went to Stanford—distance of 10 miles, and went into Camp. After we had gotten supper and were asleep—10 o'clock P.M. we were aroused again and started on the road leading to Crab Orchard. About 2 o'clock (*Wed.* Oct 15th) as we were coming very near the latter-named place, we arrived in view of the rebel campfires.[28]

They immediately opened upon us with one of their *mule* cannon,[29] but a few well-directed shots from one of our batteries soon caused them to take to their heels, after which we went forward and took possession of their camp, and were immediately ordered to prepare and eat breakfast[.]

After we had finished our breakfast and rested a few moments, we again set forward—our Brigade in front—on the road leading to Crab Orchard, now 1 1/2 miles away, but we had hardly started till our pickets encountered and began to drive the enemy. At Crab Orchard the rebels attempted to make a stand as if to give us a temporary check, but our batteries which were kept near the front opened upon them so vigorously that they gave up the town in a few moments. About a mile from town the audacious Rebels again attempted to check us and threw a few shells among our Brigade, one of which burst almost directly over our company and another a few steps in rear of the Regiment. These were the first shells that had ever burst near me, and in fact the first cannon missile I had ever heard whizzing through the air, and you may at once conclude that I was all *dodge*. We followed them this day about 15 miles, they falling back so slowly as to keep up a continual fire with our pickets and to cause our Brigade to have to march the whole day in line of battle, which rendered the march very fatiguing.

Our artillery had to be brought to play upon them almost every mile, and we were constantly expecting that they would make a firm stand and give us battle, but when we afterwards learned that they were only cavalry and not very numerous at that we did not wonder at their passing so many points that would have been favorable to a large force of them to give us battle.

Gen. Crittenden superintended this day's operations in person, and was almost all the time up with the front line giving directions, and I have ever since thought that if he could have commanded the van of our Army from the time we left Louisville, and had the proper support that Gen Bragg's Army would never have escaped from Kentucky.

We went into Camp that night about one hour after sunset, just one mile to Mt. Vernon and just as we were stacking arms the busy rebels attacked our skirmishers but a few hundred yards in advance and maintained a sharp fight for a few minutes, which caused us to again have to *take arms*, but reb' concluded that it was all foolishness and fell back, leaving us in quiet possession of our camp and the privilege of a good night's rest. We were now getting so far from our base that provisions were again getting scarce and the men were beginning to murmur considerably.

Thurs. Oct. 16th. passing through Mt. Vernon, we advanced about *5 miles*, and went into camp.[30] Some skirmishing in front to day but as other troops were in front I could learn nothing of its details, nor results except seeing a few prisoners brought occasionally to the rear.

Fri. Oct. 17th. Advanced about 4 miles through an exceedingly rough and hilly country, then halted and remained till the latter part of the day, when to obtain water we marched back and encamped near our previous night's bivouack. We could not proceed beyond the point to which we went today till the road should be cleared of the many obstructions which the rebels had placed in it— felled trees, &c. The road was filled with trees for several miles, and this rendered the passage of our wagons impassible, for the country was so rough and broken that it was impossible to make new roads. We left the Divisions in our front cutting and removing the trees from the road.

Sat. Oct. 18th. Advanced on the same road as on yesterday, but further.—crossed Rock Castle River and climbed the Wild Cat Mountain till we came to the ground where was fought the memorable "battle of Wild Cat" between our forces commanded by Col's Woolford, Gurrard and others, and the Rebels under Gen. Felix K. Zollicoffer in the previous October.[31]

We could yet find numerous evidences of the terribleness of that small but sanguinary conflict. The position that was occupied by our troops was as near impregnable by nature as could be imagined, to be at all assailable by an attacking party; and the nature of the ground at once explained the cause of the terrible slaughter of the rebels, and the comparatively small loss of our troops that occurred in the battle.

Late in the evening we returned to the opposite [bank] of Rock Castle river and encamped for the night.

Sun. Oct. 19th climbed to the summit of the mountain and advanced 8 or 9 miles along the dry and barren ridges on the London road and again bivouacked for the night, a portion of our Regiment being sent on picket; and remained here for the whole of the next day, the remainder of our Brigade being out on a scout.

Rations had become very scarce and water could scarcely be gotten at all; we had to go about one mile to procure the latter article, and then it was of that inferior article known among the boys as *coppers water*. We were very much worn out with the almost incessant marching we had done since leaving Battle Creek and now the general supposition among the common soldiers was that we would have to follow the rebels through the hills and mountains to East Tennessee. Now you may know that I dreaded it, for it was plain that as we advanced rations would become scarcer on account of the length of our communication line and means of transportation, and the Rebels would strip the country in our advance. We remained at this place for several days anxiously awaiting to know the direction of the next day's march, for we thought that would decide our fate,—if we went forward one day we would pursue the rebels to Tennessee—if we turned back, the campaign was closed.

Fri. Oct. 24th. turned our faces to the rear and started on the back trail, and went as far as Mt. Vernon; there we turned to the left and took the Somerset Road and marched that evening about 7 miles. This days march decided two queries with us, 1st, that we would not pursue the rebels any farther and 2nd, that we would not go back to Louisville, but that we would take the most direct route for Tennessee.

Sat. Oct. 25th. Marched to Somerset, the distance from Mt. Vernon to Somerset is 25 miles.

This was an exceedingly cold day for the time of year, and the scarcity of clothing and blankets among the boys aroused them to such a degree of indignation, that to obtain some revenge for their sufferings from the cold, they made a combined attack upon their natural enemy (apple jack) who could be found lurking in heavy force at almost any house in the country.

A running fight was thus kept up the greater portion of the day, and from the continued absence of our boys that were engaged in the struggle I had almost concluded that they had come off victorious, but at the approach of night they began to return to camp with blackened faces and bruised bodies which not only told the severity of the contest, but that our gallant boys had been defeated. But the victory had been dearly bought by the enemy, and their victory resulted in the complete extermination of all their forces engaged.

We arrived in camp near Somerset, a few hours before night, and just as the *snow* commenced falling.

We immediately commenced collecting large piles of wood and ere nightfall we had roaring fires in every part of the camp, and the snow falling in heaps.

There were no tents with the regiment except those of a few officers—The men were in a measure destitute of clothing and blankets and thus was our situation rendered extremely disagreeable in the immense drifts of driving snow.

About two hours after dark I attempted to prepare my bed, and after spreading my top blanket in great haste to prevent any flakes of snow getting between them, and getting between them just as I was about to pull the blanket over my head, about a hatful that had collected on a limb above fell "slap" on my head. Branches of trees were giving way under the great weight of the snow and falling at intervals through the night, which rendered it very dangerous to be in the timber as we were. Next morning we found the ground covered with about eight inches of snow, and the air of course was very cold.

We remained at this place the *26th* and *27th* with nothing to do but shelter ourselves from the cold in the best manner we could, and for which we could only keep large fires burning, but on the second day the air became much warmer, and the snow principally disappeared.

Tu. Oct. 28th. We marched 28 miles in the direction of Columbia—on the 29th marched 15 miles—on the 30th 15 miles, and on the 31st we marched to Columbia, distance 6 miles. Ever since leaving Somerset a great many of the boys had expressed a determination to go home when we should arrive at Columbia, and by the time we arrived at Columbia almost every man seemed to be seized with that resolution. It was generally believed that the army would march by the way of Glasgow and the boys thought they could go by home, remain a few days, and then meet the troops at that point, at any rate, as soon as we stacked arms near Co———— Brigade Head Quarters was besieged by a host of line officers and privates begging permission to go home. I had no idea that *all* would get to go, and I had been at home more recently that many others, I resolved that I would not attempt to go home, but would let others have the opportunity, and I just went off to myself and commenced reading a novel that I had just procured.

Presently Lieut Clark passed and told me to "be ready to start home immediately"—that Col. Beatty had taken the responsibility of granting the whole Regiment a *ten days pass*, and the Lieut handed me the following pass which was the only one I procured at all but which did as well as any. The pass was:

> Columbia, Ky
> Oct. 31st 1862
>   Wm. Woodcock has permission to go home and
> return in 10 days.
>   Silas Clark, 1st Let.
>   Comdg. Co. B 9th Ky.

All was immediately stirring and in a few moments the Camp of the 9th Ky. was vacated and we were in the town of Columbia preparing for our walk home.

Late in the evening we left that place; and went out 12 miles that night, and obtained supper and then slept a few hours.

Next morning *Nov 1st* we were up and on the road several hours before sunrise, and that day I *walked* to Tompkinsville, because the boys that were in advance of me had hired all the horses. I and my friend Holland arrived in Tompk. that night, completely tired down and obtained food and lodging with a Mr. Taylor, who treated us very kindly, and the more so because we were Union soldiers.

Sun Nov. 2nd *went home*. It is entirely unnecessary for me to again attempt to describe the pleasures and welcomes that are sure to greet a soldier on his arrival from harm after a long absence. There is scarcely an adult person in the whole nation that has not either experienced those pleasures and welcomes, or seen their effects, and a description of the "tears of Joy," "embraces of welcome," congratulations of welcome, and the many little attentions that are bestowed upon the returned soldier would be of no more importance than the repetition of an old song. Let it suffice to say that I enjoyed myself as well as could be expected of a soldier at home with the exception of an occasional guerilla alarm, but which alarms all proved to be false during our stay at home this time; and really we did not much dread them for we had been allowed to bring home our arms. I only got seriously alarmed one day and then myself and a few others lay on a hill near an important crossing but no one passed.

Chapter 5

༺༒༒༒༒༺

The Memorable Battle of Stone's River

After the Battle of Perryville, Bragg fell back to the Middle Tennessee town of Murfreesboro, thirty miles southeast of Nashville. Woodcock and his fellow soldiers of the re-styled 14th Army Corps—soon to be renamed again the Army of the Cumberland—followed to Nashville, led by their new commander, Maj. Gen. William S. Rosecrans. On December 26, Rosecrans finally marched out of Nashville to confront Bragg. Four days later, already in contact with their enemies, both generals finalized their very similar plans to turn the enemy's right. As New Year's Eve dawned, it was the Confederates who attacked first. As the Federal right collapsed, Rosecrans patched together a ragged defense along the Nashville Turnpike. It saved his army. There along the pike, Marcus Woodcock received his personal baptism of fire. Reading his breathless account, one might conclude that the battle took an hour rather than an entire day.

Two days later, the 9th Kentucky found itself in the thick of the fight once again. Maj. Gen. John C. Breckinridge's desperate charge against the Union left was one of the grandest and most terrifying moments of the entire war. In the late afternoon shadows, Kentuckians and Tennesseans reeled back and forth across Stones River, killing each other with abandon. In contrast to his accelerated memories of the first day, Woodcock's description is remarkably immediate and precise. He was a veteran now—a fact that came home to him painfully after the fight. As he stood over the body of his best friend, he confusingly felt only the joy of victory. "A battle seems to take all the firm feelings from man," he wrote.[1]

Tu. Nov. 11th Left home again and started to the Regiment in company with my friend Holland who was the only member of my company that lived near me, but we expected to find the greater portion of our company at Scottsville that night—Arrived Jimtown Monroe Co, Ky. and found Co. G assembled at that point and ready to start, going our road, and we all went together toward Scottsville. I stopped with a gentleman named Atwood for the night, just two miles to Scottsville.

Wed. Nov. 12th. Passed through Scottsville and went 6 miles on the Gallatin pike and stopped that night with an old gentleman by the name of Suttles who lived a few miles off the road. There were several soldiers stopping with him who had been left sick by their regiments, but they were now about well, and their principal topic of conversation was the prospect of their obtaining a parole; and from their manner, I judged that nothing would have been more desirable. They were continually calculating how long it would take them to go home, and whether they had money to bear their expenses &c.

We had met several since leaving Scottsville who had met with this *good luck* and were going to the rear in high glee, and it would be a shame on the character of our army for the public to know how many of it's members *sought* and *obtained* paroles during this and the two preceding months.[2]

Thur. Nov. 13th,—went to a schoolhouse just one mile below the Rock House on the Gallatin Pike and slept in the schoolhouse that night.

Some of Co. G. killed a hog and borrowed a kettle from the *neighbor* to cook it in, and this with bread that we had brought from home made us a substantial supper and breakfast.

Fri. Nov. 14th.—went 1 mile beyond Gallatin on the Lebanon Pike and stopped in the barn and lots of Judge Jas. Gill. Here we principally procured our rations for supper and breakfast from the citizens obtaining it already cooked.

Our party now numbered about 65 and was under command of Lieutenant Maize of Co. G.[3]

Sat. Nov. 15th.—Captain Bryan came up early with about 100 members of our regiment and took command of our party also, and we set out for the front, and arrived that evening at Silver Spring where we found the Brigade and in fact a large part of the army, but very few of the regiment had yet arrived, but the all that had left at Columbia *and more too* arrived in squads that evening and the next day. We also found some recruits for our regiment that had been forwarded by the recruiting officers that were sent back from Battle Creek. The wagons containing our knapsacks had also come up but the knapsacks had been unloaded and for want of proper attention on the part of somebody, everything they contained that was worth carrying off had been stolen by *somebody*, and the empty shells alone were left to our part; but a rogue will never freeze or starve.

Sun. Nov. 16th. We laid off our camp and pitched our tents for the first time since leaving Battle Creek and on this and the succeeding day drew a supply of clothing and other necessary articles.

Tu Nov. 18th Late in the afternoon set [out] and marched in the direction of Nashville till we came to Stone River and there went into camp and remained here on the 19th and 20th, changing our camp once in the meantime, but nothing of interest occurred along this portion of our march, and therefore I will say nothing.

Fri. Nov. 21st Went across Stone River and encamped about two miles beyond near a little hamlet known as spring place, and remained at this place several days, having *general inspection* the 22nd and Company inspection the 23rd.

On the 24th (?) the 13th Ky. Infantry of our Brigade was sent to the rear to go to Kentucky, and was subsequently stationed at Munfordsville. Had Company drill to day.

Tu. Nov. 25th—broke up camp in the afternoon and marched in the direction of Nashville, and encamped in a large lot on the left of the road in about two miles of that place. We remained in Camp here the two succeeding days, cleaning off, sweeping, and ditching as though we expected to remain here a considerable time. A *brigade guard* was established the first day, and in the evening of the 27th a sermon was preached by Maj. [Perry] Blankenship of the 79th Ind Vol. Inftry.[4]

Fri. Nov. 28th—marched out on the Murfreesboro Pike and encamped about one mile to the right of the road, turning off at the Lunatic Asylum.

The weather was now becoming very cold and we had to be placed where we could obtain supplies of wood.

Nov. 29th & 30th remained in camp sweeping and burning leaves and straightening out our camp generally, and making preparations to be reviewed by Gen Rosecrans who had superseded Gen. Buell in the command of our army.

Mon. Dec. 1st.—marched out to be reviewed by the Commanding General at 10 o'clock A.M. and remained in line till 2 o'clock P.M. and the General not coming we returned to camp without the pleasure of seeing him, which sight but few of us had as yet enjoyed.

Tu. Dec. 2nd. Our Divisions (5th Comded by Brig Gen Van Cleve) was again marched out and formed in order *for review*, and at 12 o'clock Maj. Gen. Crittenden and Brig Gen. Van Cleve and their respective staffs rode around the lines in double quick taking a hurried glance at the troops. Soon after this, Gens Rosecrans Crittenden, Van Cleve and their Staffs rode to the right of the Division, and presently the smiling face of the Commanding General was seen coming up the lines, between the ranks, saying a word of kindness or instruction to almost every soldier as he passed—asking one why he had no canteen, another "where is your haversack?" and still another "have you got no blanket?" and thus he proceeded along the lines creating a good opinion among the troops of his magnamity and careful consideration for those under his control.

It is needless for me to attempt a description of a *general review* with my feeble pen for it has already been made the theme of many a fireside conversation, and almost every person in the land have heard it from lips that rendered it, so sacred that any attempt of mine to comment upon the flashing of polished arms—the gaily-dressed officers—the symmetrical motions of heavy columns as they break into still smaller columns, and file with perfect military precisions past the reviewing officer,—or the gentle rustling of waving flags and soul-stirring strains produced by the bands—would be worse than useless.

After the review was over we returned to camp, and then our regiment was sent on picket.

Maj. Grider, who had been under arrest ever since the 25th of October on account of a difficulty between himself and Lt Col Cram, shouldered a rifle, accoutrements, and a roll of blankets, fell into line on the left of our company and went with us on picket, and went to the outpost, and then insisted on being allowed to take his turn at standing—this was granted and the Major was counted off in the *third relief* and I was corporal of that relief. I then offered to let him act as corporal of the relief for he would thereby get to remain by the fire all the time, but he refused the offer and stood on outpost four hours that night.

Colonel Grider, who had been under arrest ever since the day we left Somerset Ky was also restored to his command this morning[.]

Returned to camp on the 5th and on the 6th our Regiment furnished the *Brigade guard* the whole of which for a day's duty was now taken from a single regiment, and the regiments furnished in succession.

Dec. 5th. There out on picket, the Major going with us again, and performing the regular duties of a private soldier. A heavy fall of snow again came upon us today, and the wet was exceedingly cold.

Sun. Dec. 7th. Maj Grider, and Lieut Col Cram who had been under arrest for the same alleged offense, were restored to duty this morning.

Our Regiment and the 19th went out on a foraging expedition about 7 miles from camp, fill our wagons with corn and returned without any casualty. Remained in camps on the 8th and 9th without anything of interest occurring drilling regularly and in general doing well, till late in the afternoon of the 9th we heard that a forage train under the escort of the 23rd Brigade had been attacked about 7 miles from camp and that a fight was going on. Our Brigade was immediately ordered to the scene of action, and under some excitement we started in a great hurry. Our sutlers, *Kendall & Hall* each shouldered a musket and fell in on the left of our Regiment and marched out with us, but when we were about 3 miles from camp we met the trains well loaded and coming in all safe under care of the escort, though a fight had actually occurred but our troops had been victorious with but slight loss. The attacking party was a large force of Rebel cavalry under command of [Wheeler].[5]

Wed. Dec. 10th our Brigade again sent on picket, and on returning to camp the next day we found that it had been moved about two miles nearer Nashville, and established about a half a mile to the left of the road.

Next day we again started on a foraging expedition, and went beyond Stone's River on the Lebanon Pike—loaded our wagons and returned to camp without any casualty. On picket again on the

13th. The next few days we remained in camp undergoing severe drills, and cleaning up and sweeping off very extensively, and making preparations for remaining on winter quarters.

Thurs. Dec. 18th—Our Brigade again sent on a foraging expedition to Cumberland river 7 miles above Nashville and again returned without anything of interest occurring, and on the next day went on picket.

Sat. Dec 20th—returned from picket this morning. A terrible alarm was raised in our army this morning by the rebels making a dash at our pickets on the Murfreesboro Pike; but our boys happened to be awake and just ready for such an emergency, and the rebels finding that dashing "wouldn't pay" fired a few bombs into our lines, and then fell back having lost about 200 taken prisoners, and whole battery of artillery captured[.]

Mon. Dec. 22nd—for some reason unknown to me Col Kneffler took command of the Brigade to day, which had been expected some days by the members of the Regiment.

The first order he issued was to relieve the Brigade guards and cause no men to be detailed. You might hear the spicy expression "Bully for Kneffler" from any portion of the Camp while the boys were commenting on this act.

Tu. Dec. 23rd Col. Grider took command of the 11th Brigade today on account of a temporary absence of Col. Beatty. About 2 o'clock P.M. Lieut Clark was ordered by Col Grider to select 25 men from the regiment to accompany him on an important scouting[6] expedition. This detail together with another from the 19th Ohio reported to Gen. Van Cleve's Hd. Quarters where we found about 50 men of another Brigade order[ed] on the same expedition. At sunset the whole detail was placed under the command of Lieut Murdock of Van Cleve's staff,[7] and we were marched on the Murfreesboro pike beyond the pickets, then turned to the left and immediately commenced crossing fields, penetrating almost impenetrable cedar thickets, climbing rough hills and crossing deep hollows, intending to make a circuit and strike the pike in rear of the rebel outpost and effect its capture.

After ranging for several hours, and becoming as I thought irretrievably lost, we much to our surprise heard the sharp command to *halt,—who comes there*, followed almost immediately by the sudden flash and sharp crack of a carbine, and the unpleasant whiz of a minnie ball over our heads. We soon ascertained that it was one of our pickets, and that we were at that very point where we left the road.

We then started to camp I riding Lieut Murdock's horse on account of a severe sprain which I had given my ankle joint during the route, and which almost entirely prevented me from walking. We soon met a much larger expedition that had started out on a reconnaissance, and they required our party to turn back with them, but I rode the Lt's horse to Hd Qrs and rested there for the night, our detachment also soon came back.

Wed. Dec. 24th. A general feeling through the camp that we would move shortly but no positive declaration as to the manner and direction, yet all seemed to feel that we would go toward the rebels. As it was Christmas Eve, the boys were unusually noisy tonight, and several of them having procured new horns there was a general sounding of those musical instruments.

Just previous to *taps*, the buglers of the 79th Ind formed a column about their Colonel's tent and gave him a blast from their horns that was truly *funny*.

Thur. Dec 25th. All hands raised hollering "Christmas gift", "hurrah for Christmas", &c. but were soon stopped in their preparations for a gala day by an order to get ready immediately to go on picket. Were sent on picket near the Lunatic Asylum and kept there the remainder of the day without meeting with any incident of interest.

Fri. Dec. 26th.—returned to Camp early and found all hands engaged in making preparations to move—orders had been issued for all the surplus baggage to be placed in wagons and sent to the rear, but for the men to retain their knapsacks. Tents were immediately struck and rolled, cooking vessels collected about the wagons, and individuals were giving to the *lucky* sick ones, who were ordered to stay with the wagons little articles of value, to them, and the proper disposition to be made of them *"if I should happen not to get back,"* for we were confident that we were going toward Murfreesboro, and that we could not march far without fighting. About 2 o'clock, in the midst of a slight rain which had been falling at intervals through the day, we marched out in the direction we expected to. We marched that night to within two miles of Lavergne and encamped some distance to the right of the pike. Heavy skirmishing could be heard some distance in advance the whole evening, and our advance guard was reported to be now about Lavergne.[8] Rain fell the greater portion of the night after we got into Camp, and as we had no tents, we fared rather badly.

Sat. Dec. 27th. heavy cannonading on the right and in front this morning.[9] About 12 o'clock we started on the road to Lavergne. The rain soon commenced falling in torrents and as the cannonading was still very severe in our front, our progress was very slow. Finally, we passed through Lavergne and took the Murfreesboro road and travelled about two miles, when the cannonading on the McMinnville road became so severe that we turned back and took that road and marched out about three miles and went into camp. Col Sam Beatty again took command of the Brigade this morning, and Col Grider took command of his Regiment.

When we got into Camp the firing had all ceased and we kindled our fires, dried our blankets, and went to sleep without any uneasiness.

Sun. Dec. 28th. Clear and cool—remained in Camp the whole day. Considerable alarm about ten o'clock caused by some regiments on the other road discharging their guns that had become wet in the previous day's rain. The troops were unusually lively during the whole of this day. [O]ne Regiment of the 14th Brigade[10] got so funny that its Colonel attempted to drill it awhile by way of punishment. The boys very readily fell into line and the battalion was soon formed and the exercise commenced. The commands of the officers were obeyed with unusual promptness and precision, but each movement was accompanied by such a succession of yells that the scene was rendered truly interesting, and all the efforts of the officers to suppress it were vain—hundreds of troops gathered in the vicinity to see which would come off victorious, the officers or the men. After about a half hour's exercise, it was evident that the men had the best of it, and the final result was the sending of the regiment away on some duty.

Mon Dec. 29th, Clear and cool. Cannonading away to the right this morning. About 12 o'clock M. we started through the woods and went to the other (Murfreesboro) road and then marched to within about two miles of Murfreesboro that night and encamped just on the left of the road. We could hear heavy skirmishing in advance the whole evening, and when we arrived at camp it was particularly sharp just a few hundred yards in our [front] but it all ceased about one hour after dark, and everything became quiet,[11] and after drawing 20 rounds of extra ammunition which now made 60 rounds that each man had about his person we retired to rest, many a poor soldier to dream his last dreams of dear ones far away. At 9 o'clock P.M. everything was so quiet that a passerby would never have thought that two large and well appointed armies were now lying on their arms within speaking distance of each other and only awaiting the approach of daylight to begin the direful work. We were all convinced by the stubborn manner in which the rebels had contended for every inch of ground since leaving Lavergne that they would here make a desperate effort to stop our progress, even at the risk of a general battle, and we also felt confident that our gallant commander would drive the enemy from Murfreesboro or be defeated in a general battle which he was sure to stake on the issue.

Tu. Dec. 30th.—a slight rain falling this morning when we were waked up and ordered to dispatch our breakfast, which was about 3 o'clock. [A]nd at four the rain was still falling but all was quiet so far as we could judge throughout the lines, and the first cannon was not fired amid us till fifteen minutes after 8 o'clock A.M., but a heavy skirmishing had commenced in front and had extended away to the right.

About 9 o'clock A.M. a battery moved out in front of our Brigade and opened a heavy firing on the town of Murfreesboro—this action elicited about a dozen shots from the enemy. This seemed to silence the skirmishing in our front, but if possible added new [ferocity] to the same on our right, and during the evening a severe artillery and infantry firing could be heard just to the right of the pike, where the reader knows was fought in day's fighting of the memorable *five days* Battle of Stones River.

About 10 o'clock the troops were cheered by the presence of Gen'ls Rosecrans and Crittenden, who were riding along the lines taking observations. This morning one of Crittenden's Staff was killed by the explosion of a shell in the General's quarters. At 8 o'clock P.M. all was quiet again, the dark shades of the night seeming to serve the double purpose of allaying men's passions and stopping the horrible work of the day, and to afford time for rest.[12]

Wed Dec. 31st.—with a mind filled with many doubts and forebodings as to the result of this days action, I awoke and sprang to my feet at an early hour upon being aroused by the Sergeant, to make preparations for my first day's battle. I had never yet realized the horror and bloodshed that are met with in battle—felt not the usual dreads and eventual sufferings that are peculiar to the veteran soldier, for my imagination had not pictured the battle with half it's horrors—the crash of the skirmishers' musket, or the boom of the heavy cannon did not cause that feeling of uneasiness and fear to creep over my limbs as it always did in subsequent actions. I could only imagine myself firing and killing numbers of the enemy and then charging bayonets, and with breach and point just slaughtering the enemy somewhat after the manner of the fabled giants of ancient times.

At 7 o'clock A.M. an order from Gen Rosecrans was read, which paid a glowing tribute to the gallantry and patriotism of the soldiers engaged in the previous days battle, and exhorted us to be ready for the trial of courage and fortitude which "may to day decide the fate of the nation," and ordering us to be obedient to our officers in the trial hour, and to "shoot low" in which event he pledged the victory to our arms. The order was read to all the regiments separately and received hearty cheers from every throat[13]—about this time Gen [William J.] Hardee's force on our right wing commenced which came so near completely annihilating our army, and of which fact we were notified by the terrible cannonading which could be heard in that direction. Immediately after the reading of the order we were ordered to pile our knapsacks and leave a man to guard them and were then moved to the left and marched across Stone's River and took a position on the opposite bank, but during the execution of this movement the cannonading and musketry on the right was becoming terrible to hear, and to make it more serious it was rapidly nearing us along the line toward the center, and also the right wing seemed to be giving way. We had been in position beyond the river but a few moments when we were marched "double quick" back in the direction of the firing.[14] As we came upon the ground of our previous night's encampment, a sight met my eyes that to this day causes a chill to creep over my heart and a shudder through my body—we could see over a farm of several hundred acres in extent at the near edge of this a line of our troops were attempting to make a stand against the irresistable charges of the enemy, besides this line everything seemed to be falling back—whole regiments of troops, apparently hopelessly demoralized, stragglers by the hundred, staff officers and orderlies, batteries, cassions, artillery wagons, ambulances and even the very smoke seemed to be seized with a panic and were rolling in hopeless confusion to the rear. The cruel missiles from the enemy's artillery were ploughing up the dirt among the confused masses, and occasionally mowing down a score of poor fellows. Beyond our last line the long menacing lines of gray could be seen advancing with a heavy tread and good order, continually emitting sheets of flame, clouds of smoke and showers of deadly missiles upon the last line of our devoted soldiers.[15] Their artillery occupied every commanding position that was in view and were increasing in rapidity of movement, and accuracy of aim, telling fearfully in our ranks. They were now within three hundred yards of the pike—our last line already overmatched was contending with unexcelled fortitude and bravery against their irresistable columns. Amid all this there was one calm face and cool head—Gen. Rosecrans, accompanied by his numerous and significant staff was briskly riding from point to point within musket shot of the enemy, heedless of the many messengers that were sent at him and were continually cutting down the officers and soldiers of his staff—himself a prominent object for their balls.

Our Brigade was wheeled about a few times among the masses of straggling and demoralized [men] that were flocking to the rear, and who were being rallied at this point.

Then we started down the pike to the right by order of the Gen. Rosecrans, who said to Gen. Van Cleve "I want you to go and support Harker." We had arrived nearly to the skirt of woods that here cross the pike and almost to the point where our last line had given back nearly to the pike, when by some body's order we were halted and ordered to march by the "about face," and it was difficult to tell in which direction we were the worst needed, for the rebels were on the pike just to the left, and were rapidly approaching it on our right, which would literally have severed our Army in two, and resulted in its complete annihilation. We had not marched far by the left flank till we again met General Rosecrans who again ordered Van Cleve to "go and support Harker??["] We were again faced about and started off down the pike in the direction of the skirt of woods just mentioned, and just as we started we saw the last of our lines in the skirt of woods give way in utter confusion, and flee across the pike, and the rebels raise a yell and come after them in a style that was truly terrifying.[16] Our Brigade was immediately ordered to "double quick" the 19th Ohio Infantry in front and we following *in line of march* and thus we ran in between the charging rebels and our discomfited friends, accompanied by Gen'ls Rosecrans, Crittenden and Van Cleve. As we dashed into position, Col. [Lyne] Starling of Crittenden's staff[17]—as noble a soldier as ever drew sword—threw up his hat and yelled "here comes the gallant old 11th Brigade, I know we will whip the rebels now." Gen Rosecrans rode among us with his sword gleaming above his head, and tears streaming down his cheeks, and saying "boys, you must drive them." The gallant Crittenden, without betraying the least emotion of excitement, rode along among us, with apparently as much composure as if in the midst of a gay procession.

My own sensations—how can I describe them, for I do not even have an idea of the thousand bewildering thoughts that flitted through my mind as we rushed into this terrible slaughter, and the victory flushed rebels emerged from the thicket on our left and prepared to swoop down on us as the mighty avalanche that carries everything in its course.

But to resume,—when we had gotten fairly abreast the enemy and when they were rapidly nearing us, the order to *"front* and *fire"* all in one command rang through the lines and we immediately turned and poured a volley upon that advancing line of rebels that seemed to bring them to their senses, and caused them to stop as if to consider whether to come any further. We followed our first volley by a terrible "firing at will" for a few minutes that seemed to almost entirely silence the rebel musketry and cause the chivalry to hide behind the numerous pine trees and large stones that abounded in this neighborhood.

The loud and distinct voice of Col. Beatty was now heard above the din of battle, and ringing in clear and even tones was heard the command to "charge bayonets."[18]

Immediately we dashed forward with an impetuosity and force that rather astonished the shattered lines of the Chivalry, and caused them to break and flee in confusion without even *attempting* to resist our charge. We followed about three hundred yards, and then halted and dressed our lines. When the rebels seemed to be almost entirely gone, though we had the opportunity to try our skill at an occasional one as he would jump up from behind a rock or tree and run off. The second line of our Brigade now came up and passed through our ranks to the front. As the 11th Ky passed through our Regiment, and the 79th Ind. passed through the 19th Ohio, they raised a yell that I have no doubt served to accelerate the speed of the retreating rebels. They advanced slowly but firmly about 3/4 of a mile when they met another host of stragglers composing the remains of a Brigade of Infantry and a battery of artillery coming to the rear. The front line halted and suffered these poor fellows to pass through their ranks, and then they came around the left of our Regiment. They presented the most shocking and mangled sight of any body of troops I ever saw in my life. A large number of wounded were being borne off by their comrades, while many others who had received flesh wounds about the body, arms and head were bringing themselves off. Several were mounted on artillery horses who had been cut loose from the captured cannon in the great hurry to escape.

They had scarcely passed the front line when the pursuing rebels came in view of our front line,[19] and then was begun one of the most magnificent shooting scenes that was presented in that days battle. The 11th Ky with their breach-loading five shooters, and the 79th Ind. with their heavy [Enfield] Rifles poured volley after volley into the advancing Rebels in a truly gallant style.

During this time our troops seemed to gain much of the ground that had been lost on our left, and a terrible musketry had been kept up away to the right, but with what result was to us uncertain. The musketry seemed to have abated to some extent along the whole line and its place assumed by the heavy roar of artillery which could be heard increasing in vigor on both wings.

But the front line of our Brigade maintained a heavy musketry

National Colors of the 9th Kentucky, Volunteer Infantry Regiment, 1862.
Courtesy of the Kentucky Historical Society, Military History Museum.

fire in front for several minutes, when by order of Gen. Rosecrans who was on the ground in person they were moved by the left flank to counteract a similar movement on the part of the enemy. Both lines of the Brigade was now moved to the left, but the nature of the ground was such the front line was compelled to fall back nearly to ours and while we were thus huddled together moving almost in a solid mass, the rebels cut down several of our troops.[20]

It was here that our noble and gallant Color-bearer, Jno. G. Raglin received his death wound, and was borne off the field. A private soldier of his company (C.)—Moses Roark, seized the colors and was carrying them and his gun and keeping his place in the ranks when Col. Grider rode up and ordered him to throw down his gun; and promoted him to sergeant on the spot.

We moved a little further to the left till we could be properly formed then we fell back as Gen. Rosecrans ordered to give the artillery a chance. We retired slowly, occasionally halting to prevent the rebels getting in too great headway, and finally emerged from the woods into the old field, moved a little to the rear of the crest of a knoll, formed in line and *lay down*. A battery[21] then opened upon the advancing rebels and they were soon put to flight.

This was at a point where so many batteries were collected after the first grand charge of the enemy in the morning,[22] also where the retreating columns of our discumfited army had seemed to concentrate from the beginning of the fight, and was consequently now one of the most important as well as the strongest, part of our line. A large part of our artillery was still here and the whole of that part of the field seemed to be covered with our blue columns lying flat on the ground awaiting the approach of the enemy. But no opportunity was offered here during the remainder of the day for infantry fighting. But a heavy and unceasing artillery fire was kept up by both armies during the remainder of the day, and that of the rebels frequently told upon our artillery's men with fearful effect, and sometimes the merciless grape would tear through the supporting columns of infantry doing much execution. One solid shot killed two men and wounded two more in Co. C of our Regiment.

At one time in the evening, the rebels attempted to advance their line in our immediate front.[23] We could see them come over the crest of a slight elevation away in the further edge of the field—

nearly a mile distant—their lines stretching from the woods on the right to the woods on the left—so evenly did they seem to move that I fancied I could almost detect the regular moving of their feet—one line came to the crest of the ridge—wonder what is their purpose—will they stop?—no, while crossing the level of the crest they seemed to be for a moment stationary, but soon we can detect the rising ground in their rear, and this proves to us that they are advancing—we can see enough of the line to detect three regimental flags—our hearts began to beat and our nerves to string themselves for the contest—now another line is seen in their rear, at the regular supporting distance advancing in the same direction—what are our artillerymen doing?—for here is surely a fair mark for their practice—All is silent among the artillery near our position. All eyes seem but upon the advancing column of rebels—Presently our batterymen begin to prick up their ears, cast quick glances from one to another and pat their guns—one piece is discharged, all watch the course of its shell with apparently breathless interest.—it bursted apparently not more than twenty feet above and directly over the enemy's line.—every cannon in view was then leveled and aimed and almost at one volley three or four whole batteries were discharged—many of the shells seemed to burst in the rebel ranks and a portion of their column was almost completely enveloped in the smoke of the bursting bombs—one seemed to burst within the folds of one of the flags; This unlooked-for reception and accuracy on the part of our batteries put the enemy to immediate flight, and they quickly disappeared in the woods on either flank, greeted in their skedaddle by the show of thousands of our troops who were lying in view.

Oh, I shall never forget the anxious suspense of that awful afternoon as I lay there for four long hours without daring to raise my head—the rebel artillery continually throwing their cruel missiles among and killing and wounding us—the spent-balls of the skirmishes frequently striking and slightly wounding our boys,—the air very cool and the ground freezing fast, and when we first lay down was soft on the surface from the slight thaw of the middle of the day which rendered it disagreeable. No wonder if I should at any moment be torn in pieces by cannon shot—and nothing to do to drown my apprehensions, for when the soldier is up and fighting, he has no time to think about consequences,—scores of the wounded of both armies were laying in the woods in front of us and we could distinctly hear their heartrendering groans and cries for help, yet neither party could render them assistance.

Gen Rosecrans was frequently on this part of the field during the evening, accompanied by not more than two or three officers,— the look of confidence that I could see on his face reassured me notwithstanding the many reasons I had to believe that our army had gotten much the worst of it during the day.

At the approach of darkness the firing almost entirely ceased and early after dark a detail was sent to procure our knapsacks which were found unmolested although the enemy had at one time through the day held possession of the ground they were on but not for a sufficient time to pillage or carry them off. In this day's fight we lost two killed and about twenty wounded in the Regiment.[24]

This comparatively small number of casualties may be accounted for by the irregular and disorganized shape the rebels were in when we first met them.

9 o'clock P.M.—we our Brigade have moved back from the front line but rather toward the left, and we are now all desiring that the right and center of the army do without our assistance to-morrow. Gen. Van Cleve received a wound in the leg early in the day but did not quit the field till after dark. Lieut Murdock of his staff is reported killed, and I fear it is true for he is brave as a lion and is sure to be where danger is most imminent.[25]

Gen. [Joshua W.] Sill, commanding a Division, is reported killed also one of his Brigade commanders, and another wounded. Our Company has lost four wounded, and among them is Lieut Silas Clark who is shot through the leg just below the knee. I would give the names of the other wounded but it would require too much space and be considered tiring to a greater part of my readers.

We are now trying to forget the terrible scenes of the day by taking a nap, having raised large fires and spread our blankets in perfect security, as there are several lines of troops between us and the enemy. I lay down and was soon asleep, and strange to say, had pleasant dreams.

Thur. Jan. 1st. "a happy New Year to you" said my comrade to me as we awoke from our slumbers this morning, but the occasional crash of the skirmishers' musket that could be heard in front seemed to promise anything else than to verify his wish. Col. Beatty took command of the division in consequence of Van Cleve's wound, and Col. Grider took command of the Brigade, which left Col. Cram in command of our Regiment.

The morning opened bright and clear and the sun rose in all the beauty of his majesty as if in derision of the extensive operations that were being attempted by puny man to further their designs. Our Brigade is formed in rear of our battery on a commanding piece of ground near the river[26] and about a half a mile to the left and below the railroad. About 10 o'clock A.M. our Division was moved across the river at the same point where we crossed and recrossed on the morning previous and formed along a ridge about 300 yards from the stream, but the extreme of each wing of the Division was thrown back near the river to prevent the turning of the flanks in case of an attack. Our Regiment was on the extreme left of the Division and our Company was thrown out as pickets rather in rear of the left-flank but no incident of note occurred at that part of the line during the *whole day.*[27] Many rumors were afloat through the camp in regard to yesterday's operations. There was a considerable cannonading on our right during the evening, and at dark it was rumored that our troops had captured two regiments of rebel Infantry. Another report, that 3000 Rebel cavalry had made a dash at a Division of our troops which were guarding the wagon trains supposing the guard consisted of only a Brigade, and the whole Division, together with six batteries of artillery opened upon them and completely annihilated them killing and capturing nearly all.[28]

About sundown one of our pickets—J. I. Tool[e]y—shot a large fat hog from his post, and some of the boys went and brought it in, and being relieved soon afterwards by Co. G. we had a real feast that night on fresh pork.

The skirmishing in front of the center and right of our division was very severe during the whole day and a section of our artillery occasionally exchanged shots with the enemy artillery in our front. But we could hear of nothing being done today to affect the relative positions of the two armies.

Fri. Jan 2nd.—woke up all right this morning and eat our breakfasts before daylight. Skirmishing commences in front of our Division with the first appearance of daylight. 8 o'clock A.M.—there has been a severe cannonading away to our right of a few moment's duration but it has all ceased and everything but the skirmishing among the pickets is quiet.[29]

9 o'clock A.M.—another Brigade has taken the place of ours and we are now lying in rear of the right of our Division, and the skirmishers are maintaining a severe fire.[30]

3 o'clock P.M.—the skirmishing in our front has been very severe all day and our skirmishers have been compelled to give back a little. Ah the anxious and awful suspense I suffer while laying so near the enemy and expecting every moment that a battle will begin.

Sometimes the enemy doubles their fire on our pickets with such energy that I almost conclude that an attack has been made in force—many of their balls whiz low over heads which serves to increase the anxiety and unpleasant state of our situation. Notwithstanding all this we are safe from the shots while we remain in our present position, and have cooked and ate a scanty dinner and I have just finished supping a cup of coffee with my friend J. I. Tooley, who invited me with the remark "we may never again have the opportunity." We had a considerable conversation on the probabilities of our having to fight this evening, and he seemed very communicative yet he did not have any presentiment and thought— he would get through safe; but hark!—there is another volley and it sounds as if there is *something up*.[31]

Later—and there *was* something up; for it was the beginning of the grand "Breckinridge charge" that is so well known to all who have read a history of this war—it was the first volley of that heavy mass of troops who were advancing in three columns and each column six lines deep—it was the opening ball of that, one of the most bloody conflicts of the war according to the number of troops engaged, it was the herald that drove in our skirmishers and let the irresistible mass [of] daring spirits—principally renegade Kentuckians and Tennesseeans—fall with unchecked force upon our devoted little Division. On they came with deafening yells and fell with unparalleled fury upon our front line.[32]

Then everything seemed lost in the awful roar of musketry and showers of balls that were flying over our heads now.

Presently the wounded are flocking to the rear in large numbers, and the increasing terribleness of the musketry tells us that a desperate struggle is going on. The commands to *take arms* and *lie down* ring along our line, and then in an unimaginable state of anxiety we await the result.

Oh! can the front line[33] withstand the assault? God grant they may and that we will not be called on to relieve them! They breast the storm of leaden hail with a fortitude well worthy of Americans—the wounded and straggler pour through our ranks saying that their comrades are falling fast—the volume of musketry seems to increase and the volleys that are heard in the regularity of the first onset are now lost in one continual roar—the angry roar of the enemy's guns tells us that our poor fellows are by far outnumbered and that it will be a miracle if they can hold their ground, but—oh, horror, they are wavering—they have done all they can to drive back the powerful enemy, "but alas, what can valor do against equal valor,["] backed by such fearful odds,—their ranks are sadly thinned, and were they entirely repleted they could not withstand the furious onset of the powerful enemy—oh, can they? Will they carry the stars and stripes in retreat from that hated emblem of treason that flutters over the enemys columns? Yes, they cannot withstand such a charge much longer—*they are falling back* is uttered by a hundred lips in our line and here they come, the few that are left, entirely disorganized and every man guiding himself. *Attention, forward*, were the commands coolly uttered by our Lieut Col. (Cram) and we sprang to our feet and started, then *double quick* sounded and away we went up the hill through a brier thicket in the direction of the scene of conflict—the front line breaks through our ranks but so determined were our fellows to do their duty that this caused but little confusion—up the hill we went, and as we emerged from the thicket, the first line of the rebels appeared in view,[34] not more than one hundred yards distant and the intervening space clear of every obstruction to view, or the passage of a minnie ball.

They had not *entirely* ceased firing at our front line, and though their first column was badly shattered they immediately opened upon us with all the rapidity that human beings can be supposed capable of, and of course, we halted and *took issue*. Their flag was very prominent in the center of their column, and I believe it fell to the ground as many as a dozen times in the next ten minutes.[35] At our first volley their first column almost entirely disappeared the few that were left standing going off at double quick toward our right flank, but their place was quickly supplied by a fresh column, and then again in all of its awfulness commenced that awful roar of musketry that caused tears to flow at many a fireside. Oh but their balls did fearful execution in our ranks, the more so on account of our inexperience, for almost every man kept on his feet and thus offered a fair mark for the enemy, but they did the same, and there we stood, two solid columns within pistol shot of each other using their weapons of death with all the rapidity and precision their capacities would allow. The bravery of the rebel officers amounted almost to insanity, they dashed to and fro on their horses directly in range of our fire, as if they knew not the principle of fear and many of them paid dear for their temerity. Our boys were falling thick, and almost at the first volley our Captain's right arm was broken and he went to the rear. Our 2nd Lieutenant, [Benjamin M.] Johnson,[36] was wounded as we advanced up the hill,—many other companies had lost some of their officers, but the boys cheered each other with their voices, whooping and hollering, laughing and talking, and some *cursing* and *swearing*, but shooting all the time.

One *group* of our company whose capacities for quick loading seemed to be about equal, fired several volleys at the rebel banner at the cool command of one of their number, and at every volley the flag would fall. A passing shot took away my bayonet in the beginning of the fight, just after I had rammed down the fourth load. I primed and discharged the gun, but the barrel was bent so much that I could not get another load down and consequently could do nothing but stand and hoop and halloo to encourage the rest, the idea never occurred to me that I might seize the gun of some of my fallen comrades and continue my deadly work[.] A rebel battery was just in rear of the rebel line raining its deadly charges of grape and cannister upon our shattered column with fearful execution.[37]

Oh that I could depict the features, feelings, and passions of men while engaged in such terrible work! I looked about me after my gun was disabled. Some of the men were on one knee, others were nearly flat upon the ground, while others were standing up;

but all were doing their utmost as if the fate of the day depended upon the exertions of a single arm. I could not see *fear* upon a single face, some were looking calm as death, and without noticing anything else were rapidly loading and firing—some were pleased apparently, and seemed to laugh as heartily at the occasional *tumble* of a rebel as if they were viewing the gambols of a circus clown—others seemed to be wrought up to the highest pitch of anger, and every yell of pain they heard from our ranks caused them to utter curses and imprecations against the enemy, and to renew their exertions.

The rebel column was again becoming sadly thinned and was beginning to present unmistakable evidences of confusion, and it seemed that a fresh column of our troops could here have done good work by a charge, but we were the last line on this side of the river; the front was so terribly cut up that it was found impossible to rally and bring any number of them back to the contest even if we could maintain our ground a sufficient length of time for such a movement. Can we do that? If the rebels have no fresh troops to bring immediately against us our chances for holding the position are good; but a new and unlooked for obstacle to our success now presents itself.

In charging up the hill our line (composed of only our Regiment and the 19th Ohio) had by accident borne off to the left and thus left an unoccupied space of two hundred yards or more in breadth between our right flank and the river—the wary enemy was not long in discovering this gap and thousands of rebels poured into it and came down on the right flank of the 19th Ohio with a velocity and force which added to the heavy attacks from the front was too much for human nature to bear and that gallant regiment whose bravery and patriotism was unexcelled was compelled to give way.[38] It commenced falling back as Col. Beatty's official report[39] said *by files*—soon the whole regiment was retreating down the hill without the least regard to order, which was simply impossible, followed by the right companies of our Regiment.

The order to retreat rang along the line, but all seemed to think that it had been given by someone who did not have authority[40]—and ignorant of the reverse on our right, each man stood and fired at the rebels in front till the man next on his right discovered the condition of circumstances and joined in the retreat. So perfectly was this assertion made good that I think the extreme right of our Company had gone 50 yards to the rear before the extreme left discovered that anything was wrong on the right. One man who stood but three files to my right was shot down at least 15 yards in advance of me just as I commenced retreating.

We fell back down the hill and across the river in the greatest disorder, every man taking his own course and running at the top of his speed. The rebels followed so closely that the slightest stumble or accident insured the capture of the unfortunate. They followed us right up to the bank of the river yelling like the very furies and pouring showers of balls after us at every step.

As I was crossing the river the surface of the water was powerfully agitated by the numerous missiles, and as I climbed the further bank it seemed that fifty struck within a yard of me. Many of our boys were not so fortunate as to get across the river, but the rebels were so close after them that they lay down under the bank and the rebels came up and captured them. Capt Bryan who was wounded in the early part of the action was overtaken here by the enemy and just as they started with him to the rear, a ball from one of our guns pierced his brain and he fell lifeless. This was ascertained by one of the members of Co. I, who was captured with him and afterwards made his escape.

Ever since the beginning of the battle we had been listening wistfully for our artillery, but not a gun sounded near us and we had almost got to conclude that we were to be wholly sacrificed without any assistance. As I reached the river, a continued flash of lightening seemed to light up the scene, and immediately after peal upon peal in such quick succession as to form almost an unbroken continued roar, the welcome crash of our cannon (which had been massed in the rear of our right without our knowledge) greeted our ears and whir'r'r'r over our heads went grape and cannister from the gaping mouth of 56 pieces of closely-parked artillery, and for this simple reason the deafening yells of the elated Rebels were changed into shrieks and groans of dying.[41] Never before did artillery alone have such decisive effect in an open field engagement. The front line of the enemy was at the bank of the river and consequently were out of range, but ah, those in the rear caught from the artillery what we could not give them from our muskets. The first discharge of the artillery seemed to reassure our boys and every man that got across the river very readily listened to the commands of the officers to rally, and a considerable line was soon formed and ordered to lie down just behind the top of the high bank of the river. But they did not rest many moments for the front line of the enemy, entirely ignorant of the fearful execution our artillery was doing in their supporting line, prepared to charge across the river, they started,— but then we were ordered up again, and again the boys poured a terrible volley into the rebel ranks. The enemy seemed disposed to contest our right of recrossing the river, and answered us with a severe fire of musketry. Their officers advanced to the brink of the stream, cheering and hollering "come on boys, d———n 'em, we have got the run on 'em", &c. but we followed our second or third volley with a charge that gave us "the run" on the rebels—into the river our brave boys plunged, cheered by the cry of *fresh troops* who were coming onto the field by thousands[42] and waded across, and commenced a race of pretty nearly the equal of the one just made, except that a *change of direction* had been effected.[43] Many of our boys who had been captured under the further bank of the stream, and whose captors had been afraid to remove them till we should be whipped back a little farther, now turned upon their captors and made them prisoners. One member of our Regiment and three of the 19th Ohio brought over fourteen of the Chivalry and many others did the same. We followed the rebels up the hill, and the few of our Brigade that could be kept together after such a terrible handling maintained their places in the front line till dark, driving the enemy nearly one mile from the river; but obstinately did the disappointed rebels fall back after once thinking that they had already gained a victory; but our boys pressed on with such fury and determination, rendered almost desperate by the terrible loss they sustained among comrades and friends, that the now frightened rebels could not make a stand for hardly a moment at any one place against the overwhelming force of our troops.

So swiftly did our boys press upon them that ere the rebels were aware of the fact the blue coats were close on the famous Washington Battery, and ere they could draw it away so many of their horses were either killed or disabled that they were compelled to leave four pieces behind.[44]

When our line was within one hundred yards of the battery it was halted and thus the deserted guns were left between the lines. Presently the rebels raised a yell [and] started toward us as if they were going to charge and retake the battery, but their voices became fainter at every step and in few seconds entirely ceased, even before they had gotten near enough for us to shoot at them—directly we heard the yell raised some distance further off, and again they advanced a few paces but their chivalric blood was becoming too weak and again they failed to charge—soon another, but much fainter and last yell was heard from them, and then our boys advanced and took possession and dragged the cannon from the field.

Our Brigade was now permitted to return to camps. i.e. the position we occupied when the fight began and where we had left our knapsacks. We found our knapsacks unmolested although the rebels had possession of the ground for some time, but they had no time for pillaging.

We immediately proceeded to examine the battleground to collect our poor dead and wounded comrades who had so suddenly been sent to eternity, or snatched from the enjoyment of health and strength and stretched up[on] beds of pain from which many of them would never rise.

The first wounded man I found proved to be one of my company, Andrew Bray—he had been shot through the body, near the heart and was now in a dying condition.

Oh, how can I portray my mingled feelings of sorrow and pleasure as I stood and listened to the dying words of this soldier and christian.

He thanked Almighty God that he had been permitted to die so noble a death—"the death of a soldier fighting for the cause of freedom and nationality"—and that he was prepared to meet the great Judge before the bar of Eternal Justice and render a clear account of his stewardship while on earth. He prayed for the souls of mankind *and for the nation*. He insisted that I should hear him talk awhile ere I attempted to remove him. Finally, I procured help and removed him to where the wounded of our regiment had been collected—what a horrid sight here met my eyes!—amid the light of the glaring fires that had been kindled around the spot I could see 14 dead bodies and near fifty wounded and helpless soldiers,—

all of our regiment. Never shall I forget the awful thoughts that loomed up before my imagination when I looked upon those pale faces that had so recently known life and health, or when I heard the heart-rending shrieks of our mangled and suffering wounded, as they lay there far from home and their dearest friends—many of them in a dying condition. The M.D's were among them and promising to carry them away as soon as possible, and which was done ere 9 o'clock P.M.

Among the dead was my most intimate friend, Jas. I. Tooley. He was shot through the body before we commenced retreating and after going a few steps to the rear, had dropped dead. The conversations I had with him just before we entered the fight now came with peculiar force upon my mind and caused me to renew my thanks to the Great Ruler of the Universe that we had gained the battle and that I had come out unhurt.

I felt *good*; and despite the many suffering companions that were lying around I could not avoid occasional remarks of rejoicing at our success. But in truth a battle seems to take all the firm feelings from man. I could look upon the faces of my dead comrades and at the same time think of our victory with a complacency of mind that caused me to shudder at my want of proper feeling. In spite of my attempts to bring my mind to bear upon the subject in its proper light, I felt satisfied because we had whipped the rebels.

The brave and noble Captain of our company was also among the killed; also Lieut Fred Carpenter of Co. F.

Capt [Demetrius B.] Coyle of Co. G and Lieut [Algernon S.] Liggett of Co. D were mortally wounded and died the next day. Maj John H. Grider; Capt [Riley A.] Reed[,] Co. F; Lieut [Theodore F.] Heeter, Co. C; Lieut. [Benjamin M.] Johnson, Co. B; and Capt [Chesley D.] Bailey of Co. I were also wounded. Lieut [Wellington J.] Cram of Company H was severely wounded in the mouth on wednesday. I have not the official report of the losses of our regiment before me but I think the severely wounded did not far exceed 50 on this evening's battle and the killed 14. There were many slightly wounded who are not included in the above figures.[45]

There had also been several captured, but I now disremember the number. Our first sergt., Wm B. Roddy was among the number, having stumbled and fell into a clump of briars just as we

commenced retreating and so bruising himself in the fall that ere
he could disengage himself and rise he was in the clutches of the
enemy. I suppose the loss in killed wounded and missing in our
regiment must have been near one hundred on both days fighting,
but the principal loss was on this evening, for we lost nearly one-
half of the number with which we went into battle.[46]

No better could be expected than that our Brigade in a disorderly retreat of one forth of a mile after sustaining an awful musketry combat for several minutes, and then almost without halting,
turning and pursuing our enemies for near a mile at a furious charge,
would become very much scattered. This was so much the case that
when our Brigade was ordered back to camp I dont think there were
twenty of our Regiment in any one squad, and I arrived into Camp
almost alone.

The danger had now passed over this part of the field and the
time had come for the operations of that villainous and detestable
set of brutal bipeds whose highest sense of duty is to go over a battle
field and pillage without discrimination the bodies of fallen friends
and foes. They were just making an onset on the knapsacks of our
regiment as I arrived, and it required every exertion of the few of
us that were there to save the boys' baggage till more would arrive.

When we found the body of Capt Bryan some of these *villains*
had robbed his body of a valuable watch and his pocket-book which
contained a considerable amount of money. Oh, you despicable set
of inhuman wretches, what a feast to my eyes it would be to see you
tied to a cannons mouth and blown in pieces, for thus pilfering the
dead bodies of these little souvenirs which would be of priceless value
to weeping and bereaved ones who now mourn for your unexcelled
depravity of heart.

The heaps of rebel dead that were laying on every hand gave
strong evidence that they had staked a great deal on the issue of this
evening's fight, and we readily came to the conclusion that they
would not attempt to break our lines at this point any more.

Several of them came out of the thickets and into our camp a
little after dark and gave up—one of them carrying a wounded
comrade whose thigh was broken.

Sat. Jan. 3rd. Only 116 men could be mustered by our Regiment
this morning. Our Brigade was moved back across the river very

early and encamped to give us a chance to rest and reorganize. The loss of the Regiment was this morning supposed to be 125 killed wounded and missing but the arrival of the stragglers through the day who had unavoidably become separated from the Regiment reduced this computed number of losses a little. The rain fell in torrents today and much to our discomfiture, for we were on very muddy ground, surrounded by troops on every side and wholly unprovided with tents. We discharged our wet guns and put them in as good order as possible, for the severe skirmishing that could be heard along the lines during the whole day was an evidence of the probability that we might yet have to fight a little.

About 8 o'clock P.M. a considerable fight occurred on the line not far to the right of our yesterday's contest.[47]

The musketry was at one time so sharp that we were called into line and ordered to take arms and be ready to move but presently the firing died away, and the noise of the guns argued that the enemy had fallen back a little. With the muddy earth for a bed, wet blankets for cover, and the rattle of falling rain for music I *retired* to rest and to sleep soundly and dream of fields of carnage and strife, and of my poor comrades who had rendered up the last great sacrifice on the altar of their country.

Sun. Jan. 4th. Not a gun can be heard along the lines at 6 o'clock this morning, and every evidence goes to indicate that the rebels have left us to do our own fighting.[48] The sun rose bright and clear this morning to spread his brilliant light over thousands of mangled human bodies that were lying unburied over the scene of the recent five days conflict, and to view a shattered army of rebels retreating in all haste from this, to them, unhealthy place; and to witness the movements of the victorious army, which scarcely less shattered than the vanquished was laying in its works, resting from the terrible work and burying the dead of friend and foe. In the afternoon a squad was detailed from our Regiment to go over the scene of our first days fight and bury the dead, and another to go over the scene of our second day's fight for the same purpose—I was attached to the first squad. But when we arrived on the ground other parties had already collected and were preparing to bury all that could be found, and therefore we had nothing to do but look on.

Wherever we went, we found at least two rebel dead to one

United States soldier, and in many places the disproportion was much greater.[49] At one point where the rebels had followed us so closely as we fell back on Wednesday, they were laying almost in heaps and were shot or mangled in every conceivable manner, and the various features that were presented to me by this evening's ramble would be food for many a writers pen that would go on from page to page to detail the horrors of a battlefield, but I will not attempt to illustrate what I saw, for the description of such scenes have been the theme of millions of letter-writers within the last five years (1865) and I would be wasting ink to attempt here an illustration of what has already been faithfully portrayed to almost every inhabitant of the United States by a thousand pens. About 6 o'clock P.M. our regiment was sent a short distance down the river on picket, and for once had the opportunity to breathe tolerably pure air[.]

Chapter 6

Our Camp at Murfreesboro

After the Battle of Stones River, the Confederates fell back forty miles to Tullahoma, and the Army of the Cumberland settled into camp. Before pursuing Bragg and moving on Chattanooga, Rosecrans wanted to fortify Murfreesboro as a supply base, re-equip and reorganize his army, build up his cavalry, and amass supplies for a new campaign. Guerrillas could cut supply lines and ruin a campaign, as they had done with Buell; Rosecrans wanted to outwit them by supplying himself. Not eager for more fighting, soldiers like Woodcock heartily approved of their commander's policies. Among other things, it gave them time to think. It was during this encampment that Woodcock began to re-evaluate his political and racial views, a process that eventually was to make a Radical Republican legislator out of the young southerner.

Woodcock was not to spend the remainder of his war time in Murfreesboro, however. Increasingly irritated by the lack of activity, Lincoln and Halleck finally forced Rosecrans to move. After six months, on June 23, the brilliant Tullahoma Campaign began.[1]

Mon. Jan. 5th—the morning opens fair and rosy and everything looks cheerful. The air is very cold and the boys are huddled around the fires talking of the results of the late battle—the skedaddle of the rebels, for they have evacuated Murfreesboro and gone towards the "enemy south"—and the rumored capture of Richmond which somebody reports this morning, just to have the fun of hearing us rejoice at the news. Our Brigade was moved farther down the river today to obtain a more favorable place for encampment.

Sun. Jan. 6th.—waked up early this morning to find the rain falling in torrents, and the water running under me in a perfect stream. There was nothing left for me to do but to get up and take the rain straight down, but a few hours after daylight the rain ceased to fall, the clouds cleared away and we had a clear and pleasant evening. Lieutenants Clark and Johnson of our company came out this evening in a buggy to see us—were both in fine spirits and promised soon to be with us again. We were called on this evening to make out a report of the losses in the two days' fighting. The loss of our Company was the Captain and two privates[2] killed,—two Lieutenants, one corporal, and five privates wounded—and one sergt missing. So there is not a commissioned officer left to our Company and only four sergeants and one corporal.

As I have before remarked, we were principally engaged against Kentuckians and Tennesseeans in our desperate fight on Friday evening. The 6th and 9th rebel Kentucky were there as was also the 26th (?) Tennessee[3] which was commanded by Preston Cunningham of Jackson County Tenn. Cunningham was killed and the battle flag of the 26th (?) Tennessee was captured.

Roger Hanson, commanding a rebel Brigade,[4] was also killed near where the rebels made the first onset.

Wed Jan 7th—day clear and rather warm. Moved across Stone's River near the railroad bridge and through Murfreesboro, and near a mile beyond and encamped about one fourth of a mile east of the Murfreesboro pike, near a small muddy stream to which the boys were afterwards pleased to give a very comical but soldier-like name.

I obtained an Enfield Rifle today from Col. Kneffler of the 79th Ind. which was the first I could get since the battle, for at that date this species of arms was rather scarce and soldiers who were carrying the smooth bore musket would gladly seize any opportunity to get one of these guns instead. I picked one up on the battlefield on the evening of the last fight, but did not have time to examine it till next morning, and then I found it unserviceable, but it was now too late to procure another.

Thur Jan. 8th—to our great satisfaction our wagons came up today bringing with them not only our baggage and camp equippage but a large mail for us, which of course afforded us much satisfaction after passing through such trying scenes and not having heard from home in a considerable time. With much satisfaction we put up our tents and found at the approach of the night that their arrival had been very timely, for the air was becoming very cold and a slight fall of snow greeted us at night. The time was spent from this to the *12th* of the month in relating our adventures to our friends who had been left behind and engaging in that most pleasant duty to the soldier—writing letters to relatives and friends. Oh, what satisfaction did I feel as I took up my pen to give an account of my first battle to my parents, relatives, friends, and *another*! How I searched my scanty vocabulary to find the most appropriate words in which to picture the part I had borne in the battle, and to express thankfulness to my Creator that I had come safely through the storm!

Nothing affords the soldier half so much pleasure as to be in constant communication with the mailroutes, and nothing troubles him so much when he hears that the "communications are out" as the idea that he will now fail to hear from those from [whom] he may desire to hear.

How often and fervently will [he] read the last letter and devour the words of love, and injunctions to do his whole duty, and then carefully stow it away in a safe spot and anxiously await an answer to his last; and then how great must be his disappointment when he sees a heavy mail from his own post office and finds none for himself. On the *11th* we had a general feast in No. 2 on fowls of various description which the foragers had seized in the farm yards out in the country by the authority of the famous Emancipation Proclamation,[5] and on the next day we made a general cleaning up and straightening out of our camp in order that we might begin to live like soldiers again.

Wed Jan 14th—rain falling during the whole of the afternoon and evening, and as No. 2's tent is in a very leaky condition we fare very badly but still dont conclude that we can render our situation any more comfortable by grumbling. Rumors float around the camp to day (without foundation of course) that the rebels are again acting on the offensive and that will make an early attempt to dislodge our army from its present position; and after night, as if in confirmation of this rumor, I heard a few discharges of cannon, and a few musket shots away to the left of the Lebanon Pike.

Thur Jan. 15th—opened with snowing, blowing, and freezing and everything wore a dreary aspect; but as we had nothing to do

but to provide for our own comfort, we got along with these dis-
advantageous circumstances very well; but the next day was an
improvement on the former in regard to the *freezing, blowing and
snowing,* and we had nothing to do but huddle around our fires and
keep turning the frozen side of our bodies to the fire to keep warm,
and to mentally and verbally speculate on the prospect of having to
remain in this uninviting spot for the rest of the winter. On this
evening I was promoted from 1st Corporal to 5th Sergt by order
of Lieut. Col. Cram.

The next two days with nothing to do but what we choosed to
passed off as usual, except that on the first we had the first of that
long line of idle rumors that followed us through our term of service
that our Regiment was "going back to Kentucky". The 11th Ky
Infantry was started to the rear a few days after the battle and this
probably gave rise to the rumor that our Regiment was soon to
follow; but be the cause what it may, we were never in camp another
month while out without hearing some rumor of the same effect
as the above.[6]

Mon Jan. 19th—our Regiment and the 19th ohio sent out on
picket. Much rain during the afternoon and night which proves to
be very dark, but as the officers had not yet learned that strict and
rigid mode of discipline which was instituted by the prolific Rosy
so soon afterwards, we did not have very strict orders and five of
us were stationed at one outpost with orders for one to stand sentinel at a time. We soon erected a shelter of clapboards of which
we found a pile nearby and passed the night very comfortably.

The next two days were spent in camp without any incident of
interest occurring to break the general monotony of camp life.

Thur Jan. 22nd—went out 12 miles on the Liberty Pike today
on a foraging expedition—filled our wagons and returned to camp
without any casualty although a forage train was captured but six
miles out on the same road yesterday.

The next day was spent in sweeping, and clearing up, and ditching about our camp, and on the following day we again went on
picket, which began to give us reason to think that duties were
going to come on us a little thicker and faster than we desired.

We went on picket again on the 27th and it was a very disagreeable and rainy day, but our company for once got to remain on the

reserve. A considerable snow fell that night and the next day was as cold as "Binger" and the weather remained so till the 30th when we were greeted by a general thaw and a heavy mail from "old Kaintuck," and in the evening by an order to go on picket.

Sun Feb. 1st—cold raw rainy day. Our Regiment is detailed to work in the fortifications, and the nature of the weather renders this business of picking and spading doubly disagreeable, and filthy, and also renders it impossible for us to make any speed in the completion of the work. But an early completion of what is laid off is impossible, for the whole country seems covered with boards and stakes to denote where heavy forts and lunnettes are to be raised.

Tu Feb 3rd—weather still severely cold. I and Sergt [Turner] Hestand who was now commanding the company,[7] and who I was assisting in making out muster-rolls and "straightening out" the books, built a chimney to our tent, and while we were absent for a load of bricks, a petition was drawn and signed by the members of the company, petitioning Colonel Cram to promote me to the 2nd Lieutenancy which would be rendered vacant by the promotions of Lieut. Johnson to 1st Lieutenant vice Clark, promoted to Captain vice Bryan. When the petition was presented to the Colonel he informed the boys that they were a little too late as he had already recommended Hestand for promotion. This seemed to satisfy the boys, for they had become uneasy at the tardiness exhibited in the promotion to fill this office, and feared that someone was to be promoted to fill the vacancy who did not belong to the Company.

Wed Feb. 4th—go on picket—weather very cold—the position and direction of the picket line somewhat changed—snow continues falling rapidly at dark—Inspections are becoming very particular in the management of the picket line—have to remain tonight entirely without fire or shelter, and the next morning is cold as *craut*.

Fri Feb. 6th—went a foraging five miles out and two miles to the left of the Lebanon road—got a good supply of forage and returned to camp without any casualty. Remained in Camp on the 7th but on the 8th we were again placed to work on the fortifications—plenty of *pop-skull* (commissary whiskey) issued to the troops to justify some of the boys to take it into their heads that it would look decent to take a gentlemanly tight,—two of them conclude that each of them "is monarch of all he surveys" and fall out about the originality of their claims when they conclude to decide it by a pugelistic contest, this action seeming to disagree with the peaceful inclinations of their company commander, he orders them to be separated and tied down. In the evening some of the boys take it into their heads to annoy a negro who was peaceably passing by, by pelting him with light sticks and stones (rather small business, I think)—the negro not relishing such treatment returned these affronts by throwing a stone at the crowd from which most of the offending sticks and stones seemed to emanate and striking one of the members of Co. K with said stone, on the neck with such force as to nearly deprive him of life. The negro immediately broke and attempted to run off, but a hot pursuit and cries of "shoot him," "hang him," "knock out his brains" was immediately commenced from all quarters and soon the negro was in custody and preparations were being made for his immediate *suspension* when his employer came up and demanded that he be allowed a fair trial. After some hesitation, this was acceded to and the negro was carried away.

I dont know that the negro was ever tried for this act, but he certainly deserved punishment for the *manner* in which he attempted to resent these uncalled-for insults.

He should not have thrown the stone promiscuously at the crowd and thus risked the injuring of an unoffender, and the man whom he came so near killing was not one of his tormentors, but was quietly attending to his own business of shovelling dirt. But I do think that the men who were so uselessly and provokingly insulting to the negro deserved at least the contempt of all honorable men. This is rather a strong assertion for a man who was born and bred in a Southern state, but I have seen so much *little meannesses* practiced toward the negro race that I cannot help expressing my *true feelings* on the subject. There was always a class of persons in our Army who were continually croaking about the measures of the administration, and their strongest point they could ever bring up to excuse their *disloyalty* or opposition to every great and wise action of the lamented President—Abraham Lincoln—the subject upon which they lived principally to discant was the subject of *Negro Equality*, and these same *croakers* were always first to attempt to bring themselves into this hated (by them) sphere of social equality with the negro. A negro could not pass them without eliciting from them some obscene remark and a shower of hurtful missiles for which there was no excuse in the world, save that the individual at whom they were aimed was a negro. Many a time has my blood fairly boiled with rage when I have seen some of these poor fellow[s], whose only fault is a *black skin*, and the fact they have always been *slaves*, stunned by a stone thrown by some specimen of the *noble* and *magnanimous* Anglo Saxon race. And as a general thing the persons who were thus continually despising and insulting the negro, and specially those who were most forward to do so, were generally men superiors to whom in point of bravery, patriotism, morality, education, and natural intelligence could be found among the free Africans and even among the *slaves* by the hundred. This is another rather strong assertion, but if I were not prepared to substantiate such an assertion I would most certainly not make it. But as these columns are not the place for me to go into a defense of the rights of the negro I will immediately desist from this digression, but which can hardly be called a digression, as it is brought out by an incident connected with the relating of my narrative.

There was much excitement in our Regiment while at this place caused by the passing of an Act by Congress allowing the President to raise arm and equip persons of African descent to serve as soldiers and seamen in the United States Army and Navy.[8] The opposition to this measure was in our Regiment and many others, very great. I had not yet got rid of all the prejudices to the negro race that had been instilled into my mind as a consequence of living in a Southern State, and therefore I was violently opposed to having any *negro troops* in our Army. But the excitement soon ran so high and the opposition in our regiment was so universal that I became alarmed for the safety of our regiment, if not for the whole army, lest the men would disband themselves and go home.

Thinking that such a dishonorable breaking up of our regiment and probably of our army would be a greater evil than even millions of negro troops, I began to endeavor to allay the excitement among the members of our company, but in doing this, to have any effect I was compelled to take the opposite side of the question which I willingly did, thinking it no crime to argue against my principle and in favor of the laws for a few days if it would remove what I feared would lead to a disastrous catastrophe.

I handled the arguments that I could produce in favor of negro troops with all the skill and apparent sincerity that I could assume for a considerable time, when almost to my horror I found myself partially convinced of the truth of the arguments that I had been advancing simply from a motive of policy, and then by degrees I came to sincerely advocate this, one of the wisest and most prudent acts of the United States Government during the war; but as it is not my purpose to relate incidents that have already appeared in various columns as matters of history, I will say nothing further on this subject.

No incident worthy of remark occurred within the next ten days, save that our Recruiting officers who had been sent back from Battle Creek came up about this time.

Also, our Regiment was being rapidly filled up again by the arrival of persons from convalescent camp hospitals.

About this time also the Paymaster again made his appearance and then there was a stir about wall tents to get papers ready to be paid off. We were going on picket, or out on foraging expeditions almost every day, and duties were falling heavy in the general[.]

Sat. Feb. 21st—incessant raining all day which was the more disagreeable as we had to go on picket, but our Company was in the reserve and *posted in a house* which I suppose was the former resident of Hon. Merideth T. Gentry,—candidate for Governor of Tennessee in 1855 on the Know nothing ticket against Andrew Johnson. The floor of one room that had probably been his study was heaped with old papers and documents belonging to Gentry, but they were now scattered promiscuously about the house as were his books, of which there were many valuable works on law.

Sun. Feb. 22nd—an order from Gen Rosecrans was read to the troops reminding us that this was the beginning of a week that would include the anniversary of the birth of George Washington, and the resurrection of our Savior, and requesting us to conduct ourselves in a manner merited by the occasion, also directing that a national salute be fired at sundown by a battery in each Division, but it seemed to me that instead of a battery firing from each Division of the army that every battery in the army was brought out. What emotions filled my heart as I stood and viewed and listened to these deathly monsters belching forth their clouds of smoke, with their deep, heavy sounds in honor of the "Father of his Country!" What sacrifices did he make for our happiness! how long and earnestly did our forefathers toil for our liberty while suffering from all that a suffering people can be brought to endure! and now how are we repaying them for all their anxieties? We have grown too proud—have come to the conclusion that we are wiser, better and more patriotic than our illustrious ancestors—that our government is imperfect in many of its parts—our best men have almost come to shed the highest offices of the land because they are surrounded while there by so many self-interested creatures who scruple not to act against the interests of their country if they can only contrive thereby to fill their pockets with its gold—thousands are to be found in this blood-bought land who openly scout the greatest principles that Washington and our other great government makers advocated with a tenacity exceeding life.—The emotions of love and patriotism that once filled so many bosoms at the mention of American honor and glory are now unknown to millions of those who have been most favored by the great institutions of this glorious country, and these millions are now at open war with the government.—and that too to preserve the most abominable institution that ever stained the bright escutcheon of our country.

Yes, they are waging a most terrible and bloody war which is costing our country the lives of thousands of patriots and millions of treasure that they may enslave an unfortunate race which is decreed by Heaven shall be free. But we will come victorious out of this struggle, and if our country's history is stained with the black spot of one civil war, it will be the brighter by the removal of the blacker one of *slavery*.

Tu. Feb. 24th—our Brigade was sent out on a foraging expedition today several miles out on the Lebanon Pike—Two men deserted from our Regiment to day, one from our company and one from Co. E;[9] also, 9 men deserted from the 79th Ind., and desertions were now becoming so frequent that my worst fears seemed to have a good opportunity of being realized. Many of our Regiment had threatened it since the passage of the Negro Soldier Law and I feared that when a break should be made that a great many would leave.

I should have remarked much earlier in this work in regard to the reorganization of our Army after Gen Rosecrans came into command. The whole Army (infantry) had been divided into three grand Divisions called Army Corps, which were numbered 14th, 20th and 21st and commanded by Maj. Generals Thomas, McCook, and Crittenden, respectively. These Corps were again subdivided into Divisions and the Divisions into Brigades. Our Regiment was now attached to the 1st Brigade and third Division of the 20th Army Corps. The Brigade was commanded by Col. B. C. Grider of our Regiment, and the Division was commanded by Col. Sam Beatty of the 19th Ohio.

Col. Grider resigned about this time,[10] (if not several days previous[)] for from some unaccountable reason I failed to make a memoranda of the fact. At any rate, soon after its occurrance, Lieut. Col. Cram was promoted to the Colonelcy, and the command of our Brigade devolved upon Col. Fred Kneffler of the 79th Ind.

About this time many radical changes for the better were beginning to be effected in the rearrangement of the picket line. Whole organizations were no longer detailed for such service, but small details from all were made at one time. Extreme vigilance was practiced on the picket line, and orders were as severe as there were ever afterwards, even when in the face of an enemy. And the long tours and constant rigor of picket officers while at this place effected much in the efficiency of our pickets, and established a system that was ever afterwards adhered to in a great manner by our Army.

Sun. March 1st—This morning opened upon us bright and rosy, and caused many a soldier to think of his plow and the long furrows that in a time of peace he was accustomed to turn on the beautiful [days] that chance to come at this season of the year; and of all the facts that cause yearning thoughts of home and the peaceful pursuits of life, those that are excited by the first opening of spring are the most longing. We were at this time enjoying the *pleasures* of camp life: of course, our duties were very heavy but they were *regular* and not very onerous. We had ceased to work on the fortifications, that being done by some other portions of the Army while we did the picket duty, and as it was too late in the season for foraging we had nothing to do but a great deal of picket duty, and to attend to the keeping up of our camp. Our Company was commanded for a time after the battle by Lieut. B. O. Rhodes (Co. K),

but he having met with the misfortune of shooting himself accidently with his pistol while loading it and thereby severely wounding himself through the leg the command devolved upon Sergt.
Hestand who on *March 2nd* received a commission as 2nd Lieut.
in our company.

Sat March 7th. The last week has been of a character in regard
to weather very suitable to the month of march, raining and shining
alternately every few hours almost each day. But this evening it
seemed that [we] were going to have something of a more business
nature to effect the general monotony of our camp life. About four
o'clock an order was issued to the troops to have "three days rations
in their haversacks and to be ready to move at a moment's warning."
Everything immediately presented the bustle of preparations, with
the usual confusion which is inevitable after so long a quiet rest in
camp and every tongue was loaded with conjectures as to where we
were going. The most popular, or at least the most desirable conclusion arrived at was that we were going to Lebanon, Tenn. and from
thence to Ky. But night came on and finally we were informed that
"we would not move today, and that the *order* was *contrabanded*.["]¹¹

Sun March 8th,—our anxities not heightened today by any order
to move—Heavy rain and hailstorm last night, but the sun rises
clear this morning and we are cheered by the prospect of another
night's rest on dry blankets, and sheltered from the pelting storms
and cold march winds by our tents.

Mon March 9th—the sun came up fair and rosy this morning
promising a warm and comfortable day and I had just seated myself
to write some letters to various friends as this was a good day for
me to tell them that "we had fine weather and that I was enjoying
myself very much," where all my arrangements were interfered with
by an *order* to "get ready to move immediately," and raising my eyes
from the sheet before me I saw the tents of the surrounding regiments being struck and *moving preparations* being made. I concluded this was not a good day for writing letters, and shut up my
portfolio and obeyed the *order.*

Our Regiment and the 79th Ind was moved out about 12 o'clock
M. on the Lebanon Pike as far as a stream which we styled Stone
River, but which was only a tributary of that stream. A mill was at
this time standing by this stream just above the pillars of the old

Pike bridge. Without crossing we camped on a hill near the river that gave the section of artillery that accompanied us complete command of the crossing place, which was now made passable by a *pontoon bridge*.

We were surprised when we left our camp to find that only our two regiments were moving, for the whole army as far as we could see had struck tents and were ready to move: but it proved to be a general reorganization of the order of encampment, and that no permanent move was being made.

Tu. March 10th—rain fell incessantly from 2 o'clock this morning and to increase our inconvenience we are not allowed to pitch our tents, which fact rendered the general prospects more mysterious, for we had not heard that the whole army was not moving in some direction. At 7 o'clock the creek was rising fast, and the pickets had been called in from the other side of the river and the bridge taken up.

Wed March 11th—we awoke this morning with thanks to the Supreme Being that the rain had ceased, the sky cleared away and that we had the promise of another fine day. As if to aggravate our thoughts in regard to our yesterday's wetting we were ordered early to pitch our tents and to go work immediately on Pay-Rolls. The Regiment received 2 months pay a few weeks previous to this, all except our company which had failed to get pay on account of some incorrect statement in the rolls, which from the inexperience of our young Lieutenant might be considered unavoidable; yet we were pretty mad about it.

Thur March 12th.—Weather fair and warm—sent our Rolls to Murfreesboro to day for inspection—the whole regiment is to receive another two months installment.

On the next day the Paymaster came out and "paid off" the 79th Ind. and returned our rolls to be signed by the men.

Tu. March 17th—weather fair and warm as if the gay season of Spring would soon set in [in] earnest—we are much pleased with our situation and I would like very much to remain here all summer. Capt Clarke came up with us today and is in splendid health and almost entirely recovered from his wound.

The Paymaster came out today and presented our regiment with some of "Uncle Abe's Photographs",[12] probably to keep our memories sharpened in regard to that great and good man. Our Company received *four months pay* which placed us on an equality with the other companies.

Wed. March 18th—Lieut Hestand is taken very sick to day. I spent the day in writing letters to friends and reading those received this morning, and in the evening taking a walk out in the forests and enjoying myself generally.

Thur. March 19th—weather clear and almost uncomfortably warm—had to "roll up" and leave our beautiful camp this morning with all its conveniences of excellent wood and water, and beautiful trees which promised soon to afford us comfortable shelter from the scorching sun. We marched back to within a few hundred yards of Murfreesboro and encamped in a large field to the right of the Pike and near a small creek which after our camp was formed ran along near the rear of the camp [of] our Brigade. Lieut Johnson came up with us this morning but he has not yet recovered from the effects of his wound so as to be able for duty. Lieut Hestand was so very sick that he was hauled in an ambulance, but would not be carried to a hospital and when the tents were pitched in our new camp he insisted on being placed in his own tent, which was accordingly done. We were relieved from our positions that we left this morning by two regiments of the 2nd Brigade.

Friday March 20th—have to drill two hours today and it is reported that our regiments are to be "filled up" with conscripts[13] and that we will remain here till they are thoroughly drilled. I shall relish the *camping* very much, but I fear my propensities to do *nothing* will seriously interfere with those to obey orders, if such incessant drilling is required of me as is necessary to discipline a band of raw recruits. Considerable skirmishing was heard in front today on the Manchester (?) road, but I know nothing of the extent of the operations.

On the 28th we commenced drilling in earnest, four hours per day—some rain on that evening and the next day; and the next day was very cold, but the drilling was not interrupted.

Sun. March 29th—very cold this morning, and the wind is blowing with a coolness and fury never known except in the month of March, and it seems that I cannot keep warm at all. Oh with what yearning thoughts do I revert to times when I could shelter myself from such inclement weather and patiently await its abatement, but after a moments thought I chide myself for such thoughts, and cooly turn them aside by thinking, oh, I will only have the more to tell when I get home. We have a feast on flour pudding (which our cook can serve in excellent style), and this contributes to the satisfactory calming of my thoughts. Company Inspection today at twelve o'clock, but you may know that the severe cold facilitated a speedy consummation of that duty.

The next day was somewhat warmer and I had to go on Camp Guard which was the first time I served on Camp Guard since the Battle of Stone's River[.]

Thur. Apr 2nd—this was as cold windy and disagreeable a day as I ever saw in the month of april. I was rather unwell with a cold, and my mouth was so sore that I could scarcely eat anything at all except something that was cool and very soft; and as there was nothing of that description in the army rations that [we] were drawing at this time I had to live entirely upon such eatables as I could procure from the sutlers—principally condensed milk and butter crackers.

Fri. Apr 3rd—no drill to day, and it has been very irregular for several days. The 3rd Brigade has gone out on a scout, and we have to do their picketing and it takes nearly half our men to fill each daily detail. The weather continues to be very fine now for several days in succession, and had it not been for the continual details that were constantly being made on us for duty of various kinds we would have passed the time very pleasantly. As it was scarcely a day passed without almost every man being *detailed* either to go on picket or to do some kind of duty about the camp. A man that was able for duty all the time had to go on picket at least every third day and on the other days he would have some other duty to perform besides the regular one of drilling which was again revived about this time and enforced upon us with a promptness and strictness which proved that we would *smoke* now. Col. Beatty (as used to be) had returned from a short leave of absence about the time we moved into this encampment, having been promoted to Brig. General, and he now seemed determined to give our little Brigade a character for efficiency in drill. The third Brigade returned from its scout on the 7th and this rendered the picket details in our regiment a little lighter[.]

Sat. April 11th—weather still fine and has been with but little interruption for some time. We were ordered this morning to get ready for inspection tomorrow and as the severity of the inspectors had increased somewhat of late there was a general washing of clothing and cleaning of guns to day, each one determining to be out in his best colors, and on the next day we were inspected by the Colonel and of course the most of us received some words of praise as he examined our guns and accouterments one by one and said we were all right.

Mon Apr 13th.—weather nice and warm. "Get ready for inspection tomorrow." The receipt of this order caused some little grumbling among those who never want to do anything that required a little labor, and also among those who could not see the necessity of such incessant parades and inspections. But the next day was too rainy for inspection and it was therefore dispensed with.

Wed Apr 15th—drizzly, damp, and disagreeable day—weather too inclement for drill. A general investigation of the cases of some of the boys who were absent at last pay-day by a board appointed for that purpose.

Pay-masters had become much stricter than they were about Corinth in the Spring of 1862, for when I came up with the Regiment at that place I had not drawn pay on the two last payments to the Regiment on account of absence at the time of payment, and as I happened to arrive before the Paymaster had left the Brigade, I received my pay. *Now* the thing was quite changed, and if a man happened to be absent on pay-day on the day of the muster in reference to which the pay-roll was made he could not then draw any money till a general investigation of his case held and an *order* was issued from Division Hd Qrs, ordering the paymaster to pay him.

Thur Apr. 16th—We were aroused from our slumbers at 1 o'clock this morning and ordered to "have three days rations in our haversacks and be ready to move at a moments warning." This order surprised and troubled us very much, for we had almost come to the conclusion that we were going to be allowed to remain quietly in our camp for a considerable time to come, but notwithstanding our sleepiness and unwillingness we had to go.

About 3 o'clock A.M. we marched out on the Lebanon Pike to the encampment that we left on 19th of march. Arrived there about day light and found to some extent an alarm existing, at any rate the troops stationed there were standing in line of battle, and had erected barricades of the rails of all the fences in the vicinity.

About noon we were told to put up our tents which we did and remained there the rest of the day. The tents were of that peculiar cut known as Dobia Tent, of which we had drawn a supply a few days previous and this was the first opportunity we had of using them. The boys made a great deal of sport when they came to erect these diminutive domiciles, and many were the names they received by our prolific speakers.

Fri Apr. 17th—The clouds have again cleared away and the general warmth of the sun seems to say that at last we will have an earnest setting-in of warm weather.

The trees are all passing from the dead wintry appearance to a beautiful living green, and the sweet fragrance of the fresh opening buds is wafted on ever gentle breeze that disturbs the stillness of the air about the summit of the little grassy hill on which we are encamped. The birds are singing sweetly on every bough apparently with an energetic determination to cause wicked man to learn a lesson by their uninterrupted happiness. Oh how I would delight in a ramble through the forest today that I might once more alone look upon a page of the great book of nature and enjoy its beauties and the good lessons it always teaches; but it no doubt would awaken fresh thoughts of home and the pleasures of former days, and cause my mind to revert with painful emotions to times when I rejoice[d] in the greatness and glory of my country without ever once thinking that it would be called upon to free itself from the coils of one of the most sanguinary civil wars of modern times[.]

Sat. Apr 18th—Weather clear and bright. Rations growing scarce—Nothing of interest to day to change the general monotony of camp scenes and incidents except a few pugilistic contests among some of the members of the other regiments, which was brought about by a too excessive indulgence in the "water of fire". Two of the 79th Ind proved beyond a doubt that it will be perfectly impossible for a human being of ordinary physical powers to break either of their skulls by hitting them with stones, and I think it will be a needless precaution for them to attempt to shelter their heads in times of battle. This evening our wagons came out to us bringing rations which were beginning to be needed. Their arrival established the fact in our minds that we would remain here for several days, but just as the C.S.[14] began to issue the rations to us we were surprised by hearing the Brigade bugler sound the *assembly*.

Immediately the rations were thrown back into their wagons and we were ordered to "fall in," and marched back to our camp at Murfreesboro that night—arrived at 9 o'clock, and upon the whole I felt much benefited by the trip.

Sun. April 19th—cloudy and warm—we are allowed to take a good rest to day, and nothing is required of us except to furnish a small camp Guard which we managed to fill up with men who did not go out with us on our last trip.

Mon. April 20th—some rain to day. Not required to drill any as we are expecting to receive another two months pay this evening. A newcomer made his appearance in our Regiment this evening, and the rumor immediately flew around among the troops that he was to be our Adjutant. This caused much dissatisfaction in the Regiment, for the boys did not know where the "*fellow*" had come from, or what his record was, and in fact could not for some time learn his name.[15]

It *is* hard on the deserving men of our Regiment to bring men from other Regiments, or from other States and promote them to the best offices in our Regiment but I hope we will not suffer by the act. And notwithstanding the unfairness of such conduct we are *fortunate* in having a Colonel from another State (Col. Cram is a citizen of Jeffersonville Ind) who I think will make our Regiment create for itself a character for discipline and efficiency in all duties that is and has heretofore been unknown to us.

Tu. Apr 21st—cloudy with some rain furnished a heavy detail for picket—received two months pay this evening from Maj Osborne which settles our account with the government up to Feb. 28, 1864.[16]

Wed. Apr 22nd—It was about this time that Capt. Bailey (who was wounded in the Battle of Stone's River) came up with the Regiment, and found a Major's Commission awaiting him. Maj Grider who came up a long while since, had been promoted to Lieut. Colonel and the "new Comer" was sure enough promoted to adjutant, but I failed to make a memoranda of these events and therefore cannot be positive as to the precise time of their occurrence.

The new Adjutant as I have before stated was promoted against the almost unanimous wishes of the Regiment but by his good conduct and gentlemanly bearing toward everyone who came in contact with him, he soon succeeded in winning the affections of almost every member of the Regiment as an officer, a gentleman, and a brave and patriotic soldier.

About this time the heavy system of drills was again introduced and continued almost without interruption through the whole of the time we remained here. First came the *Company drill* which lasted from 8 1/2 to 10 1/2 o'clock in the fore noon. Then the *Commissioned Officers'* drill of one hour from 10 3/4 to 11 3/4 o'clock in the forenoon, superintended by the Colonel. In the afternoon the *non-commissioned officers'* drill lasted from one to two o'clock under the command of Maj. C. D. Bailey, and next came *Battalion drill* from 2 1/2 to 4 1/2 o'clock.

Thus was our time kept filled out with the drills and other little duties. Company cooks were appointed and thus we were rid of that occupation of cooking our own meals, and got to rest much more in consequence of it. We drew rations every five days by throwing the "draw days" so far apart we were saved much trouble on that score.

But the one item of picket and camp guard details bore heavily on us during the whole of our stay here, and there was never much less than one-third of our whole strength on duty. Really the camp of our whole Army seemed to be turned into a camp of instruction, and every requirement of the Army Regulations seemed to be made of us with a force that admitted of no denial. Bugles (for the first time) were issued to the Colonel by our careful and intelligent Quartermaster and soon we were greeted almost every hour in the day by the sounding of the various calls, and which at the beginning on account of the inexperience of the Buglers was the cause of much merriment among the troops but which soon proved to the satisfaction of everyone to be a source of great convenience to both officers and men.

Our Quartermaster—Frank White (who was also an Ohioan and formerly a member of the 59th O.) was a perfect gentleman in every sense of the word, and the most efficient officer that ever filled that position in our Regiment, and we had had about five or six officiating in the same office previous to his promotion (Jan. 1863).[17]

About this time I was detailed by Capt Clarke to act as first Sergt. on account of the non-exchange of our *orderly* who was captured at Stone River, and that will account for my not going on picket any more for a considerable time.

On *Tu Apr. 28th* we had to turn over our Sibly tents[18] and erect our Dobia tents instead. This was the source of much dissatisfaction among all the soldiers, for we thought the "tiny" thing would be entirely insufficient to protect us from the inclemency of the weather. But the interesting and beautiful appearance they presented, and the radical change that was effected in the form of our camp, and a few days "making out" with them caused a decided revolution in the feelings of all in regard to the health, convenience and comfort of the Dobia Tent.

They were of a size that would not admit of more than three persons sleeping comfortably in them, and thereby we were freed from the crowded air peculiar to the larger tent with its twenty occupants. By raising our beds two feet from the ground, which the slope of the Sibly would not admit we were freed from the unhealthy dampness of the earth, and which is greater under blankets continually spread on the ground. They were cleaner because those that were disposed to keep themselves clean from the dirt and *crawling filth* were not compelled to *wallow* with those who only paid such attention to personal cleanliness as they were compelled to by the strictness of military rules[.]

Thur Apr. 30th—our Regiment was mustered for pay and inspected to day by Capt. L[afayette] Harling[19] who acted as mustering officer. The next few days were bright and pleasant and everything rolled quietly and smoothly on, and it really seemed that if there could be any enjoyment in a soldiers life we were blessed with that privilege.

Our communications with home were uninterrupted, and we would now have time to pen lengthy and satisfactory letters to relatives and friends. We had very few opportunities to procure any good reading matter, and were therefore compelled to adopt a series of amusements to help kill the intervening time between the discharge of our various duties.

The weather was now getting so very warm that we could not indulge in any violent physical exercise, and really we got enough of that at drilling. We therefore had hardly a resource left but to indulge in games of marbles, or the more dangerous ones of cards, and to [that] last dangerous and demoralizing game many of our boys became addicted no doubt to their subsequent sorrow. For the mere game soon loses much of its attractions and to supply this deficiency the card player is almost certain to take up to gambling. At any rate this was almost invariably the case with the card players of our Regiment and many a green one soon was stripped of every cent of his hard earned money, and then laughed at and derided by his more fortunate friends. During the first few days of the month of April this vice was carried on to an excess in our Company that almost beggars description. Players seemed to have forgotten everything else but to be endeavoring to discovering some new trick by which they might strip their comrades of their greenbacks, and the games of "seven Up", "honest John" "Euchre" and Polka could all be frequently seen running in the shade of our tree at the same time, and a crowd was sure to be gathered around to witness the sums of money being lost and won by the hundred.

This vice of gambling was a source of great annoyance to the better disposed of our Regiment, for at the time heretofore mentioned, they became so bold as to come to the tents and carry on their demoralizing practices there, and I have frequently seen the dice being rolled down on the chuckabuck board right in the Company streets; but after a time this boldness was interfered with by military orders, and the gambling operations were in the main removed from about the camps.

Mon May 4th—a little rain to day. According to an order from the Brigade Head Quarters we commenced ditching about our tents and cutting trenches through the whole [length] and breadth of our regimental camp, and on the next day two trenches parallel to each other and about ten feet apart were cut through the whole length of the Camp of the Brigade between the two rows of tents occupied by the line and field officers. The dirt excavated to form the ditches was strewn on the space between them, thereby affording a dry and firm road in all kinds of weather[.]

A ditch was cut through the entire length of the camp of the Brigade in front also and these with the numerous cross ditches running among the tents kept the camp at all times completely drained of water. More stringent measures were now taken in regard to the sanitary condition of the camp, and at the *fatigue call* each morning everyone was compelled, under a heavy penalty, to turn out and assist in sweeping off the accumulated filth of the company street, and once in each week the whole space inside the guard line was thoroughly policed.[20] Pork Barrels was placed about the cooking places of each company to receive the scraps from the kitchen and when it was filled it would be hauled away by a wagon detailed for the purpose.

Wed May 6th A slow rain fell all through the day—and the air is so cool as to render the absence of fire tolerably disagreeable. A heavy detail was made this day and sent to the wood with wagons to procure cedar trees to be set up about our camps; and the next day we commenced this operation.

Rows of cedar trees were set all along in front of each row of tents, and around the officers' tents and a solid row of heavy-topped ones was set along each side of the Brigade walk before referred to, throughout its entire length, thus affording a pleasant place for walks, and for the exciting amusement of foot races. Our Dobia tents were so arranged that each company had a row of tents on each side of its street facing to the center, and a deep ditch was cut just under the front of each row of tents and the side next to the street gradually *sloped*, and all the dirt thrown to the center, and thus were our streets kept all the time in a comfortable condition.

I think that when all the arrangements were perfected our Brigade had one of the finest camps in the army, at least it was the most tastefully arranged, neatest and most comfortable I ever saw. But it required several days of hard labor to complete it, and I think we did not drill any from about the 1st to the 10th of this month.

Mon May 11th Weather fine and warm—still working away at our camps and have not ceased for several days except on yesterday when we suspended operations for the purpose of Regimental Inspection. Our camps are assuming a degree of comfort and beauty that I dont think I ever before saw, and the officers seemed determined that we shall leave nothing undone.

Wed. May 13th weather cloudy and rainy in the evening. Were taken out and carried through the pretty but laborious operation of *Brigade* drill today under personal command of Gen. Beatty, who now seems determined that the Brigade shall make itself as perfect as it has made its camp.

On the next day we were again carried out to *Brigade drill,* and were well paid for the wearisome performance by the grand sight of three Brigades and two other Battalions all drilling on the same field, and all of which could be seen at one time from an elevated position on one side of the farm.

Wed May 20th. Have had fine weather, good health and plenty of drill for several days. Capt. Clarke of our Company sent up his resignation to day on account of *disability*—his eye was rapidly failing him, and he was blind in one eye before he entered the service.

Sat May 23rd. Capt. Clarke's resignation returned yesterday *approved* and he will start home the day after tomorrow, consequently all hands are this evening engaged in writing letters and packing up little presents which the Captain promises to take home with him. This evening a petition from our Company was sent to the Colonel requesting the promotion of Lieut Johnson to Captain, of Lieut Hestand to first Lieutenant and of myself to second Lieutenant. The petition was returned without any comment.

Sun May 24th Regimental inspection to day at 4 o'clock P.M. After inspection Companies B and H were formed in the streets of Co. B where in front of the Companies I presented a beautiful watch on behalf of the Companies to Montraville Waddell, who was formerly a member of our Company; afterwards a member of Co. H, and was now Hospital Steward of the Regiment. He responded to the presentation of the gift and the few accompanying remarks in an able and eloquent speech—pledging himself to the exertion of every fervor he could command to add to the comfort and health of the regiment, &c.

On the next morning in behalf of Co B, I presented Capt. Clarke with a large navy pistol just as he was about to leave for home, but this was done without any parade and consequently no speech.

Tu. May 26th Weather clear and warm.—Received news that Vicksburg had been captured by Maj. Gen. Grant, and that with it there had been surrounded several thousands prisoners and many pieces of heavy artillery.[21]

The Regiment marched out and gave three cheers for the good news, as did many others in the vicinity, but almost everyone said the news was "too good to be true." The next day and the next news came that Vicksburg was not captured but that Grant had fought several bloody battles in advancing upon the place, in all of which the rebels were defeated with great loss, and that he had succeeded in completely surrounding the city and reducing it to a state of siege. This much was satisfactory and confirmed by the few succeeding days dispatches as beyond all doubt.

Fri May 29th. Went to the woods to day and procured several wagon loads of the branches of green trees, together with forks and poles suitable to our purpose and with them we erected comfortable shades over the whole of our Company streets which serves very much to increase the comfort and health of our camp. The cedar bushes really were more ornamental than useful, for it was impossible to cut ones of sufficient size to create the solid and uninterrupted shades that the present arrangement afforded.

Sat May 30th considerable rain last night and enough to day to completely saturate the ground, which was very welcome as the ground was getting very dry and dusty. Rumor through the camp that a rebel reinforcement has been sent off in the direction of Vicksburg from the army in our front and that causes us to expect that we may shortly have to move.[22] Lieut. B. M. Johnson sent up his resignation this evening, and as it will in all probability be accepted—we then will be left with but one commissioned officer in our company, and, of course another promotion will be made.

Wed. June 3rd. Last night we were visited by a very heavy thunderstorm. A tree was torn in pieces near our camp, and two of our Company who were at their posts as camp guard received such severe shocks as to be for a time perfectly insensible, but were finally revived by the falling rain, and in the midst of the shower came staggering into the company streets perfectly proving by their mental and physical maneuvers that they were not yet completely recovered from the effects of the shock by a deal, but they have since gotten all right and are making sport today over the adventures of last night. An order was received this evening for us to be ready to march tomorrow morning with three days rations in our haversacks and four in our knapsacks.

The news from Mississippi during the last few days corrects the false impression we were laboring under,—that Gen. Grant's army had invested the city of Vicksburg, but according to the dispatches received to day our army is rapidly nearing Vicksburg and will either completely surround it or annihilate the rebel army in a few days. We place much importance by the capture of that city and think that when that is effected by the "backbone of the Confederacy["] will be broken[.]

Thur. June 4th—Weather windy. Lieut Johnson set out for home to day, his resignation having been returned *approved* on yesterday—Considerable cannonading this evening in the directions of Lavergne and Franklin, and the general impression among the men is that in a few days we may have to in a few days try our skill in handling muskets and pointing them at rebels.

Fri. June 5th. The whole army (except our Division) is reported to be under marching orders, and a portion of it is said to be marching out on the roads leading southward this morning, but it seems that no one has gone over to satisfy himself as to the correctness of this operation. Only one General is to remain at this post with a Division of troops (3 Brigades), and that duty is said to have been conferred on General Van Cleve and our Division, but as our Brigade is commanded by a General he will have to go on the campaign and Mrs. Rumor says that he intends to get our Brigade attached to another Division so he can remain in command of us.

This caused much dissatisfaction among the boys, and many indecorous remarks were made on the subject, proving that some men are always ready to raise themselves to a high pitch of excitement on the mere strength of rumor, that they may have some excuse for giving vent to their feelings of dislike against some commissioned officer, or against the whole *set*, for some imaginary injustice received by their orders. I was very much dissatisfied with the arrangement—if such arrangement did exist—but I always think it best to not act on the strength of a camp rumor, but wait for some confirmation. It would certainly have been unjust to have detached our Brigade from a Division to whose honor we had greatly contributed, and that in a time when we supposed the Division was going to be favored though I dont think such thing was ever contemplated by any of our Generals.

Sun June 7th. rain this evening. Gen. Van Cleve says our Brigade shall not be transferred—regimental inspection at 2 o'clock P.M.

The 17th Ky Vols came up from Nashville to day and was attached to our Brigade. As it is a large and fine regiment, our Brigade will now have a more respectable appearance; for we had only three very small regiments. The 17th also brings a *fighting* record that causes us to at once decide it *worthy* to become a member of the 1st Brigade.[23]

Mon June 8th. Continue to drill very regularly and our Regiment is rapidly acquiring the proficiency and efficiency so necessary to a fine Regiment, and is becoming so expert in all the exercises that it is actually becoming a pleasure to partake in the exercises, and I think we are now second to but one regiment in our Division in the point of prompt and regular executions of commands while on *battalion Drill.* Gen'ls Crittenden and [Thomas J.] Wood passed this evening while our Regiment was on Battalion Drill and paid us the compliment of lolling on the ground and attentively watching us during the rest of the exercises.

On the next day I received a commission as 2nd Lt. vice Lt. Hestand promoted to 1st Lt. same date, and by occurrence of another incident that morning the Sergt. Maj. as he handed me my commission ordered me to take charge of the company.

The next few days were spent as all days are in camp, with nothing of interest to break the dull routine of ordinary camp duties. The weather was becoming almost oppressively warm and we did but little besides the duties, that came as regular as the days, but to be continually attempting to devise some plan to protect us from the almost intolerable hot weather; also something to keep our minds employed and relieve the continual anxiety we were under to hear something from Vicksburg.

About the 13th or 14th I was so badly poisoned by the ordinary poison oak vine that I was for several days utterly unfit for duty, and suffered much during the time.

Mon June 15th—weather growing to be almost intolerably warm but my poison is getting a little better. *Ough* if we should be ordered to march now I hardly think I could come it. "Vicksburg is yet Vicksburg" is now the frequent salutation of officers and soldiers and is becoming almost like an old song, and we are anxiously hoping that something decisive will occur in that quarter soon. A member of Co. A of our Regiment was some time since sentenced by a

General Court Martial to be "shot to death" for the crime of *desertion* and tomorrow is appointed for his execution.[24] A petition was sent to Gen. Rosecrans from our Regiment to day signed by nearly all the officers asking for the reprieve of the prisoner but the petition was not granted, and this evening we are ordered to prepare for the execution tomorrow, and our Regiment is required to furnish one man to form one of *the twelve* who will shoot the prisoner. The company commanders were collected at the Colonel's tent about 8 o'clock P.M.—nine blank tickets were put into the hat and one marked one and then each one drew out a ticket. Capt. [Henry F.] Leigget of Co. A[25] got the marked one and consequently had to furnish the man who was to do the shooting.

The next day which afforded me the opportunity of witnessing one of the most solemn scenes known to mortals was the hottest one that had yet occurred in the season.

Early in the day our Division was marched out to a large field and placed in the form of a hollow square with one of the lines of the square left vacant.

Hundreds of spectators were on the ground to witness the execution, and but for the nature of the scenes that were about to take place I could have relished much better the imposing appearance of the Brigades as they respectively moved on *en masse* into their respective positions. After waiting a considerable time the ambulance supposed to be conveying the prisoner hove in sight accompanied by the Provost Guard: but judge of our surprise when as they approached nearer we saw the prisoner, entirely unsupported, walking with a firm and steady step between two of the guards, and seemingly entirely unaffected by thought of the trying ordeal through which he must directly pass, and the bare thought of which had already made me almost sick. Oh awful thought—to see a man who was so soon to pass the broad gulf that separates Time from Eternity, and who will soon enter the dread uncertainties of the awful Hereafter, and there to live by the past and not the future: and yet he appears so little concerned. Before leaving Headquarters and when the officer of the guard proposed to place him in an ambulance; he remarks "O no, I think a walk will make me feel better."

The guard entered the square and commenced to make the circuit of the whole of the inner columns. The prisoner closely attended by guards and supported by Lt. Pipkin (Co. A) and Chaplain Smith (?)[26] proceeded immediately by his coffin, and accompanied by the solemn tones of the band playing the "Dead March"(?) and with his head slightly bowed but with a firm step followed around the whole square without the least faltering in his step. I took one glance at him and turned heartsick from the scene, anxiously contemplating the awful scene that must follow, and which I would be almost compelled to witness.

The circuit completed and the prisoner placed about the center of the open side of the square, a short prayer was next uttered by the Chaplain and thus the prisoner was secured to his coffin in a sitting position and the twelve were marched up a short distance in front of him and brought to a front.

I involuntarily turned my eyes away from the scene and waited several seconds which seemed like hours, of the most tormenting suspense when the almost death-like silence was broken by one of the poorest and most irregular volleys I ever heard, and a glance toward the prisoner told me that he was no more. All stood a moment as if in breathless suspense and then a long breath apparently from each one broke the spell of suspense and immediately we were deployed and formed into *columns of companies* and marched in this order over by the spot where the victim lay and then filed off toward the camp.

A great many executions of this kind occurred during our stay at Murfreesboro and the good effect it had upon its *deserting portions* of our army was conclusive evidence that we would not have had to report so many "absent without leave" for the last several months if this experiment had been tried at least a year sooner. And fewer examples would have had the desired effect at the first organization of our Army by far than were now required. For the last fifteen months men had deserted and returned almost with impunity, and till Gen. Rosecrans came into command of the army the punishment hardly ever so severe that anyone would not have undergone it voluntarily to have obtained thereby a short furlough to go home. The punishment was most commonly a simple "stoppage of pay" for the length of time the prisoner was absent, and who would not give 13 dollars per month for a few months to be allowed to go home after a protracted absence from friends.

The next few days were passed over without any incident of

interest, but we were kept very closely at the regular duties, and these served to fill our time in the most pleasant portions of the days, for the weather had now become so warm that no attempt at drilling was made during several hours in the hotter time of the day.

Some of the boys becoming *musical*, a violin was purchased by the combined contributions of our company and this afforded much sport after night would set in and the air become cool enough to admit of the pleasing but laborious exercise of dancing. We were frequently visited by a vocal band from another regiment (the 79th Ind Inftry, I think) and the combined musical favors of the two regiments, seconded by the "*almost superhuman*" exertion of the dancers afforded us much pastime during the weary and lonesome evenings.

On the evening of the 21st I went to a prayer meeting which was conducted in a beautiful arbor that had been erected by the members of the 19th ohio near their camp. I was seriously impressed with the religious solemnity that seemed to clothe every item of the proceedings of the meeting, and I resolved that I would attend these meetings regularly during our stay here if they should be kept up. Capt. Miller[27] (G) was present and addressed a short discourse to the meeting, and seemed to take a great welfare in its prosperity, and the good effect it might possibly have upon the morals of the members of the Brigade.

Mon June 22nd—I was detailed to go on picket, and it was the first time since the putting forth of the leaves that I had been outside the precincts of our Brigade Camp. Therefore, I was almost surprised and very much pleased to find that my post was in a delightful shady grove, the ground being covered with a beautiful and fresh grass that had been preserved from pasturage by the nearness of the picket line and the rigidity of the orders of the picket officers.

I cannot tell how much I enjoyed the absence of the bustle, confusion, continued noises, dust, impure air, sounding bugles, rolling drums, occasional quarrels, and sometimes independent fights of the camp. I could now enjoy the pure air, cool shades, and the pretty chatter of the numberless birds with a pleasure I never realized to such an extent before. My duties were of a nature that kept me from being responsible for the conduct of any man except myself, and therefore I enjoyed the pleasures of my position very much. But

I can never come to the contemplation of any pleasure without the thought of better days rolling before my mind and causing a pang of sorrow to pervade my heart.

I cannot avoid reverting to the once prosperous, glorious and happy condition of my country, and to the days when a man could and did by his own conduct entail happiness or misery upon himself.

Tu. June 23rd—weather tolerably cool. Returned from picket early in the day—indications of a general move by the Army—preparations going on in every quarter which furnish unmistakable evidence that ere long we will have to leave our beautiful camp, and once more undertake the toilsome march and probably the dangerous battle field.

Chapter 7

To the Other Side of the Tennessee River

Under pressure from Lincoln and Halleck to march against Bragg and prevent the latter from reinforcing Vicksburg, Rosecrans finally led the Army of the Cumberland out of Murfreesboro on June 23, much to Marcus Woodcock's displeasure. Rosecrans hoped to get in the Army of Tennessee's rear and force a decisive battle on his terms. That battle never took place, but with two brilliant turning movements, Rosecrans compelled Bragg to fall back to Chattanooga. With only 560 casualties, Rosecrans's Tullahoma Campaign seemed to the general—and to modern scholars—a great success.

From Washington, however, came only demands for a new triumph to match the victories at Gettysburg and Vicksburg: the capture of Chattanooga itself. Six weeks elapsed as the methodical Rosecrans resisted pressure while again amassing supplies and repairing his supply line. On August 16, the Army of the Cumberland once again took to the road. Rosecrans's new plan was as daring as the one that had preceded it. While Maj. Gen. Thomas L. Crittenden's Corps feinted against Chattanooga from the north, the rest of the army would flank the city to the west by marching into the rugged mountains of northern Georgia.

At first the plan seemed to be working splendidly. On September 8, Bragg abandoned the vital city and retreated into Georgia. Rosecrans blithely assumed that his counterpart was falling back to Atlanta. In fact, Bragg was hatching a plan of his own. Securing reinforcements from as far away as Mississippi and Virginia, Bragg determined to destroy the separated elements of Rosecrans's suddenly vulnerable army, as they struggled and straggled through the mountains. Three attacks failed due to confusion among subordinates, yet, by September 18, Bragg was poised to smash the Federal army along Chickamauga Creek.[1]

Wed. June 24th—a light rain falling during the greater portion of the day. The whole army, except our Division, moved from their camps today taking various routes leading off to the south. The 20th Corps marched on the Shelbyville road; the 14th A.C. on the Manchester road, and our corps moved out on the Liberty pike.[2]

As before remarked our Division did not move out with the main Army but about noon, amidst a steady rain, we had to strike tents and move over to a position near the railroad bridge over Stone River, and encamped.

It was on the drill ground of a Brigade that had moved out that morning, and was very much torn up by the frequent passing that had been made over it during the day, thus it seemed the mud and rain were using their combined efforts to render us as disagreeable as possible; but we cheered each other with the hope that we would get to remain here during the summer, though I cannot say that hope ever assumed a very large sphere in my list of aspirations. Yet we could not imagine why we left here if it were not to guard the post, for all the army, so far as we could ascertain, had gone out this morning, and we *know* that the defenses, stores and bridge of this point are so important that they would not be left entirely unguarded. But we went to sleep that night without ascertaining what was to be our fate.

The rain continued to fall in torrents the next day and the mud about the camps became almost impassable from its great depth, and its being on every spot of ground about the camp. The next day (26th) the rain fell in more moderate quantities, and we thought we could safely indulge in a hope that it would cease entirely by to-morrow. But we heard no news from nor no cannons at the front, and were compelled to retire to our *bunks* equally as wise in regard to the general proceedings of the outer world as we were in arising that morning.

On the 27th we received orders to be ready to move at a moments warning, which completely dispelled the vain hope that many of us had indulged in that we would remain here as post guards. But notwithstanding all these troubles, the rain continued to fall in heavy showers through the most of this day, and we retired to our bunks on this night under the firm convictions that, rain or shine, we would have to move to-morrow.

Sun. June 28th—some rain in the forenoon of the day. In the afternoon our Brigade and a portion of the second Brigade set out on the march along the Manchester Pike, as escort to a heavy ammunition train which it was said we were to carry to Dept. Head Quarters. After a weary and toilsome march of ten miles we arrived at ———— creek[3] about midnight being almost completely [exhausted] by the heavy pulling we had been compelled to make through the mud.

Mon. June 29th. Started early this morning but the wagons started being very heavy loaded and our advance was necessarily very slow, and added to the already many disadvantages for speedy marching, a heavy rain set in early in the afternoon, which at once rendered the roads nearly impassable, for the continually passing wagons soon cut the road into numberless gullies and holes. A great many wagons broke down and with their loads were of course lost; for there was no remedy. In many instances the teams failed to draw their wagons across difficult places without the process of "double teaming" and this of course greatly retarded our advances.

We only gained eight miles in the whole days [march] and at night the train was parked in two different places, some miles apart. Our Regiment was camped about 3 or 4 miles beyond Beech Grove.

Nothing could hardly exceed the disagreeableness of this days work. We had been compelled to wade mudholes, and roll at wagon wheels till we were so nearly exhausted that I for one could scarcely hold out till we arrived at camp, and then when we did we were so completely bedaubed with mud and sand that sleep was almost out of the question. But we were finally halted on a pleasant hillside which offered too good an opportunity for rest to be left and we remained here all night.

Tu. June 30th. The rain had ceased falling this morning but the roads were in a sad plight indeed, and under any other circumstances than the present I think we would have found it impassable. The troops composing the escort were by far the muddiest and most discomfited fellows I ever beheld; this with the dampness of the night rendered a refreshing sleep an impossibility and consequently we rose from our blankets this morning feeling very sensibly the effects of yesterdays march.

Some time in the forenoon we set out again but with a continual whooping and hollering, and tugging at wagon wheels we were only able to advance 4 1/2 miles in the whole day, i.e. our regiment only advanced that far for the 17th Ky. which was in advance arrived near Manchester that night; as to the remainder of the command they did not catch up with us in the whole day but encamped some miles back to the rear. The train was parked in *open order*— or on every favorable spot of ground for some miles along the road.

Wed. July 1st—Weather clear and very warm, but the roads were still very much in need of repair, especially for our business. Our regiment arrived in Manchester today and encamped in a beautiful grove near town in the yard of a gentleman whose name I have now forgotten. We can get but little news from the front, which is now at least twelve miles ahead of us, only that the rebels are evacuating all their important posts with such little resistance that it has been the origin of a rumor among the boys that Bragg with the greater portions of his Army has gone to Virginia to occupy Richmond while Lee with his "invincibles" pulls on and crushes "old fighting Joe Hooker" and the gallant army under his command.[4] All now agree that the rebels will fall back without any further resistance to the other side of the Tennessee River. Cos. A & B go on picket tonight and after much stumbling through bushes and crossing hollows finally got a good position, and for the first time since leaving M——— a comfortable place for rest.

Thur July 2nd—We returned from picket early this morning, being relieved by a detail from the several companies of the regiment. Co. A caught four straggling Rebels this morning and one of our videttes[5] shot at a squad of three. The woods are reported full of them trying to get to their home in this state and Kentucky without getting into our lines. Think we have reason to be very much cheered by the flattering success our army has met with since leaving M———, and [if] the Army of the Potomac could now give old Lee a similar chase Jeff Davis might begin to think seriously about using some of his stolen pieces of gold to close the eyes of his Confederacy. Oh that the Great Ruler could in his wisdom say that this war should immediately end as it inevitably must, and save the shedding of rivers of blood that I believe are yet destined to flow!

On the next day we remained in Camp striving to render ourselves as comfortable as possible on a hot sultry day. We were very anxious about the movements of the various armies but as we could get no news on account of the irregularity of the mails, we could come to no definite conclusion as to the general condition and position even of our own army.

Sat July 4th—weather clear but very hot and sultry. A national salute was fired at the usual time of the day by a battery in town, but no other demonstration by the few troops left at this place. Receive [mail] after dark to night, but no newspapers, and consequently still remain uninformed as to the true condition of affairs.

The next day we heard reports that Gen Hallack had been succeeded as commander-in-chief by Gen McLellan and that Gen Hooker had been superseded by Gen Meade in command of the Army of the Potomac.[6] This was the cause of some rejoicing among us, for we knew that with a change of commanders there would be at least an *attempt* to do something whether it succeeded or not, and we could only hope for its success.

On the 6th I with several others went to the woods in search of huckle berries. We had a most agreeable and pleasant ramble of some miles through this country of heavy undergrowth of bushes and briers, and procured a bountiful supply of berries of different kinds. I got separated from the rest of the party and we only protracted our walk by a few miles in whooping and hallowing and using other means to ascertain each other's whereabouts, but finally we all came together at an old mill, and without any injury in either life or limb we returned to camp.

Wed July 8th—good news to day from every quarter. Vicksburg was surrendered with its whole garrison to Gen Grant on the 4th inst.—Gen Meade is manfully closing in with old Lee and is reported to have captured a great many prisoners. The rebel generals, A. P. Hill and Longstreet are reported the former killed and the latter wounded.[7] "Hurrah for the Potomac Army" is on every tongue this morning, and if these reports only be true we may hopefully listen for something decisive from that quarter soon.

Thur July 9th—Set out for McMinnville to day, where the other half of our Division has gone under Gen. Van Cleve.

We are very much pleased with the idea of a move for the country about Manchester is so effectually stripped of everything fresh in the line of eatables that it is simply an impossibility to procure forage even to the amount of a mess of potatoes. And as McMinnville lies rather out of the general field of operations we calculate that when we get there we will find plenty in the country, to mix with and make our army rations go better; and also as it seems to be rather out of the general line of march we hope that we will get to remain there a considerable time.

We camped that night nine miles from Manchester. On the 10th we went to McMinnville, distance 14 miles—arrived in sight of town and on the banks of the stream near that place (Known I believe as Caney Fork) and which stream we were submitted to the necessity of wading. As it was tolerably broad and as the bottom was covered with sharp flinty stones this mode of ferrage was at once very disagreeable and painful, for we were ordered to take off our shoes.

There very much pleased with the country through which we passed to day, as it promises great recompense to foragers, and as some citizens informed us that the people are *largely* secesh we will not be very scrupulous about taking what we actually need, but I heartily condemn anything that pertains to the destruction of private property let it belong to whom it may[.]

We remained in camp the next day (11th) but the weather was so disagreeably warm and sultry that we did scarcely anything towards cleaning up or otherwise working at our camp so as to make it comfortable.

Sun July 12th—I went on picket this day, and was well repaid for the duties it calls forth by the regular feast I had on potatoes and buttermilk; and in the evening on a portion of a "shoat" that attempted to carry away one of the boy's haversacks and who paid for his temerity with his life.

Genls. Rosecrans and Crittenden, with their respective staffs, came out to "our town" on the 13th and spent a short time in looking about.

During the next few days nothing of interest occurred in our camps, for as the orders on picket lines were very severe, and as there was not any beating ground within them, we could not find food for the productions of interesting incidents. We broke up our camp and moved over to the North East side of town on the 15th and again settled down, and then went to work at straightening out our camp in real earnest; and in a few days were again very comfortably situated, and ordered to commence drilling.

On the 18th I went out 7 miles on the Chattanooga road on a foraging expedition in charge of the train escort, and after filling wagons with corn, sacks with potatoes, pockets with peaches and apples, and hands with chickens, and getting considerably alarmed at the rumored proximity of a squadron of rebel cavalry we returned to camp.

About the 21st we began to hear stirring news from the North, and almost fabulous stories in regard to the great freebooter John Morgan, Brig Gen. C.S.A., who was reported to [be] fairly turning over the states of Indiana and Ohio, and who was being hotly pursued by Genls. Judah, Hobson and Shackleford.[8]

When we first heard that this daring and powerful robber had crossed the Ohio we fairly chuckled, for we were confident that he would never get his neck out of the halter into which he had so recklessly thrust it; but when we began to hear of the repeated masterly runs and inevitable depredations of this great robber-chief, who it seems could never be caught, or headed we began to fear that he would make a masterly raid through "the States" and finally escape to Virginia.

On the 23rd, the Paymaster (Maj. Osborne) arrived in our camp and we immediately making out a new set of pay rolls, in order to be ready to receive our "share" of the ever-acceptable "greenbacks," and on the next day the 19th Ohio received pay, and on the next day the 79th Ind. and still on the next day (sunday) we received our installment.

Mon July 27th—warm weather, and a dry day, and plenty of money, and consequently plenty of potatoes. Received a dispatch this evening stating that "old Morgan and his whole force is finally captured.["] This news was particularly gratifying to the members of our regiment for he was the particular horse stealer, and alarmer of helpless women and children in our particular country.

Wed. July 29th—weather cool and pleasant. I am on picket to day and have again had a good feast on the various delicacies of the season.

Soon after our change of camps Gen Van Cleve had issued a

circular regulating the price of the various articles of trade that were being daily exchanged for or sold by the citizens and soldiers, and regulating the manner in which their dealings should be carried on. This proved to be a wise thought of the general for previous to this many of the citizens had demanded and received enormous prices for their various articles of sale; and in other instances some of the soldiers had forcibly or by other means defrauded citizens to some extent, and in a most shameful manner.

Citizens were now not allowed to cross the picket line till 9 o'clock and then only were they allowed to come to the *picket reserve*, and there they were compelled to all the trading that they [did] with our troops. The picket officers were furnished "price lists" and it was their duty to personally superintend the dealings of the various parties and to see that everything was conducted fairly and squarely according to *orders*. These prudent regulations caused many of the citizens to bring in various articles which were very acceptable to the troops, and for which the soldiers were always eager to exchange either greenbacks, or their rations of sugar and coffee. The articles generally brought in by the citizens were potatoes, beans, peas, milk, butter and eggs, fruits of almost every kind, cooked meats of every description, fowls, fish and really anything that a fruitful country could be expected to produce.

Taking everything into consideration I think that we fared better in every respect and enjoyed ourselves better during our stay at McMinnville than at any other time or place while in the service. The citizens (if many of them *were rebels*) were by far the most courteous and deferential as a whole that we ever found; but we ascertained that a large portion of the population were Unionists and that they had suffered many prosecutions on account of their patriotic devotion to the "old flag". Our duties were for a time very light, consisting principally in going on picket and *occasionally* drilling. But the picket officers soon became so lenient in their requirements that it almost became a real pleasure to go on picket.

The small number of troops stationed there and the great distance by which the different Brigades were separated prevented the air from being filled with those nauseous vapors that are inevitable to a large army. The water was excellent, and the stream beforementioned afforded good opportunities for healthy bathing. But we were almost totally deprived of the *luxury* of reading news-papers, for while we were in Murfreesboro, Gen. Rosecrans issued an order prohibiting news dealers selling western papers for more than five cents per copy, and the prices of eastern papers were regulated accordingly. This order was a considerable "dig" into the profits of those concerned, and the consequence was as before-stated.

The weather, after the first few days, was generally very cool and pleasant for the season, and we had but little rain.

Tu. Aug. 4th The weather was now growing warm very fast. In the afternoon our Brigade received an order to be ready to march on a scouting expedition, and set out at 5 o'clock P.M. We took the road leading to Sparta, and traveled about 15 miles halting near midnight at Rock Island, the point where the Sparta Road crosses the Caney Fork River.

I afterwards learned that the design of the expedition was to march to this point and capture the rebel force by surprise that were stationed here to guard the ford, and then to move on the town of Sparta, which was at this time occupied by some rebel cavalry. But as our advance guard was not able to take the rebels by a complete surprise, and only effected the capture of a part of them, it was considered useless to go any further and therefore the expedition was abandoned, and on the next evening amid a shower of rain, and being very sore and much wearied we arrived in camp with the happy consolation that we had our trouble for our pains.[9]

Sat. Aug. 8th our Regiment, the 21st Ky Infantry, and the 44th Ind. Infantry were moved across the river near the railroad bridge and organized into a pioneer Brigade, and place under the command of Col. [Samuel W.] Price of the 21st Ky.[10] We did not much like the idea of changing our pleasant camp for a new one where we would be compelled to undergo the necessity of again devoting a week's work to digging and shading; and when we came to learn that we had been moved across there for the purpose of erecting fortifications our dissatisfaction rose as fast and extensive as the Confederate troops fell about the first day of April 1865. And the intensity of this dissatisfaction was not in the least decreased by the almost intolerably hot weather which was now pouring it to us with all the force of an almost boiling sun[.]

On the 10th we worked hard all day at our camps and got things as nearly completed as possible,—ditching shading, &c.—for we were informed that we would have to commence work on the morrow, and sure enough we did, by breaking ground just in front of the Brigade. From the general direction of the stakes that were set up as marks by the engineer we concluded that there was at least a months digging in store for us, and I tell you I dreaded it. But if there had been no such organization as Granger's Reserve Corps[11] we could have comforted ourselves with the thought that we would get to remain and occupy our works when they should have been completed and the last of the Division gone on the great Southern Campaign.

We remained here and dug hard till the 15th with constant rumors of a forward movement, and numerous curses and imprecations among the boys at the thought of being compelled to work so heavily in this intolerably hot weather with the daily prospect of leaving for some other point.

But notwithstanding the general displeasure we had some real pastime and among other incidents of *no* interest was the settling of a dispute between our Regiment and the 21st Ky as to which regiment could show itself to the best advantage. I need not say that the palm (if there was any) was awarded to the "old 9th" and *justly* too, though I don't recollect that any of the members of the "Twenty onesters["] conceded the point.

Late in the evening of the 15th we received the order to "be ready to march tomorrow morning at 6 o'clock A.M.["] The news was received by many of the boys with violent volleys of curses and imprecations, and whole vocabularies of impolite epithets, which exceeding hurtful missiles were hurled at the innocent Reserve Corps with all the vindictive energy that could be expected of disappointed and overworked humanity; but notwithstanding this gallant and able defense the fate of the poor fellows were sealed—the firmness or *absence* of the originator of the order would not relax in the least and we were left to no other alternative but to go or stay, and accordingly got ready.

We bade adieu to McMinnville with its many pleasing attractions the 16th (Sun) and started out on the Pikeville road with 10 days rations in our company wagons, which by the way were very much loaded for we were reduced to the competency of one wagon for two companies. We marched to the foot of Cumberland mountain (distance 5 miles), having waded Caney Fork in the meantime, and encamped. A pleasant shower of rain fell during the evening which rendered the air very cool and refreshing.

Mon Aug 17th—weather warm and clear in the forenoon—I was detailed early in the morning to take charge of a squad detailed from our regiment, and to assist Lt [Isaac W.] Stubbs (since Captain) of the 79th Ind[12] in directing the operations of a detail made from the whole Brigade for the purpose of getting the ammunition train up the mountain, the ascent of which we began to climb almost as soon as we started to march—after much hollowing and whipping, and much heavy and laborious pushing, and sometimes pulling—frequently a rope would be attached to the tongue of the wagon and passed forward between the mules when about twenty men would get hold of it and take it over difficult places—we finally about twelve o'clock reached the summit of the mountain, which was about two miles from our previous night's encampment. The ammunition train then passed on while we remained near the summit of the mountain waiting for the rest of the wagons and the troops to come up. Then the third Brigade soon came up and passed on, but our Brigade did not get all their wagons up till near night, and then we moved out about two miles and encamped. The third Brigade had gone about five miles further on.

Tu Aug 18th—Weather tolerably cool and pleasant. Marched 13 miles to day, and as the roads were very good we got along with our wagons tolerably well, and found water to be tolerably plentiful, which rather surprised us as we had some very rough experience on this same ridge but much farther South (Aug. 1862).

To night, as on the other occasion of our crossing this mountain, we had a very exciting alarm, which originated from a cow that was browsing about among the tents, knocking down a stack of guns. As on the former occasion the whole Regiment was aroused, and kept for some minutes in anxious suspense in consequence of no one knowing what was the cause of the alarm, but finally without anyone scarcely knowing the true cause we all lay down again to sleep. All hands decided that Cumberland Mountain was certainly attended by some evil spirit, or had some other reason for being very prolific of exciting alarms.

Thur. Aug 19th—Weather very warm. We marched early and

soon went down the mountain into the beautiful and productive Sequatchie Valley, beyond which and not more than five miles away Waldrund's Ridge[13] could be seen rising in all it's rough beauty, forming an agreeable background to the broad fields and narrow strip of wood that interspersed each other over the valley.

Weary, foot-sore, and dusty, we arrived at Pikeville late in the afternoon, and were encamped in a beautiful grove of trees just above town, and which was surrounded by numerous fields of corn which was now in that state so favorable to the soldiers' facilities for cooking and eating—roasting ears; and soon every man's kettle was filled with the tender, nourishing ears of corn, and all in good spirits over the prospect of a good supper.

Pikeville was neither large, nor populous, nor thriving nor beautiful; and judging from all appearances it undoubtedly got its growth soon after its first settlement. Though as an excuse for this it may be truthfully said that it has no advantages by which it can acquire the above-named attractions. The valley in which it is situated, though very productive is very narrow and stretches out several miles both above and below the town thus almost entirely cutting off communication with the outer world. I can say nothing for or against the inhabitants of the town and surrounding country, for during our stay we had very little intercourse with the citizens, and that principally with the rough inhabitants of the mountains, who were generally a pretty good representation of the first settlers of our country. One of them came in one day bringing some fresh venison for sale. Some of the boys asked him where he killed it at upon which he remarked "over at the back of Uncle Ike's field."

Fri Aug 21st—The weather was now rather cool and consequently very pleasant. A train started back to McMinnville for supplies today. The 4th Michigan Cavalry[14] had a skirmish with the Rebels last night some distance up the valley.

Mon Aug 24th—weather again very warm. Our Regiment started back to McMinnville to day to escort a supply train—Marched to the summit of the mountain and some distance farther on where we halted at a small stream and I found myself more completely exhausted from excessive heat than ever before but here the whole Regiment was mounted into the wagons and from this we travelled very easily and made our day's journey about twenty miles.

Tu Aug 25th—rainy last night and a very hard shower this morning—Marched early and about the middle of the afternoon we met the train that had left Pikeville on the 21st returning with a very slender escort. The four left companies of our Regiment were detached to return with this train which was under the command of Maj. [John S.] Clarke of the 8th Ky. Inftry.[15] We got our train up the mountain that night, and camped not far beyond where the road reaches the top, and spent a very disagreeable night on account of not bringing our "doggeries" (tents) with us, for the rain fell through the greater portion of the night, but under every consideration we were very much pleased that we did not have to go all the way to McMinnville.

Thur Aug 26th—weather very cool and tonight the air is disagreeably so. Marched back on the Pikeville road to day to within three miles of the brow of the mountain and went into camp—Our detachment encamped in an orchard the trees of which were loaded with choice fruit and of course we spent a very agreeable evening, but our appetite for fruit had been considerably [assuaged] through the day. the boys who could not content themselves by plodding along the road with the wagons had branched off into the few farms that were scattered along the road, and they returned almost invariably loaded with the most delicious and elegant peaches I ever ate.

I had to go on picket to night but did not suffer any inconveniences therefrom except being compelled to sleep by my self and with no bed or covering except the cold ground, the friendly branches of a majestic oak and a gum blanket.

Sat Aug 28th—Col Cram returned from home where he had been on "leave of absence". The right wing of our regiment returned to day. Receive[d] the cheering news that lines of our main Army are now established on the Tennessee River. About 8 o'clock P.M. an old cow that was poking about in the Camp of the 17th Ky became frightened at something, and blinded by a fire that was burning near, she dashed off—ran over and knocked down a whole row of "dog-tents" in some of which the owners were lying gently asleep. This incident brought an immense volley of loud whoops and huzzas from the witnesses, which was immediately taken by those in the neighborhood, and yell upon yell, louder and louder, soon commingled into one prolonged yell the awful tornado swept down upon our devoted regiment striking us with such force that it called forth a succession of loud yells from almost every one— I had just retired to rest, but when I heard the awful rushing, as if of a mighty wind, I sprang from my bunk and rushed forth into the open air, and throwing my head slightly backward, and standing at my full height, and assuming as nearly a "show action" attitude as possible, I opened my head and manufactured a few first-rate young-lion-roars as quickly as possible and then quietly returned within my tent. The storm passed throughout our Brigade and by Gen Beatty's head quarters producing everywhere the same startling effect as in our regiment.

After it had in a manner ceased and the boys were talking over the results, they were as suddenly astounded by hearing the *assembly* sounded from the bugles at Brigade head quarters, and quickly repeated by the regimental buglers. Every one knew that this was the signal for our punishment. Some of the boys came in and *waked* me, and you may judge of my surprise when I learned that the boys had been exercising their lungs a little too freely and now were in immediate danger of being punished for it. But there was no help for it and the whole Brigade was compelled to stand in line two hours, some of the boys said as a *recompense* for the terrible damage we had sustained in the recent tornado though they did not all put it up so well and some grumbled severely.

Sun Aug. 30th—Weather clear and warm—I was detailed to go out with a guard to a forage train to day—went about five miles down the river and simply loaded our wagons with corn and re-turned to camp without anything interesting occurring to pay my trip except that I stopped in at a house while the wagons were being loaded and had the to me almost inexpressible pleasure of hearing a beautiful young lady play (on her piano) and sing "The Star Spangled Banner", &c.

On Monday we had rumors all day that we were on the eve of making another general move, but our anxieties were not relieved till a very late hour in the evening when we received orders to "be ready to march at 6 o'clock in the morning.["] I supposed we would march in the direction of Knoxville and earnestly hoped so, for I believed that the main army under Rosecrans would soon attempt to cross the Tennessee River and therefore if we joined him I thought we would stand a very good chance to get into hot places, and I tell you, Stone's River had effected a complete cure of any propensities that I might have had in that direction. However we packed our trunks and knapsacks, separated those articles that we would carry with us from those we intended to leave with the wagons, and made other preparations necessary to a long march:

Tu. Sept. 1st—weather tolerably warm and roads very dry and dusty, and marching consequently very disagreeable—marched 14 miles down the valley, without yet being satisfied as to whether we would march on throughout the entire length of the valley or turn across Waldrund's Ridge in the direction of Knoxville.

The next day we marched 18 miles, passing through a little hamlet termed Dunlap, 6 miles from our previous night's bivouack. Several men gave out from excessive fatigue and heat and were placed in ambulances.

On the 3rd, we marched to Jasper, distance 14 miles. Here we suddenly found ourselves within the lines of the main army, and Gen Crittenden's headquarters were at this place. We also found ourselves in a portion of country that we had occupied before (Aug. 1862) and had since evacuated it for the purpose of following Bragg into Kentucky—Passed the very house where I saw the first example of house-pillaging by a part of a thievish set of scoundrels who joined the army to obtain the privilege and opportunity of robbing negro-kitchens and ladies ward-robes. We found also that we had arrived just in time to partake of a great movement of some kind that was being made by the main army. The 14th and 20th Army Corps were reported to have already crossed the river and disappeared in the mountains beyond and gone "no man knew whither[.]"

Fri. Sept. 4th. This is the twenty-first anniversary of my birthday, but I am so hurried by orders to march and marched so far that I have hardly had time to think about it; though it always is food for much and very serious reflection, and will generally lead into reflections of such a nature that it causes the thinker to form many resolutions which if kept, will generally tend to make them better, wiser, and more useful persons.

We were aroused early and ordered to prepare to move, and by the time the sun was peeping over the spurs of the Ridge, we were marching in the direction of the Tennessee River at Shell mound. Arrived at that place, or rather at the bank of the river opposite that place about 10 o'clock and by noon nearly the whole of our Division had been crossed over in flatboats.

This was rather a slow mode of crossing compared with the facilities offered by a pontoon bridge, but it was conducted in a very safe manner, and I did not hear of a single accident occurring in the whole Division while crossing. After we had gotten across, we were moved up into the mouth of a valley and encamped not very far from the celebrated Nicki Jack Cave.[16] I paid a visit to the cave in the evening and found some points of admiration in the grand opening at its mouth—the extensive saltpetre works that had been erected by the agents of the Confederate Government and in the numerous little skills of every almost every description that could be gathered about the works. I went in a little beyond the reach of daylight, but as my curiosity had not been careful enough to cause me to provide myself with the materials for a torch ere I left the camp I did not venture further, for I did not choose to extend my explorations in this subterranean passage without having the partial advantage of the use of my optical organs. There were scores of torches in the hands of soldiers going and returning, but by their light I could distinguish nothing beyond my position except the carriers, yet I did not choose to explore further without the torch in my own hand.

Sat. Sept. 5th. At 5 o'clock P.M. we were *blowed* together again, and marched about ten miles that night in the direction of Chattanooga over an indescribably rough road, and encamped just beyond the well known Whiteside bridge.[17] We now begin naturally to come to the conclusion that the present operations were being directed against Chattanooga, the place that I had long considered as almost impregnable, and as I had not yet began to calculate on the great flanking powers of Gen. Rosecrans, I could think of no way for us to obtain possession of this general stronghold of the Confederate Armies but by a direct assault.

"But where is the rest of our army?" was a question very frequently asked by almost everyone and it of course unanimously remained unanswered. We had no definite news from the 14th and 20th Corps for several days, and had not *seen* either of the other

Divisions of our Corps though we felt tolerably certain that they were in our advance. Retired to rest that night—conscious that we were within a day's march of C——— but not dreaming of the many barriers that could be thrown in the way of our progress.

Sun. Sept. 6th. Marched about three miles and encamped on the Trenton road in Georgia. The weather was now becoming very dry and the roads were so dusty that it rendered marching very difficult[.]

On the next day we remained in camp—could occasionally hear a cannon away up the valley which indicated beyond a doubt that somebody had found somebody and that somebody was trying to pick a fight with somebody. In the afternoon our company elected two Sergeants, and the elections were approved by the Colonel. The men elected were Corporal J. W. Hinson and Corporal J. M. Holland. Passed the time as merrily as soldiers usually do when they are expecting a battle soon[.]

On the 8th we advanced about three miles and encamped on a steep hillside in plain view of the famous Lookout Mountain, but were too far up the valley to obtain a view of the point, and were utterly unconscious that we were so near Chattanooga, and as much so of its topographical position. Thus to sleep that night in *blissful* ignorance of the whereabouts of the other Corps, and of the operations of the Confederate Army.

Wed Sept. 9th. Our Brigade was aroused and started on the march early this morning, it was said with orders to "clear Lookout Mountain of rebels". After marching and counter-marching in the valley through fields of corn and high weeds, we finally (near sunrise) struck the right road near the foot of the mountains and commenced the toilsome ascent. The mountain was not very high, and we ascended at a kind of low gap, but there were no level spots along the side of the mountain, popularly known as benches, to interrupt the one long steep ascent that continued from the very foot of the mountain to the summit, and consequently the assent was very fatiguing and we were in constant expectation of being fired upon by the imaginary enemy on the summit.

Not a single vehicle of any description accompanied us, and in fact such thing would have been impossible. We finally, much to our surprise, reached the summit of the mountain about 2 hours after sunrise without meeting any obstacle in the shape of an armed foe, and were halted and allowed to rest awhile. A detachment from the signal corps had accompanied us and they soon had their glasses poised and flag waving, endeavoring to attract the attention of the occupants of a signal station near the site of our previous night's encampment, but I think they finally did not succeed on account of the air being filled with dust that was raised by long trains of wagons and lines of troops that we could now see going down the valley in the direction of the Point Lookout. About 10 o'clock A.M. we started in the same direction on the ridge of the mountain, and were near sixteen miles from the Lookout House.[18] We suffered much from the great heat, and scarcity of the water, which was also of a very inferior article, and tasted strongly of coppers. Weary, hot and thirsty, we arrived at Lookout House late in the afternoon, and as we were marched down in front of the principal dwelling and so near the edge of the awful precipice that abruptly breaks off from the level of the top of the mountain, I cast my eyes in an easterly direction and, oh ye admirers of the beautiful scenes of nature! a sight here met my astonished gaze, that for extent of territory, variegated beauty, and diversity of scenery, far exceeded anything it had ever been my fortune to witness. Almost beneath my feet a high ridge ran through the valley almost parallel with the one on which I stood, but the height of which was so scarcely perceivable from my elevated position that simply resembled a forest level in common with the surrounding fields. Some miles beyond this long, evenly carved Mission Ridge rose in gentle hills above all the surroundings and seemed to form the first line of the beautiful background that rose ridge behind ridge, higher and higher for many miles, till the beautiful train was gradually hid from view by the lovely azure that seemed with a spirit of jealousy to interfere to curtail the extent of my vision, as if it were hiding something beyond too sacred for morality to behold.

I turned my eyes toward the mouth of the valley and saw the placid, and now beautiful Tennessee River winding in gentle curves among fields and forests, and finally losing itself from my view behind the swell of the mountain. My eyes then went back up the stream and soon fell upon what! do my senses deceive me? is the jewel for which we have so long and arduously toiled to be so easily won when we had expected that the greater part of the price was yet unpaid? is our Army to be allowed to march in and quietly take possession of what has been considered the main joint in the backbone of the Confederacy? No, my eyes did not deceive me for away up the river, so far off that the largest houses looked scarcely larger than a "dog tent", and which all almost hidden from view by the intervening trees—so much so that it hardly had the resemblance of a town—I saw Chattanooga; but was much disappointed in its general appearance. I had expected to see numerous lofty spires; steam puffing from a hundred engines; columns moving about the scanty rifle pits; huge redoubts seeming by their very weight to defy all assault; rebel banners floating from every tree; but of all these I saw nothing. But one or two spires were visible; scarcely enough smoke was ascending from the city to justify the belief that it was inhabited; no heavy columns of rebels and scarcely a living being was visible about the city; a few lines of rifle pits seeming to be mere marks could be seen above the city. But why could we see no rebels? Borrowing a glass from a comrade for a few moments I looked over to the right of the city and saw a cavalry force marching under the stars and stripes and dressed in blue.[19] This explained all without the need of the further evidence I obtained on casting my eyes down almost under my feet and there seeing our Corps coming around the point of the mountain and marching off in the direction of Rossville. The joyful reverie into which this beautiful scene and the good news was fast hurrying me was suddenly interrupted by hearing the cries of [a] female who appeared to be much excited. I turned my head and saw a woman—moderately young, of ordinary beauty, possessing a considerable degree of intelligence and some education, probably never celebrated for possessing an excessive amount of modesty, finely formed, unmarried (for she spoke of a sweetheart), and altogether neither attracting nor repulsive in person or manners.

She had become greatly enraged, it seemed, in consequence of our presence on the mountain, and the rebels' *non*-presence in Chattanooga, and she was holding forth in violent strains of ———— to a crowd of "eager listeners" who had gathered around the doorstep, and who were seemingly much edified by her discourse as the loud peals of laughter in which they frequently responded to some ridiculously unreasonable or funny remark of the fair orator.

She discussed the merits of the respective armies, told us that her sweetheart was an officer in Bragg's army and had promised to pay her a visit in three weeks "and he *will* come";[20] she gave it a strong emphasis and gestured in a manner that was almost bewitching to behold. It was truly interesting to witness the amazement and diversion of our boys as they would happen to be passing and catch sight and sound of this principal supporter of the rebellion. Some of them would pass and with astonishment listen a few moments and then with an indescribable (but which I think will bear the definition of suppressed contempt) G-d d-a-m-n would turn away, wondering if Barnum wouldn't give a handsome [sum] for such a prodigy. Others would attempt to reply to some of her sarcastic expressions, but they were all taken aback by the rapidity [and] volubility with which her tongue kept up a continual chatter, and which did not give an opportunity for the wittiest of our boys to slip in a word edgewise.

She raved, and clapped her hands, and stamped her pretty feet, (oh, if [I] was a shoemaker), and performed other wonderful feats with such energy and in such rapid succession that she about worked herself into such a pitch of excitement that I feared for her life, but she soon began to perspire freely and her excitement began to give way to great exhaustion and she was compelled to sit down upon the floor, but she still continued our "services," but we were prevented from hearing or seeing the catastrophe to this wonderful living drama by the bugles sounding *attention*. We started down the mountain some minutes before sunset and marched to Rossville that night over one of the dustiest roads it has ever been my fortune to travel, and arrived in camp about 9 o'clock almost suffocated with dust, and almost worn out by our days march, which could not have been much less than thirty miles, and ascended a mountain and traveled near 16 miles with almost no water.

We had expected when we discovered that the rebels had gone that the campaign would cease for awhile and that we would again get a few days of rest, but every movement this evening seemed to indicate that active operations would continue. Why were we not marched to Chattanooga instead of Rossville? and why are we ordered to retain our extra ammunition and to procure more rations when we have two days supply on hand? and more than all, where are the 14th and 20th Corps?

Thur. Sept. 10th—Received letters from home stating that my father is at the point of death and all hopes of recovery given up.[21] It is useless for me to attempt to describe my feelings at this news; but after a first pang of sorrow it seemed that my heart suddenly became dulled against it and all the other tormenting anxieties that I had suffered in the last few days, and for several days following this [I had] a kind of feeling of disregard for any misfortune that might come upon me. I was so near a hypochondriac state of mind, that I rather welcomed than dreaded the evident prospects of a battle, and so much had my mind sunk under the mental suffering of the last few days that I fancied I rather preferred than wished to avoid death; but these foolish fancies were destined to be vanished at an early day, and sad experience was soon to cause me to gladly avail myself of the friendly shelter of a tree or log to avoid the whizzing bullets and murmuring shells as they went crashing by.

Our Corps moved out early this morning in the direction of Ringgold Ga. and traveled about 5 miles and then formed into line of battle and encamped. The Division in advance of us were keeping up a sharp skirmish with the enemy when we went into camp, and the advance guard, composed of about 60 men of the 3rd Ky Infantry, had been captured near the present skirmish line.[22] A sharp picket firing was kept up during the most of the night and many of our soldiers were wounded. We retired to rest that night still in ignorance, but very anxious about the whereabouts of Thomas & McCook.

Fri. Sept. 11th—March early on the Ringgold road and almost simultaneously with the command *forward* the skirmishing is resumed and was kept up with slight interruptions till we reached Ringgold, and here the enemy attempted to make a stand, and our artillery was ordered to go forward and throw a few shells into the enemy's line; that soon caused them to again start off down the railroad toward Dalton. At this place we were joined by Col. Wilder's Brigade of Mounted Infantry,[23] and they drove the enemy on in advance some 5 or six miles, but could not hurry them fast enough to prevent them setting fire to every trestle work and bridge along the railroad, and as the continued dry weather had rendered all woodwork very combustible, it was useless to attempt to extinguish the fires. Wilder lost 2 men killed, and captured two dead and two wounded rebels.

We encamped about two miles beyond town near the railroad in a pleasant grove of trees and feast[ed] like kings through the night on Georgia Pork and mutton, seasoned with U.S. salt and "washed down" with U.S. Coffee. By this time I actually began to feel very uneasy that our Corps should be away out here in the vicinity of the whole rebel army and much scattered out that to watch different points, and the other Corps gone to—Rosecrans knows where. I wisely concluded that our general knew his business and strove to not suffer it to puzzle my brains any further.

Sat Sept 12th—march back through Ringgold early this morning and take the road leading to Lee and Gordon's mills, at which place we arrived about three o'clock in the afternoon, and that the first Division of our Corps had gone there on the morning of the previous day and had a severe skirmish with the enemy who happened to be at that place.[24] We cross[ed] the stream (Chickamauga River[)] just below the mill, then moved up a few yards and encamped, and there many of us accepted the *tempting* opportunity to take a bath in the mill pond.

Sun. Sept. 13th—Our Brigade was sent out this morning to feel the enemy to ascertain if possible his strength. We had scarcely cleared the picket line ere the skirmishing began with considerable warmth on both sides, but the rebels fell back slowly for about one mile, and then opened a battery upon our skirmish line. Capt. Drewry (Chief of artillery of our Division) immediately ran one of his batteries from the road onto an adjacent cornfield, and by a careful movement, and sheltered by the tall green corn he got a commanding position over the enemy and the first shots started them off in a considerable hurry. But while riding around seeking a good position for his guns Capt Drewry was severely wounded by a rebel sharpshooter, and was borne off, as we thought in a dying condition. We then followed them about two miles further, skirmishing all the time, when we again were ordered to halt by receiving the fire of the enemy's artillery. They were behind a skirt of woods that was so filled with underbrush, that our artillery men could not get sight of them though I think the two batteries were not more than three hundred yards apart. The rebels worked their cannons with great fury for a few moments, and fatally wounded two men of the 19th Ohio, which Regiment was lying near our *battery*. Our artillerists soon got range of the enemy's guns and then they put it to them in such style that they soon ceased to annoy us. We then returned to camp, but were compelled to march in line of battle and keep skirmishers deployed in our rear for the rebels followed us at a respectable distance till we regained our lines. Lieut. Clark of the 79th Ind was wounded by a rebel sharpshooter. There were no casualties in our regiment.

We had been out to *feel* the enemy, and the unanimous decision of the boys, when we returned to Camp was "that they didn't feel very good."[25]

Mon Sept. 14th. Our Corps was marched across the country in the direction of Chattanooga valley.—Stopped on the road about noon and remained till near dark, then went into the edge of the valley about six miles from Lee & Gordon's mills and encamped.

This movement puzzled us all very much, and served to increase our perplexity as to the whereabouts of Genl's. Thomas and McCook.[26] In fact affairs began to be a gloomy aspect, which the joy at the recent capture of Chattanooga could not entirely dispel. Rations were for some unaccountable reason growing very scarce, and we were reduced to the necessity of subsisting (in the meat line) almost entirely upon Georgia pork and that principally without salt; but we were yet receiving tolerable liberal quantities of "hard tack" and sugar and coffee, and when a soldier has plenty of these he hardly ever grumbles, especially if he is on a march. It had now been weeks since a drop of rain had fallen and therefore the roads were becoming intolerably disagreeable, and the dusty sand that would accumulate on our bodies in one day's travel, greatly interfered with our rest at night. I was sent on picket that night, and had to establish the line myself, and that in one of roughest *roughs* imaginable, that can be composed of steep rocky hillsides and an almost impossible underbrush assisted by the darkness of a very dark night.

Tu. Sept. 15th—marched back in the direction from which we came on the previous day about four miles, and encamped near the celebrated Crawfish springs.[27]

After we had stacked arms, and before we received the command to *break ranks*, Colonel Cram pointed to a drove of hogs that were grunting and munching but a short distance from us, and which were very numerous, and large and fat, and remarked "I have bought all the hogs in this country, boys, but if you are mean enough to take them from me I can't help it, break ranks." The boys were not so dull of perception that they could not at once see that this was a hint for them to make some *provision* for their empty haversacks and hungry stomachs; consequently the last command of the Colonel was the signal for a general charge upon the unlucky representatives of the swinish population of Georgia, and they made it with a yell that would have been worthy of a much more difficult and dangerous undertaking, but which resulted in the speedy Killing and dressing of a sufficient quantity of meat to feed the regiment bountifully for some days. Some of the boys found a sufficiency of salt in a neighboring barn. Our camp here was in a pleasant situation and the water was of the first quality, as everyone knows who has ever drank of the clear and cooling water of Crawfish springs.

We remained at this place the next day, and finally began to hear some correct rumors as to the whereabouts of the other two Corps, but the news did not serve to satisfy us any when we were informed that Thomas was twenty, and McCook at least forty miles away, for we believed, from the actions of the enemy, that they were reinforcing heavily, and had hardly the confidence in our little Corps that it could withstand an attack from the whole rebel army. Gen. Rosecrans came to the Springs and put up his headquarters on this evening, and this event raised our spirits to some extent[.]

On the 17th the air became much cooler, but still we had no rain. There was a little skirmishing in the evening on our front, but nothing of unusual interest occurred, and we remained in our camp throughout the day.

Fri. Sept. 18th. There was much skirmishing along our whole front on this day, and occasionally some cannonading.[28] A shell from a rebel cannon passed through Col. [Sidney M.] Barnes' (Col. 8th Ky now comdg. 3rd Brig. of our Division)[29] marquee early in the evening. This incident caused me to give way in a degree to the impression that our commanders didn't know exactly what they were at or where the rebels were at. About noon our Division was moved to the left, and thrown into position near to and facing the river just below the mills. Sharp skirmishing throughout the evening in our immediate front, and a heavy cannonading away to the left. Late in the afternoon ambulances loaded with wounded began to come from that direction, and we learned that Col. Minty's Cavalry Brigade had had a severe battle with the enemy, and that they were finally hard pushed and nearly surrounded by Infantry and after being sadly cut to pieces were compelled to retire.[30]

About sunset the forces who had defeated Minty made a keen attack upon the left of our Division, but as they found our boys wide awake and laying on their arms they quickly gave back, but not until they had received two or three terrible volleys from the 44th Ind and the 59th Ohio. Our Brigade was moved in double quick toward the scene as soon as the firing began but ere we could reach the spot, the firing had ceased.[31] The direction of the line was somewhat changed and we were ordered to stack arms, and "every man to lay near his own gun.["] The left of our regiment rested upon the road. The night was exceedingly cool and from the fact that I and my bedfellow had left our woolen blankets with the wagons we slept but little, and even if we could have been comfortably warm, re-freshing sleep would have been almost an impossibility, for troops were passing the road and going on to the left by thousands at intervals through the night, and the immense clouds of dust that were raised by their weary dragging feet rendered breathing ex-ceedingly disagreeable, and sometimes almost painful. These troops were a part of the lost Corps[32] and we were now revived by the thought that our Corps would not have to contend single handed against the whole rebel army.

The extensive preparations that were being made through the night—the occasionally dull rattling of a arriving battery,—the almost incessant tramping of galloping horses—the watchfulness that seemed to be kept up by various commanders—the passing troops, and in fact every indication was that we would have a severe fight on the next day. And the occasional crash of an enemy picket sentinel's musket told too plainly to admit of any doubt that the rebel army was confronting every portion of our line and was un-doubtedly strong enough to ably contest the issues of tomorrow with us. But the night passed off quietly without a single alarm occurring to interrupt the slumbers of those that *could* sleep.

Chapter 8

❧

The Hills and Thick Forests
of Chickamauga

"Chickamauga," according to legend, means "river of death." A river of blood flowed during two late summer days in 1863, as the men in blue and gray killed and maimed each other in the dense woods of northern Georgia. The battle began early on September 19, when a Federal reconnaissance encountered Nathan Bedford Forrest's dismounted cavalry just west of Chickamauga Creek at Jay's Mill. More and more units were swept into the vortex of battle, and soon a general engagement had broken out along the La Fayette Road. At the end of the day, despite bloody fighting, often hand to hand, neither side had gained an advantage.

The second day was different. By morning, Bragg's Army of Tennessee had been augmented by five additional brigades, Army of Northern Virginia veterans under the command of Lt. Gen. James Longstreet. Longstreet and the last two brigades arrived during the night. At 11:30 A.M., his wing of the Confederate force hit the Federal line just at the point where Rosecrans inadvertently had left a gap. The result was a disaster. Confederates smashed through the breach and rolled back the now-terrified Federals. Rosecrans, Crittenden, and several thousand others fled to Chattanooga. Only Maj. Gen. George Thomas's dramatic stand on Horseshoe Ridge, coupled with the timely arrival of Maj. Gen. Gordon Granger's Reserve Corps, saved the Army of the Cumberland from destruction.

Chickamauga spelled wounded pride as well as bloody battle for Woodcock and the 9th Kentucky. On both days, the regiment broke in the face of fierce Confederate attacks. On the evening of the nineteenth, Woodcock wrote that "we had been compelled to retreat in a very disorderly manner." That was nothing, however, compared to his regiment's near-complete disintegration the following morn-

ing. It was the chaos of the second day's rout that separated Woodcock from his regiment, left him "considerably demoralized," and
placed him in line on Horseshoe Ridge.[1]

*Sat Sept 19th. This day is famous in American history as the first one
of the most unequal struggle that* the gallant and (hitherto considered)
almost invincible Army of the Cumberland was ever called upon to
make. This was the day on which many a brave patriot, and rebel
drenched the soil in their blood, without any definite result except
to warm the ardor of their friends and cause them to rush pell mell
into the awful scenes of the succeeding day.

The sun rose clear and beautiful, and shed his cheering warmth
over our dusty soldiers, and quickly driving away the chilly vapors
of the preceding night, only to replace them with his more uncomfortable heat.

The unusual stillness of the morning was first broken into by
a furious cannonading commencing on the left of our Corps, about
7 o'clock A.M. It was not kept up a great while and we were informed that the enemy had charged upon our troops but had "met
with a most magnificent repulse."[2] As the heavy booming of the
artillery died away we could hear a deep and heavy rolling of a
continual discharge of artillery away to the right, but could not
conjecture what it meant, and began to feel very apprehensive that
the enemy were attempting to turn our right and enter the Chattanooga valley. This soon in a measure died away and then for a
time, all was comparatively quiet; but it was only that lull in the
storm from which it breaks forth with renewed vigor and over-
whelms everything in its onward and resistless course. Though we
could not for a considerable time hear more than an occasional
boom of cannon, yet all seemed forcibly impressed with the con-
viction that we would have some awful work to do ere nightfall.
The soldiers sat pensively in their places clutching their deadly rifles
and casting apprehensive glances on every orderly that rode past,
as if they thought he was bringing an *order* for our advance.

They listened with eager interest at each discharge of a gun as
if they expected it to be followed by a volley; and with anxious
countenances they would turn to each other and talk concerning
the probable strength of the enemy and the result of the battle.

About 10 o'clock the rebels again charged upon our army away to the right and were again repulsed, and then so far as we could hear, everything again assumed a comparative quietness, though the fierceness of the skirmishing was increasing with a rapidity that evidently proved that the crisis must soon come.[3]

Oh how can I portray the anguish of mind the soldier suffers while he is waiting in dread expectation of a battle!

What were my feelings as I lay there on that gloomy morning and calculated the chances that I felt I would certainly have of being a bloody and mangled corpse before night? How my heart was rung with conflicting emotions as I looked around upon my beloved comrades, and wondered which of them would ere night have received the fatal messenger and be called abruptly from us to realize the awfulness of Eternity! If I should live, how many of my comrades had spent their last happy hour on the earth, and with whom I had spent my last agreeable moment? I endured such heart-rending thoughts as these till I actually prayed for the battle to begin, for then one has no time for meditation, and when it is over his agonizing apprehensions are to some extent converted into less painful but stern realities. But these meditations were again broken into about noon by the enemy making another grand and heavy charge on our left.[4] The heavy boom was soon almost lost in the incessant and increasing volume of musketry, which was now getting louder and louder as additional troops came into the contest, and the volleys were soon lost in one continual roar, proving to our anxious minds that the fight had now begun in earnest;—that the opponents had now so far committed themselves to the struggle that neither could withdraw without acknowledging a defeat, and therefore the reason for knowing that the battle had really begun[.] All ears were now listening with intense eagerness to see if they could distinguish by the sound whether either party was gaining ground, and all eyes were bent in that direction to detect any stragglers that might happen to be leaving the scene. Presently a staff officer dashes up to Gen Van Cleve's head quarters; and then one of his staff to Gen Beatty's head quarters—The bugle sounds *attention*—the boys *straighten* themselves for they had sprung to their guns upon the commencement of the fight—our Division was going at "double quick" "left in front" away down the road toward the conflict.[5] Nearer and nearer we approach the awful conflict which seems to be going on without any relaxation or gain on either side—directly we found ourselves a few hundred yards in rear of our line—here we pass Gen Crittenden and staff who were quietly halted in the road, as if awaiting the issue, but now our road took a turn, and soon brought us upon the scene just on the left of our engaging line; as the Regiments were moving "left in front" they had nothing to do as they cleared the other line but just to *front* and "pitch in" to shooting. We were almost completely exhausted by the long run we had been compelled to make (nearly two miles) and at a short distance our troops looked very similarly to "grey backs." Our Brigade fronted, regiment at a time those that fronted first commencing a musketry fight with the enemy till our regiment (which had been on the extreme right) came into line, and then the whole Brigade made a general charge, driving the enemy back for several hundred yards and capturing a battery of four guns in the meantime.[6] We then halted and commenced a general musketry upon a new line of rebels that made their appearance in our front, as if to shelter their flying comrades.[7]

We fired at them a considerable time when they disappeared from view, and for a moment there was a suspension of the firing in our Brigade. We almost began to come to the conclusion that we would not be molested further during the evening, and if such should be the case we considered ourselves lucky though we had lost several wounded in the Regiment; but we had not rested many minutes till we saw, away through an opening in the woods, heavy columns of rebels going to the right—Where are they going?—is our right properly protected?—Those movements foretell that the storm will soon be on us again in all its fury. The gallant Capt. [Alanson] Stephens with his ——— battery[8] comes right up to our line and asks what he must do—No General, but Col. Cram points to the heavy columns moving away to the right and advises the Captain to give them some of his "most suitable pills[.]"

He immediately wheels and has his battery unlimbered to the front,—one piece almost in the midst of my Company and opens a furious cannonading upon the enemy, throwing grape and cannister among them at a fearful rate.

This seems to *awake* a rebel battery which was in our front and much closer than was comfortable, and the answering showers of grape and cannister whizzed with *hurting* sounds over and through our ranks, and occasionally doing execution. Presently the rebel infantry fell with resistless force upon our right,[9] but our boys met them with a determined resolution well worthy of a better arrangement of troops; but the enemy's line is advancing almost at right angles with our right, and consequently they are subjected to a heavy front and flank fire—with intense eagerness we watch this unequal contest (for the woods were so open that we could see to a considerable distance)—but soon our line begins to waver, and then to fall back in great disorder, upon which the rebels set up a deafening yell and bound forward in the pursuit, like so many grayhounds when they first catch sight of the wearied line. Eagerly do we cast our eyes back on the supporting line relying upon us now to save the day to our arms, but oh! the supporting line has disappeared;[10] it has been deployed on the right and left of the Brigade and consequently there now was no supporting line, and the rebels, unchecked, came down upon the right of our regiment with the fury of a tornado, and we were immediately subjected to a most murderous raking fire. Capt Stephens stood gallantly to his guns and poured the deadly missiles upon the enemy with terrible effect. At this critical moment, one of our batteries,[11] away in the rear of course, commenced throwing shells into our regiment and Captain S———'s battery with commendable accuracy and terrible effect—one of the shells bursted in the midst of Cos. G and K and severely stunned Lieut Rodes and several men. Never have I seen our regiment or any other act with such extraordinary coolness at any other time as ours did this evening. The clear, calm, and steady voice with which Col. Cram uttered his commands seemed to reassure everyone, and although the enemy were now almost upon us, and had us partially surrounded and our boys were being killed and wounded by the score yet they plied their muskets with a resolution that seemed to say "we will stand till ordered to retreat or die in the attempt." Every since we commenced fighting early in the forenoon, the various commands had been given (as much as practicable) by the bugle, and the promptness and precision with which they were obeyed seemed to create a kind of mutual confidence among the members of the regiment.

But the right of our regiment soon found it too hard pressed to stand any longer, and really it would have been evident to a casual observer some minutes previous to this time that we must either soon fall back, surrender, or be completely cut to pieces, yet Capt. Stephens never attempted to limber his guns till our regiment began to fall back, and just then a shell from one of our batteries (before referred to) bursted in the midst of his horses and killed and wounded several, and so completely frightened the rest that it was impossible to bring off but two of the guns; for simultaneously with the first wavering on the right of the regiment, Col. Cram gave the order to *retreat* and away we went in great disorder for near one fourth of a mile, when a partial rally of our regiment and some others is effected.[12] As the rebels had stopped shooting for a moment, no doubt to reform their lines we got a sort of a line rallied. Just then Corporal Clarke of my Company asked me to come to him, upon which he pointed through an opening in the timber, and not more than three hundred yards off, I espied the rebel line advancing[13] and their flag was distinctly visible. Clark said "do you see that G———d d———nd yaller rag? oh, how I would love to shoot its bearer." I was almost amused at the fellows earnestness, and disgust upon seeing this traitors emblem, but we had no time for meditation, for just then this line opened a terrible volley upon us again which was too much for our thin and straggling line to withstand and after giving them an answering volley we again broke, if possible, in greater disorder than before.[14]

Adjutant Shepperd wounded. The rebels followed in *close* order, but we soon passed through several batteries that were parked along a low ridge in an open field[15] and which gave the enemy a momentary check till fresh troops began to arrive from the right and we were soon freed from further work during the evening, and well was it for us, for we were so badly cut to pieces and scattered that I dont think one half of the Brigade was present when we halted some distance in the rear and bivouacked for the night. It was truly discouraging to witness the condition of our Division as we were compelled to fall back that evening, and I at one time almost came to the conclusion that the whole army was retreating. But on dark many stragglers who had been lost in the retreat came in, and we found that our regiment had suffered comparatively small loss either in killed or wounded. We had lost one killed from our company[16] and had been compelled to leave him on the battle field and as we supposed the ground to be now in possession of the enemy we had to suffer the painful uncertainties of his receiving even a desent soldiers burial. But the battle raged if possible more fiercely than ever after we fell back, and after dark we, from our camps, beheld one of the most magnificent scenes that is ever witnessed in any battle, to wit, a heavy musketry and artillery contest just a few hundred yards to the front and slightly on the left of our position.[17]

In the contemplation of the awful grandeur of the scene I for a moment forgot the imminent danger of the actions, and that incidents were occurring every moment that would send sorrow to many a peaceful and happy fireside—that these thousands that were now seemingly getting up a scene for fancy's eye, were momentarily experiencing sufferings of every grade from the slightest pain to the awful pang of death every time a fresh volley served to increase the redness of the broad red glare that seemed to hover over the heads of the contending lines, it carried death faster and thicker among the suffering troops; but at length the sound of battle died away and with the advantages of the struggle on our side.

Notwithstanding the fact that *our* Division had been roughly handled during the evening, and that we had been compelled to retreat in a very disorderly manner, and had suffered very heavily in killed and wounded, yet we were satisfied with the news that we got from the rest of the army. It seemed that on almost every other part of the field our troops had come off victorious, and every passerby had a long story to tell about the great doings of his regiment or Brigade—all were flushed with what seemed to be a victory, or at what they were sure was only the beginning of a victory for to-morrow.

But the suspicion of one fact was the source of much earnest conversation and of many doubtful surmises among the boys, and that was a general belief among all parties that Bragg's Army had been largely reinforced by troops from Virginia, and that belief had received confirmations this evening. A forest of rebels charged upon Davis' Division (?)[18] of the 14th A.C.—They came on with a grand rush and panther-like yells which seemed to the *Regular Brigade*[19] to greatly exceed a similar movement by any portion of Bragg's *former* army both in irresistible force and human-frightening ferocity; from the fact that the terror of their yells was "Eastern troops"—

"Bull Run", &c. These cries (or something else) so frightened the Regular Brigade that they broke and fled in confusion leaving their battery in full trim and ready for operations, minus not a single horse. Next in rear of this Brigade lay a volunteer Brigade, the front line being composed of the 9th Ohio and 2nd Min. Vols. As soon as the demoralized regulars had cleared this line to the rear, it rose with a "damn your Eastern troops" and made such a terrible counter-charge upon the enemy that he was soon discomfited and driven from the field

I retired to rest late at night on a steep hill side,[20] with no bedding but two gum blankets, and a fence rail on the lower side of me to prevent me from rolling down the hill in my sleepy hours. My bed-fellow of the preceding night (1st Sergt William B. Roddy) had been severely wounded and carried to the rear during the fight, and I now had to fill his place with another member of the company who had also lost a companion wounded in the same fight. But a soldier is rarely known to entertain gloomy thoughts just after a battle, no matter what may have been its results, consequently I enjoyed a fine nights rest, and had pleasant dreams of terrible hand-to-hand struggles, in which our banner was always covered with the laurels of victory and the enemy completely exterminated. Oh, how uncertain is life!—on that night thousands sought the welcome arms of Morpheus, and enjoyed the soothing refreshment of a good nights rest as if unconscious of the many chances there were for a battle on the next day—full of hope, and without those torturing presentiments that frequently visit the poor soldier on the eve of battle many a gallant heart beat uninterruptedly through that long night while the body was calmly reposing from the labors of the previous day, and which was on the next day to receive the fatal messenger, that was either to bring death or severe suffering to its unfortunate possessor. Calmly did many a mind wander away to distant homes and firesides; to the anxieties of fond parents; to well-wishing brothers and sisters; to beloved wives and little ones; or to some gentle maiden, whose last word was love and hope, and a promise to not forget.—Calmly did they mentally speculate upon the prospects of their living through the service, and relating to these dear ones the many dangers and hair-breadth escapes they had undergone. But at midnight all was comparatively quiet, and the picket firing was probably more scattering and infrequent than on the night previous.

Sun. Sept. 20th. There was a heavy frost on the ground this morning, and the air was very cool, but the rising and unclouded sun soon dispersed the cool vapors, and we were greeted with the prospect of another warm day.

Early after sunrise our Division was marched back into a hollow and received three days rations of meat and *hard* tack.[21] Wagons were here collected thickly in all parts of the valley, and we saw one almost complete regiment of rebels (17th Tenn) who had been captured on the previous evening;[22] besides these, we saw several other squads of prisoners. For a time after sunrise everything was unusually quiet and at one time I began to think that some change had been made in the rebels programme or that they had probably concluded to decline a battle.

The skirmishing would sometimes break out afresh and for a time seem to indicate that something was going to be done but then all would die away again.

Sometimes a battery would peal forth in thundering tones for one or two successive rounds, without apparently having any more effect than to disturb the general stillness of the scene. Soon our Division was moved forward to the crest of the ridge, and the different regiments formed in "column of Division" that they might easily be deployed into line of battle. This position gave us a view over an extensive field and we could see our troops moving to and fro in every direction as if making preparations for some great undertaking.[23]

About this time the skirmishing began to increase in severity, and the frequent vollies told that the combatants were becoming warmed up to their work.

From the position that had been assigned to our Division, we all naturally came to the conclusion that our duty was to act as a reserve force to our Corps, and we knew that the expected battle would have to assume a desperate character if we were called into the struggle; therefore we had a two-fold reason for desiring that we would be so lucky as to not have to participate in the engagement of the day.

It was a sad scene to look upon our Division, so greatly decimated that Brigades were scarcely larger than full Regiments, the men stiff, sore, and battleworn from the almost super-human exertions of yesterday, and yet conscious from the increasing severity of the skirmishing and an occasional heavy volley away to the right or left that we would have to again come in for our share of the terrible work. Suddenly the skirmishing became unusually severe in our immediate front and extending away to the left, and everyone seemed to at once conclude that an attack was being made by one of the opposing armies.[24]—The bugles sounded *attention*, and we were moved a few yards toward the front—Staff officers were now flying in all directions, as if carrying the last order for making dispositions for the final struggle—Batteries of artillery were parked along the ridge in our rear, and the cannoniers were standing at their pieces anxiously looking to the valley below where the battle was soon to rage in all its fury, and attentively listening for a command to commence firing upon some point.

Presently the battle opened away to the left, and soon afterwards we could hear that the work was going on away to the right; it seemed that the fight was raging at two or three different points along the line but as yet not very near to our position. Our Division was moved down nearer to the front line.[25] About eleven o'clock A.M. the enemy made a furious attack upon the left of our corps, and soon the sound of musketry and artillery assumed an extent of volume and fearfulness of rapidity that is rarely exceeded; louder and more frequent grew the vollies till they were lost in one continual roar proving to us that a desperate effort was being made and oh, how anxiously did we await the issue. It soon became evident that our troops were hard pressed, for they seemed to be falling back—A Division was called up from the line just in our front and went away to the left, and again for a moment it seemed that our boys were likely to hold their ground; but soon we discovered this to be a mistake; we cast our eyes in that direction and could see thousands of stragglers in a confused and helpless mass pouring to the rear through a skirt of timber, and emerging into the open fields in a state of hopeless confusion. At this critical period of affairs— with our right and center greatly weakened to reinforce the left, and the left already hopelessly broken. Our Division was ordered to the left; changes of directions were immediately effected and we had just received the order to "double quick," but just as this order rang along the line a new event occurred that caused it to be immediately, and before we could commence to carry it into execution, countermanded.[26]

A heavy attack was made on our immediate front, and extending away to the right;[27] our Division again changed directions, but by the time this movement was effected, the deadly grape and cannister were flying so thick through our ranks that we were ordered to lie down and await the result of the contest that might be made by the slim line now in our front—On the enemy came with a valor that was worthy of men fighting for any cause, and with a force that was only to be checked by unexcelled valor and countless numbers.

We knew that bravery and patriotism were in our front, but alas! it had but few representatives—our thin lines were swept down before the mighty storm of grape and cannister and musket balls like chaff before the whirlwind.—They made a gallant struggle, but everyone could see that they must soon give way. The rebels were now so close on our front line that the deathly missiles of every description were flying thick over and around us, and we were compelled to shield ourselves by lying close to the ground branches of trees cut off by the flying cannon balls, were flying thick in every direction presently the front line broke[28] and back they came in helpless confusion running over us as we lay upon the ground, and kept on their way to the rear next came the front line of our Brigade,[29] which was so badly demoralized by the issue of the contest in front, and by the unearthly yells of the now rapidly approaching and victory flushed rebels that they came running back in as demoralized a condition as the front line, and unceremoniously running over us they also followed in the wake of the others—next came the caissons of a battery that was rapidly working in our front, and heedless of our inability to be run over by the heavy wagons without the probability of being smashed they also made a dash to pass through our recumbent column.[30] This was more than human nature could bear—we had already submitted to the humiliation of being run over by two columns, and many of us could test that members of this column were *weighty* and wore new shoes, but when we saw the caissons coming toward us, we instinctively began to *open in-*

tervals to give them room to pass to the rear—This movement was misunderstood by many as an intention to join the retreating columns, and followed by the remainder of course, they immediately broke and even we were rolling in a confused mass to the rear, but this was too much for the 9th Ky many a soldier yelled out "never let it be said that the 9th Ky ran without firing a gun."—Our gallant Colonel spurred his horse in advance of us, and then whirling around and waving his sword over his head he called out for "one more effort to be made by the 9th Ky." Obedient to his command the regiment halted and about faced, and was soon placed in tolerable order, and then with as loud a yell as two hundred men can raise we again dashed at the now invincible enemy. This was a trying moment to any participant in the struggle. As far as we could see to the right and left our troops were falling back by thousands, and being closely pursued and continually shot down by the countless number of the enemy, who had not yet emerged into the open field. Those in our front seemed astonished at our rashness in attempting to check such a heavy and impetuous movement, but they had come to a halt, and as we charged forward at a run, they poured an awful fire of musketry and artillery into our ranks, but onward we went, our regiment alone with the exception of a gallant handful of the 19th ohio who with their colors and *one officer* (promoted to Adjutant after the Regiment re-enlisted)[31] who had rallied on the left, and seemed determined to die or remain with us. Oh the terrible feelings that must have possessed the heart of any witness of this scene—there were less than three hundred men, regardlessly throwing themselves into the scale against thousands of the enemy, who were rendered more furious by their recent success on our front lines—every man seemed willing to sacrifice his life if it would in any way retrieve the fortunes of the day which we now saw was surely lost without some almost superhuman effort.—I saw tears streaming from many an eye as the poor boys would cast their eyes to the right, left and rear, and see unmistakable evidence that the day was lost.

But onward was the cry and forward we went near two hundred yards when we came to a small barricade that had been occupied by our front line in the beginning of the engagement.[32] Here we found a battery that had not yet been deserted by its brave cannoniers, but who had been so nearly all shot down by the now closely approaching rebel infantry that there were only enough left to work two of the guns.[33] They raised a feeble but cheerful yell as we came up and seemed to redouble their exertions, yet hoping that the enemy might be driven back and that they might *save their guns*, for their horses being all killed it was now impossible to haul off the pieces. I never shall forget to my dying day the anxious look that was depicted on the countenances of these powder-blackened artillerymen as they heroically worked their cannons, and swore they would not leave as long as their ammunition boxes contained a shot.

When we arrived at the barricade the rebels were not many yards beyond, and were keeping up a terrible fire—we poured a scattering volley into their ranks, and it seemed to have a momentary effect upon them, for they seemed to hesitate a moment, but then they only parted in the center and made a dash at the wings of our short line. A section of Rebel artillery had advanced into the open field within about 150 yards of the barricade and was working rapidly when we came up,[34] but we soon compelled it to hide itself in the trees to the rear. We remained here about five or ten minutes, and struggled hard to maintain our position, but we soon discovered that was worse than useless, for we could distinctly see that the rebels had cleared our line in the rear, both on the right and left, and were rapidly closing in to cut off our retreat.

The command to *retreat* was heard along the line and then we started to run the gauntlet, from which we could not hope to be free till we had retreated at least half a mile. I cast a longing look at the brave artillerists (before mentioned) but they still stood to their guns, and I have no doubt they were either killed or captured to a man.[35] Presently we came to a wide gully that ran along in rear and nearly parallel to the barricade. This gully had been crossed by us as we made the charge, and was at the time literally filled with men who were so cowardly that they would not raise their heads above the surface lest they should be shot, and as we passed over them we tried to induce them to go forward with us, but they never heeded our solicitations. Now we were retreating and when I was in about ten yards of the gully I yelled out to its occupants "retreat or you will be captured," but they only seemed to crouch lower to the ground, and I determined that at least one of them should have an excuse for being captured, so when I was in about three yards of the gully I strung every nerve to the effort and made as lofty and extensive a spring as I possibly could, considering I was greatly retarded by my baggage; but I calculated correctly, and came down on one of the occupants of the gully with a crushing weight, planting my right foot right in the small of his back, and no doubt rendering it necessary for his [captors] to bear him from the field. As my foot struck his body, I brought it around on a kind of a twist and bending that knee and as suddenly straightening it I was soon many yards beyond. If that man is yet living I have no doubt that he has a legible print of my shoe heel on his back, but I am at a loss to know how he will account for it to his friends[.]

When we had fell back about three hundred yards our regiment was so badly scattered that no man could have decided which way it was going, and by some means I had lost sight of the colors, but just as I came to the edge of the open field I saw a flag a short distance to my left and apparently nearly a regiment had rallied around it—I concluded that this was our flag and with a few others turned and took position on the left and commenced firing at the advancing rebels. I soon discovered that this was neither our regiment nor our flag, and looking all around I could see not a single organization or flag of any description, except the long gray lines of rebels who were climbing the ridge away to our right—and now, for the first time, the idea of the possibility of being lost in battle forcibly struck me.

For a moment I was completely bewildered and undecided as to what course to take, but I was soon relieved of any embarrassment by the organization with which I had rallied breaking and flying confusedly to the rear, and it took me no time to decide as to the proper course to take and I immediately commenced a race that would have taken the premium from almost any biped that ever strode the earth. I climbed the hill entirely alone and as I perceived that the rebels in my rear had halted a moment probably to dress their lines for another heavy surge I halted a moment and cast my eyes away to our right proper to see the rebels charging on one of our batteries that was planted on the crest of the hill.[36]

The front line of the enemy was within one hundred yards of the battery which was pouring mines of grape among them with fearful rapidity and apparently doing much execution for at every discharge of a cannon some portion of the rebel line would be completely enveloped in the cloud of dust that was raised by the flying missile, but the enemy seemed to bow their bodies as if in defiance of anything a cannon could do. They were rapidly approaching nearer to the battery which seemed destined to only defend and then be captured, and I was anxiously awaiting the grand catastrophe, when a shower of whizzing balls about my ears convinced me that I had enemies in my rear and that they had again discovered me, and I again beat a hasty retreat up the hill and arrived at the top almost overpowered with heat and exhaustion. I here found a gallant band of near 500 men who seemed to have been gathered from all regiments, and I assure you they were well off and they had formed a solid line at right angles with the ridge and were awaiting for the enemy who were coming from the right to reach the summit of another elevation about 100 yards to the front.[37] Stragglers were joining them continually and they were halting those that evinced a disposition to pass on. I took a position on the left of the line and sat down to breathe a few moments. Just then an officer rode up to me and ordered me to assist in rallying stragglers. I told him I was too nearly exhausted at that moment but would assist him in a moment. He said I was a d———d poor officer and rode away. Soon after the rebels arrived at the crest of the previously mentioned hill, and opened upon us with a heavy volley of musketry—I turned and saw the *brave* officer who had just a few minutes previously spoken to me in such an insulting manner, now going to the rear as fast as his suffering horse could carry him. Just then if I had a loaded rifle I should have taken the pains to spare one rebel, and subtract one from our list of cowards; but other matters called my attention for the rebels had gained the desired position, and the gallant band of stragglers with whom I had rallied had poured a destructive volley into them, and followed their volley with a yell and a charge that sent the rebels pell mell down the hill and across the fields to the woods beyond. We advanced to the spot from which we had drove them, and formed our line again and lay down to let circumstances develop what we should do next. Presently we saw a column emerge from the woods away to the right and advance toward our position at right angles with the original direction of the lines of the two armies in the morning. They were near a half a mile away and exactly resembled Federal soldiers, at least a great many thought so, myself among the rest.[38] The front line had not come far into the field till another came out in its rear and advanced in the same direction. Immediately there was a verbal conflict in our ranks as to whether they were yankees. A Lieut. Col. (the ranking officer present)[39] said they were U.S. troops and ordered us not to fire upon them. A Major said they were rebels and ordered the men to fire. There was but one flag visible in the whole of the two columns and it very much resembled the Kentucky State Flag, hence the ground for deceiving us.[40] They continued to advance toward our position and uncertain what to do, our commander ordered one of the several flags that were with our party to be waved at them to see if they would recognize it, but they did not; still many of us were firm in our belief that they were Federals and used our endeavors to keep the men from firing. When the front line had advanced to within about two hundred yards of our line, several of our boys who were convinced that they were rebels, discharged their muskets at them.

The rebels concluded that their trick had failed, and opened on us with a volley that caused many a brave fellow to bite the dust. I think it did more execution than any volley I ever saw fired, and we all at once saw the necessity of retreating, which we would have done sooner had we not been deceived by the enemy's *blue coats* (for I yet believe they were dressed in something that approached near to the U.S. uniform). This time we were hopelessly scattered by the want of organization and the many banners that were in our squad. I went over the ridge and through the woods about a half a mile to the rear, when I came upon a squad of stragglers, numbering about 50 men who had been rallied by a Colonel. They were placed in charge of a Captain and myself, and we again soon started for the front, taking a path that led in the direction of the point of where I had last seen the enemy, but we had gone but a short distance when we were fired upon by the enemy's skirmish line from a direction that we had little expected. The whole squad immediately broke, with the exception of one or two who stopped to give the enemy a parting shot, and fled, every man in his own direction. The Captain took off up the hill in a line leading most directly from the enemy, and I followed at a speed which I would have considered wonderful, had I not had so much better specimen of the sport just in advance of me, in the rapid movements of the Captain. Reader you may as well know that by this time I was getting considerably demoralized, and I was afraid to move in almost any direction lest I should receive a shot from some rebel, for I began to believe that the woods were literally alive with them.

I could have gone direct to Chattanooga without any danger, but I could not yet get the consent of my mind to go to the rear without making another attempt to find my regiment. Soon after this occurred, I came upon Capt [Orson O.] Miller of Gen Beatty's staff,[41] but he could give me no definite directions as to how I could find my regiment, and this left me almost without hope as to whether I ever would find it at all that day. But I set out according to the *supposition* of Capt. Miller, and had not gone far till I passed through the right wing of a *skirmish line* that was advancing in front of Granger's Corps, and some of the men told me that they had not yet been engaged throughout the whole battle, though it was now at least 3 o'clock in the evening.

I now felt confident that I was at any rate safe from a surprise by the enemy, and concluded to sit down and rest a few moments having had scarcely a moment's rest since the battle with our Corps began in the forenoon and was of course by this time very much exhausted, and finding myself for a few moments out of danger, the excitement in a great measure left me and I stretched myself upon the ground.

But I had not lain there long till I heard but a short distance from me, field officers giving commands to battalions and looking down a hollow that stretched off in the direction of the left of the main line of our army I saw two fine and fresh looking Brigades moving up in rear of the skirmish line that I had just passed through. It was Gen. Steadman's Division of Granger's Corps[42] and they were preparing for an attack on that part of the Rebel line that was just in front. As I had lost all my taste for fighting away from my regiment I immediately effected a change of position and moved to the rear of the line formed by this Division.[43] They moved quietly up to within a few paces of the brow of the hill, and of their skirmish line, and then with a loud and continued succession of yells they charged forward toward the enemy, who soon received them with a heavy fire of musketry and artillery. A short and terrific fight ensued which resulted in the enemy being driven back about 1/4 of a mile, but our troops suffered severely, as the numerous wounded who were borne to the rear gave ample evidence.

A short lull then occurred in the storm of battle, and it began to appear that these gallant troops were going to be allowed to enjoy the fruits of the victory without any more trouble, but it was only a verification of the old song "A calm precedes the most violent storm", for they had not rested many minutes till the enemy made such a charge as was not to be repelled by any but the most obstinate fighting. They bore down upon our front line with almost irrestible force, and judging from their audacious yells and heedless advance they did not expect that our troops would make the slightest attempt to check their progress, but they were for once deceived.[44] The gallant Steadman and his heroic Division received them with galling fire and heroic counter-charge that brought the impetuous rebels to their senses, and caused them to decide to act in a more cautious manner. They made a temporary halt and commenced pouring a destructive fire into our line and making a slow but cautious advance on our line. Our troops were now borne down by the mere force of numbers and compelled to commence a reluctant retreat, and in this way they kept a severe and destructive fight with the enemy for near 1 1/2 miles. Sometimes the enemy would make a dash at our line as if they would force it to break and begin a more rapid retreat, but our boys always received them with an obstinate coolness that seemed to say "I'll die ere I run." The rebel battery[45] would sometimes advance to within a very short [distance] of our line and then for a few moments the destruction would be awful. But still our gallant soldiers still continued to slowly fall back and keep up a continual fire upon the enemy which was beyond all doubt very destructive in their ranks. Finally the enemy seemed satisfied that they could gain nothing by pursuing this line and they came to a halt and left the poor fellows a few moments to breathe. After this struggle ceased I started off in the direction of the left of the army but had not gone far till I came to a road that was literally filled with stragglers going back in the direction of Chattanooga.[46] Wounded men of every description, some traveling without assistance—some who were able to walk were being supported by their comrades, and in many cases had not less than a half a dozen for immediate attendants—Some were being borne upon litters of hasty construction, sometimes a blanket or piece of tent serving as a stretcher—Officers and soldiers of nearly all ranks and departments of the service—squads of rebel prisoners—occasionally a single piece of artillery or a caisson, and in fact there was abundant evidence that a large portion of our army was routed and making a most disorderly retreat. With a heavy heart I joined this throng and for the last time that day turned my face to the direction of Chattanooga and bewildered and confused I determined to go to the rear and trust to Providence to place me with my Regiment.

Soon another road coming into ours from the right of the army was reached, and it was if possible more crowded than the one we were on, and the general crowd of meeting thousands, and numerous wagons rendered this road for a considerable distance beyond, almost impassable.[47] At this point I found I was joined by one member of our regiment, Sergt [David H.] Butram of Co. E;[48] but he could tell no more of the whereabouts of the Regiment than myself for he had become separated from it at the same time I had. We travelled that night to within one mile of Rossville and encamped on the ground of Granger's recent encampment, having found two others of our Regiment in the meantime. Oh what a discouraging sight presented itself! Hundreds of yards in every direction was covered with the innumerable campfires of thousands upon thousands of straggling and disordered troops—without any regularity or organization existing among them. The air was filled with the constant voices of men calling for their regiments, and with the moans and groans of many wounded who were scattered about the camp in charge of their friends.

We could find no one from which to obtain any reliable information of the condition of affairs at the front, but as we could find representatives of almost every Division in the army on every hand; we naturally thought that the whole army had sustained a terrible defeat, and that if the enemy improved their advantages that our army would be completely annihilated. But still I felt hopeful for from the various reports I knew that they had not given away at a single point till they had dealt death to scores of the enemy, and thus I hoped they would not be able to follow on the next day.

Only about 40 men and a few officers of my regiment had been rallied under the Colonel after I became separated from it, but these fought hard till night closed the scene. They were stationed at the point of a ridge from which lines of troops extended back in two directions, and thus they were exposed on two sides to the assaults of the enemy, and they were many and vigorous.[49]

In one instance they made such a desperate assault that our troops at one part of the line near the point gave way for a moment—one of the rebel color bearers leaped over the low barricade that had been erected and waved his colors and called to his comrades to follow. The sight of this hated rag so enraged our wavering troops that they rallied and with a desperate struggle regained their position and drove the Rebels down the hill. The color bearer was killed, but his colors were snatched from across the works and borne off. This was at a point between Granger's Corps and the left of Thomas' Corps, and the fight raged fiercely at short intervals till near dark, when our regiment fell back with the rest of the line and soon joined in with the retreating throng and encamped that night near Rossville.

Thus closed one of the most eventful days that it has ever been my fortune to witness, as well as the most sanguinary that the Army of the Cumberland was ever engaged in. Our army, as every person interested in American affairs well knows, had gained nothing at a single point, but had been driven from the field at all points except that occupied by the troops under the invincible Thomas. Through the whole of that terrible day he had maintained his position on the main road leading from the scene to Chattanooga and had received and repulsed charge after charge from the best disciplined Corps in the Confederate service; but knowing that this was the key to the whole position, and that upon its protection depended the salvation of our army, Gen Rosecrans had sent Division after Division to Gen. Thomas' aid until he had the flower of the army under his command, and with them he won imperishable laurels, and gained another step on the ladder of fame, which he finally ascended to such a height as to become one of the four master spirits of the war.

Though our whole army was compelled that night to give up

this gory field with its precious load of gallant dead and wounded, and leave them to the *uncertain* care of the enemy—Though we had suffered greatly in killed, wounded and prisoners—Though several Divisions of our army had been badly demoralized and scattered in all directions—Though we had lost an immense amount of artillery, small arms and military stores generally; yet as I plodded my way back toward Rossville that night I could not feel that our army had received what is generally termed a whipping, nor could a man be found that would acknowledge it. All seemed confident that if we could be reorganized again before the enemy could catch us that we would yet prove to [them] that their dearly bought victory had not lessened the valor or damped the order of our Army, and all seemed anxious for an opportunity to convince them of this fact. Notwithstanding the discouraging turn affairs had taken, and the dismal scene that presented itself in our camps that night, yet all seemed to be in high spirits on every hand and we could hear them with a soldier-like pleasure recounting the many incidents of the day, and telling how they mowed down whole ranks of the enemy as they made their last effort to hold their positions. Every one was confident that the enemy had suffered dreadfully, for he had through the whole day fought with a strange bravery and heedlessness of danger as if depending alone upon the mere strength of numbers.

Mon. Sept. 21st. The sun was clear and beautiful again this morning, but the air was not cool as on the morning previous and was soon exceedingly warm, the disagreeableness of which was doubled by the clouds of dust that were continually being [raised] by hundreds and thousands of passing and repassing troops. I was at Rossville by sunrise where I came upon Gen Crittenden and his staff. I asked Col. Starling (chief of Staff) for information in regard to my Division, but he could tell me nothing, but gave it as his impression that it was encamped at the Tennessee River near the foot of Lookout mountain. After beating about for another hour and learning nothing more certain, I joined a small detachment of the 79th Ind. under Lieut. Co. [Samuel P.] Oyler,[50] and we set out in the direction of Lookout Mountain, but when we arrived at the place indicated by Col. Starling we could not find a single vestige of our Division, and the road was filled with thousands of stragglers who were as yet unable to find their commands.

Wearied almost to exhaustion, foot-sore to an extent that nearly rendered me unable to walk, over powered with heat, and suffering a continual near approach to suffocation from the clouds of dust, I turned my course for Chattanooga hoping that I might there gain some information.

I came into the town about 11 o'clock A.M. but you may be sure that I met nothing there to revive my now drooping spirits. Every street and all the vacant grounds, and approaches to the river was choked with wagons, all directing their course toward the trestle bridge that had been erected across the river. Disorganized soldiers flocked by hundreds through the streets; houses of every description were closed and apparently untenanted except the hospitals, and they were numerous, for though we had left many of our gallant wounded on the battlefield, yet many had been borne away, and it is a significant fact that numbers of our wounded were borne from the battlefield to Chattanooga by the manual exertions of their comrades. By some accidental source I learned that our Division was camped on the river just above town, and I set out to find them. They were encamped near an unfinished rebel fort that subsequently took the name of Fort Wood and on the extreme left of the line that was subsequently formed by our army around Chattanooga.

I found our regiment badly cut up, and there was yet considerable numbers missing, but all were in high spirits and seemed not to be apprehensive that the rebels would not fail to follow up the advantages already gained. The Division was camped without much regularity and seemed to be only resting. The ground about the Camp was covered with a thick thorny underbrush, but most of the larger trees had been used for fuel or other purposes. Night closed upon us without our receiving any definite news from the front, but the occasional arrival of someone who had been reported among the missing, informed us that Gen Thomas was still out in the hills to keep the rebels in check,[51] and also that the rebels showed no great disposition to follow up their victory. This was encouraging to us, for notwithstanding our usual good spirits, we could not see the philosophy of our defeating the rebels here in the open fields about Chattanooga, when we could not maintain our ground in the hills and thick forests of Chickamauga.

It is true that we were in constant expectation of a heavy rein-forcement, composed of Gen Burnside and his whole army, but his proximity had not yet been realized.[52] "Burnside will be here ere night-fall" had been the cry throughout the evening of the previous day, and many a poor soldier cheered by this hope stood to his post till he received his death wound.

Chapter 9

The Storming of Mission Ridge
Was a Fearful Undertaking

Defeated at Chickamauga, the Army of the Cumberland retreated to Chattanooga. Tardily, Bragg followed, closing off the city save for one treacherous mountain road that ran to the railhead at Stevenson, Alabama. Woodcock and his fellow soldiers now faced the very real possibility of starvation. Luckily, help was on the way. First, Maj. Gen. Joseph Hooker raced to Bridgeport, Alabama, from Virginia with two corps. Then Grant, the hero of Vicksburg, arrived in the city on October 23 to take personal command, having already sacked Rosecrans in favor of George Thomas. Before the month was out, Grant had opened a new supply route, the so-called "Cracker Line." When Maj. Gen. William Tecumseh Sherman and 17,000 men fresh from Mississippi finally reached the city in mid-November, Grant was ready to fight his way out of the city. Bragg, in contrast, foolishly weakened his factionalized army by sending Longstreet, his rival for command, into East Tennessee.

With little faith in a Cumberland Army that he viewed as demoralized, Grant relied on Hooker and Sherman in conceiving his strategy. On November 24, one day after Thomas's men seized Bragg's forward lines at Orchard Knob, Hooker dramatically stormed Lookout Mountain. The next day, Grant attacked the main Confederate lines along Missionary Ridge. Thomas was supposed only to demonstrate against the Rebel center, while Hooker and Sherman did the real work of rolling up Bragg's flanks. The latter's attacks bogged down, however, and late in the afternoon Grant ordered Thomas to take the Confederates' first line of trenches. Incredibly, and against orders, the men of the Army of the Cumberland swept up the ridge and drove Bragg from its heights. Grant had misjudged them. Chattanooga was relieved, and Chickamauga was avenged.[1]

Tu. Sept. 22nd We commenced fortifying our position to day after we had been formed in the proper order, as best we could by collecting together the few remaining logs and filling up the crevices with rocks, billets of wood, &c. About noon we received a small number of picks and spades to each regiment and commenced tearing up the ground and throwing dirt on our imperfect works.

With our limited number of tools and the almost impenetrable firmness of the ground, rendered so by the continued drought, our progress was necessarily very slow, and the men having fully recovered from the devil-may-care excitement that always succeeds a heavy battle, had now began to feel some of the unpleasant emotions of despondency and did not seem to work with their usual good will. About an hour before sunset a squadron of rebel cavalry attacked our pickets and for a time a severe skirmish ensued in which the rebels appeared to rather have the best of it, for our line was compelled to give back some distance, but that seemed to arouse the fears of our troops, and to open their eyes more sensibly to the condition of our situation, and receiving a fresh supply of intrenching tools, they commenced their work with a new energy and determination.

We worked by reliefs through the whole of that night, and when the sun rose on the following morning we had sheltered ourselves by a tolerably respectable rifle pit, but we were not satisfied with that for we were morally certain that they would have to receive the heavy thumps of huge artillery missiles, therefore we continued our work throughout the whole of the day without interruption, and the order was "never let an implement be idle[.]" Early in the afternoon we could see the rebels coming over the crest of Mission Ridge, and pouring down its green sides along the winding roads leading into Chattanooga Valley by the thousand. We now began to feel certain that we would be attacked within the next 48 hours, but it was now beginning to be an event more to be wished for than dreaded, for our works were rapidly advancing to such a state of perfection that gave us confidence that we were masters of the town, and that we could repel any assault of the enemy. We also knew by the tardiness that the enemy had exhibited in pursuing us that we had taken heavy toll out of his ranks while he was driving us from bloody and disastrous Chickamauga, and another encouraging fact was that through the whole of this day their pickets did not show

the least disposition to encroach upon our lines, and as a consequence the skirmish lines were very quiet.

The stragglers had now all come in and we could make a correct
estimate as to our losses in the recent battle.

Our Regiment had lost three men in killed[2] and about sixty
wounded, and several captured. Co. B lost one killed, 5 captured
and several wounded. Thus our losses footed up much smaller than
I had expected; but the losses in that battle were generally smaller
than usual, and can be readily accounted for by the fact that our
army fought all the time on the defence, and partially sheltered had
received the heavy and daring charges of the enemy, and that fact
also accounts for the heavy loss of the enemy. Combining all the
circumstances we could not give up that we had been badly whipped.

Thur. Sept. 24th The weather that day was dry and warm as
usual. The pickets commenced fighting pretty warmly early after
daylight and continued it throughout the day, and at one time a
yung [young?] battle was brought on by a Division (Wood's, I
believe) making a reconnaissance in front of our corps.

Gen Rosecrans passed along through the lines on the night
previous, and made many encouraging remarks in the presence of
the boys. Among other things he said that he intended to stretch
a *trip wire* in front of our works and that we could then shoot the
rebels with a more unearring aim as they would fall over this device,
and true to his word the wire was stretched that evening. The next
day I went on picket but no adventure occurred worthy of note
except an ineffectual attempt by the Rebels to discomfit our picket
line by throwing shells at us from a little *mule cannon*. The next
morning I returned to camp without anything to tell. On that evening
Gen Rosecrans made us another visit, this time stopping and making
a short speech to each regiment as he passed, which was received
by long and loud cheers.

Sun Sept. 27th Weather still very dry. The rebels seem to show
no disposition to make an attack on us and we are beginning to
apprehend the troubles and uncomfortable necessities of a long
siege. It is true we are not entirely surrounded, neither do I believe
we will be, but the enemy have retaken Lookout Mountain and
their line now stretches from the river above town to the river below
town, thus effectively cutting off all rail-road communications and

rendering it necessary for our supplies to be transported in wagons across Cumberland Mountain from Stevenson, and of course we will soon be on short rations, although as yet we are receiving plenty. But then we are cut off from all the avenues for procuring forage, such as fresh pork, or beef, potatoes and vegetables of any kind, or corn meal, or in other words we are reduced to the necessity of feasting entirely upon the dry salty army rations.

We can now have no long agreeable walks through shady forests inhaling the pure country air that infuses a fresh spirit of life in every vine but we are confined to the narrow limits of our camp and the dull, uninteresting town of Chattanooga, which of course after having been submitted to the straggling pillage of two armies offers but few opportunities for pleasure or information. Every thing is changed as if by magic into a resemblance of the army or its attackers, or rather every object displays the spoiling hand of the conqueror. No house in town is occupied as a business house by any of its citizens, but all are filled by Sutlers, Clothes dealers, Quartermasters, Commissaries, Christian Commission agents,[3] Sanitary Commission agents, Staff Officers, and many other sects that are innumerable. We are also without mail, and we since the battle have been under the promise of receiving it in a few days. Flags of truce were exchanged to day between Gen Rosecrans and Bragg, no doubt with a view to some arrangement or disposition of our wounded that are in the hands of the enemy, probably an exchange of wounded prisoners will be the result.

On the 29th our pickets were ordered to cease firing entirely unless the rebels should attempt to advance, and the rebels in general did the same, but our pickets were considerably annoyed by some rebel sharpshooters who were posted in a house entirely beyond the reach of our guns.

Wed Sept 30th For the first time in a long while we had some appearance of rain and fine mizzling rain fell for some hours during the morning. The pickets remained quiet throughout the whole of the day, and the general and usual monotony of camp life was only broken by an occasional report from the gun of a rebel sharpshooter, yet they did comparatively no damage.

The long wished-for rain fell that night and the next day in considerable quantities, rendering everything more comfortable

notwithstanding the general gloominess that always attends a rainy
day in autumn, and the unusual disagreeableness of matters it generally creates in a military encampment, where "dog tents" are the
only covering, and your own natural heat is the only in door warmth.
But we were encouraged by the rumored arrival of many pieces of
artillery to replenish our depleted batteries, and by seeing two long
steel rifled 32 pounders driven up to Fort Wood and their gaping
mouths thrust through its embrasures and pointed toward Mission
Ridge as if staring defiance at everything it might support.[4]

Fri. Oct. 2nd The weather on this and the next two days was
very fine, and the pickets of the two armies remained generally at
their posts within full view of each other. They made a kind of
agreement that they would not fire at each other, except in case of
an advance by one of the lines, and this agreement was strictly
adhered to during the whole of the remainder of the time that we
were kept cooped up in that desolate camp.

Almost immediately after this agreement was entered into the
pickets commenced exchanging papers, and for several days we were
regularly supplied with the latest southern newspapers, from which
we gleaned many interesting pieces, interesting from the tendency
they all seemed to possess of giving the most exaggerated accounts
of the prowess of the Confederate arms, and of the inexhaustible
resources of the South. But they all joined in a wailing over the
dearly bought victory of Chickamauga, and did not conceal the fact
that there their armies had lost thousands of its best soldiers, and
almost a score of Generals of different grades, and they openly
declared that if Bragg did not succeed in capturing our army, and
of course Chattanooga, that the Battle of Chickamauga was *really*
a victory to the U.S. arms.

On the night of the 5th Gen Rosecrans came around to see us
again and had many of his little encouraging and sometimes comic
speeches to deliver to us, but we were not now in dread of a battle,
for we knew the enemy too well to think he would attempt to storm
our works, but we were dreading the consequences of a protracted
siege, and the probabilities of the enemy cavalry running in on our
single line of communication, and so interrupting it that we would
be compelled from sheer starvation to either surrender to the enemy or vacate the city, for it was a plain case that our little army

could not even *think* of storming the enemy in his lofty and apparently impregnable stronghold.

On the 6th we moved our tents back from the works and regulated our camps in regulation order, for previous to this time each tent had stood just where its owner desired it to since our encamping at this place, and as this entirely dispersed all thoughts of an early battle, we began to sink into that listless monotony that is inevitable to persons in our situation.

About the first of the month I began to be troubled with an irregularity of the digestive organs and it was now assuming the form of a diarrhea, and caused me much suffering. I lost my appetite for everything that we received from the commissaries, and as the sutlers had been all banished to Bridgeport I was greatly put to my wits to procure something to eat, and the first result was that I ate scarcely anything at all, and kept daily dwindling down to that second rate species of skeleton so often visible in long-tenanted camps, and which so plainly says *chronic diarrhea*. Sickness was the only situation in which I could be placed in the army to cause my spirits to sink below the proper medium, and this was I think the worst of all sickness to bring about a hypochondriachal state of mind. I was all the time longing for something nourishing, something that I could not get; and at one time I felt that if I could get a can of peaches that I would be satisfied, but finally a sutler ran the gauntlet of red tape gallows, and brought up a full stock of goods. I procured a supply of his most desirable articles of food, principally fruits, and although they seemed to agree with my digestion organs [better] than poor beef or crackers, I was still not satisfied.

Between the 5th and 10th of the month our rations began to grow scarce, and simultaneously with this event we began to receive *wormy* bread and occasionally stinking bacon, and beef of the leanest quality, and from this I might date the beginning of hard times for from this time our rations grew gradually and "beautifully less" till, I think for the last two or three weeks of the siege, we did not receive more than one quarter rations, and this small quantity combined with the generally inferior quality tended to render our condition truly unenviable.

The pies and cakes that were sold by the bakers in the city commanded almost fabulous prices, and were not a mile towards supplying the wants of the army. Every device that that inventive *genius* "hunger" could produce was called into practice to satisfy the continually craving vitals, but still the men were almost continually hungry. When a beef was slaughtered every part of him except his hide, hoofs and entrails was messed for the table. Even the tail was skinned down to its extreme end of flesh and bone and eaten with smacking lips and appreciating appetites. Though we to some extent suffered for want of rations, yet I think upon the whole that the health of the troops was better than if they had been receiving plenty; for the provisions were not so scarce as to produce hardly a single degree of emaciation, and it is probable that if we had been kept in that condition for months that we would have fair finally become so accustomed to it as to have suffered no inconvenience from it.

Wood became very scarce soon after our occupying the place, and we were reduced to great straits to procure a sufficient quantity of this article to keep us thoroughly warmed, but it finally increased our favorable ideas of the comfort of a Dobia tent. The boys would draw their tents close to the ground and then an oil cloth was fastened across one end, and the other filled with a kind of mason-work which somewhere contained a flu that led up from a small fireplace in the interior of the tent.

A few coals from the cook's fire would be thrown on this model grate which were fed by small particles of wood, soon diffusing a general warmth throughout the small apartment and rendering comfortable its two or three occupants. The stumps of trees that stood near the camp soon were nearly all leveled to the ground, and the *abbatis* that was formed in front of the line of works, suffered materially ere we could procure larger quantities of wood. Not a floating piece of wood of any description that came in reach of the shore escaped the vigilance of our soldiers and much wood was obtained by dragging it ashore as it was floating past. A considerable quantity was also procured by crossing to an island adjacent to our camp and bringing the desired article across in a small flat-boat.

On the 9th of October we were greatly relieved by a rumor that Gen Hooker had arrived at Bridgeport in command of two Army Corps (11th & 12th)[5]—the first impression was that we would now undoubtedly in a very short space of time be able to act on the offensive toward the enemy. Since the Battle of Chickamauga and up to this time it seemed that a general reorganization of the Army had been going on. The 20th and 21st Corps had been nominally consolidated under the title of the 4th Corps and was to be commanded by Gen. Granger. The Reserve Corps was, I suppose, distributed between the 14th and 4th Army Corps.[6] Our Brigade was consolidated with what was formerly the 2nd Brigade of our Division, and which for the last several months had been commanded by Col. [George F.] Dick of the 86th Ind. Our Brigade was now composed of eight Regiments, namely the 9th and 17th Ky; the 13th, 19th and 59th Ohio; the 44th, 79th and 86th Ind. The Brigade was in command of Gen. Samuel Beatty, and was styled the 3rd Brigade of 3rd Division of the 4th Army Corps. The Division was commanded by Gen. Thos J. Wood. The 1st and 2nd Brigades were commanded by Genl's [August] Willich and [William B.] Hazen respectively.[7]

Gen Crittenden left the Army on the tenth first passing quietly to the Head quarters of each Regiment and taking a formal farewell of its Commander. He was, so rumor said, going to Indianapolis to attend a court of inquiry that had been convened at that place to investigate the conduct of certain General Officers in the Battle of Chickamauga.[8]

I was truly sorry that Gen. Crittenden was about to leave for I had ever considered him a brave and efficient officer; but as to his conduct at the battle of Chickamauga, I had *no* opinion for I saw neither him or any other General after the grand charge of the rebel army about 11 o'clock A.M. on the 20th till the next morning when I arrived at Rossville.

The soldiers had begun to be naturally apprehensive lest the *releiving* spirit that had so long seemed to curse the Army of the Cumberland, would now take possession of the immediate rulers of the affairs of the Army of the Cumberland. We thought that the mere fact of a man losing a battle was a poor plea upon which to have him arraigned before a Court Martial in defense of his character as an officer, and we feared that if this mania did sweep over us that we would lose "Rosy" in the operation "and who can succeed him?" was the question that always followed this result of our verbal speculations.

Though there was no general determination of feeling yet I

think that many of our soldiers were loath to part with General Crittenden. But he was not going alone.—Gen. McCook of the 20th Corps was, as rumor said, releived by the same order and ordered to report to the same court,[9] and many dark hints were whispered about the camp that Gen Rosecrans would come in for his share of censure. This caused many unpleasant apprehensions but the soldiers generally seemed to be loaded with thoughts of the inner man, but little was said about governmental affairs.

Gen Van Cleve, formerly of our Division was assigned to the post at Murfreesboro, and notwithstanding his inability for active field service on account of old age and partial blindness, yet many of us were not satisfied to exchange him for Gen Wood, about whom we had heard all kinds of stories as to his tyranny, hard marching, &c. Though wherever we met up with any member of Wood's old Division he expressed regret at losing his commander.[10]

On the 11th our little short Regiment was for the first time since the Battle, drawn out on inspection, and presented a striking contrast with what it did less than six weeks previous to that time. The next four days were raw, rainy disagreeable ones, and we could do no more than roll around in our tents and comment upon the probable result of the Ohio Gubernatorial election, which was held on the 13th; and also discuss the merits and designs of soldiers— U.S. soldiers—who had fought for two years and had sadly felt the need of having thousands more troops in the field—who voted for the 2nd epistle to Jeff Davis, in *treason*, if not in *crime* to wit, C. L. Vallandigham.[11]

On the 15th I made the following entry in my Journal: "Rain all last night and to day, and nothing to do but eat wormy crackers and shiver with cold—Narrator suffering much from diarrhea."

On the 16th I was for the first time detailed to work on the fortifications that were then just beginning to be marked out on the numerous commanding eminencies near the city, and which have since assumed a magnitude of strength, and exhibit such perfect engineering as to render them among the most formidable that were built by the Cumberland Army. The next day we resumed the old camp orders to the extent of a dress parade.

Tu Oct. 20th Weather clear and cool.—Our Brigade moves down to the left of our Division which throws us on the extreme

left of the army, our Regiment being on the left of the 2nd line.—
To day the rumors that Gen Rosecrans has been superceded is so
current that we are almost forced to believe it, and really if the
change is made I dont think there will be much murmuring for one
reason, while we are giving away a good man from the head of the
army, we are receiving another equally as worthy.

We had not forgotten how the gallant Thomas had saved our
army at Chickamauga, neither had we forgotten the other long list
of heroic achievements where deserving a place on his banners.

On the evening of the 22nd, the *orders* creating the Military
Division of the Mississippi, and placing Grant at its head; and also
relieving Gen Rosecrans of the command of the Cumberland Army,
and placing Gen Thomas in his stead was read to the troops, with
eliciting scarcely a murmur of either approbation or dissatisfaction.
"Several shells were thrown at the rebels from our works during this
evening without obtaining any reply,["] which we rather desired,
for we were almost dying for the want of some excitement—anything that would indicate a change. We felt confident that some
effort to change the relative positions of the two armies would be
ere long attempted as soon as the order was issued announcing Gen
Grant as our Commander, for he was growing high in our esteem
as he was in that of the Nation, and at any day I believe the soldiers
would have gladly responded to the order to make a direct assault
on either Mission Ridge or Lookout Mountain[.]

Fri. Oct. 23rd Cold and rainy during the whole day, bad tents,—
but little fire,—no mail at all—no news of interest—no prospect of
a move, either forward or backward,—no probability that the enemy will quietly fall back to Dalton and leave us free—no prospect
that we will get plenty of wood, rations, clothing or supplies of any
kind, and in fact there seems to be *no nothing*.

About the 25th there was much talk of consolidating our Regiment into a Battalion and uniting with the 8th Ky. Inftry. which
was first to be consolidated in the same manner. A majority of the
officers of our regiment was in favor of it and accordingly an application was made to Head Quarters for permission to do so.

Tu. Oct. 27th Considerable cannonading the day[12] from Lookout Mountain and our batteries on the opposite side of the river,
and some fighting farther down but we dont know to what extent,

or the number of troops engaged. Rumors late at night that Lookout Mountain is in our possession and that the steamer Paint Rock has gone to Bridgeport for rations[.][13]

The 28th was raw and rainy, and our Regiment had to go on picket. That night for three hours following midnight we heard a heavy cannonading and musketry away down the river, and were much puzzled to know the nature & result of the contest.[14]

Sat. Oct. 31st—much cold but no rain—heavy cannonading to and from Lookout Mountain—rumors that our boats are coming up the river within six miles of this place and that we will soon have full rations—Hooray.

On Wednesday the 4th of November our Regiment went on picket. I, on account of ill health was unable to go and consequently remained in camp. For the next few day[s] following nothing of interest occurred except that mails began to arrive much more frequently, and at an earlier date after starting, which proved to us that the boats were running and caused many hungry soldiers to hope that in a few days we would be in the receipt of full rations.

The firing from Lookout Mountain on the front of which the rebels had stationed one or more pieces of artillery some time in the month of October, was continued each day till as long as the rebels occupied the territory, and thus hundreds of shots were thrown toward our camp without ever, to my knowledge, having killed or wounded a single man. For the first few days after the battery was established it was a source of some annoyance to our boys, but they soon became apprized of its harmless effects, and would amuse themselves by watching the smoke puff from the crest of the point, and counting the number of seconds till the report of the piece would reach us, or till the shell would burst.[15]

Fri Nov 6th—an unusually warm, clear, and pleasant day. The shells from Point Lookout burst lower down than usual and indeed in some instances today their proximity to us was alarming[.]

Sat. Nov 7th—weather still exceedingly beautiful—Battery on Lookout Mountain works away with its usual regularity—Rations growing much plentier—Hurrah for that.

Sat. Nov. 14th—wood, wood, is the cry on every hand. We have burned almost every stick of wood inside our lines, and what will we do if it should turn cold ere we can push the rebels back far enough for us to procure a supply. The Pay-master has been here several days, and we have made out Pay-rolls and he has them in his possession; therefore we are expecting soon to receive another installment of green backs, which, added to our increasing supply of rations serves to render the boys gay and high-spirited[.]

Sun. Nov 15th—Weather a little cooler than yesterday. Inspection to day at 10 o'clock—a few shots from Lookout—a mess of dried beans for dinner—Hurrah for dried beans.

Wed Nov 18th—Our Regiment went on picket on that day. That portion of the line which our Regiment occupied, stretched in from the river bank along a small creek[16] that here emptied into the river, and by establishing the line on the creek it caused the left of it to be thrown a considerable distance to the rear, and greatly injured the appearance of the line as well as requiring many more men to fill the posts, yet it had heretofore been considered by our picket officers imprudent for our line to be advanced beyond the creek lest its high banks and the depth of the stream should be the means of some of our boys being captured. This evening our Company and Co K were crossed over the stream on a bridge that had been previously constructed, and the first platoon of each Company deployed and made a dash at the enemy's line. The enemy simply fired one scattering volley, and then run, a portion of them throwing down their guns and one of them threw himself down and remained till we came up and then surrendered. Ere many minutes had elapsed we saw the rebel line again established about three hundred yards in advance but they evinced no disposition to fire at us, and thus the matter passed off quietly, and the general peacefulness of the picket line was not in the least disturbed[.]

Fri Nov. 20th—about 12 o'clock M. the officers of our Regiment were notified to report to regimental head quarters. When all had assembled the Colonel proceeded to inform us that we were to attack the enemy to-morrow, and then he unfolded the whole programme to us, which strange to say the General Commanding for one time thought proper to communicate to all the officers in the Army. The Colonel then proceeded to give us the general instructions that were to be adopted[17] and finally closed by ordering us to be mute on the subject to any one.

This news raised my feelings a considerable per cent for I could now see a termination to the many troubles and inconvenience we had suffered since being hemmed in this place. The most ignorant man in regard to military operations that could have been found in the army would have at once pronounced the place of our attack on the enemy a good one, and the sequel proved that their judgment would have been correct.

But they told me on all hands that I would not be able to participate in the struggle, and I was myself conscious that my physical strength would fail on the very commencement of any arduous undertaking, yet I had been pent up so long, and had suffered so much, that I resolved to go with the Regiment as far as I could[.]

At 5 o'clock P.M. we received orders to have two days rations cooked by morning, and to be ready to move early next day. We also received the usual number of extra rounds of ammunition. At 7 o'clock this order was *countermanded* and we were ordered to return the extra ammunition.[18]

A steady rain fell through the night of the 20th and the whole day of the 21st. There were no fresh indications of a fight, and I began to think that the plan had fell through. There was much verbal speculation in camps about the intentions of our Commanders; yet as all knew that Sherman had come up to the opposite bank of the river, and had heard rumors that Longstreet had gone to Knoxville, they believed that victory to our armies was as certain as we made an attack.[19]

Sun Nov 22nd—weather clear and moderately cold—Inspection today at 1 o'clock—Get ready for *the movement* tomorrow—Each man must carry 100 rounds of ammunition and two days rations, and one blanket, leaving the knapsack behind. This begins to look like active operations, but I feel worse in health today than usual and unless a change for the better I will have to *remain behind*[.]

The first incident that occurred on the next morning of interest was the order to *turn over* the extra ammunition.

This almost led us to the conclusion that our commanders didn't exactly understand themselves; but about noon the ammunition was again issued and the troops ordered to march immediately, and as everyone knew that the movement was *to the front*, and that they could not go far without fighting, there was an unusual bustle and confusion among the troops as they made a disposition of long treasured souvenirs and valuables to those that were remaining behind, and hurried to buckle in the accouterments of war, and march from the quiet camp, and almost at a single step find themselves in the midst of a general battle.

Soon our Corps was in front of our ranks, and in heavy columns commenced moving down the gentle slopes that led into the level valley, and where, not more than three fourths of a mile away, could be distinctly seen the rebel picket line quietly looking on. I almost fancied that I could see their countinances (even at that great distance) betray signs of puzzled curiosity and amazement. And prisoners that were captured that evening avowed that they thought that our Army was coming out on *grand Review*, and indeed for a time such an idea would have been justifiable; for the long, heavy columns moved out in slow and steady movements, with good order prevailing throughout the whole. Richly dressed staff officers dashed from point to point, as if they were apprehending any danger of their soon being conspicuous marks for the enemy's sharpshooters.[20]

Generals with their numerous staffs rode each with his respective Brigade or Division, without any of the usual precautions generally taken in such cases. No wonder the enemy, thought the Union Army was coming out for a *review*. On the side of the enemy we could see no unusual movement occasioned by our movements. The pickets still remained listlessly at their posts as if inapprehensive of danger—struggling men and animals were seen moving about the naked face of the Ridge, apparently looking on with wonder at the grand display that was being made by our troops.

Soon the columns began to close up in rear of the picket lines— The enemy's pickets seemed to straighten up and step forward as if to fully satisfy themselves of our intentions. Soon our picket line began to advance, and then the enemy's line was seen to jump into their pits or behind trees, now fully comprehending the designs of our troops. For a moment they waited as if still anxious to avert the contest that must inevitable ensue unless our troops should soon come to a halt, but no, they still advance. Presently they commenced a hot skirmish fire on our troops, to which our boys respond with a yelling charge that soon causes the enemy to break and fall back. Gen Willich who commanded a Brigade to the right of ours found some serious opposition in his front, but he went ahead over every obstacle and soon succeeded in capturing almost the whole of an Alabama Regiment that was stationed on his front.[21] Almost simultaneously with the first fire the whole scene was changed in the rebel camp. Drums beating the *long roll*, and bugles sounding the *assembly* could be distinctly heard rallying the Rebels to resist our attack. Mounted men were dashing up and down and along the face of Mission Ridge—Wagons were going up the Ridge by every road that lead from the valley, and upon the whole there was considerable evidence that they were not expecting us to attack so soon.[22]

A heavy skirmishing fire, occasionally interspersed with volleys from whole regiments was kept up during the whole evening till dark closed the scene, when our line had been firmly established about one mile in advance of the original picket line. Our Regiment had lost only two men wounded, Sergt Riley Hudson of Co. B, severely in the groin, and ——— Robinson of Co. D. Some other Regiments had suffered more severely and in some instances had lost several killed.[23]

Those that returned to camp for various reasons seemed to be highly pleased with the result of the evening's engagement, and anxious for to-morrow to come to see what it might bring forth. The enemy had lost some killed and wounded that fell into our hands, and several prisoners besides one almost complete Regiment.

With an anxious mind I stood that night and viewed the fires on the summit and along the sides of the Ridge and occasionally caught a glimpse of dark forms passing and repassing between me and the fires; fondly hoping that ere night again went and come that there would be a change in the prospect thus afforded—that either there would be no fires, or that they would give warmth to people of a different purpose.

Tu. Nov. 24th—was one of the important days in the Battle of Mission Ridge. All was quiet along the center and left during the whole day, except an occasional picket shot. The steamer Dunbar went up early in the morning out of sight above the city without attracting the attention of any of the enemy's batteries, and remained above nearly the whole of the day and then, late in the afternoon, returned.[24]

Late in the forenoon we began to hear sharp skirmishing all around the base of Lookout Mountain near the Point, and at about

11 1/2 o'clock the firing became so severe that we knew that something important was being undertaken in that quarter. The firing continued, sometimes with great severity, and at others slackening down to an ordinary skirmish till late at night. The day was slightly rainy and unusually foggy, sometimes the summit of the mountain would be enveloped in a dense rain cloud and at others we could see the bleak point rising out of the unremitting fog, that kept the base continually hidden from view, like a barren & rocky island rising abruptly from a tempestous sea. We fancied that at times we could catch glimpses of dark lines fighting their way up the mountain side but we could not be positive, and the distance was too great to distinguish by the ear whether locality of the firing was being changed. When darkness came on we could occasionally catch a dim view of the flash of a gun and from their increasing proximity to the summit of the mountain we rightly judged that our troops were gaining ground, and that if it was possible to reach the top anywhere near the point that they would soon be there.

Had it not been for the thick heavy fog this battle would have presented one of the grandest battle scenes ever witnessed, but as it was, nature interfered and cut off the pleasure of witnessing such a scene, lest we should become too much elated over its sublimity, and the welcome news we received next morning that "Lookout Mountain was in our possession[.]"

Wed Nov 25th—This eventful [day] was exceedingly clear and beautiful—the air was cool and bracing just to the extent that is disagreeable—scarcely any wind was stirring and indeed all the turbulent elements of nature seemed to withdraw themselves from the scene as if to give wicked man a fair field over which undisturbed, he might shoot and butcher his fellows for having a different way of thinking.

The air was perfectly light, and clear of all mists which tend to obstruct the vision. The smoke from the thousands of camps and bivouack fires seemed to ascend with a speedy velocity above the line of the horizon. Really nature in every respect was favorable to the operation of both armies.

I sprang from my cot early and was soon out to catch a view of the scene that might present itself. With considerable anxiety I strained my eyes to catch a view of the northeastern extremity of

Mission Ridge, hoping to ascertain if Sherman's corps had yet crossed,[25] but the distance was too great, and the darkness not yet sufficiently dispelled by the increasing daylight to render objects visible, but a little while before sunrise our ears were greeted with the heavy boom of cannon and the crashing roar of musketry away in the direction indicated and we then knew that Sherman had crossed and was now falling upon the enemy's right flank. As the sun began to peep over the crest of the long barren Ridge, we could see away to its termination on the extreme left, a battery seemingly on the last knoll working vigorously and throwing its charges at another battery on the next swell of the Ridge to the right, but at the great distance they seemed to be not more than 100 yards from each other. Oh how elated I felt when I saw this evidence of the maturity of the plan that had been previously explained to us! and as I stood and looked at the now dark smoke curl up between me and the bright sun I felt confident that Sherman had obtained a foot-hold and that the victory would eventually be ours.

With anxious emotion did I listen to the fearful combat that Sherman made this morning as he three times attempted to break the enemy's line, and was as many times repulsed—anxiously did I watch to see the batteries momentarily cease firing, and change positions, for by that alone could I form an estimate of the probable results of the contest, but they remained apparently immovable for several hours, and almost without intermission continued to emit their deadly missiles. At times each battery seemed to be almost completely enveloped in the smoke of the others shells. I knew that the contest was a terrible one and oh, how anxiously did I await the result. I did not know that Sherman was losing men by the hundred in dangerous but unsuccessful charges upon the enemy's works, neither did I know that Gen Thomas had sent Gen [Absalom] Baird's Division[26] to reinforce Sherman and that Sherman had ordered him to return with the laconic remark "I know what my men can do.["]

The battle raged heavily in that quarter till about noon without my being able to ascertain who were getting the better of the struggle though I had occasionally caught a slight view of dark moving lines in the fields near the batteries and had once seen what bore a strong resemblance to a shattered column flying down the side of the hill, but we were unable to distinguish what army they belonged to.

About noon there was a general lull in the storm of the battle, and I began to tremble with anxiety for the fate of Sherman's Corps. Scarcely a gun could be heard in any direction, and a general calm seemed to assume the place of all the noise and confusion that had reigned supreme in the left of the army throughout the forenoon[.]

But the center and right had remained very quiet up to this time, and seemed as if they were awaiting to see if Sherman's single corps could defeat the whole rebel army. The center (our Corps) had been shifting and moving about all the forenoon, and occasionally advancing a short distance, meeting with only a slight resistance from the enemy's lines.[27] The boys said that they were never before so eager for the fray as on this occasion, although the storming of Mission Ridge was truly a fearful undertaking. But they were encouraged by the great amount of Generalship that everyone could plainly see our Generals were exhibiting. They had seen column after column of the enemy pass along the crest of the Ridge in their immediate front and go on to the assistance of those who were battling with Sherman—They had seen heavy columns leave the works in their immediate front and therefore they knew that this part of the enemy's line was materially weakened, hence this eagerness to storm the ridge. Our Regiment was on picket or rather on the skirmish line about six or seven hundred yards from the base of the Ridge. One solid line of the enemy occupied a line of works about 500 yards in front of our line, and Col. Cram thought they could be easily dislodged.[28] The boys said he solicited an order from Generals Beatty and Wood to charge this line—at any rate he received such an order, and the signal for the beginning of the charge was to be the firing of six guns from Fort Wood[.]

The gallant Colonel read the order to *Reserve*, and remarked "pretty heavy boys but we can go if any can". Soon the sharp, but deafening peals of the long steel 32 pounder was heard issuing from the embrasures of Fort Wood,—The first five shots came in quick succession, as if to not give the boys time for a single thought between the first and the starting. Then there was a moment of awful suspense, but only a moment between the firing of the last two shots.

The sixth shot pealed forth upon the thin air, but before its keen notes were reverberated from the distant hills our Regiment (and others) bounded forward to the charge. They had a fearful race to make. The 500 or 600 yards that lay between them comparatively open ground and every foot of it in plain view of the score of batteries along the crest of the Ridge.

Therefore the moment our boys emerged from the woods into the open ground they attracted the attention of these batteries which immediately turned their whole fire upon our advancing line. Then was presented a scene for painter and poet that defies all description. The whole line of the summit of the Ridge seemed to be the continuous crater of one immense volcano. The white smoke curled up from the mouth of the cannons in almost one dense cloud, but the lightness of the air lifted it rapidly and thus the beauty of the scene was heightened. The pieces were worked with truly commendable rapidity, and terrible was the shower of shells and shot that were poured upon our advancing line. At times the smoke of the bursting shells rose almost in clouds from the open spot of ground across which our line was advancing.

This was the great danger that our boys apprehended before advancing, and consequently they advanced across the fields at the top of their speed, and in this manner they were continually just below the range of the cannon-shots, and consequently the front line suffered but little by the enemy's artillery, though it gave them a close race, and ploughed up the earth in great ugly furrows just after our troops would have passed over it[.]

When our Regiment arrived in about three hundred yards of the enemy's works at the foot of the hill its occupants[29] delivered a scattering volley upon our advancing line, and immediately broke and fled up the hill in confusion, and soon afterwards I could catch an occasional view of a glistening bayonet as they neared the summit—Finally our boys, almost faint from exhaustion, reached the enemy's works, and literally rolled into its ditches to catch a safe moment to breathe. But they could not remain long, for soon the depressed pieces of the enemy's artillery were raining their destructive missiles in their midst, ploughing up the works, throwing the timbers about with great force, and rendering the situation truly critical. Gen Wood rode along through this storm of lead, attended only by his color bearer, and came up to where our Regiment was lying. He said "hurrah for the 9th Ky["]—the 9th Ky. responded with three cheers, then bounded over the works and commenced the fearful and painful ascent. They were almost exhausted from their previous exertions, but they were now in the midst of a sea of whizzing lead, with no way to extricate themselves except by advancing up the rugged sides of the hill in face of the enemy or by falling back to their original position and this they could not think of. Then commenced that contest of physical strength and courage between the various regiments of our front lines for the fame of being the first to reach the enemy's works. The hill was very steep in many places, and was covered with patches of scrubby undergrowth, and the branches of fallen trees, which rendered the ascent very laborious.

The rolling shape of the face of the hill prevented our boys from being very seriously annoyed till they were near the enemy's works, and then every time one would show his head above the parapets he received the leaden messenger that deprived him of life and carried desolation to some fireside. The rebel line was so weakened by the great number being sent away to the right to withstand Sherman that after a short but severe struggle with our wearier boys they fell back over the rest of the ridge in great confusion.

But in some instances not until they had made a momentary resistance with clubbed muskets and the staves of the defences. In many cases the contest was so close that when the enemy gave way our officers threw down their swords and hurled stones after the retreating enemy. One number of our regiment (Alfred Cook, Co. A) killed one man with the butt of his rifle as he mounted the parapet. The rebel had fired at him and grazed his ear, though he was so near that Cook was powder burned by the flash of his gun, when he perceived that he had not laid Yankee he threw down his gun to surrender, but Yankee told him he was too late about it and that he "could not quit," and served him as afore-mentioned.

The first *stragglers* had not been many moments on the enemy's works, till the Yankees were pouring over to the right and left by the thousand. As Capt [James M.] Simmons[30] arrived in the works he and another officer of our regiment[31] (have forgotten whom) hastily loaded a piece of artillery, primed it with a musket cartridge and whirled it to fire on the retreating enemy, but ere they could level the piece the way was blocked up by thousands of Yankees and they were compelled to desist.

Now came the exciting part of the eventful battle—Gen. Wood had arrived at the top of the hill and made a short speech to the boys, telling them that they had ascended it without his orders and now "if they didn't stay there he would have them all court-martialed." This was responded to with a hearty cheer and the boys continued to advance down the rest of the ridge in pursuit of the flying enemy. They were apparently as much scattered as the enemy, and without heeding the rallying commands of the officers every man was acting on his own hook. They were so elated with success that they seemed to have forgotten that any precautionary measures were necessary, but considered themselves invincible. Many of the retreating rebels, still seemed to entertain hopes of effecting something yet to change the fortune of the day, and they stubbornly contested every inch of ground, from behind every tree as they fell back before the myriads of Yankees, but they were swept along as the chaff before the whirl-wind. Presently they met with a returning surge, or in other words the heavy masses that had been sent to engage Sherman.[32] They now, partially vanquished with Sherman pressing heavily on their rear came sweeping up the crest of the ridge with a strength and velocity that seemed to defy all opposition and fell with incompa-rable fury upon our disorganized thousands. For a few moments the conflict was terrible—the rebels fought with the determination of men who believe life is at stake, and doubt seemed to be accumu-lating in the scale of victory. The main body of our troops could not immediately engage the desperate enemy on account of the eager ones that were scattered promiscuously in advance and were manfully striving to check the coming storm. But this seemed to have only a momentary effect, and soon overpowered by numbers they came falling back on the main body. A few moments then decided the day, for there was a perfect wall of Yankees many lines deep across the crest of the hill, and while those in front received the desperate enemy with terrible volleys of musketry, and slight counter-charges, those in the rear were building a barricade in order to be prepared for the worst. But ere this dreadful carnage had been going on many minutes, the enemy began to waver and were soon retreating over the hills in hopeless confusion. Our army was too completely exhausted with the exertions of the day to immediately follow up the advantages already gained, and this only saved the rebel army from complete annihilation. Thus terminated the ever-memorable battle of Mission Ridge; which resulted in one of the most complete victories that had ever been known to the United States arms during the war. The enemy had been driven in confusion from a position that was considered by nature almost impregnable. He had suffered an immense loss in artillery, small arms, and military stores. He was now convinced that he could offer no formidable opposition to our advance into the heart of the Confederacy. The backbone of the Confederacy (Chattanooga being one of the joints) was now effectively broken, and its recovery was hopeless.

Our army was no[w] freed from the white prison in which it had been confined ever since the battle of Chickamauga—Our soldiers were no[w] freed from the pain of seeing themselves corralled by a wall of gray by day, and a wall of fire by night—they would no longer chafe under the half confinement to which they had been subjected by the tenacious enemy—the losses and reverses of September 19th and 20th were doubly and trebly atoned for, as far as was in the power of man—indeed, it seemed like making a single step from bondage to freedom, from starvation to plenty.

Our tired and battle-worn troops sank exhausted upon the ground where they exchanged the last shots with the discomfited enemy; but a moment sufficed for their pant, and then they were up talking in all the glad excitement of victors who knew they have done a great work. I could fairly catch the sound of their animated and joyous cheering as they caught sight of some favorite Officer, or heard of fresh fruits of the victory on other parts of the field. As every one had been his own commander from the time of reaching the crest of the hill, each one had some exploit to narrate to his comrade. When night set in the firing had ceased in every part of the field evincing conclusively that the rebels were all gone, and soon bright bivouac fires were gleaming from the crest and sides of the hill, on the very spot occupied but the night before by the enemy; but they now seemed to shine with ten-fold brightness.

The enemy had suffered greatly in killed and wounded ere they left their works on the summit of the hill, and the ditches were lined with their bodies.[33] Thousands of small arms of every description were scattered in all directions, also accouterments and equipment were lying almost in heaps, as if the rebels had stripped themselves for the contest and had forgotten to gather their property in the hurry of their retreat, and many of our soldiers feasted that night with a keen relish, on the fresh baked *"corn pone"* and fat *"shote"* that had been thus unceremoniously thrown aside by the frightened enemy.

The loss of our regiment was comparatively trifling, considering the conspicuous part the[y] bore in the action, and the great length of time they were under fire. Its loss was five killed and thirty wounded. The killed were Lieut William Barton of Co A, William Kirtland of Co. C, William Mitchell of Co. D, Thos. M. Arturburn of Co. G and another whose name I have forgotten.[34] Col. Cram received a very painful wound after arriving at the top of the hill. The ball entering the top of his shoulder and coming out on the shoulder-blade bone. Capt. [Toliver] Moore of Co. E[35] was severely shocked, bruised, and to some extent wounded by a shell bursting, somewhere in his vicinity. One of the fragments had gone through his hand, another had dreadfully torn his clothing on the side opposite his wounded hand, and in fact almost every part of his person bore marks of his proximity to the bursting missle. When he undertook to explain the manner in which he received his wound, he would proceed with clearness till he came to the bursting shell and then said he "I felt might *queer* for a moment" and then knew no more. Lieut [David W.] Pope[36] was severely wounded through the body. Other officers were slightly wounded—many of the men severely, but upon the whole the losses did [not] by far come up with the expectations of eyewitnesses on the scene.

Thur Nov 26th—That was a bright and cheerful day, and a joyfully spent one by every member of our army who was able to be on his feet and moving. Scores of stories were related of thrilling incidents and hair-breadth escapes that had been enacted on the previous day.

Wagons were out collecting the valuable muskets and accouterments that had been captured on the battle field, and frequently two or three pieces of artillery drawn by mules could be seen coming into town. The slightly wounded, who had come to camp, were relating thrilling stories of the scene. About 9 o'clock P.M. our Brigade returned to camp. I and the mess cook had made preparations to the full extent of our abilities, to give our mess a worthy reception, and rendered cheerful by the result of the late battle it was a considerable time ere the boys could sufficiently calm[ed] down from their great height of story telling to eat supper but we finally discharged this *perilous* duty and retired to rest with the weight on our minds of a rumor that on the morrow we would have to start to East Tennessee in pursuit of Longstreet.

Chapter 10

The Famous City of Knoxville

Bragg's stunned army was in retreat toward Dalton, Georgia, but one threat remained in Tennessee. Longstreet, having moved toward Knoxville, had besieged Maj. Gen. Ambrose Burnside's Army of the Ohio inside the city. Grant accordingly ordered Woodcock's IV Corps, under the command of Gordon Granger, Maj. Gen. O. O. Howard's XI Corps, Brig. Gen. Jefferson C. Davis's division of the XIV Corps, and Sherman's Army of the Mississippi to relieve Burnside. Six days into the march, Sherman learned that Longstreet had tried unsuccessfully to storm the Knoxville fortifications and then had lifted the siege. Sherman and most of the column then turned back to Chattanooga, but Thomas J. Wood's division of the IV Corps proceeded on to Knoxville to keep an eye on the Confederates. It camped fifteen miles beyond the city, on a cold, windy hillside. It was miserable and boring duty.

The division's winter quarters provided Woodcock, increasingly emaciated due to his chronic diarrhea, with an opportunity to go home and recover his health. Little did he know that the journey itself would almost kill him. Invariably, his luck failed him, and what could go wrong did so. At least he kept his sense of humor through the ordeal.

Woodcock's political views continued to evolve during this period. Much to his own surprise, the ambitious young Democrat discovered that he could find no good reason to support likely Democratic presidential challenger George B. McClellan. Quietly, he had become a Republican.[1]

Fri Nov 27th—Weather warm and cloudy—a rumor in camp this morning that on yesterday Gen. Palmer defeated a large body of rebels on the old Chicamauga battle ground and that he captured many guns and prisoners.[2] The continued reports of the complete demoralization of the rebel army cheers us greatly, and were it not for having to go to East Tennessee we could make a finish of Bragg and then go into winter quarters. Late in the morning we received orders to be ready to march at 6 o'clock tomorrow morning.

Sat Nov 28th—Weather cloudy and warm. We did not march as early as was ordered on the previous evening, but were instructed to keep in constant readiness to start at any moment.

I contended that it would be best for my health for me to undertake the trip for it was every day becoming more evident that I could not live much longer in Chattanooga. I knew that if I gave out on the march that I would not be left behind, and also that the exercise change of water and diet would be beneficial to me, therefore I made arrangements to accompany the expedition.

Late in the afternoon we started from Chattanooga and traveled 6 miles on the Cleveland road, arriving in camp about sunset. A little after sunset the air began to turn cool and the winde to blow very chilly, but my friendly and able-bodied mess had soon erected a tent and kindled a large fire at one end of it, and I was soon comfortably seated in a warm place feasting on some sweet potatoes that had been hastily boiled.

Sun Nov 29—Weather very cold but partially clear; We marched to Harrisons landing fifteen miles above Chattanooga. A portion of the road was exceedingly swampy, and in some instances was scarcely passable, but about two miles from Chicamauga creek we struck firm ground and for the rest of the way had a very fine road.

Mon Nov 30—Weather exceedingly cold—Gen Beatty says "the coldest day since I have been in the service." We marched twenty miles, and encamped for the night within one mile of Hiwassee River, but had scarcely gotten into camp and kindled our fires till our Regiment had to go on picket. But after mature deliberation we concluded that it was best to not get mad about it, and made the best of it that could have been done by slaying several animals of different kinds and appropriating their flesh to fill our flesh pots.

To day we began to find some of the people that were so long the prominent subjects of rebel tyranny—loyal East Tennesseans. All along the road they seemed to welcome us as deliverers and received us with all possible demonstrations of joy. The first Union flag was hung out near Georgetown. Our Brigade band went down to the house and played the lively and soul-stirring tune "The star spangled banner." The family was so much affected at the sight of the dear old flag borne by national troops and the sweet notes of one of our national tunes that they all shed tears.

I rode on horseback the greater portion of the day, which with the keen air, caused me to feel much stronger than usual.

Tu. Dec. 1st Weather still very cold. We remained on picket all day. The Corps being halted for some purpose. In the morning we drew a very limited supply of rations, and could hear it occasionally hinted about that it was unknown where we were to get any more. That we would now have to forage for a living for some time to come. Early after 9 o'clock P.M. we moved down to the river and after standing on the bank for some time we were finally taken in and ferried to the other side by the steamer Dunbar. After we got across, we stumbled about through the brush for nearly a mile and then went into camp in a little field.

Wed Dec 2nd—Weather clear and a little milder than on yesterday. Marched twenty two miles in the direction of Kingston and camped on a rebel Captain's farm. Our march lay through a rich and productive country, and as the boys knew that they were now thrown upon their own resources to provide provisions, they were not slow to embrace the opportunities that were afforded to day; and as a result we had for supper fresh cuts of almost every description.

Thur Dec 3rd—Weather very warm and pleasant but as a result of that the roads are exceedingly soft and muddy, which renders marching very disagreeable.

After marching around twenty five miles we found ourselves in the pretty little railroad village known as Sweetwater where we encamped for the night. Just as we were going into camp we heard a sharp skirmish a short distance beyond a skirt of woods that lined the fields. We soon learned that it was the result of a collision between a party of our independent foragers and a company of rebel cavalry. But our boys proved to be as good at fighting as foraging and the rebels soon skedaddled.

Fri Dec 4th—Weather warm and very pleasant. I walked all day and began to think myself much stronger, as we had marched 15 miles. Our march lay through a very fruitful country, but the people were not so unanimously loyal as on some other days. A detail of twenty men was made from each regiment this morning to forage, each detail for its own Regiment during the day. Our detail did not procure scarcely anything and as a consequence we turned in at night in no enviable state either in body or mind.

Sat Dec 5th—Cloudy and a little rain. We marched about 5 miles and crossed the Holston river at Morgantown and marched about ten miles farther in the direction of Knoxville. We crossed the river on a small hastily constructed bridge and it broke down just after the troops and headquarters train had gotten across, and therefore we had to do without our blankets through the night, which was of course a severe deprivation. The citizens of Sweetwater informed us that Longstreet had made a fierce assault on Burnside, and then went on to give a tolerably clear account of the affairs. As their stories all seemed to agree we all settled down into the conclusion that it was certainly true and thus were relieved of the agreeably sudden joy we would have felt had we received the news by an undoubted source at first.[3]

On the 6th we marched to Little River—distance of ten miles, and on the route, passed through the little old town of Marysville. The forage detail did much better than usual to day and brought in considerable quantities of flour, meal, salt, potatoes, &c., and as the commander of the detail (Lt. B. O. Rodes) belonged to our mess you must know that I came in for a full share of all these good things. Since the weather had began to have warmed my health had begun to grow much worse again, and I was now rendered to great straights to procure anything suitable for my condition.

On the 7th we crossed Little River at Rockford and marched to within 1 1/2 miles of Knoxville and learned to a certainty that we had had our long and tedious march without any prospect of being repaid for our suffereings by a chance to chastise that famous Army Corps of Longstreet. We had traveled over 130 miles in ten days—through a rough hilly country—with scarcely any rations but such as we procured from the country through which we hurridly passed—in the most inclement weather—very indifferently clothed on account of the "blockade" at Chattanooga, and in fact we had everything to render the expedition at once disagreeable, except the thought that we were marching to the relief of our suffereing brethren. Yes, the gallant Burnside and his noble little army were surrounded and cut off from all chance of escape by a large and well appointed force of the enemy and this thought that our timely arrival might effect some great object rendered our march comparatively an easy one.

But we did not have the remotest idea of the amount of suffereing and weariness from constant constant watching. We had no idea that Burnside's noble little army was surrounded on all sides and reduced to almost no rations,—and above all, we thought that that army was at least twice as strong as it really was; but small as it was it had sucessfully repelled one of the most [?] and bloody assaults recorded in the annals of modern warfare. Though worn down with hunger and fatigue they had manfully maintained possession of the city, and in the last desperate attempt of the enemy had come off victorious.

But where were the rebels? "The nest was there and warm, but the bird had flown;" yet he had left abundent evidence of his rashness. All around the parapets and in the ditches of one little fort could be seen the marks of a recent desperate conflict—desperate in every sense of the word for there a chosen body of heroes had attempted in one single charge to decide the fate of an army, and they had acted in every way worthy of the occasion. But it is already known to the world how Longstreet attempted to reduce Burnside's army to such a state of destitution that it would have to surrender, and how when he heard the fourth Army Corps was coming he attempted to take the city by assault, and how he met with an awfully bloody repulse, and how he concluded to let Burnside alone, and how he pulled up stakes and went on further East.

We remained on picket the night of the 7th and the whole of the 8th till late in the afternoon when we were relieved by the 17th Ky. and then we went into camp about three miles from town.

We remained at this place several days without anything of interest occuring except an occasional order to move and equally as frequent counter manding ones. Though we had plenty of such rations as the country afforded, yet we could not be said to be faring well, from the fact that we had not suitable vessels for preparing bread, and the indifferent manner in which we were compelled to cook and eat it caused some sickness in our ranks. The boys were sadly destitute of shoes, and to remedy this defect, leather was issued to the various regiments to repair the shoes of those that had any, and raw-hides to make moccasins for those that were entirely destitute. The last was a source of much amusement among the boys, but I believe I never saw anyone try the experiment of raw-hide moccasins.

During our stay we also received an order of thanks from General Burnside: "heartily thanking Gen. Granger and his gallant Corps for the gallant promptness with which they had marched directly from one bloody field to participate, if necessary, in another to save his Army from inevitable anihilation[.]"

On the 15th I procured a horse and went over to have one peep at the famous city of Knoxville. I had spent the day very pleasantly and was just thinking of starting to camp when Hazen's Brigade came marching through town. This rather hurried me up and I immediately hastened to camp and found our brigade just *going into camp* where I had left them.

They had had orders to march, but after the tents were struck they received orders to wait till morning. We began to wonder "war secret" for from the movements of Hazen's Brigade we were sure that our destination was somewhere above Knoxville; and previous to this we had almost began to hope that we would go into winter quarters, vain hope, for no more did we enjoy winter quarters while we were in the service.

On the 16th we passed through Knoxville and 15 miles beyond in the direction of Blaine's Cross Roads, and encamped on a very steep and thickly wooded hill side. There were now many rumors afloat in regard to the strength of the enemy at the front, and our cavalry were undoubtedly falling back, therefore we began to suspect that we might yet get satisfied with the notorious Longstreet.

The air was so warm that my mess lay down without pitching the tent, and sometime after midnight when the rain began to fall we [were] reduced to the awful necessity of breaking into quiet naps a sufficient time to clear off ground, erect and ditch around a tent.

Ooh, it is so disagreeable to be awakened from a pleasant nap by the rain falling on your face and then to stand around in a hard shower till you are thoroughly drenched to the skin! On this night it was particularly so. I was so emaciated from disease at this time that I could scarcely walk, and no one can imagine the heavy yearning I felt for home as I stood on that steep hillside, the rain falling briskly, the night exceedingly dark, I exceedingly tired, sleepy and sick. As I looked through the already inky darkness with imagination's eyes, I almost fancied I could see warm, soft beds, bright firesides, pleasant sofas, the old armchair, and many luxuries rolled up before my mind as if to make me feel more keenly the dis comfiture of my situation. But those days are passed now. The soldier no longer makes heavy marches, and tentless bivouacks, and breadless suppers; and those that have suffered from these causes can scarcely realize the fact, since they have returned to the happiness and comforts of home and friends much less those who have never seen a battlefield or a soldier's bivouack can have a correct idea of what the soldiers of the late war endured for the salvation of this great and glorious Republic.

I believe that the loyal portions of this Nation feel all the gratitude that is possible toward its defenders and I believe also that they sympathized with the soldiers while they were in the field, for in proof of that fact many evidences could be brought out.

But if they could have a correct idea of the *real* toils and privations that a soldier is compelled to undergo, and of the many self denials he is compelled to make in order to befriend his country they would never cease to shower laurels upon his head, and speak words in his praise.

About an hour before daylight on the morning of the 17th, we received orders to be ready to "march or fight" at daylight, but daylight came on in due time without any other company save a slow rain, and deep mud, and a desolate scene generally. The 17th Ky.[4] came up during the day and brought a *few* rations, but rations now began to grow scarcer for we were in a country that had been foraged over by Longstreet's and Burnside's armies, and could not reasonably expect to find a great amount of forage left. On the 18th, Cos. B and G were sent out under Capt. Simmons to escort a forage train for hay and feed corn, and on their return they fetched persimmons and apples which pleased my fancy very much, for it is the nature of persons afflicted with chronic diarrhea to crave fruit of any kind. The air was very cold during the day, but that just suited me for every time the weather became cooler there would be a temporary improvement in my health.

The weather was a little warmer on the 19th and so scarce had become the fighting news that Co. H of our regiment was sent some distance in the country to guard a grist mill. Large wagon trains and droves of cattle passed on to the front and from all indications we judged that Longstreet had finally given up the idea of being able to accomplish any thing in this end of the earth and had gone to try his hand with the Yankees of the Potomac.

About the 20th I begun to entertain serious thought of attempting to procure a leave of absence, for I had given up being able to conquer my disease if I remained in camp. I finally went to Old Dr. Jeffray Brigade Surgeon and asked his advice as to the course I should pursue he told me that I might either "resign, obtain a leave of absence, or die," and I thought he was going to add "and I don't care which you do" but he did not. I concluded that I "must have time" to make up my mind as to which I should choose and accordingly returned to my tent about as wise as when I left; for my friends had been repeatedly urging me to resign or obtain a leave of absence for a month.

On the 21st we recieved a large mail, which I believe was the first since leaving C———, but it was very old, yet a letter is never to old to be desirable and interesting to a soldier.

The 24th (Christmas Eve) rolled around and found us on the same steep hill side, but under many obligations to an All Seeing Providence for the enjoyment of such general health and good spirits among the troops. It also found us in the midst of a considerable excitement in regard to re-enlisting as *veterans*. Almost the whole of the 19th Ohio that was present had reinlisted, and the fever was extending toward our Regiment, in which there were many ready to veteran *provided* they could make choice of the arm of service in which they might serve. But somehow or somehow else it never got a right start among our boys, and though I would not encourage anyone to reenlist, yet I felt that it was one of the great politic strokes of our rulers by which our army was to be kept filled and discipline and experience retained.[5]

Had I been healthy at the time I expect I should have attempted to induce Co. B to "go veterans[.]" I also expect my efforts would *not* have been crowned with success.

Christmas was cloudy and some warmer than usual, but on account of the scarcity of chaplains and *other materials* we could not have the usual holiday sports, and the proper religious exercises. After dark the other regiments of our brigade got up such a scene by throwing firebrands and turpentine balls, and such a racket by any and every means that could be invented for creating noise that they were brought out and compelled to stand two hours in line of battle. This is one of the sorest punishments that is known to the soldier, but on this cold night the regiments seemed to defy it its facilities for creating anything but pleasant feelings, by giving a deafening yell just as they were dismissed from parade.

Amid varied scenes of camp life we passed the next few days at this place, but time passed as cheerlessly and sluggishly as I ever knew it. The weather was at times very cold, and again it would be warm; and the rain falling in torrents rendering our conditions in many ways disagreeable. We were getting no rations at all except as we procured them from the country and then it was in exceedingly small quantities and the meat was generally of the most inferior quality—The animals which were driven in for meat being generally of the very leanest order.

To add to the disagreeableness of the situation we hardly ever received any mails, and when we did they would have been en route for many days. We almost entirely lost communication with the general current of events in the outer world, and had not the remotest idea as to what progress was being made by the various departments of our armies. We once or twice received a limited supply of clothing and shoes, but not, by far, enough to supply the increasing wants of our ragged and barefoot soldiers.

"*Thur Dec. 31st*—weather warm and rainy. I made application for leave of absence this evening in consequence of my very low and swiftly declining state of health; though many have urged me to resign as they think that I will never again be able for service; but I think that if I can get home that I will soon recover my usual good health."

About ten o'clock in the evening of the 31st the wind commenced blowing with a violence that seemed intent upon sweeping every movable thing in its face, and with such coldness that seemed to pierce the very bones, so sudden was the change from a very warm state of air. Many of the tents were blown down and not a few were blown entirely away, and the whole valley seemed to burn a perfect blaze of light, produced by the flying sparks of the agitated camp fires. The men generally had left their tents and were standing on the company street enjoying the piercing wind and yelling at the top of their voices, as if they would drown the roar of the wind.

Notwithstanding the piercing wind, the flying sparks, the falling tents, the hungry stomachs, the naked limbs, and shoeless feet, yet the boys seemed to enjoy the sport amazingly. The next morning was the coldest I ever experienced. A slight snow had fallen the night previous and this aided by the still driving wind rendered the cold exceedingly severe, and the wood began to disappear from our side of the hill with such a wonderful rapidity that we knew that it would not be long ere we would be compelled to move camps to be near a supply of that article. We had rumors of every description in regard to our going back to Chattanooga but they all proved to be unfounded, yet we never could see why we were kept here so many miles from any kind of transportation, and where we had foraged over the country till it was almost completely stripped of all the necessaries of life for either man or beast.

On the 4th we suddenly received an order to be ready to march at a moment's warning, each man to be supplied with 100 rounds of ammunition, but we never heard any more of it. On the 5th, Gen. Grant passed up the road in the direction of the front and rumor said that he was going through the mountains to Kentucky. We received a small mail again on that evening, but no papers. On the 6th I recieved a leave of absence for *twenty* days, which I told the boys I thought would probably last until I could reach home, and I could then get it renewed till I should have recovered my health.[6]

I concluded to not start home till the baggage train should arrive from Chattanooga which I had heard was on the route, for we had all been compelled to leave the greater portion of our baggage at Chattanooga.

The 7th was cloudy and cold, and in the evening we had about 1 1/2 inches of snow; but we could not yet get any definite news from the train and, of course began to grow very impatient.

On the 9th we again heard from our train, and it had not yet left Louden. My [im]patience now knew no bounds and I immediately resolved to be ready to set out for home on the next day. Gen Wood and staff had gone on a few days previous and I now regretted that I had not gone with them as far as Chattanooga, for I expected that transportation to that point would be rather difficult. Early on the next morning of the tenth I informed the boys that I was ready to receive anything they wanted to send home, and soon found myself encumbered by a roll of money amounting to nearly 2500 dollars, and it principally in small bills. I then set out for the depot accompanied by my brother officer and mess-mate B. O. Rodes. We traveled on horseback and went to Strawberry Plains. The train had just arrived from Knox ville and as there was no convenient place for me to rest till it would commence its return, Rodes assisted me into the car where he said that I would be comfortable, and unmolested. I would have been well situated, but the Conductor soon came along, and informed me that the cars had to be moved some distance by hand to get the locomotive to the other end of the train and therefore ordered me out. Rodes saw me coming out, directly ordered me to return, and also cursed the conductor for his (as Rodes called it) impudence. I was not molested any further.

Train arrived at Knoxville about sundown, and the first thing I did was to procure a bill of transportation to go by the cars to Louden the next day, and then I looked for some place to stay all night. I went to one hospital and procured supper, and was expecting to sleep there when the surgeon in charge came in and informed me that I better report to the Medical Director. I repaired to his office immediately, but he was not in, and another surgeon that was in the MD's room said that he knew that he would do nothing for me if he were there.

I next, by the advice of an old gentlemanly looking citizen went to a house of a widow woman near the river and which was a boarding house, but here also failed to procure any quarters, but the "good woman" gave me a substantial and nourishing supper. After knocking at half a dozen other houses, I finally obtained quarters in Hospital No 1. Where I was kindly cared for by the surgeon in charge, who seemed to be as solicitous for my comfort as if he had not been used to seeing hundreds of men in my condition and worse almost every day.

On the next day I took the cars for Louden and after a jolting, rocking and altogether unplesant ride I arrived safely at my destination from which I expected to travel to Chattanooga by boat, but when I arrived the last boat had gone out of sight and another was not expected for two days. Feeling rather vexed at this I immediately started in search of the baggage train which I supposed was still somewhere near the place, but I soon met up with the last of the escort just marching off in the direction of Knoxville. The train had already gone, but the private baggage had all been left at Chattanooga. There was a considerable squad of my Reg. along, accompanied by Lieuts [James] Goad and [Demetrius B.] Coyle,[7] and the few minutes that we spent together was spent in their telling me of a fight that they had in Charleston as they came on. And their account of Gen. Wheeler's unsuccesful attack on the "Quinine Brigade["] was truly interesting, slightly bordering on the ludicrous.[8] And I would that I had space to give a full account of this interesting little affair.

I went to the camp of the 3rd Ky. Infantry and procured transportation for the next boat that should pass down the river and there in company with a Lieut. of the 15th Mo. whose name I will not mention[9] and Capt. Miller, Commissary on Gen. Wood's staff[10] we crossed the river to Louden and for the modest sum of one dollar we procured a dinner of corn bread and coffee. Then we recross the river and bivouack under a large shelter lest the boat should come and go during the night. I was very much annoyed by the close attention of the Missouri Lieut. and felt some apprehensions as to the honesty of his intentions for I could tell by his remarks that he believed my pockets would be worth rifling. Capt. Miller warned me to be on my guard and was so kind as to extend me a portion of his blanket which his careful ideas of comfort had caused him to bring along.

We remained on the river's bank during the whole day of the twelth, without being greeted by the anxiously expected boat and with an inpatience that was scarcely endurable I turned in to my humble breakfast of cold beefs liver and corn bread, which my cook had been so careful as to prepare for me before I left camp. For dinner the Missourian went and made arrangements with the mistress of a house in the vicinity, and soon we were there and seated at the table loaded with—whew! I seated myself at the table, and feeling no sense but hunger I piched into some cannister biscuits, and black flesh, but a few mouthfuls of this satisfied me and I finished my meal in short order by taking a few sups from a cup of coffee and then sat back. I then began to look around the room to ascertain if possible by what kind of people I was surrounded. It was a mixed collection of old and young women, dirty girls and boys, and in fact they were the most rottenwitch family that I ever beheld. One corner of the room which to all appearances contained a loom was literally piled with ragged uniforms broken chairs, stinking raw hides, one or two beef heads, several articles of questionable appearance, and right under my chair I discovered a sheepskin with the legs attached, and judging from the pale color of the fleshy side, it was originally a covering for the identical meat that I had just partaken of on the table.

This heightened my disgust and caused an almost uncontrollable desire to eject that which I had just eaten, yet the Missourian ate on as if he were dining at the most elegant saloon in any large city. Presently an anti-silvery voice asked me to eat more, and looking around, I saw a fat, dirty, greasy, black eyed, red faced, yellow complexioned, indolent, dissipated, and self centered specimen which I beleieve some folks call a young lady. A throng of dirty, ill-raised children were on every side of me and were charging into the dish of meat and plate of bread with a rapidity and veracity that would have soon left nothing for me to eat, even if I had been so disposed. I dont think I ever in my life saw such an ignorant, degraded, uneducated family of persons. They seemed lost to all the finer feelings of humanity, and were rolling in dirt and crawling filth, in the happy state that lets every day provide for itself. But I cant repress a feeling of mingled loathing and regret to this day.

Despairing of hearing of the boat that night, I went to the camp of the 3rd Ky Infantry, and soon found the cabin of an old friend, J. M. Akin, and with him I spent the night after eating a rough but *decent* supper.

Wed Jan 13th. Lieut. Christie[11] came down early in the morning and invited me to his cabin, and requested me to remain with him as long as I should stay about the camp. And as he had the best table and my friend the best arrangements for sleeping, I made my arrangements accordingly.

On the 14th I was again doomed to the disappointment of not seeing a boat arrive, and oh, but I began to grow impatient—my furlough was rapidly shortening—my health gradually declining—and really the fates seemed to conspire against my welfare. We had no news through the day to relieve the painful monotony except a cheering telegraph from Kingston to the effect that the Steamer Chattanooga had gone to Bridgeport for repairs and that the other steamers were too heavy draught to come up in the present low stage of the river. The weather was now *disagreeably* nice and clear, for you may judge that I now wanted to see heavy rains. The next two days were of the same impatience creating nature, and I begun to get so low spirited that my health became rapidly worse, but on the coming of the second day Gen [George D.] Wagner and staff came down from Knoxville, going on leave of absence, and then I summed up all my powers of patience to see if I had as much as a ★. On the morning of the 17th a sick man of the mess with whom I had been sleeping began to break out with small Pox, and of course this incident did not increase my satisfaction, considering that I had occupied the same bed with the sick man for four previous nights.

Late in the evening I joined a party of seven officers of different regiments and 18 privates principally of the 3rd (?) ohio cavalry (veteran) who were preparing to start to Chattanooga that night in an open *ferry boat*. This I considered to be a rather hazardous undertaking especially as the river was very low and filled with many rapids that would render night traveling in such a frail conveyance both disagreeable and dangerous; but I felt willing to incur any risk or inconvenience in order to be travelling toward home. Accordingly, about 6 1/2 o'clock P.M. a jolly crowd had assembled at the river bank preparing to start on the perilous voyage. Generally they seemed to anticipate a fine time during the voyage and were as busy about their leave-taking with men whom they had never seen till a few hours previous, as if they were starting on a voyage across the Atlantic, and were taking a last sad parting with dear relations and friends. Soon we had completed our preparations and amid the shouts of a dozen spectators and the firing of a pistol we started down the river. Not a single passenger of the boat was in any way aqauainted with the river, but we knew that before starting and had heroically concluded to "go it blind." There were twelve stout men among us and they agreed to work the oars by reliefs, and they would keep the boat at a swift enough speed to give steerage way.

I, and a few others (being unable to row) were placed at the bow of the boat to look out for snags and shoals, &c. and soon we had every possible regulation made to insure a quick and safe voyage. We steered around many rough places, which we could distinguish in the darkness by the roar of the water lapping around the rocks. At one time we found ourselves so close to a rapid before discovering it that we saw no other way of escape but to go straight over or under, and the helsman called for a "hearty pull" at the oars, intending to run over in a manner to prevent swamping. We wheeled to the left and over we went broadside, where the water made a perpindicular ascent of nearly three feet, but which we had judged from the roar of the water to be much worse. As it was, our boat took in water frightfully, but finally we cleared the "breakers" and were again in smooth water. When we had been out two hours, and just as we were making a turn in the river we espied a sight ahead which would have been an exceedingly welcome one a few hours since, but which now called for a volley of half-malicious oaths from many of our *river-sick* passengers. It was the steamer Kingston coming up the river, but she was some distance off and we did not pass her for another half hour. Then the usual hails were passed and some of our boys were just laying in a volley of jests upon the passengers of snail-traveling steamers, when we found ourselves in its waves and they came very near sinking our clumsy vessel. A hasty consultation had been held when we came in sight of the steamer relative to whether we should hail the steamer and be taken on board or "go ahead." The former alternative, after considerable discussion was agreed upon, but the officer of the steamer refused to recognize our hail, and we soon found ourselves in the wake of the steamer irresistably drifting down the current which was at this place remarkably strong. Our crew then for as few moments indulged in a torrent of oaths and imprecations that would have carried the palm from any large beer saloon in the time of a Dutch

festival, and they swore they would "go ahead" in our present conveyance or die in the attempt; But after the steamer was lost from
view we began to calculate how long it would take our boat and the
steamer to make the trip to Chattanooga, and finding a vast difference in favor of the latter we resolved to land at the first suitable
place and make our way back to Louden.

After having been in the water for about three hours we "hove
to," and learned from a citizen that by the river we were twelve
miles from Louden, and only seven by land. Several of us at once
resolved to return to Louden that night, hoping to get there ere the
boat would leave—Hired a wagon and away we went. We arrived
at Louden about 5 o'clock A.M., but the guards would not suffer us
to cross till after daylight, and as the rain had begun to fall we
repaired to the Moss hotel and bided our time. At daylight we
crossed over when to our intense mortification and chagrin we
learned that the boat was intending to make a trip to the *White
River shoals* and return before going through to Chattanooga. We
could do no more than go to the camp of the 3rd Ky and *wait*. Gen
[Robert B.] Potter came down the night previous and was going
home on leave of absence.[12]

Early on the 19th a rumor was spread through camp that the
post was threatened with attack by a large body of rebel cavalry, and
in another Col. H. A. Dunlap (3rd Ky) received a dispatch ordering
him to retain all persons that were now stopping at his camp, regardless of rank or condition. When this communication was published, I began to feel "kind o' *mad*" and if I thought there was the
least chance for me to receive my health in camp, I should have started
at once to return, but I mentally resolved that I could endure as much
detention as any *two* Generals, and concluded to stay and with them
share the worst of consequences. But presently another order came
allowing those officers to pass who were not in command of detach-
ments, and of course I was free to go if the boat ever returned.

About 9 o'clock in the evening the boat again came puffing up
the river, and in two hours she had discharged her cargo (it was very
small) and we were winding our way down the *ugly* Tennessee, and
I was commencing one of the most disagreeable steam boat rides
it has ever been my fortune to make. There were no rooms for
comfort except for the regular crew, but the dining room, and that

was filled with the two generals and their appendages and a few others. There were about 500 officers and soldiers on board, principally veterans and that of course completely deprived me of any chance to get within the small circle of heat that surrounded the engine.

I was so weak I could scarcely stand, and as there was no place to sit but the floor I just lay down and drew my coat-cape over my face and lay all night almost pierced through and through by the chilling wind.

The next morning I was scarcely able to move, but the kind cook passing and seeing my desperate condition, took me to his room and soon had me feeling much better, and eating hot coffee and butter toast. I was not the only sick person on board, by a large number or probably I would have fared better than the night previous.

We continued to steam away down the river through the whole of that day; the boat seeming to travel more slowly on account of our truly deplorable condition. About ten o'clock we arrived at Chattanooga, and I soon found my former mess cook, William Sprave, who had been left to guard the baggage, and through his prescription, I was soon in the enjoyment of a very fine sweat. Oh, but I did feel so comfortable after I had donned a suit of new clothes and was wrapped in warm blankets, and *laid aside* to sleep.

The cars had been running to Chattanooga but a very short time, and were so crowded with "veterans" and other classes that I did not get away for the next two days, but was compelled to submit to the device of Fates, which seemed to be that I should not get home. But on the morning of the 23rd I by an extraordinary strategic stroke managed to get aboard a freight train, and for one more time felt like I would see mother. We arrived at[.]

Arrived at Stevenson, Ala. about ten o'clock A.M. and was then informed that there would be no train for Nashville till 6 o'clock in the afternoon. I got out to walk about a little while, and suddenly found myself with the 21st Ky. Reg. which had reinlisted and was going home as "veterans" and were going up the road that evening by a 6 o'clock train.

I was aquainted with several of the numbers and at once resolved to cast my fortunes with them till we should reach Nashville. Sure enough, at six P.M. we were "under way."

The Twenty Onesters were in high glee at the prospect of seeing home, as veterans usually were while it was a new thing, and not-withstanding it was a very cool night the greater portion of them remained on top of the cars the whole night, whooping and yelling and having a gay time generally. By the kindness of Capt [John G.] Evans,[13] I was stowed away in a large roll of blankets and passed the most comfortable night that I had done for many. I slept the whole night perfectly unconscious of the bumping and jolting of the freight cars and of the swiftly passing mountains, valleys, rail-road stations, rivers, creeks, &c.; all of which were plainly visible in the beautiful moonlight.

We arrived in Murfreesboro the next morning about daybreak and took breakfast, but the train did not start again till about 9 A.M. Then, without any occurance of interest except a temporary loss of a portion of the train which caused much merriment at the expense of the boys that were on the *left* boxes, we, about 12 o'clock arrived at Nashville.

I then went immediately to the Capitol, registered, obtained a city Pass and then put up at the Commercial Hotel, eat my dinner, and then started out to make some purchases when, to my chagrin (I must say it) I found it was sunday and that I would be compelled to remain in the city the next day.

It was wholly out of my power to get away on the train the next morning and therefore I was compelled to remain the whole day in the City, which is never pleasant to a stranger and sickman, and worse than all there were no evening passenger trains. I went to the depot anyhow and found the 42nd Ind veterans just starting for Louisville, and I was "kindly taken in" and at midnight I alighted from the train at Bowling Green Ky. I went to the various Hotels, but after a series of knocks and yells I failed to gain admittance and repaired to the Public Square where I had seen a fire. This was, under the circumstances, a real treat.

It was the guard fire of a Company of the 49th Ky Infantry and who by the way, had at that time seen very little service, and the boys were very perceptibly shocked, when they saw me (an officer) stretch my blanket before the fire and lie down. It seemingly had never ocurred to them that an officer could rest on the ground, but I guess they saw my conduct repeated by some of their own shoul-der straps ere they were done "riding the elephant."

Notwithstanding my pleasant bed I was up early the next morning and procured a good "country breakfast" at the "Moorehead House["] and began to cast about for some means of conveyance home which was yet forty seven miles away. By the kindness of ex-Col. and Lt Col. B. C. and J. H. Grider I was supplied with a horse from the livery stables and in company with Mr. S[amuel] Carpenter of Scottville Ky[14] and a young lady I set out again. After an invigorating, and rushing ride of twenty five miles (travelled in five hours) we found ourselves in Scottsville, and as it was late I put up for the night. Next morning I failed to get away till about 10 o'clock A.M. and had not been gone from town an hour till it was attacked by a band of about three hundred guerillas, who soon compelled its heroic little garrison (one infantry company) to surrender, but not till they had exhausted their supply of ammunition. The rogues burned the dwelling and another house of my host of the previous night, mr. S. Carpenter, and scaked the town, taking all their horses. This was another pretty narrow escape of mine, and the reader (especially if he is a citizen of a Northern State) will wonder how I could have any pleasures in going home under such circumstances.

Our Country was at this time completely run over by these desperadoes, and the life of the lone soldier was never safe. Even citizens could not go about their common vocations of life without a feeling of dread lest the rogues should come upon them and rob them of property and perhaps life, which was not an uncommon occurrence.

They never felt safe at any time unless they were in view of some Yankee detachment, which was a thing of very uncommon occurrence. Many of the most prominent and wealthy citizens had been compelled to leave their homes and become refugees in Northern States, or members of the Army to save themselves from cruel deaths. I knew all this before I left home, but so far away was I that I could not realize the fact in a sufficiently strong light to deter me from coming. I did not arrive home until sometime after dark, and before I got home I met Tom (my big brother) who with several other boys had started to a party. Before making myself known to them I attempted to give Tom a little scare, and my efforts were crowned with success, for in about one tenth of the time it takes a frog to catch a fly, I felt an unpleasant punch against my breast and needed no instruction to find out that it was a pistol. I took down my scaring colors in a hurry, and raised a flag of truce, but had liked to have been too late, for Tom was really scared and in another moment he would fired.

I felt thankful that the affair turned out no worse and made up my mind that scaring folks "didn't pay."

The reader knows, of course that I got home that night, and knows that the old folks, and young ones to were glad to see me, and that I was glad to see them, and he would not be any more strongly convinced of that fact were I to write pages after pages on the enjoyments, comforts, pleasant associations, and early recollections of Home: Or if I were with the pen of a Shakespeare, Milton, Byron, or Burns should to meditate on the endearing and heavenly name of mother. Novelists alone could take up my subject at this point and make my stay at home occupy several pages of interesting material. But as I have not their great powers of composition, nor their remarkable fluency of words, nor their ready command of the pen I would in the beginning despair of success.

The next day I started my Bowling Green horse for home in care of a trusty man, but he met up with a Battalion of Yankees who were pursuing the rogues that robbed Scottsville the day before, and they took his horse from him and supplied him with an old broken down concern. So you see that my usual run of good luck continued without any abatement from the time I left camp till I got home. But once there I felt grateful to the All Seeing being that I had come through with life and was now at home, among relations and friends, with a kind mother to administer to my wants, beloved sisters to help while away the weary hours till I was able to walk around.

Let it suffice to say that I spent an agreeable term at home and that after a long period of uncertainty I began suddenly to rapidly recuperate and in a short time was fat enough for meat, and stout enough to march with any regiment.

I had my leave of absence extended *three times*, which made the whole leave amount to eighty days;[15] though I reserved 16 days of the last twenty for the purpose of travelling to the regiment; or in other words started back just 16 days ere my time had expired not troubled by guerillas while at home.

On the 14th of March after packing the extra concerns of my

William Marcus Woodcock with grandson Wilson Wiley Woodcock, Jr.,
and son Wilson Wiley Woodcock, Sr., 1913.
Courtesy of Mary Elizabeth Cain.

trunk with various little packages, sent by wives, mothers, and sisters, to husbands, sons and brothers, and taking leave of dear relatives and friends I again set out for my regiment. On the 17th I took the cars at Franklin, and that day evening found me in Nashville, where, among the first items, I learned that the Nashville and Chattanooga Rail-road had been cut by guerillas near Tullahoma and that the road would not be repaired so I could go ahead, till the evening of the next day.

I got aboard the train at 9 o'clock P.M. on the 18th, and we were soon bumping away toward Chattanooga. Finding no one near my seat who seemed to be of conversational turn of mind I fell into a sound slumber a little while after dark, and with short interruptions slept till near daylight the next morning, when on arousing, I found we were just enetering Stevenson, Ala.—Halted a little while and then *tooted* away again and by 10 o'clock arrived in Chattanooga having had a rather long spell of car-riding, but was very much vexed to see the Knoxville train move out of the depot and go rumbling away to the northeast just as we came in sight, but had no way of helping myself, so I calmly alighted from the train and put up at a boarding house to await my time.

The next morning we drove down to the depot at 9 1/2 o'clock to be ready to start on the 10 o'clock train, but imagine our unexpressible joy and surprise when we learned that the *schedule* had been changed and that the train had left at 7 o'clock. With many kind feelings for the rail-road agents we drove back to our boarding house and spent the day as best we could which was not so disagreeable after all, for my companions in misfortune were all interesting and intelligent personages.

On the next morning (*Mon March 21st*) we were at the depot at a very early hour, but there was no passenger train we got on a train with the 19th OVVI which was just new units returning from its "interim furlough." The boys seemed to be in a high state of forced merriment, and were wisely commenting upon the hard bargain they had made in giving three more years of hard service for a furlough of thirty days. But as a general thing they were with great cheerfulness submitting to the consequence of their patriotic but severe bargain.

We had a slow and exceedingly rough ride till we arrived at Loudon; 3 1/2 o'clock P.M. And as the bridge had not been built across the river we were carried over in a "two mule" ferry-boat; again mounted the train, and arrived at the Knoxville depot about 8 o'clock P.M. For want of hotels in the city we were compelled to accept the exceedingly rough and disagreeable fare and lodging at the Rail-road Eating House for the night. The next morning I went to the Convalescent camp and found it commanded by Col. Cram of my regiment.[16] As there was a good prospect for the early setting in of disagreeable weather, and as I had several days to return to my regiment, I resolved to stop at this camp for a few days, and accordingly had my baggage transported thither.

Snow now commenced falling very early and continued to fall till it was nearly five inches deep. This of course caused me to be very much satisfied with my action of remaining a few days.

I remained here three days with no other object than to let the snow pass off, for I did not like to have such a disagreeable time for commencing to again harden myself to camp life.

Sat March 26 I set out for my regiment, but was far from having a pleasant forenoon, as I was compelled to sit on the top of a car, and enjoy the cold drizzling rain. I arrived at Strawberry Plains about noon, and obtained a dinner of Lt. Frank White R.Q.M. 9th Ky, and then mounted a wagon that was going to the regiment, which was last heard from as being encamped in Richland valley about 3 miles above Blaine's Cross roads. I arrived at the camp of the regiment, but learned from the cooks and wagoners that it had started that morning on a scouting expedition and would be absent for the next two days—didn't care much, for I wanted to recover from the fatigue of my journey ere I attempted the heavy task of shaking hands with all the boys[.]

From the accounts of the boys I was satisfied that my furlough had relieved me from some of the hardest service that the regiment had yet seen.[17] On the evening of the 28th the regiment arrived in camp after having a most fatiguing scout in which they had effected nothing except but the killing of one and the capture of a few more bushwhackers. The reader (especially if he is a soldier) knows that I felt great pleasure in meeting with the boys after having been so long separated: and we had many remarks of mutual interest to exchange. I to tell them about affairs at home and they to tell me about what they had seen and suffered in my absence. The weather that night and the next day was very disagreeable, and I now began to feel the effects of my rough initiation in the shape of a violent cold. But I contrived to adapt myself to the circumstances with the greatest possible grace, and wouldn't have cared a wit had not the boys been continually asking me annoying questions (good-naturedly though) as to how I "liked camp life—your dog tent is not as comfortable as your father's house, etc."—"wouldn't you like some milk and honey for dinner?"—"going home is a great deal better than coming back ain't it?" and many others of a similar nature as though I were but a raw recruit and had not seen as much hard service as any of them.

I found my kind 1st Lieutenant in excellent health and spirits, and immediately after my arrival he made an application for a twenty-day leave to go home.

On the first day of April our brigade, in command of Col. Kneffler as Beatty was on leave of absence set [out] on a scout—crossed Clinch Mountain and travelled several miles up Flat Creek

Valley, making our whole day's march about 16 miles. Met with no enemy to our comfort or cause except a rough road, heavy rains and swollen streams. But the rain ceased falling about night and we went into camp on a rocky hillside and enjoyed a very pleasant night's rest.

On the 2nd we advanced seven miles further up the valley, which brought us to within twenty-seven miles of Cumberland Gap, then drank a cup of coffee to the health of those enemies we were seeking, and set out to return, and camped that night on the same spot as on the previous night. The boys managed to collect some of the "delicacies of the season" in our camp, and upon dividing the spoils among other things that fell to my share, I found a large lump of maple sugar and *seven fresh eggs*, all of which I securely deposited before going to sleep.

The next morning we set out to return to camp. The day was pleasantly warm and beautiful; after a toilsome ascent we reached the summit of Clinch Mountain, when, on casting my eyes away to the east I caught a limited view of the famous Smoky Mountain, the snows of the winter still remained undissolved on its distant but lofty peaks, and their appearance was a strange contrast to the greener ridges that showed themselves in the intervening space.

The 4th and 5th were very rainy disagreeable days, so much so that we were kept closely confined to our little "doggerys," which are very disagreeable places to remain in a great while, as a man cannot even straighten himself, and that of all days is the one in which exercise would be agreeable. In the afternoon of the 5th Lt Hestand (Co B) received his leave [of] absence and immediately announced making preparations to start for home the next morning.

The next day (April 6th) was one of those exceedingly pretty and lovely days which generally herald the first approach of spring, and are rarely ever seen except in this mediating month. Our Company had gone on picket the night before, but were relieved at daylight this morning, marched to camp, and ordered to be ready to move at a moment's warning.

The whole division marched by a little after sunrise, and of course wondering what could be the object of the move, we marched that day to Strawberry Plains, distance of 11 miles.

The general opinion of the boys was that we were going back

to the old department of Cumberland, but I thought that I had every reason to form an exactly contrary opinion.

Lt Hestand took his departure for home in the evening leaving me in command of the company.

The 7th was very cloudy and cool, but we marched through Knoxville and about 4 miles beyond in the direction of Loudon and encamped, making the day's travel about 22 miles. We had a pretty strong indication this evening that we were going to leave the country, in the shape of an order to send back to Knoxville and fetch up all the "surplus baggage" which had been stored away there for near two months. Still many of us thought that surely our time had come, if it ever was coming, to have the privilege of doing some kind of Post duty. The other two divisions of our Corps (S & O)[18] had been guarding the rail-road during the whole winter between Chattanooga and Knoxville and another of them was larger than ours we thought that one of them would be relieved and supplanted by ours. But alas, for the soldier's hopes of ease and pleasure! we were *all* relieved, yet I will not anticipate. On the 8th we advanced only 5 miles, but on the 9th we travelled 14 miles and in the evening halted at Lenoir Station, which was probably once a pretty little rail road station, but now presented many effects of the restless hand of civil war.

Thus far we had had but one or two pleasant days in the month, rain falling most of the time, rendered the roads so muddy as to cause marching to be exceedingly disagreeable and irksome, yet we were not hurried, and felt certain that if we *should* have to go on to Chattanooga, that it would be made in slow and short marches, which in pretty weather is almost as agreeable as laying in camp.

On the 10th we arrived in Loudon, and as there was no means of crossing the river except by a small ferry boat, the whole day was consumed in crossing the 2nd Brigade, and ours and the first encamped for the night on a hill some distance up the river to await our turn on the morrow.

On the 11th we moved down to the river early, and as the steamer Kingston had arrived we were crossed over in a very short time and moved out about one mile from town and encamped.

We were much cheered during the evening by a rumor that we would be transported to Cleveland on the cars, for Wood's Division

had done slow marching, forced marching, dry marching, wet marching, and every other kind of marching till it was no novelty in any
of its forms, and as the regiment had never yet had a trip in the cars,
we felt very desirous to undertake the trip; but in this as in every
other good thing we were doomed to disappointment.

This was a pleasant day, but in the evening the rain again commenced falling and we could not do otherwise than pass a disagreeable night, but to recompense us for this we were allowed to remain
in camp the whole of the next day, and a great many of the boys
improved this respite from marching by making a fierce attack on
some barrels of "pop skull" that were fortified at Brigade Headquarters, but after a bloodless, yet nevertheless sanguinary conflict
which lasted through the whole day, the patriotic pop skull came
out victorious, but the victory was dearly bought, as the lightness
of his ammunition boxes notified. The boys had suffered severely
in wounded and disabled, and in evidence of their valor many helpless
forms were stretched over the *spewy* field.

Wed. Apr. 13th—The weather was pleasantly cool and beautifully clear. We breathed the pure fresh morning air, we felt that
gentle spring had in reality visited us at last with all her gentle and
soothing influences; her leafy trees and grassy fields, her pleasant
odors being waf[t]ed in every breeze from myriads of sweet-scented
flowers, and the genial productiveness; all of which is gladly welcomed by the soldier; for summer is always preferable to winter, no
matter what may be his circumstances.

Early in the morning we broke up camp and marched out; and
by slow and easy marching reached Sweetwater ere nightfall.

This clearly proved to us that our Division would do no railroad
guarding, for if such had been the purpose a portion of it would
have been left at Loudon, but such was not the case. Thus were all
our hopes of an easy summer dispelled, and we mentally began to
prepare ourselves for bearing, at least, our share of the operations
of the main portion of the Department during the next probable
campaign.

We felt no disinclination to do all that our Generals required
of us, yet we thought that if any garrison or rail-road duty was to
be done that we were entitled to the positions.

On the 14th we marched to Athens, and encamped on a high

fine hill near that place. The day was cloudy and cool but my mess made up for the lack of fine weather by having a real feast on sweet milk and "sole leather pies" procured from some of the citizens.

We marched through Athens early next morning. It presented no point of peculiar interest except one, and in that it bore a strong resemblance to Elizabeth Town, Ky. Coming square to the truth and without speaking disparagingly of anyone, I will simply state that this peculiar item of interest was no other than the large number of good looking ladies that showed themselves at the doors of their houses. It seemed that there was more at this place than I had ever seen any where, according to the population of the town. They did not make such demonstrations of patriotism as did the ladies of Elizabeth Town, Ky almost two years previous, but I suppose this may be accounted for by the difference of the circumstances by which the two places were surrounded on the different occasions. When we passed through Elizabeth Town in the fall of 1862, the place had been just a few hours before left in the rear of the numerous hosts of Bragg's Army, a greater part of which passed through the little village. And it is a reasonable surmise to suppose that the *loyal* people were doubly gladdened at the farewell of the rebels and the arrival of the Yankees, so much so that they made every possible sign of welcome to us.

Now, as we passed through Athens, we were not objects of special attention, for the rebels had been expelled from its place many months since, and a garrison of U.S Soldiers kept at the place. We camped that night at Charleston, after crossing the river— distance 14 miles.

Sat. Apr. 16th. We marched early, our regiment in front, and Co's A and F acting as advance guard under Capt. [Riley A.] Reid of Co F.[19]

We travelled about three miles, and then halted to rest, and while stopping were much amused by seeing Co's A and F come up from the rear, and, amid the jests and cheers of the crowd pass on to the front—they had taken the wrong road, and were then thrown behind. As it was only 11 miles to Cleveland we marched out at a cheerful step expecting to stop when we arrived at that place, but were again deceived, for when we arrived there (11 o'clock A.M.) we were marched directly through town without halting, and

over desolated farms out among the ruins of once pleasant home-
steads we continued our march six miles further, and went into
camp near McDaniel's Station.

We remained at this camp for several days undergoing that
refurnishing re-equipping, and redrilling that we had long been
sadly in need of. The first thing was to make requisitions for full
supplies of all kinds of supplies that were needed, and next we
proceeded to fix up our camp; i.e., ditching, sweeping, &c. And so
well did we learn the art at Murfreesboro that we soon had an
exceedingly beautiful and pleasantly arranged camp. As I was by
myself and my wall-tent had been lost, I [?] *in* with Capt Simmons
and Lieut Coyle of Co G, and we soon had a substantial cabin
erected, and roofed with a tarpoulin that had by some strange "nick
o' forturn" came into Capt. Simmon's possession.

When we had spent a few days in this manner, our attention
was called by a *general order* to drilling. The program was that we
should drill three hours each day. The time being divided equally
between Company, Battalion, and Brigade drill.

This, from the variety and shortness of time was rather a pleasant duty than otherwise, and everything went on smoothly. Another matter that added greatly to the good humor of the troops
was the regular arrival and departure of the mails. Nothing affords
more pleasure to the soldier than to be in regular communication
with home and friends, and no matter what may be his condition,
his circumstances may be in never so adverse a state, he may be
prostrated on his rude couch by the restless hand of disease, and
may have sank into that despondency that knows no hope, and in
this state if he receives a letter, you will always see the smile of
pleasure flit across his brow, and a sigh of satisfaction as he peruses
the welcome missile. Letter writing also affords much amusement
and pastime, when the soldier is in regular camp and no reading
matter to beguile the lonely hours that intervene the hours of duty.

But amid all our ease and pleasure the most careless observer
could see that efforts were being made for our extensive movement
the character and direction of which were yet a mystery. Maj. Gen.
Grant had some time previous to this been raised to the merited
position of Commander-in-chief, and was succeeded in the command of the Military Division of the Mississippi by Maj. Gen.

Wm. T. Sherman. The 11th and 12th Army Corps were consolidated and the command given to Maj. Gen. Hooker. Maj. Gen. O. O. Howard formerly of the 11th Army Corps had been assigned to the command of our Corps in place of Gen. Granger, who had been relieved.

Maj. Gen. Phil. Sheridan had been relieved of the command of the Second Division of our Corps and removed to the East, and his place supplied by Maj. Gen. Nelson. The whole army had been (to use a bookkeeper's phrase) over hauled, and completely reorganized, and we felt confident that the new commanders were becoming anxious to make another move. *Grand reviews* and inspections were matters of daily occurrence, and every move indicated an active campaign at an early day.[20]

On the 22nd a grand review of our Division by Maj Gen. Howard was appointed for the next day, but at a later hour the order was countermanded "for the present[.]"

"*Sun Apr. 24th.* According to detail on yesterday evening, 5 officers, 24 non-commissioned officers and 150 enlisted men of our regiment went on picket for the whole brigade." This was a new way of doing things, and really if an observer had only marked the orders of our Brigade Commanders he would never for one moment have entertained the idea that we were preparing for a campaign.

The Brigade picket guards, and the Brigade camp guards, the stiff salutes of the sentinels, and the limber (pop skull) recognitions of "the shoulder straps", the daily shoe-blacking and dress parades, the weekly company and regimental inspections, and the universal order to "snap" all seemed to indicate that we were preparing for a season of "stylish doings".

We had a pleasant time while out on picket, for there was quite a change in the popularity of that *institution* within the last twelve months. The natural horror that we all felt for sleepless nights, and prowling rebels when we first entered the service had now been entirely dispelled, as it afforded a relief for that day and the next from the irksome and monotonous duties of camp. It was almost a complete step from the rigid restraint of discipline to the pleasures of freedom. In the evening as one of the boys was testing the flexible properties of a pine sapling that was near the picket station, it suddenly snapped off some five or six feet from the ground, and as the stump suddenly flew back into its perpendicular position a splinter was detracted from it and struck one of the boys that was standing near. A "genius" that was standing near instantly perceived the prospect for fun and siezing the stump, he bent it to nearly a horizontal position, and laying a small piece of wood on its end, and like any other experienced gunner, calculated the distance and direction of a squad of boys that were standing near and suddenly "let fly". The "chunk" flew with wonderful precision and told with much effect among the designated squad.

This exposed the trick, and soon *whole batteries* were bravely dealing out their missiles on their foes.

In the evening I smuggled some of the boys across the lines, and was soon rewarded for this breach of discipline by receiving a canteen of buttermilk—Officer of the day came along and asked by what means I had procured the milk—told him I caught a man attempting to slip across the lines from the outside, and that I gave chase, and was rewarded by him dropping the canteen of milk[.]

Col. Cram came up the next day from Knoxville where he had been in command of Convalescent camp. He was in splended health, but was still suffering from some chronic (?) affliction in one of his feet which had been troubling him for a great while.

On the 26th in compliance with an order from Capt Taft I went to Division H Qrs and appeared before a Military Commission and had my leave of absence and surgeon's certificates investigated.

On the 27th we received orders to make out Muster Rolls for the last and present month, and to make out Pay Rolls also, as the Paymaster was expected to be along soon after the 30th, but if he came *I* didn't see him nor get any of his greenbacks.

April the 28th we were ordered to commence the interesting duty of "practice firing". It had been already in operation in many parts of the army, and was decidedly a prudent move of our generals, if it had only been commenced in time for us to prosper by the exercise. But in consequence of its not doing so, it only afforded us some good amusement, at the hours of our previous Company drills, but it proved to the boys that they had all along previous to this been very much mistaken in regard to the general accuracy of their firing.[21]

On the 29th, the Division was reviewed by Maj. Gen. O. O. Howard, but it passed off as reviews generally do—weather hot— very dusty—long lines of blue—gaily-dressed officers—no end to the ceaseless marching—and a world of style. The only interest attached to the affair by the boys was their eagerness to get a glimpse at the one-armed General, of whom we knew almost nothing either in regard to soldierly qualifications, and dispoitions, or personal qualification. The General put the matter through in a more dash- ing and military manner than any I had ever before seen, and by this, if nothing else, he created a good impression, for soldiers are always glad to be relieved from *review*.

The reader is aware that for a considerable time previous to this the soldiers had been gradually bringing themselves into campfire discussions in regard to the future Presidential Canvass, though that event was yet some distance off. Yet, the soldier had no better way of employing his time than to think, and his condition natu- rally led him to calculate as to who should be the next President, and how the soldier's condition was to be affected by his election.[22]

They had, previous to this time (as had almost every man in the nation) decided that the issue would be between our then Presi- dent, and Gen. McLellan. The reader knows also the many posi- tions and reasons for doing so that were assumed by the soldiers as well as the citizens. I felt that if the issue should be as I expected, that I should be for McLellan.

At the time of which I am writing the excitement had become pretty strong in my Regiment, and I, hoping to do good, resolved to take up my pen and defend my position, which was assailed by all the loyal citizens of my native county. I wrote, and studied, studied and wrote, for some days, preparing an address for the citizens of my county.

My first point was to defend the political and military character of my Champion, and also to enumerate his qualifications and merits. After having written several sheets on this part of my subject, I then came to consider the objections that I had to the course of the President,—the immortal Lincoln,—the man who stands second only to washington in American history, and not even second to him in magnanimity and statesmanship—The man who proved himself equal to emergencies of the country, when it was more

bitterly assailed than was ever known of a country for it to ultimately succeed; and the man who, after he had rescued the Union
from its greatest troubles, and had restored that peace that had been
so long by the world, and was now prepared to enjoy all its fruits—
was brutally murdered.

Notwithstanding his greatness I *boldly* lifted my pen to make
one of the many disgraceful assaults that were malignantly hurled
at him[.]

But I could make no point. I wrote line after line, and page after
page but still not a single objection was defined. I saw the unten-
ability of my position yet I determined if possible to hold my ground,
and closed my address by saying that "I cannot assert that Lincoln
has, as yet committed any very objectionable act toward the people,
but we must not vote for him for fear he *may* do something wrong."
As soon as I completed the sentence I mentally asked myself what
McLellan might do were he to be elected. The result was that in
a short time afterwards I tore up the message lest it should be seen
by some Lincolnite Abolitionists, who however were very scarce in
my regiment, and I soon discovered a complete change in my principles, but I did not have the courage to mention it for a considerable time after this date.

Chapter 11

❧

Our Destination Was Atlanta

In March 1864, U. S. Grant returned to Washington, both to take command of the entire Federal army and to devise a plan to end the war. Grant soon assigned Sherman two key missions—the destruction of the Confederate Army of Tennessee, now commanded by Gen. Joseph E. Johnston, and capture of the vital manufacturing city of Atlanta. A new campaign was a prospect that Woodcock clearly dreaded, however; Atlanta would mean hard fighting.

Neither commander wanted to risk an all-out battle. Johnston relied on the rugged terrain of northern Georgia, choosing seemingly impregnable positions, fortifying them heavily, and daring Sherman to attack. Sherman, in response, usually resisted the temptation and flanked Johnston back to a new stronghold, almost always remaining in contact with the Western and Atlantic Railroad, his tenuous supply line. Sherman called what followed "a big Indian war," but in fact the campaign of skirmishing and maneuver was punctuated by several sharp fights at the division or corps level and one major battle at Kenesaw Mountain. Sherman finally reached Atlanta in July, but for Woodcock, the campaign ended on May 27 in the blunder of a battle that one participant, Ambrose Bierce, later called "The Crime at Pickett's Mill."[1]

On the first of May we were ordered to turn over all surplus baggage. But one wagon was to accompany the regiment to haul officers' baggage. This was positive proof that we were going to move in some direction and soon.

On the 3rd we received orders to be ready to move at 12 o'clock on that day, and then with the desperation of humans who know that they are now "gone up" we hurriedly packed up and cooked our last dinner at this camp. The weather was exceedingly cool for the latitude and season of the year, though the forests had forced out enough green leaves to give them the lovely and glorious appearance that they always present at this time of the year, but they were not so green as if the weather had been warmer. The two or three next previous nights had been so cool that we expected to see frost on each morning; but to resume[.]

We set out about one o'clock P.M. and marched about seven miles in the direction of Ringgold and encamped near a good stream of water. This confirmed our worst apprehensions—we men knew that we were destined to occupy Dalton,[2] or acknowledge a defeat from the enemy, but we had not yet learned the true character of our commander; neither did we have the least idea of the great extent of his plan of operations, or the broad field he contemplated engineering. Had we known this, we would almost have shrunk from the undertaking.

The next day our march lay through a wild wood country, the increasing green appearance of which almost made us believe that spring had opened in earnest. Many wild flowers were growing among the brambles, or from the rocky hillsides that gave beauty to the scene. Birds were singing sweetly on every bough, and had it not been for the dusty roads we would have concluded that all nature was striving to contribute to our comfort.

We passed Catoosa Springs and encamped about one mile beyond (day's march 8 miles). We were here informed that the rebels were only a few miles in advance, and that they were skirmishing with our pickets, but we also learned that we were near the camps of the main army which had begun a forward movement.

Catoosa Springs presented the natural attractions for an inland watering place of great distinction, but it lacked the many artificial additions, which seem to be unknown about the places of amusement in the South. The variety of springs was great but I have forgotten the exact number, and as the marks that had been set over them were in many instances destroyed I will simply give those that remained, as follows; Healing Spring, red sweet, white sulphur, Blue sulphur, Emilie, Ahalybrate, Congress, Red Sulphur, Black Sulphur, White sulphur, Bedford, Coffee, Alkali, Trustone, Excelsior, About mobousca, and Lowder.[3]

On the 6th our Regiment went on picket, but as the rebels had all disappeared from our front we had the privilege of passing off the time very quietly and pleasantly. I took a ramble through the fresh leafing forests, which were now the more welcome on account of the great heat, and among my wanderings was surprised to find myself at the very spot where we had encamped one night the preceding September after passing through Ringgold, for I did not think we were so far in advance of the latter place. When we came to the pickets of the 14th A.C. we could see a few rebels away on in advance on vidette duty. Lazily did they sit on the horses, unconscious of the hard summer's work that lay before them. Little did they dream that on the next day the first gun of one of the most energetic, persevering and lengthy campaigns of American history was to be fired. Little did they think that not another day for five months would be one of rest unless they should meet a soldier's fate in the shape of death.

And little were *we* bothered with thoughts of a similar character. We had generally arranged a *programme* the end of which was the capture of Dalton, and a month's encampment at that place.

The whole army, so far as my knowledge extended, moved early in the day in the direction of Tunnell Hill and met with no opposition except the felling of a few trees across the roads which only served to remind the Yankees that it was more comfortable walking in the woods than in the dusty roads. Thus the advance of the army, which was some miles ahead of our Division had a skirmish at Tunnell Hill, but I could hear nothing but a few discharges from artillery,[4] and after filing out into the woods and fields we found ourselves ere long on the summit of Tunnell Hill, and overlooking all the dangers of the far famed Rocky Face, and great barriers to the advance of an assaulting army that were presented by it and contiguous gaps.[5]

The crest of the frowning and impassable row of cliffs (R. Face) in our immediate advance was crowded with rebels seemingly anxious to catch a glance at the advancing columns of our army which, as the heads of the different Columns entered the broad and desolated fields around the base of Tunnell Hill, presented one of the grandest scenes I ever witnessed. The troops on this occasion were in a splendid condition for casual observation—fresh from camps where most of them had known months of *style*, their polished arms, shining accouterments, and bright uniforms presented a sight that's seldom if ever witnessed. As I from this hill looked upon these moving columns of human forms and it struck me that each was a living creature—a man. I could not help exclaiming ["]How many of you will live to see another week?["] Although I did not know of the indomitable energy of our Commander still, I knew that we were now at a point where no standing or returning from would be admitted, even if possible.

We were roused early on the morning of the 8th and ordered to prepare a hasty breakfast, "roll and file our baggage" and be ready for operations by sunrise.

Soon after breakfast we were called into line and the whole brigade formed for an advance. Col Baily[6] then informed us that the object of the movement was to make a diversion in favor of Maj. Gen [John] Newton[7] (2 Div. 4th Corps) who it was expected would charge up the mountain away to our right.

Every thing was announced as ready and about 9 o'clock our brigade moved forward in line of battle toward the foot of the mountain. Skirmishing commenced simultaneously with the movement, and was kept up pretty regularly throughout the whole day. We advanced near one mile and halted in a field till near twelve o'clock, and then fell back to a skirt of timber and enjoyed a little spell of quiet rest, but after shading for about two hours we again moved forward to the base of the mountain and remained under arms till about sundown when we were ordered to bivouack for the night and send back for baggage, which consisted only of the personal portables of the men, but were considered too cumbersome in case of a fight.

Our rest that night was one of comparative uninterruption and but for the frequent crash of muskets we would have had no cause for complaint.

The next morning (9th) opened bright and rosy with an occasional pop shooting along the line. We were ordered to "pile our tricks" some distance to the rear and make ready for the day's work as it might present itself. About 8 o'clock we heard what was reported to be a desparate charge by the 23rd Ky Inftry on our right against the rebels occupying the summit of the mountain. Imme-

diately after this we were formed and moved forward to the immediate base of the mountain and we then moved a considerable distance
up the side of the mountain in a left oblique direction, where we
halted about 100 yards in the rear of our skirmish line (composed
of the 59th O.V.I.) which was pop-shooting at the rebels on the
summit now only about 300 yards away.[8]

We had just gotten settled in our positions, and embraced the
scanty shelter from the Rebel balls that was offered, when, suddenly, to our surprise and without any perceptible cause here came
our skirmish line down the hill at a rate of swiftness that was for
that reason (If that alone is to be considered) truly commendable,
thus leaving our front completely exposed. Our Lieut. Colonel (Col
Cram had been compelled to remain behind when we left McDaniel's
station on account of disability) saw the exigencies of the moment
and ordered three men forward from each company in the regiment
to fill the place of the absconding line. The *runners* saw their mistake and at the earnest solicitations of their officers they finally
returned to their posts.

We remained at this point till near 4 o'clock and then were
moved down the mountain and about one mile to the right; but in
excuting this movement we were severly annoyed at one point by
rebel sharpshooters from the summit of the mountain though the
effect of a rifle at that great distance was not heretofore much
dreaded. Yet, they succeeded in fatally wounding Geo. W. Star 1st
Sergt. Co. E; having shot him through the Femoral Artery of the
left thigh. We halted in considerable proximity to [Mill Creek]
Gap and remained there till near sundown.[9] The skirmishing on
our right was very heavy during the latter part of the afternoon. We
finally moved back to the site of our previous night's encampment,
and again bivouacked. [Levi] Tinsley of Co. C of our Regiment,
and who was a member of the Pioneer Squad was also mortally
wounded during the evening by a sharpshooter from the mountain
top at the distance of three fourths of a mile. This seemed incred-
ible, and as many others had been wounded at equally as great a
distance we began to fear lest the Rebels had a very superior kind
of gun and marksmen; but such incidents became matters of no concern ere the close of the campaign. We had an uninterrupted night's
rest which was destined to be the last of that character in that place.[10]

We were very much annoyed by sharpshooters through the whole of the next day though we still remained in the same position.

John I. Rhoten Co. G. was severely wounded in the arm;[11] also a member of the 79 Ind. also the horse of the Ass't Surgeon of the 17th Ky Infantry. The danger was so great and the relative position of ourselves to the rebels so peculiar that we were compelled to remain closely sheltered behind trees during the whole day, which position was the more disagreeable on account of the rain that was almost all the time falling. And toward evening we began to wonder why we were kept so near the rebels without being offered an opportunity to show them a hand while they were annoying us, or in other words, we thought that if we were destined to fight why were we not put at it at once, for at that early stage we had not learned Gen. Sherman's manner of whipping an enemy. A very heavy rain fell on the night of this day, and thus the disadvantages of our situation were much increased, and we were compelled to add the bad feelings of a sleepless night to the fatigue of one annoying and disagreeable day.[12]

The next day (11th) opened warm and cloudy, and without a cessation of the arrivals of sharpshooters' balls in our midst. Hazen's Brigade which lay near our right flank lost four men in killed soon after daylight. This was the more disagreeable from the fact that we could not in any way return the compliment but simply had to lay and take it. About 8 or 9 o'clock we were moved back out of range and for a time enjoyed a temporary rest. About noon Maj Genl's Sherman, Schofield and [S]toneman[13] passed through our camp, and soon after Gen. Howard. We judged from this that some unusual activity was pending. Our Regiment went on picket about dark.[14]

The next day was clear and exceedingly cool—we remained on picket all day away up the side of the mountain within about 300 yards of the top, and had plenty of work to do all the time in order to be up with the rebs. [Henry C.] Carver private of Co F was killed at his post by a shot through the head,[15] and some thus were struck by spent balls. About 8 o'clock P.M. we were relieved and returned to camp to learn that our brigade was at the Northern end of the mountain, at least four miles away, and away we went to find them which we did in due time, and they were well fortified. Rumors were very prevalent through the camp that the main rebel army were gone from Dalton and only a few were left back to make feints.

The first news we received on the morning of the 13th was that the rebels had all gone and that the 11th Ky (who relieved us from picket the night previous) were on the top of the mountain.[16]

We marched around the left of the mountain, and down the valley through late rebel encampments, and numerous rifle pits, redoubts, lunettes, abbattis, and every concievable obstruction to the advance of an attacking army, but we felt gay and light-hearted. The rebel stronghold which many of us had looked upon as attainable only at the cost of a fearful loss of life was now ours, and as an army of victors we were taking possession. But Dalton was farther from where we started than we expected and we cast many a longing eye towards its imaginary spires and domes ere they appeared in view, for we expected to encamp about the place for, in all probability the whole summer. But we were doomed to a double disappointment.

Instead of the flourishing rail-road town which we had anticipated we found only a few dilapidated buildings besides the public ones. After a temporary halt in the streets, during which our boys helped themselves to the contents of the knapsacks of the 54th Ga. Regt., which were unfortunatley *behind time* in the general rush. We moved on, not just beyond town and then into camp, but we went *six miles*, and late at night turned off into camp, much fatigued and dispirited, and sure that we would have to oust the enemy from at least one more position ere we could go into camp. Rumors were rife ere we got to sleep that the enemy would make his next stand at the Oostanola River, yet that did not cause us any great anxiety, for we felt confident that the position was no stronger than the one just given up.[17]

On *Saturday May* 14th was fought the first of the bloody two days' battle of Resaca. Our Division was moving towards the front a little after sunrise, and after travelling about 4 miles we found ourselves near the main lines of our army which were preparing for battle. A heavy skirmishing was being carried on as far as the ear could reach to the right or left, and everything indicated preparations for a battle. But for one time our Brigade lost its share of the fighting (when the rest of the division was engaged), and was detailed to guard the flank and rear of our Corps or more particularly the ammunition train. About 2 o'clock P.M. the 1st and 2nd Brigades of our Division together with other portions of the army advanced with deafening yells upon the enemy's lines, and soon the action became general and severe, and continued so with short intervals, for near three hours. We learned from members of the Ambulance corps that our division had captured two lines of rifle-pits, but at a fearful loss of life. Our two Brigades had lost six hundred in killed and wounded and others had suffered still more severely.[18] Gen'ls Kilpatrick and Geary were reported to be severely wounded.[19]

A little while after sundown the fighting became much heavier away on the left, and our artillery was playing with a rapidity, the equal of which I had hardly ever heard.

Presently the most terrible succession of volleys of musketry imaginable was heard to commence, and for a few moments we stood about clutching our firelocks in a state of awful anxiety, for we knew that a desperate effort was being made, but in a few moments the firing ceased almost as suddenly as it had commenced and all was still, but still we were in suspense for we did not yet know the result, but presently we heard our gallant comrades giving cheers of victory, which were responded to along the whole line, and which we joined with a hearty good will.[20]

The next day (15th) was one of almost incessant fighting from morning till night, but as my Brigade was not engaged, I will puzzle myself nor weary my readers to go through with a history of its details. Our Brigade did not move through the whole day, although on the night previous we had received the usual complement of extra ammunition, and *reville* was sounded at 3 1/2 o'clock, A.M.[21]

About 3 o'clock P.M. Gen. Willich 1st Brigade was carried to the rear suffering from a severe and dangerous wound which he had received while leading his "childs" on a desperate charge.[22] The battle temporarily ceased between four and 5 o'clock P.M. and without realizing or knowing the horrible scenes that had attended the day's operations we felt a momentary sense of relief, for all reports were that our boys had seized ground at almost every point, but were not decisively victorious. Late in the night, after we had all retired to rest and were enjoying a fine and comfortable rest from the labors of the toilless day we were suddenly awakened by a fearful fire of artillery just in our front and at the front lines. It was accompanied by the ominous roar of musketry, and so great was the exertions that were being made, and so faithfully did everyone seem to perform his part that the whole heavens in that direction were lit up by the flashing pieces; but for the intervention of a skirt of timber we would have been greeted with one of the most magnificent scenes offered. But while we listened with wonder to the awful roar our minds were filled with anxiety as to the effect that was being accomplished by these monsters. But, when after a time the firing died out and all became quiet.[23]

Without sending in any stragglers[?], we felt confident that we were destined to hear of no reverse, and after consulting around our fires for a few moments we again crawled into our tents and surrendered ourselves to the charms of the enchanting Morpheus.

On the 16th early in the morning we were greeted with the gratifying intelligence that the reb's had all "vamoosed," and gone on further south in search of the last ditch leaving us the undisputable proprietors of Resaca and its numerous "rifle pits".[24]

We left our camp pretty early and soon came upon the scene of the recent conflict, but as the dead had nearly all either been buried or carried off it was relieved of half its horrors and vivid realities. The ground that the Rebels had occupied during the furious cannonading of the night previous, was literally plowed up and was ready to receive grain of any kind so far as looseness is concerned; and was covered in every direction with cannon balls. Not a tree stood near the works that had not the marks of a bullet, and I noticed one green pine tree about three feet in diameter that had four holes through it made by cannon balls. But, save the fortifications, scarcely a vestige of the recent proximity of the rebels was left.

They had with great care carried off nearly every one of their dead and wounded, and we were only now and then greeted with the scattered contents of a caisson, a dead horse, a few muskets or probably the accouterments of some unfortunate one. Without having any time for observation we were marched directly over the scene, and straight forward to the little rail-road station of Resaca. There we saw considerable evidence of the rebels having left in a considerable hurry. Large quantities of Corn meal, and "goober peas" were lying at the depot but which were unfortunately behind lines, and as we halted here for some time, we replenished our haversacks with a supply of these desirable articles—I choosing the latter, of which I am particularly fond.

Also they had left a considerable amount of ordinance stores and among other things two new pieces of artillery which had not yet been mounted, but all the parts were scattered around and I suppose this nice favor was fully appreciated by some of our *red striped* comrades.[25] We also saw about two hundred prisoners, and conversed with them. They were still *loyal* to the Confederacy, but looked upon their cause as a hopeless one and said they did not desire to fight any more.

While we were stopping, much to our surprise a construction train came up from the rear, and cheered us with one of its loudest. This began to open our eyes to our General's ingenuity and the harmony with which the various departments were working. We now began to appreciate the master spirit that we had at our head. By his management we had driven the enemy from two of his strongholds in a remarkably short space of time, and now were pressing again close in his rear, yet the cars had jumped over burned bridges and ploughed out filled cuts and were now right with us, and "ready for duty". Of course we had no fear of starving for another day or two. The long and high bridge across the Oostanula had been burned, but we had no doubt that ere we needed another issue of rations that the train would spring over the gap and be at our sides. We went about four miles further that evening, or within about two miles of Calhoun, making our day's march ten miles.[26]

With tired limbs and minds well satisfied with the developments of the day we retired to rest; though not entirely free from apprehension of an unpleasant character as to the developments of the next day, for the skirmishers muskets were plainly audible, but a short distance in advance.[27]

Tuesday May 17th was clear and warm in the forenoon, but the afternoon was rainy. We advanced 8 1/2 miles along the railroad passing through Calhoun, and encamped at ——— River just 71 1/2 miles to Atlanta.[28] Our division met with but little opposition during the whole day, but the 2nd Division (immediately on our left[)] skirmished all the time, and about 2 o'clock P.M. they fired into a U.S. Telegraph train, mistaking it for the rear of the retreating rebels. Our flank guards were immediately sent out to ascertain the true state of affairs, and they also were fired upon by the skirmishers of the 2nd Division, the foggy state of the evening preventing the different parties from recognizing each other's uniform.[29] The 59th O.V.I. was then sent out to support the skirmishers and their colors exposed the true state of affairs and corrected the mistake. When we arrived near the ———— River, the skirmishing on our front became severe, so much so that the whole Division was thrown into line of battle, but just as this was effected the enemy began to throw shells into our midst. Robert Hogan of Co A and member of the pioneer squad was instantly killed, and Sergt. [Jonathan] Wilson of Co. B slightly wounded.[30] The skirmishing on our left, together with the heavy firing of artillery almost warmed into a general battle, and the rebel shells were beginning to drop in our midst with a precision that we would not at that time very well appreciate. But after an unusual delay Capt Bridges' famous battery[31] [unlimbered], and at the first round completely silenced the enemy's artillery. The second shot dismantled a rebel cannon and so demoralized the others that were bearing upon us that they were quickly taken out of view. This was the closing scene of the evening, and darkness found everything quiet[.][32]

The next day was warm and clear, and we embraced the fine weather by marching out early. We arrived in Addairsville about noon and there made a temporary halt, and arrangements for a further advance. Our Company was deployed about 400 yards to the right and parallel with the road as flanking skirmishers. I seated myself under a friendly tree by the side of another road to await the order to advance. Soon after I seated myself I saw an officer coming up the road from town alone, on foot, his head cast down and his arms locked behind his back. He wore a dress suit which seemed "rather the worse for wear", and upon the whole there was nothing striking about his appearance. I cast a momentary glance at him when he was some distance away and then continued my scribbling in my memorandum book.

When he arrived opposite me in the road, I again *diegned* to give him a glance and was not a little surprised to see two stars on the shoulder nearest me, and the identical face of Gen. Sherman on the front of his face. He continued his walk about 200 yards further out along the road and then stopped and acted altogether as if he were expecting someone to come down the road. Soon a cloud of dust in that direction foretold that his expectations were to be realized and in due time Gen. McPherson and staff came riding down the road, followed by the Army of the Tennessee.

The two Generals exchanged cordial greetings, and after a hearty shaking hands came on down the road—Sherman stepping as lengthy and briskly as a farmer coming in from feeding on a cold morning.

After they had passed, the cook brought me my dinner which consisted of a pot of hot coffee, and a frying pan of bacon. With the aid of the hard tack carried in my own haversack I discharged my duty toward the before-mentioned articles, and at the close felt that my digestion would not in any way be improved by the fact of my discovering a very large bug in the bottom of the frying pan with the gravy trickling from him as fast as from a fat goose. Next, the 5th Ky Cavalry came along, and as it was from the same localities as ourselves, we spent another half hour very agreeably in exchanging salutations with old friends but this was soon cut short by the order to advance.

We advanced about five miles further and just at dark came upon the rebel cavalry rear guard, and exchanged a few shots with them, upon which they left and we went into camp with our regiment on picket.

That evening we received very encouraging news from Gen. Grant and the Potomac army, which added to our own success tended to cheer us very much, and we began really to feel that a few more heavy blows would sound the death-knell of the Confederacy.[33] We had made pretty good time in the last two days, and although the rebels were reported to be awaiting us at Kingston,[34] we anticipated no very serious resistance, and began to look to the Capture of Atlanta as the object of the campaign, and as an event which must happen ere we could expect any rest.

Thus far we had not found Georgia the rich and productive country that we had expected, and but for having persons along who were acquainted with other portions of the state, we would have readily adopted the opinion that "Georgia aint much[.]"

The citizens were nearly all gone south, and on every side our eyes were greeted by abandoned homes and deserted fields of rich young corn and wheat, presenting a scene of desolation that was painful to witness. I conversed with a quick little lad of ten summers in Addairsville. I asked him if there were any union men in the

country. He said there were. *Q* Why did they not express themselves as such? *A* They were afraid to. *Q* Why were they afraid to?
A Because two men were hung in this town for doing that thing.
Q What's the name of this County? *A* [Bartow], it was named in
honor of [Lewis Cass] but he fled north at the beginning of the war
on account of Union sentiments, and for that reason the name of
the county was changed.[35]

About a hundred deserters came into our lines this evening, and
among them a Captain and Lieutenant. They said that large numbers of the enemy would desert did they not fear some kind of
retaliation for the Fort Pillow massacre[.][36]

On the 19th the weather was clear and very warm, and the roads
exceedingly dusty, rendering marching of course disagreeable. We
moved early, and about noon arrived at Kingston, at which time we
could hear heavy skirmishing in front. After taking a hasty dinner
we again moved forward, and after advancing about two miles, as
we came to the summit of a large hill, the larger, level, and open
tract of country that lay between us and Cassville burst upon our
view. Some distance out in this field the rebel skirmish line was
plainly visible stretched across the opening from one skirt of woods
to another. Our troops were moving down and deploying out into
this open field—[.][37]

One of our batteries was firing *by sections* at the Rebels, and at
each discharge they were enveloped in clouds of dust raised by the
ricocheting balls. Our Division was thrown on the extreme right
with our Brigade far into the woods, and every disposition made
for a grand advance. We then advanced about two miles over exceedingly rough and hilly ground without being able to see any
other portion of the army, but we suddenly found ourselves in the
open ground, and on a hill that commanded a fine view of our
advancing lines, and the little town of Cassville.

We here commenced making preparations to camp for the night
but were soon interfered with by an order to get ready to move. By
the left flank we moved down into the valley, and then joining in
with the rapidly concentrating columns we moved forward about one
mile. During all these movements the artillery was becoming warmly
engaged, and the infantry skirmishing was assuming a character
that seemed to say "we are in for it now." The 16th A.C.[38] came

up and formed on our right and then the arrangements being completed (though it was near sunset), the whole line again moved
forward, presenting a strikingly grand and interesting picture for
the gaze of the free observers, and notwithstanding I expected soon
to be engaged in the deadly conflict, yet I could but admire the
scene. It was very different from a *Grand Review* or any military
gotten up for show alone. Instead of gaily-dressed officers, shining
plates and glistening accouterments, and a monotonous move in
the parade of all the troops, we here had a different scene.

Real excitement rendered any assumed appearance of interest
wholly unnecessary,—staff officers galloped from post to post because
they had *something to do.* Shining buckles and glistening accouterments
were accounted for by dusty knapsacks and full cartridge boxes, and
a pleasing variety was given to the scene by every Division General
advancing his lines according to his own tactics, only they all kept
their places. Some advanced their regiments, deployed at full length,
others in columns of divisions, and others in echelon. The 17th Ky
was thrown forward as skirmishers for our Brigade. We advanced
about a mile further the enemy maintaining a heavy and murderous
skirmish fire all the time, but were forced to give way before the
obstinate inpetuosity of our valient skirmishers. Darkness now began
to close around the scene, and we were halted and ordered to throw
up rifle pits. We could distinctly hear the sounding of implements in
the enemy's camp which told that they were also engaged in the same
precautionary measure. But ere two hours passed away we had two
lines of substantial breastwork to oppose to the enemy's assaults. The
skirmishing continued very warm till a very late hour. The 17th Ky had
lost severely in killed and wounded, considering it was only a skirmish. Three were killed and about twenty wounded, and among
[them] were the brave and lamented Capt. Landrum, and the color
Sergeant. The 79th Indiana had also lost a Captain wounded[.]

We slept on our arms expecting that we would have to commence the bloody work with the first approach of the next day, and
notwithstanding our anxities, friendly sleep came to our aid, and
we were not interrupted through the whole night[.]

The first news that we learned on the next morning was that
the rebels had again gone to "parts unknown," and that if we wanted
to see them we must necessarily "pull up and follow."[39] But we

remained in camp all day, and embraced the opportunity of donning clean clothes and writing letters for home, the first since leaving McDaniel's Station. It was a day of the most complete rest we had enjoyed since the day we arrived at Tunnell Hill (7), and we heard but few shots from artillery a long way off. But we knew that our respite was only temporary. It was now a settled fact that our destination was Atlanta and that we would either reach that spot or be annihilated in the attempt before any more rest would be given us.

The object was indeed desirable, but I tell you I accepted the conclusion with much hesitancy.

Sat May 21st was a clear and very warm day. We remained in camp discussing the various rumors in regard to the direction the enemy had taken and the course that our army would next pursue. The fact that we heard scarcely a single cannon during the whole day convinced us that the enemy was either making a longer flight than usual or that our Generals were puzzled in regard to his movements. But strong rumors were afloat that the rebel army had divided and gone in different directions, and that our army would divide so as to follow the different parties. Our Corps was to go into North Carolina[.]

Our regiment was sent on picket early in the day, but were relieved near night on account of 20th and 23rd A.C.'s being encamped in our immediate front[.]

The next day was spent pretty much in the same manner as the previous one. I wrote a letter for home and in that letter I stated that "I would either go to Atlanta or get a whipping ere I wrote another," and my words came much nearer being verified than I anticipated at the time of writing. On this day we learned that twenty days rations were being loaded in the wagons, and we, of course, concluded that something important "was up". I prepared myself for "hard times". We were also ordered to box up and label all baggage that was not urgently necessary for our use and have it carried to the depot, for strange as it may seem the cars had jumped or otherwise cleared the bridge at Resacca, and was now bringing supplies to us in great abundance.

Tu May 23rd was a very warm and dusty day, and rendered the marching very disagreeable. Early in the morning we saw indications that plainly indicated a move and a little after sunrise the 20th A.C. which was in our front, began to pass back to the rear, and about noon, when this Corps had gotten ahead of us, we were marched out and put to the road in their wake. We traveled on the "back trail" but a very short distance, and then turned off to the left in a southerly direction, and marched about eight miles. After we got across the Etowa River at High Tower Bridge, we struck an exceedingly beautiful and productive country, though but little of it was under cultivation at this time. We camped that night almost in a wilderness, or at least it seemed so, for now we were away from the rail-road it was no difficult matter for us to lose our reckoning. For our lives we could not imagine any cause why we were brought away around this way leaving our "base" so exposed, for it seemed reasonable that the reb's would subsist as well away from their base of operations as we could from ours, and it also seemed reasonable that if we went around them to capture Atlanta that they would go around us and take Chattanooga. But the result proved that "Billy" understood flanking, at least, a little better than us.[40]

The next day we continued our march about 8 miles in a South Easterly direction through a very rough barren, and uninhabited country. We saw a few citizens but they would not give us the least information in regard to the whereabouts of the enemy, and some of them really seemed surprised to know that there *was* an army at all, so little information did they derive from the outer world. The forenoon was clear but the evening was cloudy, and the night slightly rainy[.]

Wed. May 25th was cool and cloudy till about dark when a very disagreeable rain set in. We marched 12 miles.

Just before we arrived at Pumpkin Vine Creek (about 4 o'clock P.M.) we heard a suddening opening of a heavy artillery and musketry fire some distance in advance, which seemed to be the report of large bodies of troops engaged in conflict. The road in our front was so filled with troops and wagons that all seemed to be concentrating at this point that our progress was very slow, and so did not reach the creek till after dark, but then the firing had all ceased, and we learned that the scene of conflict had been some distance ahead, and that it was brought on by Gen. Geary's Division of the 20th Corps, and had been terrific in the extreme, our troops suffering dreadfully, but had resulted in the repulse of an attempt by the rebels to surround and capture the Division before other troops could cross to their assistance. Just enough rain had fallen to make the hard beaten road slippery, and we found great difficulty in ascending the hill from the creek. We then advanced by slow degrees a few miles further, and after being almost wearied to death by continual standing we were finally (about 10 o'clock P.M.[)] ordered to bivouack by the roadside just in the order in which we had marched.[41]

We now knew by the great activity of the staff officers, and the frequent crack of the enemy's muskets at the picket line that we were again in the vicinity of the rebel army and also we knew that it would be able to make a very firm stand out in these wild woods; and when I rolled myself up in my blanket that dismal night to snatch a few hours of sleep, I felt that the time was near when our regiment would be called to take a more active part in the proceedings of the campaign than it had previously done[.]

The next day was cool and clear, and early in the morning we were greeted with the assuring sight of Gen. Sherman leisurely sauntering up and down the road, on foot, and attended by only one of his staff Brigadiers.

Soon after sunrise our Division was moved on to the left of the line and deployed in order thus extending the line still further to the left. Soon after the 23rd Corps moved past and deployed on our left, and then advanced the line considerably, the movement eliciting some severe skirmishing. Soon after they had gotten into position, [Richard W.] Johnson's Division of the 14th Corps went on to *their* left and took position.[42] These movements consumed the greater portion of the day, and we had nothing in the fighting line except the continual pop-shooting of the skirmishers which was vigorously maintained at all points. At one time during the skirmishing, the rebels dropped a few shells very near to our position but they did no harm.

Friday May 27 was a warm clear and beautiful day, but destined to be tarnished by one of those rude contests that result from the unrestrained passions of men. About noon our Corps moved to the left of the 23rd Corps, and deployed into line, but we had scarcely completed this movement till we were again marched off in a left-oblique direction, over rough hills, across deep hollows, and through almost impenetrable thickets of undergrowth for about three or four miles without meeting with any opposition, and I was almost coming to the conclusion that we were destined to surprise the enemy at some point where they did not expect us.[43]

We finally halted near Picket's Mills, and our Division was formed for battle, six lines deep, with our Brigade (3rd) composing the two rear lines, and our regiment composing the left of the extreme rear line, but as yet we had *smelt* no enemy. Just as the arrangements were completed, and we had halted to breathe a little, the boys discovered some rebel scouts in rear of our lines, as we were then formed, and, without orders, poured a scattering volley among them which caused them to scamper off in splendid style, and our boys to laugh heartily at their flight. A brigade of Johnson's Division then passed on to the left, and immediately after they had gotten into position, a heavy skirmishing commenced in our immediate front, and soon warmed into all the awfulness of a general battle, accompanied by the heavy booming of vigorously working artillery from the enemy's side, but none from ours. Then our lines began to advance, and when we came to the summit of the hill we were greeted with a shower of grape and cannister, also the presence of Genl's Sherman and Howard taking observations of the fight that was going on at our front lines.[44] Our line was ordered to lie down, and there we remained for a few moments suffering from the most terrible anxieties known to the soldier—viz, the viewing of a bloody carnage and knowing that you will in a moment have to participate in it.

There was a small rugged eminence between us and the scene of conflict that shut the whole affair from our view but we could distinctly hear the cheers of our gallant comrades as they heroically and successively, line after line, but alas! unsuccessfully charged upon the enemy's works, and met as often with bloody repulses. Many of them shed their last blood on the enemy's parapets.

We remained in our position till the other two Brigades had spent their strength upon the rebel lines, and we saw them come flocking back over the hill in great disorder.

Then at the sound of the bugle we sprang to our feet and crossed the hollow and ascended the hill, both of which were completely swept by a terrible enfilading fire of the enemy's artillery, and for which no preventative could be found; for up to this time, none of our artillery had been able to come up on account of the roughness of the country through which they had to pick their way.[45]

We met the gallant but defeated heroes of the front lines just as we commenced ascending the hill. They presented all the marks of a defeated, badly cut up, but unwhipped force; and they met us with cheers and exhortations and invectives on the rebels that would have reassured the minds of any but the most timid, and hundreds of them joined our ranks and returned to the contest. We arrived at the top of the hill, and then down the other side, when our front line soon found themselves in close conflict with the victory-flushed and advancing rebels. This brought us to a halt, and thus (a few moments before sunset) was commenced one of the grandest musketry fights I ever witnessed. The two lines of our Brigade were soon merged into one, and then having advanced to a little securer position we commenced pouring a continual volley of balls into the enemy's ranks that soon caused him to stop and take some consideration for his own safety, and soon afterwards to fall back a short distance for the cover of the timber. But this being done he seemed to be immovable, and despite every effort that could be made by our double line they maintained their position, and kept up a constant fire. We saw that the contest would be a lengthy one, and knowing that no ammunition wagons had ere come up we soon ceased to fire so rapidly, but with a considerable reserve of fire we could still keep up a continual volley; for as before mentioned, we were literally "piled up" along the fence that formed our barricade. The rebels had possession of a high hill just on our left and from this they poured a severe crossfire into our lines, which the troops on our left were neither able to check or draw from us[.]

About sundown I was struck on the right thigh by a ball which penetrated the flesh about one inch and then bounced out again without cutting my clothes. I looked down and saw my pants were stuffed into the incision, and quietly pulled them out, thinking that I was not much hurt, but the blood immediately began to flow freely, and I went back a few yards and lay down behind the friendly upturned root of a tree *to get sick*. I lay there a few minutes and not feeling any symptoms of fainting I went back to the lines and joined my company.[46]

Notwithstanding the precautions we had taken in the early part of the engagement, our ammunition was almost all gone at dark, and for a few moments we had to cease firing. Then our ears were greeted with a sound more heartrending than can be conceived, viz, the groans of the many wounded that were scattered over the field in our front, between ours and the rebel lines, and which had been repeatedly fought over during the evening. They were sending up the most pitiful prayers and lamentations that I ever heard from the lips of human creatures, and many of them were begging to be shot. The field was literally strewn with them and our boys availed themselves of the cover of darkness to assist many of the poor fellows into our lines and have them carried to the rear.

We went into the fight with 60 rounds of ammunition to the man and had received about 15 additional rounds but we now only had a few shots in reserve for the last emergency. Silently did we *sit* at our posts and anxiously await the movements of the enemy. We had yet enough ammunition to defeat any *feint* on their part, but should they make a real charge we knew that we would be compelled to give way. Presently they did make only a feint but the volley that we fired at them was so scattering and irregular that it only exposed our weakness, and in a few moments, the enemy bore down on us with a fury that was in our then circumstances, simply unresistable, and therefore after giving them our last shot we hastily fell back across the hill, but on account of the darkness and roughness of the ground we were not pursued. We halted and found that in the darkness a great many had got separated from us, but we soon found the greater number of the lost ones.[47]

After moving about for a considerable time apparently without aim or purpose we finally found ourselves enjoying the order to *stack* arms and *rest* and soon were trying to snatch a few moments, but my wound was becoming so sore and painful that I slept but very little that night. Our regiment had lost 3 men killed and 18 wounded, and the other regiments of our Brigade lost in about the same proportion, but the 1st and 2nd Brigades were horribly cut up, having lost, killed and wounded by the hundred.[48] When we consider our losses and the apparent results of the fight we really felt discouraged at the prospects, but not any the more elevated in regard to the ability of the enemy to eventually thwart our plans[.]

Sat May 28th was a clear and very warm day. I was waked up about 8 o'clock A.M. and found the boys cutting a barricade along the lines, simply as a precautionary measure. My wound had so stiffened my leg that I concluded it would be better for me to go to the Steward and get it dressed. When this was done the Surgeon (Dr McFaddin of the 79th Ind.) advised me to go to the hospital which was about 4 miles away. The ambulances were at that time all gone off with a load of wounded, but, feeling a desire to put as much territory as possible between myself and that point, I immediately hobbled out on foot in the direction of the hospital accompanied by a private soldier of the 79th Ind who was wounded in the finger. But we soon met an ambulance, and were taken in and conveyed to the field hospital. This was the first of which I had ever been an occupant, and I fervently hope that I may never be called upon to increase my knowledge or experience in regard to them.

This hospital was in a beautiful grove of timber and in addition to the shade thus afforded large arbors had been constructed, and every possible arrangement made for the comfort of a large number of patients, all of which proved to be a timely precaution, for since sundown of the day previous over a thousand maimed, crippled, and otherwise shockingly mangled soldiers had been brought from the battlefield to share these comforts.

I alighted from the ambulance near an amputating table, and the sight that greeted my eyes turned me perfectly sick. Arms and legs, hands and feet, fingers and toes, that had just been detached from their quivering stumps were recklessly strewn on every side. Three tables had been continually occupied with subjects for amputation [since?] midnight and continued to be filled for the following two days. Many horribly mangled fellows were apparently in the last agonies of death, and some of these were receiving no attention, for in the present emergency all hands of the hospital were engaged with those whom they could *hope* to save, and then they could not receive a tithe of the necessary attention. Several corpses were lying at the dead yard and the grave diggers were very hard at work. The principal Surgeons occupied the amputating tables, while others were moving about over the camp carrying their utensils and dressing mutilated fingers and toes which needed smoothing off. The nurses were busily engaged dressing the wounds of all and keeping those of the helpless wetted with washes to prevent inflammation. I found several of my regiment in a squad at the farthest part from the kitchen who had not had a morsel of food since they were brought there, and in addition to that had their haversacks stolen immediately after their arrival. The truth is the managers were not prepared for such a great influx of patients, and consequently the field of labor was too extensive for the limited number of attendants.

A very heavy fight some distance to the right could be distinctly heard during the greater part of this afternoon, said to be McPherson and through the whole day a heavy picket firing was kept up along the whole line.[49]

I remained at this hospital the next day, hobbling around among the poor wounded fellows rendering them whatever assistance that I could. A heavy fight occurred just in front of our hospital the night previous, and thought I was again awakened by an awful roar of musketry in our front. We were so close to the lines that an occasional stray ball would fly over heads, causing us some anxiety. After enduring the tormenting suspense for a considerable time, the fighting in a measure ceased and we turned over for a new nap.

On the 30th a large number of the slightly wounded were started to the rear in those pleasant vehicles known as army wagons, and some anxious badly-wounded were carried along also. After traveling about 8 miles over what I thought to be the roughest road I had ever traveled, we went into camp at midnight.

The next morning I had the good fortune to procure my trunk from the baggage train. We jolted off about twenty miles that day and at night encamped near New Harlan.

The two days riding in army wagons had proved very painful and tedious to us, and many of those who were the worst hurt sensibly feeling the effects of the continual jolting. But those that had come with this party were generally a persevering set and no complaints were heard, especially as we were all to take the cars on the next day and be carried further from these scenes of bloodshed and suffering.

On Wednesday June 1st we drove to Kingston (6 miles) and there procured a dinner from the Sanitary Commission that would made any hungry soldier rejoice. It was composed of mush, made from Ga. Corn meal and milk, and was extremely nourishing, and for dessert, Canned peaches.

Late in the afternoon we were mounted on a freight train, 15 in each box, all wounded, and without a single attendant. A box of crackers was thrown into each car, and we were told to subsist on this till we should get to Chattanooga.

Our situation was truly miserable. I had not donned a clean suit since the 22nd of May, and now I knew it was useless. All of us had a share of crawling filth which in this crowded car promised soon to accumulate to an enormous amount. No rations but hard tack till we could reach Chattanooga and probably Nashville, and no one to assist us to procure water or any other necessary article. Those that happened to be wounded in the arm performed these little errands for us, and those that were slightly wounded otherwise would dress the wounds of the car. At sundown we were aroused from our lethargy by the keen whistle of the locomotive and were soon being jolted along over the road to the North at a snail pace. I kept awake till a very late hour, but then found that we had only arrived at Adairsville, and having no hope of reaching Chattanooga soon I rolled up in my blanket and soon fell into a sound sleep, from which I did not wake till morning[.]

I waked the next morning when we were within about ten miles of Chattanooga, and at about 10 o'clock A.M. we arrived in its large depot. We here procured a dinner from the soldier's home and spent the time that the cars were standing in conversing with our old *pioneer* friends, one of whom (P. A. Wakefield)[50] kindly furnished me with money to defray expenses lest I should not be able to draw when I arrived at N. Late in the afternoon, amid a refreshing shower of rain, we again took off in the direction of Nashville, and feeling much delighted with the fact for we had all along feared that we would be halted at Chattanooga. But an unpleasant fact still clung to us, and that was that there had been no change whatever made in our situation in the same car in which we left Kingston. We arrived at Stevenson about sunset, and here procured another meal from the Soldiers' Home.

I found one of my company who was stationed here as recruiting officer for the 2nd Ala Cavalry,[51] and he furnished me with an excellent supper of fresh bread and country butter.

About an hour after dark the cars again rolled off in the direction (as we supposed) of Nashville, and as a very heavy shower of rain was falling, we closed doors and soon fell into a sound sleep.

On waking up the next morning, we were much surprised to find that we had just passed through Huntsville, Ala, and were equally mortified at the thought of having to remain another day in our loathsome cell. When we arrived at Athens, we went through the form of a breakfast at the soldier's House, but the supplies had already been exhausted by the numerous cargoes of wounded that had recently passed on.

We soon left this village of *red headed* and *blue eyed* Africans in our rear, and passed Columbia, Tenn at 4 P.M.; but soon after leaving that place one of the trains ahead of us ran off the track, and when I went to sleep at 9 o'clock P.M. we were perfectly still in the road without any prospect of getting on any further. This was trying one's patience with a vengeance and I almost began to wish myself back at the old field hospital in Georgia. We had no grub except the box of crackers that was given us at Kingston.

The next morning (June 4th) we arrived at Franklin about 6 o'clock, but failing to get any breakfast, we steamed ahead and arrived at Nashville about 11:00 A.M. Three of the occupants of our car had been so nearly helpless as to be compelled to lie down during the whole trip, and when they were lifted from their blankets the floor of the car under them was found to be literally covered with maggots, although we had rendered them every possible attention[.]

Epilogue

Woodcock's wound was not severe, and after a week in the hospital he obtained a furlough and headed home to Macon County. He got only as far as Bowling Green, however, before stopping. Reports of Confederate guerrillas kept him in that city for two weeks, and it was only on June 29 that he arrived at his parents' home. After two pleasant weeks, he started back to his regiment, depressed at the thought of more fighting. On July 26, he rejoined the 9th Kentucky west of Atlanta.[1]

The next month passed tensely as Sherman tightened his grip on the city. Almost daily, Woodcock wrote in his journal of picket duty, skirmishes, and dodging Rebel shells. Aside from a foraging expedition to Buckhead, however, the regiment held its position until the night of August 25. On that date, the IV Corps moved, ordered to swing south of the city and cut the West Point Railroad at Red Oak Station. "There is something big a brewin' as sure as a gun," Woodcock wrote.

On September 1, during the Battle of Jonesboro, Woodcock's division was held in reserve. That night, Gen. John B. Hood finally abandoned Atlanta and made for Lovejoy's Station. The city was Sherman's, yet the Army of Tennessee remained dangerous. The following day, Woodcock's forebodings proved justified, as Sherman ordered an attack on Lt. Gen. William J. Hardee's formidable entrenchments. The task fell to the divisions of Wood and Brig. Gen. Nathan Kimball. At 6 P.M., Wood ordered Brig. Gen. Frederick Knefler's brigade forward. Across the field waited familiar foes, Maj. Gen. Patrick Cleburne's corps, whom the 9th had fought at Pickett's Mill.

Knefler, allegedly drunk, foolishly ordered his brigade to attack the main works. "We forward and carry the pits in our front with small loss," Woodcock wrote, "and if we had stopped there, all would have been well. '[B]ut somebody blundered' and hallowed for us to charge the main works and forward went three little regiments of our Brigade; 9, 19, 79, through the thickest shower of balls I ever encountered, about 100 yards and lay down a moment, then up and forward again, but alas, what can valor do against equal valor with such fearful odds?" A few Federals actually reached Cleburne's entrenchments, but soon most of the bloodied brigade was racing back to their own lines. Some, however, including Cram and the regimental colorbearer, lay outside the works until dark.

The 9th Kentucky suffered seventeen casualties at Lovejoy's Station, including Lt. Col. Chesley Bailey, shot through the femoral artery. Only one man had been killed, but for Woodcock it was a devastating loss: his friend Turner Hestand. "He led his company till everything else wavered," Woodcock remembered, "and then said 'boys, let us get back,' and was almost shot instantly through the heart. . . . He never sought fight, but when ordered was always in the van, but he is gone. A board bearing this inscription: 'Lt. Turner Hestand, 9 Ky. V.I., killed Sept. 2nd, 1864' is all that denotes his resting place. We console ourselves with the thought that he has gone to where he will live in perpetual enjoyment without war."

After three days, the 9th Kentucky passed through Atlanta and camped on the other side. "I now think the old 9th has been in its last fight," Woodcock hopefully wrote. The men wanted to go home but furloughs were denied, they believed, because they had refused to re-enlist as veterans. Their service was not done, however. On September 29, Hood slipped into northwestern Georgia to cut Sherman's supply line. The latter followed in order to protect his railroad. The 9th Kentucky marched out on October 3 for Marietta.

The blue column reached Pine Mountain on October 6. Relieved from picket duty, Woodcock decided to climb the mountain and enjoy the view. There, for the second time, he encountered Sherman, "walking back and forth abstractedly smoking his cigar and looking as ordinary and homely as ever." This time, however, the young lieutenant had a conversation with "Uncle Billy." Wrote Woodcock: "He says that Gen. Thomas whipped the Rebels yesterday at Altoona Pass giving them a severe repulse. Also, he says that they have only 4 days' rations from this morning and that they intended to chew our crackers at Altoona but didn't do it. Also, he says they fight like Indians now. 'Don't make any fires, but they han't got any coffee to make no how'. . . . Hurrah for Sherman, with his tan coat tucked up with a pin and mud-bespattered pants." If Woodcock said anything in return, he did not record it.

The Federals continued their pursuit for the rest of October. The 9th Kentucky passed through Cartersville, Calhoun, Resaca,

William Marcus Woodcock at his desk at the Baptist Sunday School Board, c. 1910.
Courtesy of Mary Elizabeth Cain.

and Summersville, crossed into Alabama, marched back to Georgia, returned to Chickamauga, and on October 30 found themselves back in Chattanooga. There, much to Woodcock's joy, they boarded trains and rode to Pulaski, Alabama, where they would remain three weeks.

While encamped at Pulaski, the men of the 9th Kentucky cast their votes for president. Tennesseans such as Woodcock were compelled to find a Tennessee regiment with which to vote. With pride, he cast his ticket for Lincoln and Andrew Johnson. He apparently was in the minority, however. "We cannot get the vote of our Tennesseans," Woodcock wrote, "but the Kentuckians vote 45 for Lincoln and 90 for McLellan."

On November 21, with joy and apparently several barrels of "popskull," the 9th Kentucky cheered the news that the regiment had been relieved from duty. Boarding trains, they passed through Nashville two days later, and on November 25 arrived in Louisville, where a riot nearly broke out when the Kentuckians discovered that they were to be quartered with black troops. Woodcock went to work preparing muster rolls and completing other necessary paperwork. Later there would be questions, and during the following summer Woodcock would end up paying out of his own pocket for missing ordinance, quartermaster's stores, and camp equipment. His eagerness to finish probably led to carelessness.

On December 15, 1864, Marcus Woodcock was mustered out of the United States Army. He had expected to feel joy, but instead, "I almost feel a pang at parting with the service. I think of the many warm attachments I have made; of the many friends with which I am parting, and that I will never see them all together again. And I think of my country and of the claims it still has on my services, and at this thought a shudder passes through my mind to see the old 9th, the pride of her General Command, on leaving the service, but she has done her duty. Nobly has she stood up and done battle against the traitors to save her country."

Woodcock left Louisville on December 22, boarding a train bound for Cave City. There, he caught a coach headed for Glasgow. From there, he walked. He came home on Christmas Day.

Notes

Abbreviations

AGR *Report of the Adjutant General of the State of Kentucky*, vol. 1, 1861–66 (Frankfort, Ky.: John H. Harney, 1866).

Boatner Mark M. Boatner, III, *The Civil War Dictionary*, rev. ed. (New York: Vintage, 1991).

Faust Patricia L. Faust, ed., *Historical Times Illustrated Encyclopedia of the Civil War* (New York: Harper and Row, 1986).

NA National Archives and Records Administration, Washington, D.C.

OR *The War of the Rebellion: A Compilation of the Official Records of the Union and Confederate Armies*. 70 vols. Washington, D.C.: Government Printing Office, 1880–1901.

Univ. University.

URK Speed, Thomas. *The Union Regiments of Kentucky, Published Under the Auspices of the Union Soldiers and Sailors Monument Association* (Louisville, Ky.: Courier-Journal, 1897).

Van Horne Thomas B. Van Horne, *History of the Army of the Cumberland, Its Organizations, Campaigns, and Battles*, 2 vols. (Cincinnati, Ohio: Ogden, Campbell, 1875).

WC William Marcus Woodcock Collection. In possession of Martha Teschan, Nashville, Tenn.

WMW William Marcus Woodcock.

Editor's Introduction

1. Richard Nelson Current, *Lincoln's Loyalists: Union Soldiers from the Confederacy* (Boston: Northeastern Univ. Press, 1992), esp. 29–60, 133–57, 195–218.

2. Information on the Woodcock family is taken from an untitled genealogy, WC; Manuscript Census, Tennessee, Macon County, Schedule I, 1860, NA; and Harold G. Blankenship, *History of Macon County, Tennessee* (Tompkinsville, Ky.: Monroe County Press, 1986), 4, 11–13, 20–21, 37–38, 40–41, 46, 49–51.

3. Stephen V. Ash, *Middle Tennessee Society Transformed, 1860–1870: War and Peace in the Upper South* (Baton Rouge: Louisiana State Univ. Press, 1988), 4–9; Blankenship, *Macon County,* 14, 65, 165, 167, 171; Mary Emily Robertson Campbell, *The Attitude of Tennesseans Toward the Union, 1847–1861* (New York: Vantage, 1961), 13, 258–59, 263, 270, 273, 276, 279, 286, 289, 292; William Lynwood Montell, *Monroe County History, 1820–1970* (Tompkinsville, Ky.: Tompkinsville Lions Club, 1970), 1–2, 10, 28, 80. The information on WMW is taken from an untitled reminiscence in WC that WMW wrote from memory in 1911 at the behest of a daughter; cited hereafter as WMW, *1911 Reminiscence.* See 26–27.

4. WMW, *1911 Reminiscence,* 15–16. For Macon County, see Blankenship, *Macon County,* 171–78. For the state as a whole, see Robert E. Corlew, *Tennessee: A Short History,* 2d ed. (Knoxville: Univ. of Tennessee Press, 1990), 284–300.

5. Merton Coulter, *The Civil War and Readjustment in Kentucky* (Chapel Hill: Univ. of North Carolina Press, 1926); Lowell H. Harrison, *The Civil War in Kentucky* (Lexington: Univ. Press of Kentucky, 1975), 1–16; John E. Kleber, ed., *The Kentucky Encyclopedia* (Lexington: Univ. Press of Kentucky, 1992), 192–93; Blankenship, *Macon County,* 176–78; 9th Kentucky Infantry, Combined Service Records, RG 94, NA; AGR, 787, 789.

6. For Woodcock's political career, I consulted the following issues of the state's leading Radical newspaper, the *Knoxville Whig*: Feb. 22, Apr. 19 and 26, May 10, and June 7, 1865; Jan. 24, Feb. 28, May 2, and July 25, 1866; May 8, Oct. 23 and 30, Nov. 18, and Dec. 18, 1867; Jan. 29 and Oct. 21, 1868; Feb. 24, Aug. 11 and 18, 1869. Also useful were several items in WC, esp. four of WMW, Journals, nos. 1–4, 2d ser., covering Feb. 4, 1865–Dec. 15, 1866. Other helpful items included two drafts of WMW's 1864 "Letter to the Citizens of Macon County, Tennessee," his initial political salvo; WMW, public letter supporting black suffrage, Feb. 4, 1867; Tenn. Secretary of State A. J. Fletcher, letter naming WMW a Grant elector, Nov. 24, 1868; "Mr. Woodcock's Protest," undated broadside concerning WMW's opposi-

tion to the so-called Railroad Omnibus Bill; and WMW, *1911 Reminiscence*, 13–14. A most useful secondary source was Thomas B. Alexander, *Political Reconstruction in Tennessee* (Nashville, Tenn.: Vanderbilt Univ. Press, 1950), esp. 16–215.

7. See WMW's licenses to operate as a claims agent, Apr. 24, 1867, and Apr. 18, 1868, WC. See also WMW, Journals, nos. 1–4, 2d ser.

8. WMW, Journal, no. 1, 2d ser., Mar. 12, 1865; and WMW, Journal, no. 2, 2d ser., July 10 and 28, Aug. 2, 1865.

9. WMW, Journal, no. 1, 2d ser., Mar. 12 and Apr. 5 and 6, 1865.

10. Gerald F. Linderman, *Embattled Courage: The Experience of Combat in the American Civil War* (New York: Free Press, 1987), 3, 266–97 (quotation from 3); Stuart McConnell, *Glorious Contentment: The Grand Army of the Republic, 1865–1900* (Chapel Hill: Univ. of North Carolina Press, 1992), 97–100, 109–10, 167–75, 181, 187.

11. This information comes from Wilson Wiley Woodcock, Jr., interview by Kenneth W. Noe, Monteagle, Tenn., May 15, 1993, notes in collection of Kenneth W. Noe, Carrollton, Ga., as well as from two genealogical items, one labeled "Woodcock" and the other untitled, WC; and from WMW, Journals, nos. 1–4, 2d ser.

12. Martha Teschan and Betty Margaret Thomas interviews by Kenneth W. Noe, Monteagle, Tenn., May 15, 1993, notes in collection of Kenneth W. Noe, Carrollton, Ga. Martha Teschan interview by Kenneth W. Noe, Nashville, Tenn., Mar. 26, 1994, notes in collection of Kenneth W. Noe, Carrollton, Ga. WMW, *1911 Reminiscence*, 25–26, 30.

13. WMW, *1911 Reminiscence*, 14–15, 19–21, 32–33; *Missionary Messenger*, Nov. 1910, WC; *Baptist and Reflector*, Feb. 5, 1914, WC; Interview with Wilson W. Woodcock; Interview with Martha Teschan, Mar. 26, 1994; Manuscript Censuses, Tennessee, Davidson County, Schedule I, 1900 and 1920 NA.

14. *Baptist and Reflector*, Feb. 5, 1914, WC.

15. Gary W. Gallagher, ed., *Fighting for the Confederacy: The Personal Recollections of General Edward Porter Alexander* (Chapel Hill: Univ. of North Carolina Press, 1989), xxvii.

Author's Introduction

1. The manuscript in fact ends on June 4, 1864, just after WMW's wound.

2. Joseph B. McCullagh of the Cincinnati *Commercial*. See J. Cutler Andrews, *The North Reports the Civil War* (Pittsburgh: Univ. of Pittsburgh Press, 1955), 296–301.

Chapter 1. I Would Enlist in the U.S. Armies

1. In addition to Coulter, *Civil War and Readjustment*, 18–145; and Harrison, *Civil War in Kentucky*, 1–16; see William C. Davis, *The Orphan Brigade: The Kentucky Confederates Who Couldn't Go Home* (Baton Rouge: Louisiana State Univ. Press, 1980).
2. The muskets were "Lincoln guns," supplied to Kentucky Unionists by the administration through Lt. Nelson. OR, ser. 1, vol. 4:546; Harrison, *Civil War in Kentucky*, 10.
3. WMW means "Henson." AGR, 786–87.
4. Joseph H. Lewis, one of Buckner's lieutenants, established a Confederate recruiting station at Cave City, Ky., on Sept. 20, 1861, and there recruited the 6th Kentucky Infantry (C.S.A.). Davis, *Orphan Brigade*, 31–32, 37–38.
5. A false rumor, as Nashville did not fall until Feb. 24, 1862. Corlew, *Tennessee*, 308–9.
6. WMW's ch. 1 ended here. By "Hayes," WMW meant Henry W. Mayes. *URK*, 365.
7. WMW means 1864.
8. Camp Robert Anderson was established by Unionist John M. Fraim on his Indian Creek farm. Confederate soldiers destroyed it on Nov. 12, 1861, soon after the 9th Kentucky left for Columbia, Ky. OR, ser. 1, vol. 4:265, 457, 546; Montell, *Monroe County*, 22.
9. Bluford M. Fishburn of Co. C. AGR, 791.
10. Jonathan W. Roark was captain of Co. I. AGR, 801.
11. Henry C. Martin and Gilbert M. Mulligan commanded Cos. F and C, respectively. By "Fraim," WMW means Pennsylvanian George H. Cram, regular army veteran, captain of Co. H, and later regimental colonel. AGR, 786–87.
12. Fraim's home functioned as camp headquarters. OR, ser. 1, vol. 4:546.
13. At the time, Moore was a 2nd lieutenant in Co. C. AGR, 794–95.
14. William *T.* Bryan. AGR, 789.
15. When Buckner threatened Greensburg, Brig. Gen. William T. Ward fell back to Campbellsville and called for the region's newly-formed Federal regiments to join him there. OR, ser. 1, vol. 4:307, 316.
16. McRea's Crossroads. OR, ser. 1, vol. 4:546.
17. WMW struck through the phrase "eight miles to Edmunters (?) Metcalf Co." Willis Grissom is found in the Manuscript Census, Kentucky, Metcalf Co., Schedule I, 1860, NA.
18. A member of Co. H, according to AGR, 786–87, but identified below as a member of WMW's Co. B.
19. A fugitive slave. Faust, 161–62.
20. One of Tennessee's three Unionist congressmen in 1861. Corlew, *Tennessee*, 299.

21. WMW struck through the words "and left us to do what he thought best."

Chapter 2. An Attack of Measles

1. For the effect of disease in general, see George Worthington Adams, *Doctors in Blue: The Medical History of the Union Army in the Civil War* (New York: Henry Schuman, 1952). For the 9th Kentucky, see AGR, 787–805.
2. WMW's ch. 3 began with this sentence.
3. AGR, 798.
4. The 13th Kentucky fought next to the 9th Kentucky in Brig. Gen. Jeremiah T. Boyle's 11th Brigade, of Brig. Gen. Thomas L. Crittenden's division, on the second day of the battle. Boyle praised their gallant charge against enemy guns. OR, ser. 1, vol. 10, pt. 1, pp. 356–62.
5. The "Bull Pup" was "Burnett" of Col. Sidney S. Stanton's 25th Tennessee Infantry (C.S.A.), at least according to a receipt for expenses dated Oct. 14, 1861, in U.S. Army, 9th Kentucky Volunteer Infantry, Quartermaster Files, Kentucky Dept. for Military Affairs, Frankfort, Ky. The phrase "seeing the elephant" (or, as WMW later writes, "riding the elephant") refers to one's first experience in combat.
6. WMW originally identified the culprit as "a drunken soldier."
7. Created by wealthy northern civilians in June 1861, the commission provided care for ill and wounded soldiers and their families. It eventually operated convalescent camps, field hospitals, and hotels. Boatner, 720; Faust, 656.
8. Duncan would resign in mid-Jan. 1862 and be replaced by Thomas R. W. Jeffray. AGR, 786.
9. WMW means "physio-medical," a type of medical practice that utilized only natural, herbal remedies. Doctors such as WMW's father particularly denounced the use of mercurial medicines such as Calomel. Ultimately, the army agreed and discontinued them from use in 1863. Adams, *Doctors in Blue*, 38–39.
10. Col. John W. Head commanded the 30th Tennessee Infantry (C.S.A.), a regiment raised almost entirely from Macon County's secessionists. It was active in the region until transferred to Fort Donelson in mid-Nov. 1861. *Tennesseans in the Civil War: A Military History of Confederate and Union Units with the Available Rosters of Personnel*, pt. 1 (Nashville: Civil War Centennial Commission, 1964), 238.
11. Manuscript Census, Kentucky, Adair Co., Schedule I, 1860, NA.
12. Tennessee's Gov. Isham Harris had mobilized the state militia and ordered it equipped for Confederate service. James Walter Fertig, *The*

Secession and Reconstruction of Tennessee (Chicago: Univ. of Chicago Press, 1898), 32–33.

13. Battery B, Kentucky Artillery. URK, 681–83.

14. WMW's ch. 4 began here.

15. Possibly Margaret Scott, although her husband was alive in 1860. Manuscript Census, Kentucky, Adair Co., Schedule I, 1860, NA.

16. Col. Frank L. Wolford's 1st Kentucky Cavalry (U.S.A.) was one of the state's most celebrated units. Coulter, *Civil War and Readjustment*, 102; Harrison, *Civil War in Kentucky*, 62, 90.

17. Lt. Col. James D. Bennett's 7th Tennessee Cavalry Battalion, another largely Macon County unit, actively scouted in Macon and Monroe counties during winter 1861–62. *Tennesseans in the War*, pt. 1, pp. 28–29.

18. While neither the Manuscript Census, Tennessee, Macon Co., Schedule I, 1860, NA; nor Blankenship, *Macon County*, 37–38, 49–51, identifies the Woodcocks as slaveholders, Parson Brownlow described WMW as "formerly a slaveholder" in the *Knoxville Whig*, Apr. 26, 1865. Moreover, the remains of slaves are buried in the family cemetery. Perhaps the Woodcocks, like many yeomen, moved in and out of the slaveholding class.

19. Kidney stones.

20. *Lobelia inflata*, an emetic.

21. Manuscript Census, Kentucky, Adair Co., Schedule I, 1860, NA.

22. Rush was a Baptist. Manuscript Census, Kentucky, Hart Co., Schedule I, 1860, NA.

23. Jeremiah T. Boyle was at the time WMW's brigade commander. Boatner, 77.

24. Probably John J. Bragg. Manuscript Census, Kentucky, Metcalf Co., 1860, NA.

25. Engaged on the Federal left during the battle's second day, the regiment lost 15 killed and suffered 92 total casualties. Wrote Grider, "Many of them acted like heroes, and more determined bravery and coolness could not be exhibited." OR, ser. 1, vol. 10, pt. 1, pp. 107, 300, 354–65 (quotation from 361).

Chapter 3. Between the River and Corinth

1. This account is based on James M. McPherson, *Battle Cry of Freedom: The Civil War Era* (New York: Oxford Univ. Press, 1988), 414–17, 511–16; and the more positive assessment of Halleck in Herman Hattaway and Archer Jones, *How the North Won: A Military History of the Civil War* (Urbana: Univ. of Illinois Press, 1983), 170–71, 179, 181–82, 187, 206–8, 214–17.

2. Holland is listed erroneously as "James" in AGR, 789.

3. WMW's ch. 5 began with this sentence. He did not divide the remaining manuscript into chapters.

4. Henson resigned on Apr. 17, 1862, "for the purpose of Resuming my old position as Captain in said Regiment." However, another hand resembling Grider's added: "This resignation will be for the benefit of the service." He clearly wanted Henson out. WMW describes Henson's later activities below. 9th Kentucky Infantry, Compiled Service Records, RG 94, NA.

5. WMW made a marginal note here to insert a comment on "southern chivalry," but he did not follow through. Roberts, a merchant, is identified as "C. Roberts" also in the Manuscript Census, Kentucky, Barren Co., Schedule I, 1860. His wife's name was Sarah.

6. Possibly Maj. George E. Flynt, George Thomas's assistant adjutant-general. OR, ser. 1, 17:81.

7. Pennsylvania Volunteer Infantry.

8. Brig. Gen. Lovell H. Rousseau, Mexican War hero, Indiana legislator, and prominent Kentucky attorney, then commanded the 4th Brigade of the Army of the Ohio. OR, ser. 1, vol. 10, pt. 2, p. 149; Boatner, 710–11.

9. Sommerby at the time was a member of Co. A. AGR, 803, 805.

10. Underwood resigned in June 1862. AGR, 789.

11. Pipkin served in Co. A. AGR, 788–89.

12. Either James M. Proffit, George M. Slaughter, or Henry M. Slaughter, all of whom were non-coms in Co. G. AGR, 798–99.

13. The Legal Tender Act of Feb. 25, 1862, had just authorized the use of paper money as legal currency. Faust, 323.

14. WMW's future brigade commander, Col. Samuel Beatty of the 19th Ohio Infantry, reported that the brigade only moved two miles that day. It probably did seem longer to the relatively green WMW. OR, ser. 1, vol. 10, pt. 1, p. 702.

15. Surfaced with branches or trunks of trees. Boatner, 176.

16. Brig. Gen. Thomas L. Crittenden was the son of Kentucky's U.S. Sen. John J. Crittenden, author of the ill-starred Crittenden Compromise, and brother of Confederate Maj. Gen. George B. Crittenden. At this time Thomas commanded the 5th Division of the Army of the Ohio. Faust, 192–93.

17. WMW originally wrote "3 o clock in the afternoon."

18. Maj. Gen. John Pope, the hero of Island No. 10, commanded the Army of the Mississippi in the Corinth campaign. As WMW indicates below, Pope was a notorious braggart. Boatner, 658–59; Faust, 593.

19. Cram had been promoted on May 10. Boatner, 206.

20. John H. Grider, brother of the regiment's colonel, had been regimental adjutant. AGR, 786–87.

21. Lt. Col. Allen J. Roark actually had died of an illness in Nashville on April 17. OR, ser. 1, vol. 10, pt. 1, p. 360; AGR, 786–87.

22. May 21, according to OR, ser. 1, vol. 10, pt. 1, p. 702.
23. The .577-caliber Enfield, standard rifle of the British army, was used extensively on both sides of the American Civil War. Union soldiers preferred it to the American-made Springfield as more accurate and reliable. Flanking companies received rifles when the others were armed with smoothbores. Boatner, 266; Faust, 243–44; Albert Castel, *Decision in the West: The Atlanta Campaign of 1864* (Lawrence: Univ. Press of Kansas, 1992), 106–7.
24. A sergeant in Co. B. AGR, 789.
25. WMW apparently refers to the water gum tree, which tended to grow in damp sandy soils or in swamps. When submerged, the bases of such trees would swell with moisture. See *Gray's Manual of Botany* (New York: Van Nostrand, 1970), 1048–49.
26. May 28, according to OR, ser. 1, vol. 10, pt. 1, p. 702.
27. WMW is guilty of anachronism, as his army, notorious for its poor medical care, had no ambulance corps until Maj. Gen. William S. Rosecrans replaced Buell later in the year. The "yellow rag" was a hospital flag, a yellow square with a green "H" in the center. Adams, *Doctors in Blue*, 83, 89; Faust, 9–10.
28. The Army of the Tennessee, in effect commanded by Maj. Gen. George H. Thomas after Grant's hollow elevation to second-in-command. Boatner, 176.
29. Fortifications. *Abbatis* consisted of felled trees, with the branches facing the enemy. *Lunettes* were two- or three-sided field fortifications, open to the rear. Faust, 1, 454.
30. A variation of an oft-repeated southern boast. McPherson, *Battle Cry of Freedom*, 316.
31. On Sept. 19, Rosecrans defeated two brigades of Maj. Gen. Sterling Price's Army of the West and compelled Price to retreat toward Corinth. Boatner, 428–29.
32. The Kentucky Infantry Jacket, similar to the better-known shell jacket but rounded at the bottom. *Journal Junior* 1 (Mar. 1992): 3.
33. WMW's footnote: "I have no correct idea as to the name of the station or the distance from Tuscumbia but I know it was just 5 miles to Courtland."
34. While bridge burnings were common during the campaign, none are mentioned during these days in the OR. The delay probably was caused by a small guerrilla band who on July 8 cut the telegraph to Decatur, burned several water tanks, and tore up track. OR, ser. 1, vol. 16, pt. 1, pp. 124–25.
35. Henry G. Davidson commanded Cos. A and H at this point. All were captured on July 25, leading Buell to blast the unfortunate Davidson. OR, ser. 1, vol. 16, pt. 1, pp. 819–29.
36. Alabama Capt. Philip Dale Roddey was one of the great Rebel horse-

men of the war. At this time, he commanded a detachment of the Army of the West's Cavalry Brigade. OR, ser. 1, vol. 16, pt. 1, pp. 825–29.

37. AGR, 792.
38. A ferry before the war, the U.S.S. *Tennessee* had failed as a "cotton clad" gunboat but proved a useful military ferry at Decatur. OR, ser. 1, vol. 16, pt. 1, pp. 485–86.
39. Belle Mina, Ala.
40. The Memphis and Charleston Railroad met the Nashville and Chattanooga Railroad at Stevenson. The town was to have been the supply depot for Buell's descent on Chattanooga. Francis F. McKinney, *Education in Violence: The Life of George H. Thomas and the History of the Army of the Cumberland* (Detroit, Mich.: Wayne State Univ. Press, 1961), 142–43.
41. Probably the First Seminole War of 1817–18. *Dictionary of American History*, 6:260–61.
42. AGR, 793, 795–96, 800.
43. Maj. Gen. Alexander McDowell McCook. Faust, 457.

Chapter 4. In the Direction of Perryville

1. Hattaway and Jones, *How the North Won*, 217–19, 225, 247–62; McPherson, *Battle Cry of Freedom*, 515–20. James Lee McDonough, *War in Kentucky: From Shiloh to Perryville* (Knoxville: Univ. of Tennessee Press, 1994), appeared just as I completed editing this volume.
2. OR ser. 1, vol. 16, pt. 2, p. 397.
3. The Second Confiscation Act had passed on July 16. Confederates who refused to surrender within 60 days could be compelled to forfeit all property, including slaves. Unionists and border state masters were exempted. Faust, 157.
4. A corruption of *D'Abri tent*, better known as the shelter or (later) pup tent. "Clothing, Camp, and Garrison Equippage in Co. B[,] 9th Ky. Inf.[,] on the 30th September 1864," WC, confirms this usage.
5. Mexican War veteran Samuel Beatty served as captain of the 19th Ohio Infantry until he replaced Boyle as brigade commander on May 27. Boatner, 54, ranks him as one of the best western generals. See also Ezra J. Warner, *Generals in Blue: Lives of Union Commanders* (Baton Rouge: Louisiana State Univ. Press, 1964), 28–29.
6. WMW refers, somewhat incorrectly, to the Antietam campaign. Lee had defeated Pope at Second Bull Run on Aug. 29–30, and at this point had just crossed the Potomac into Maryland. Boatner, 17, 104–5.
7. Mayhugh served in Co. D. URK, 386.
8. WMW means Goodlettsville.

9. Col. Joseph Wheeler and 700 men of the 1st Alabama Cavalry and 1st Kentucky Cavalry (C.S.A.), who had been waiting to ambush the column. OR, ser. 1, vol. 16, pt. 1, pp. 893–94.

10. OR, ser. 1, vol. 16, pt. 1, p. 1054.

11. Wheeler reported that, when the ambush failed, he withdrew his men two miles to rest and eat. Ibid.

12. Black laborers in Confederate service commonly were clothed in privates' uniform jackets. James H. Brewer, *The Confederate Negro: Virginia's Craftsmen and Military Laborers, 1861–1865* (Durham, N.C.: Duke Univ. Press, 1969), 25.

13. First besieged on Sept. 14, Col. John T. Wilder actually surrendered Munfordville and its 4,000-man garrison on Sept. 17, after receiving a tour of the powerful Confederate force guided by a chagrined Buckner. The men were disarmed and sent into Buell's lines. WMW notes his error below. McDonough, *War in Kentucky*, 158–84.

14. Pvt. Leonard Jones of Co. D. AGR, 794.

15. WMW's footnote: "We drank water from ponds principally after passing B.G. [Bowling Green]."

16. Louisville had been reinforced with raw recruits under the command of William Nelson. McDonough, *War in Kentucky*, 191–92.

17. WMW's footnote: "The whole of Buell's army reinforced by several thousand new troops was now moving out on different roads to attack Bragg or compel him to retreat." The army marched toward Bardstown and Harrodsburg in three separate columns, with Crittenden in the center. A fourth column made a demonstration toward Frankfort. Boatner, 642–43; Hattaway and Jones, *How the North Won*, 253–57.

18. Brig. Gen. Horatio P. Van Cleve, of the West Point Class of 1831, commanded the 2nd Minnesota Infantry at the beginning of the war. He had taken brigade command in June. Boatner, 866; Warner, *Generals in Blue*, 521–22.

19. WMW's footnote: "Col. Fred Knefler." Frederick Knefler, born in Hungary, had taken command of the 79th Indiana only six days before. Boatner, 466.

20. Glenville. OR, ser. 1, vol. 16, pt. 2, p. 577.

21. Unaware of both Buell's plans and McCook's desperate fight, due to the meteorological phenomenon of "acoustic shadow," Thomas refused to allow Crittenden to attack. McKinney, *Education in Violence*, 164.

22. Public opinion in fact largely censured Buell, leading to his dismissal on Oct. 30. Boatner, 96.

23. A military commission called to investigate Buell's conduct met Nov. 24, 1862–May 10, 1863. The results appear in OR, ser. 1, vol. 16, pt. 1, pp. 7–726.

24. In fact, it was McCook's brother Daniel who opened the battle. At 2 A.M. on Oct. 8, under orders from Gen. Philip Sheridan, Daniel

McCook's brigade surged forward to seize Peters Hill and Doctor's Creek. Sheridan, in turn, was following orders from Buell to seize desperately needed fresh water. Buell at that time was planning an attack later in the morning, but ultimately he decided to postpone the assault until Oct. 9. In the meantime, Bragg attacked Buell. McDonough, *War in Kentucky*, 217–26, 234–35.

25. WMW's footnote: "It was one of the bloodiest battles of the war in proportion to the number of men engaged." Bragg suffered 3,396 casualties, 21% of his effectives; while Buell lost 4,211, 10.5% of his effectives. Boatner, 644.

26. Rosecrans successfully defended Corinth against an attack from Earl Van Dorn on Oct. 3–4. Boatner, 176–77.

27. A major Federal training center, Camp Dick Robinson had opened in Garrard Co. in Aug. 1861. Harrison, *Civil War in Kentucky*, 11.

28. Bragg's rear guard, commanded by Wheeler. Harrison, *Civil War in Kentucky*, 55; *History of the Seventy-Ninth Regiment, Indiana Volunteer Infantry, in the War of Eighteen Sixty-One in the United States* (Indianapolis, Ind.: Hollenbeck, 1899), 51. The latter work on the 9th Kentucky's sister regiment, largely based on the diary of William H. Huntsinger, is a useful source for following WMW's regiment.

29. Presumably a 12-pounder mountain howitzer, designed to be disassembled and carried by two mules. Jack Coggins, *Arms and Equipment of the Civil War* (New York: Fairfax, 1983), 75.

30. They were near Big Springs, according to *History of 79th Indiana*, 51.

31. Also known as the Battle of Rock Castle Hills, it was fought on Oct. 21, 1861. The victorious Federal commander was Brig. Gen. Albin Schoepf. "Gurrard" was Col. T. I. Garrard of the 7th Kentucky Infantry. Van Horne, 1:51.

Chapter 5. The Memorable Battle of Stone's River

1. Here I have followed Hattaway and Jones, *How the North Won*, 314–23; and McPherson, *Battle Cry of Freedom*, 561, 579–83. The best histories of the battle are Peter Cozzens, *No Better Place to Die: The Battle of Stones River* (Urbana: Univ. of Illinois Press, 1990); and James Lee McDonough, *Stones River—Bloody Winter in Tennessee* (Knoxville: Univ. of Tennessee Press, 1980).

2. WMW bitterly refers to soldiers who allowed themselves to be captured by the Confederates so that they might be paroled and sent home. Paroled men swore an oath that they would not fight again until officially "exchanged" for a captured Confederate. Faust, 558.

3. 1st Lt. Henry W. Mayes. AGR, 798.

4. It was a Thanksgiving Day service. *History of 79th Indiana*, 1, 55.

5. Although Wheeler, commanding mounted infantry and artillery as well as cavalry, attacked Col. Stanley Mathews's brigade three times, the train made it back to camp, albeit with over 40 casualties. Van Horne, 2:215.

6. WMW crossed out "foraging."

7. Lt. T. F. Murdock was one of Van Cleve's aides. OR, ser. 1, vol. 20, pt. 1, p. 575.

8. On the morning of the 26th, Crittenden's left wing left Nashville for La Vergne. Eleven miles out, Col. John Kennett and three cavalry regiments, riding in the advance, encountered Confederate pickets, resulting in a "sharp" skirmish. Later in the day, Crittenden reported: "Two miles from La Vergne the enemy met us in considerable force." After an artillery duel "without much result," Brig. Gen. Charles Cruft and Col. Walter Whitaker, each leading two regiments, drove the Rebels into the town. OR, ser. 1, vol. 20, pt. 1, p. 446.

9. Rosecrans ordered Crittenden to send a detachment down the Jefferson Pike to secure a vital bridge. Col. William B. Hazen drew the assignment. WMW heard his artillery. OR, ser. 1, vol. 20, pt. 1, pp. 446–47.

10. WMW means Col. James P. Fyffe's 2nd Brigade, 3rd Division, its new designation. OR, ser. 1, vol. 20, pt. 1, p. 181.

11. About dusk, Rosecrans ordered Crittenden to occupy Murfreesboro with one division. Brig. Gen. Thomas J. Wood's 1st Division was chosen, although Wood protested that a night crossing was too risky. Rosecrans eventually agreed, but not before Col. Charles Harker's 3rd Brigade, accompanied by Capt. Cullen Bradley's 6th Ohio Battery, had crossed Stones River and skirmished with the enemy. OR, ser. 1, vol. 20, pt. 1, pp. 448–49.

12. Crittenden reported that "my line of battle was formed . . . skirmishing during part of the day was very heavy." He had held Van Cleve in reserve. OR, ser. 1, vol. 20, pt. 1, p. 449.

13. Reprinted in OR, ser. 1, vol. 20, pt. 1, p. 449.

14. Rosecrans's original plan included having Crittenden send two divisions across the river to hit Bragg's right. Accordingly, at 7 A.M., Crittenden ordered Van Cleve across. Beatty had crossed and deployed before Van Cleve called him back. Beatty was then ordered back to the pike to form on Rousseau's right. Van Horne, 1:236; McDonough, *Stones River*, 75–78, 110.

15. Maj. Gen. J. P. McCown's division, attached to Hardee's corps. Cozzens, *No Better Place to Die*, 144–45.

16. Brig. Gen. M. D. Ector's brigade of dismounted Texas cavalry, part of McCown's division. Cozzens, *No Better Place to Die*, 144–45.

17. Starling was Crittenden's adjutant.

18. Cozzens, *No Better Place to Die*, 145, indicates that Rousseau gave this order.

19. Maj. Gen. Patrick E. Cleburne's division. Beatty faced Cleburne's own brigade, commanded by Brig. Gen. Lucius E. Polk. Ibid., 147–48; McDonough, *Stones River*, 120.

20. Rosecrans redeployed the 9th and 11th Kentucky regiments on the right of the Pioneer Brigade. Cozzens, *No Better Place to Die*, 148.

21. The Chicago Board of Trade Battery. OR, ser. 1, vol. 20, pt. 1, p. 586.

22. These were Rousseau's massed batteries, joined by the Chicago Board of Trade Battery, on the modern site of the Stones River National Cemetery. Cozzens, *No Better Place to Die*, 135–36, 148–49.

23. Cleburne's division again. Cozzens, *No Better Place to Die*, 148–50.

24. Grider reported 3 men killed and 21 wounded. OR, ser. 1, vol. 20, pt. 1, p. 586.

25. Lt. T. F. Murdock in fact was not wounded. OR, ser. 1, vol. 20, pt. 1, p. 213.

26. More exactly, in a hollow just below McFaddin's Ford. Cozzens, *No Better Place to Die*, 174–75.

27. Crittenden moved the 3rd Division across the river to block Maj. Gen. John C. Breckinridge's division of Hardee's corps. Van Horne, 1:247.

28. The first rumor was false. As for the second, the cavalry of Wheeler and Col. Gabriel Wharton had attacked a total of five supply trains between Dec. 29 and Jan. 1. The Federal victory did not occur. Boatner, 807; Cozzens, *No Better Place to Die*, 171–72.

29. Moses's Georgia Battery briefly shelled Col. Samuel W. Price's 3rd Brigade, which was located just to Beatty's right. Cozzens, *No Better Place to Die*, 179.

30. Grider ordered the 9th Kentucky, now commanded by Cram, to wait in reserve "under cover of hill about 200 yards from the upper ford of Stone's River." At 1 P.M., according to Beatty, the regiment was "ordered to cross the river . . . forming near the hospital . . . to protect our left flank." Col. William Grose's 3rd Brigade of Palmer's division then took the Kentuckians' original position. OR, ser. 1, vol. 20, pt. 1, pp. 576, 590.

31. In later years, WMW told a different story. In his *1911 Reminiscence*, 3–4, he wrote: "Tooley remarked 'Mark we are going to have a fight this evening and I shall be killed.' I tried to divert his mind from it by all kinds of suggestions but could not succeed. The last thing I remember him to have said was 'you know I am not afraid.'"

32. Earlier in the day, Bragg had ordered Breckinridge to assault the Federal left, despite the latter's rejoinder that the position had been reinforced and was too strong to carry. The attack began at 4 P.M. Ten of Breckinridge's 25 regiments were from either Kentucky or Tennessee. McDonough, *Stones River*, 175–85, 250–51.

33. The front line consisted of the 35th and 79th Indiana regiments, the 8th Kentucky, and the 51st Ohio. OR, ser. 1, vol. 20, pt. 1, p. 577.

34. The Orphan Brigade, commanded by Brig. Gen. Roger W. Hanson and consisting of the 2nd Kentucky, 4th Kentucky, 6th Kentucky, and 41st Alabama. Davis, *Orphan Brigade*, 154–61.
35. Cram reported that the colors fell "no less than three times." OR, ser. 1, vol. 20, pt. 1, p. 591.
36. AGR, 789.
37. The 5th Battery of the Washington Artillery. See WMW's comments below.
38. In fact, only fragments of the 2nd and 6th Kentucky regiments (C.S.A.) and the 16th–25th Louisiana had crossed the river, without orders to do so. Cozzens, *No Better Place to Die*, 188–89.
39. OR, ser. 1, vol. 20, pt. 1, p. 577.
40. Cram gave the order. Ibid., 588.
41. Capt. John Mendenhall, Crittenden's chief of artillery, had massed the artillery on a hill overlooking the ford. The actual number is disputed, with estimates ranging from 45 (Cozzens, *No Better Place to Die*, 191–92) to 57 (Faust, 723; McDonough, *Stones River*, 180) to 58 (Boatner, 807; Van Horne, 1:249).
42. Col. John F. Miller's 3rd Brigade and portions of Col. Timothy F. Stanley's 2nd Brigade, both of Brig. Gen. James S. Negley's division. Van Horne, 1:249–50.
43. Along with the 19th Ohio, WMW's regiment was the first to recross the river. OR, ser. 1, vol. 20, pt. 1, p. 591.
44. The Washington Artillery was perhaps the best-known Confederate artillery unit of the war. Batteries 1–4 served with the Army of Northern Virginia. Grider reported that the 9th Kentucky shared with the 19th Ohio in capturing the guns. OR, ser. 1, vol. 20, pt. 1, p. 588; Boatner, 893–94.
45. WMW's estimate of casualties is correct. AGR, 788–805.
46. One intriguing bit of evidence suggests that casualties among those attached to the regiment may have been higher. On Jan. 27, 1863, the Eldress Nancy, a member of the Shaker community at South Union, Ky., wrote in her diary that William Grider, a slave owned by the regiment's colonel, had been there telling a shocking tale. According to the diarist, during the battle "a company of rebels dashed round and Captured near one hundred negroes and Griders waiter with the rest; They were placed in line to be shot." The waiter escaped when "Federals dashed on to them," but "he says there were nearly one hundred shot, that he was one of the last." To my knowledge, this has not been confirmed. Certainly WMW never mentioned it. The Eldress Nancy, Diary, Kentucky Library, Western Kentucky Univ., Bowling Green, Ky. See also *Journal Junior* 2 (Winter 1993): 2–3 and *Journal Junior* 2 (Fall–Winter 1993): 2. The regiment also lost their regimental

colors to the 28th Tennessee (C.S.A.). OR, ser. 1, vol. 20, pt. 1, p. 809.

47. Thomas ordered the brigades of Beatty and Brig. Gen. James G. Spears forward to drive the Confederates from the woods in front. Van Horne, 1:251.

48. The Confederates had started before midnight on the previous night. McDonough, *Stones River*, 216.

49. In fact, casualties were all but even: the Federals lost 12,906 and the Confederates 11,739. Boatner, 808.

Chapter 6. Our Camp at Murfreesboro

1. This account follows Hattaway and Jones, *How the North Won*, 324–25, 356–57, 359–60, 378, 387–91.

2. Capt. William T. Bryan, Pvt. Andrew Bray, and WMW's friend James I. Tooley. AGR, 789, 791.

3. WMW means the 28th Tennessee Infantry. OR, ser. 1, vol. 20, pt. 1, pp. 659, 678.

4. The Orphan Brigade.

5. The men were guilty of either error or wishful thinking, as the proclamation said nothing about foraging. WMW makes the same mistake below.

6. Rosecrans indeed had proposed sending both the 9th and 11th Kentucky regiments to Bowling Green to recruit, but in the end the 9th remained in Murfreesboro. URK, 382.

7. AGR, 789, 791.

8. The Emancipation Proclamation said that African Americans would be "received into the armed service of the United States." White Kentuckians in general were opposed. Boatner, 584–85; Harrison, *Civil War in Kentucky*, 89–91.

9. WMW is in error, as two of the deserters belonged to Co. D and the third to Co. C. AGR, 793–94.

10. Grider resigned on Feb. 2, citing "the condition of my family & business." 9th Kentucky Infantry, Combined Service Records, RG 94, NA.

11. WMW's footnote: "Soldier's phraseology for *countermanded*." Rosecrans had received an erroneous report that part of Bragg's army had slipped past and was entering Kentucky. OR, ser. 1, vol. 20. pt. 2, p. 307.

12. Lincoln was on the $10 bill. Gene Hessler, *The Comprehensive Catalog of U.S. Paper Money* (Chicago: Henry Regnery, 1977), 44, 125–26.

13. Congress had passed the Enrollment Act on Mar. 3. Boatner, 172.

14. Commissary sergeant.

15. John H. Shepherd, late of the 104th Illinois. The rumor was true, as

WMW notes below in the entry for Apr. 22. AGR, 787; 9th Kentucky Infantry, Compiled Service Records, RG 94, NA.

16. WMW means 1863.
17. White replaced Francis M. Cummings on Mar. 2, 1863. AGR, 786–87.
18. A large conical tent, designed to sleep twelve. Boatner, 760.
19. Harling was Captain of Co. D. AGR, 793.
20. WMW's footnote: "Army phrase for sweeping or cleaning a camp."
21. This false rumor circulated on May 25, according to *History of 79th Indiana*, 74.
22. The rumor was correct. The Tullahoma Campaign that followed was designed at least in part to prevent Bragg from sending more. Hattaway and Jones, *How the North Won*, 385–91.
23. The regiment had fought with distinction at Fort Donelson and Shiloh. URK, 449–53.
24. William Minix, a chronic deserter. AGR, 789; *History of 79th Indiana*, 76.
25. AGR, 788.
26. James C. Rush remained the regimental chaplain; I have not identified a "Chaplain Smith."
27. WMW means James M. Simmons, AGR, 798–99.

Chapter 7. To the Other Side of the Tennessee River

1. See Hattaway and Jones, *How the North Won*, 402–4, 446–50; McPherson, *Battle Cry of Freedom*, 668–70; and Peter Cozzens, *This Terrible Sound: The Battle of Chickamauga* (Urbana: Univ. of Illinois Press, 1992), 1–120.
2. Van Cleve's division remained behind temporarily to garrison Murfreesboro. Van Horne, 1:304.
3. Possibly Pan Handle Creek. OR, ser. 1, vol. 23, pt. 2, pp. 470, 473.
4. Lee already had crushed Hooker at Chancellorsville. In fact, on July 1, the Battle of Gettysburg had begun.
5. Mounted sentries. Faust, 785.
6. The McClellan rumor was false. George Meade had succeeded Hooker on June 28. Boatner, 333, 524.
7. Hill actually had been wounded slightly at Chancellorsville. Longstreet was not injured. Boatner, 400, 490.
8. This was Brig. Gen. John Hunt Morgan's Ohio raid of July 2–26, 1863. Morgan and his men slipped out of Tennessee, rode across Kentucky, and crossed the Ohio River on July 7. The Confederates galloped across sections of Indiana and Ohio before the last of them were trapped at New Lisbon, Ohio, on July 26. Gens. Henry M. Judah, Edward H. Hobson, and James M. Shackelford pursued Morgan during

the raid, and Hobson made the capture. Boatner, 403, 446, 566, 558–89, 734.

9. The only reference to this in the OR (ser. 1, vol. 23, pt. 2, p. 601) is a message from Rosecrans mentioning a cavalry attack against "the rebel advance" at Sparta on Aug. 8.

10. URK, 500.

11. Rosecrans created Brig. Gen. Gordon Granger's Reserve Corps on July 8. Faust, 182.

12. *History of 79th Indiana*, 24.

13. Walden's Ridge.

14. Gen. Palmer's escort. Cozzens, *This Terrible Sound*, 82.

15. OR, ser. 1, vol. 30, pt. 1, p. 844.

16. Nickajack Cave had been a popular tourist attraction since it was first explored in 1818. Adiel Sherwood, *A Gazetteer of Georgia, Containing a Particular Description of the State; Its Resources, Counties, Towns, Villages and Whatever Is Usual in Statistical Work*, 4th ed. (Macon, Ga.: S. Boykin, 1860), 56–57.

17. This Nashville and Chattanooga Railroad bridge was 780 feet long and 116 feet high above the river.

18. Built just before the war, the Lookout Mountain House was a hotel located on the east bluff of Lookout Mountain, at the end of the Whiteside Turnpike and near the Point. John Wilson, *Scenic Historic Lookout Mountain*, 2d ed. (Chattanooga, Tenn.: Chattanooga News–Free Press, 1977), 58–60, 75–76, 78.

19. Wood's division, which occupied the city around noon. Van Horne, 1:318.

20. WMW's footnote: "I was forcibly struck with the force of this remark when it occurred to my memory within 12 days from this time."

21. WMW's father in fact recovered and lived until 1891. Untitled Woodcock genealogy, WC.

22. WMW means the 1st Kentucky, which had led Charles Cruft's 1st Brigade, 2nd Division, to Pea Vine Ridge until overwhelmed by Rebel cavalry. Van Horne, 1:321; Cozzens, *This Terrible Sound*, 82.

23. John T. Wilder, who earlier had surrendered Munfordville, Ky., now commanded the 1st Brigade, 4th Division, XIV Corps (the "Lightning Brigade"). Col. Robert H. G. Minty's 1st Brigade, 2nd Division, Cavalry Corps, also was present. Van Horne, 1:325; Cozzens, *This Terrible Sound*, 539, 543–44.

24. Col. Charles G. Harker's 3rd Brigade of Wood's division had skirmished with Confederate cavalry on the evening of Sept. 11. Cozzens, *This Terrible Sound*, 76–77.

25. WMW did not know the half of it. Van Cleve's reconnaissance toward Lafayette, notable for its aggressiveness, convinced Confederate General Polk that Crittenden's force was much stronger than previously

believed. Thus Polk refused to attack the isolated Federal corps, as he had been ordered to do by Bragg. Van Horne, 1:325; Cozzens, *This Terrible Sound*, 81–85.

26. Rosecrans had ordered a concentration of his scattered army along the vital roads to Chattanooga. Van Horne, 1:327.

27. Directly opposite the Gordon-Lee House, this was the most important source of fresh water in the area. Cozzens, *This Terrible Sound*, 92.

28. Bragg had ordered a dawn attack against Crittenden, but it never took place, due to the intervention of Federal cavalry. Boatner, 151.

29. URK, 351.

30. Minty's brigade had clashed with Brig. Gen. Bushrod Johnson's division, Buckner's corps, at Reed's Bridge and held out for four hours before falling back. Cozzens, *This Terrible Sound*, 101–14.

31. Johnson assaulted Col. George Dick's 2nd Brigade at 9 P.M. Cozzens, *This Terrible Sound*, 113–14.

32. Thomas's corps. Cozzens, *This Terrible Sound*, 115.

Chapter 8. The Hills and Thick Forests of Chickamauga

1. Hattaway and Jones, *How the North Won*, 450–54; McPherson, *Battle Cry of Freedom*, 671–74; Cozzens, *This Terrible Sound*.

2. Brig. Gen. John M. Brannan's 3rd Division, XIV Corps, had encountered and driven back Nathan Bedford Forrest's cavalry. Cozzens, *This Terrible Sound*, 131.

3. Two Confederate brigades, commanded by Col. Claudius C. Wilson and Brig. Gen. Matthew D. Ector, unsuccessfully attacked Union forces at Jay's Mill. Cozzens, *This Terrible Sound*, 121–38.

4. Maj. Gen. Benjamin F. Cheatham's attack against Palmer's and Richard Johnson's divisions in the Brock Field, east of the Lafayette Road. Cozzens, *This Terrible Sound*, 152–66.

5. Crittenden had ordered Van Cleve to support Palmer. OR, ser. 1, vol. 30, pt. 1, p. 803.

6. WMW's regiment formed on the left of the brigade's second line. The Confederates were Brig. Gen. Henry D. Clayton's brigade of Alabamians, Maj. Gen. Alexander P. Stewart's division. The battery was Capt. William Carnes's Tennessee Battery. OR, ser. 1, vol. 30, pt. 1, pp. 808, 811, 813; Cozzens, *This Terrible Sound*, 179–85, 230–32.

7. Brig. Gen. John C. Brown's brigade, also of Stewart's division. Cozzens, *This Terrible Sound*, 232–35.

8. Stevens (not "Stephens") commanded Battery B, 26th Pennsylvania Light Artillery. OR, ser. 1, vol. 30, pt. 1, pp. 819–21.

9. Dick's brigade held the right. OR, ser. 1, vol. 30, pt. 1, p. 808.

10. Col. Edward King's 2nd Brigade, 4th Division. Cozzens, *This Terrible Sound*, 235–36.

11. Capt. Samuel Harris's 19th Indiana Battery. OR, ser. 1, vol. 30, pt. 1, p. 808.

12. Cram reported: "We fell back across the road where a battery (Fourth U.S. Artillery) had taken a position on a slight rise" (OR, ser. 1, vol. 30, pt. 1, p. 813). This was just west of the La Fayette Road on Brotherton Ridge.

13. Clayton's brigade again, joined by Bushrod Johnson's brigade. Cozzens, *This Terrible Sound*, 250–54.

14. The regiment gave way under fire from the 25th Tennessee Infantry (C.S.A.). Cozzens, *This Terrible Sound*, 253.

15. The western edge of Dyer Field, along the Glenn-Kelly Road. OR, ser. 1, vol. 30, pt. 1, pp. 808, 813, 816.

16. Alexander W. Short. AGR, 791.

17. Maj. Gen. Patrick Cleburne's division attacking the Federal divisions of Johnson and Brig. Gen. Absalom Baird in Winfrey Field. Cozzens, *This Terrible Sound*, 263–79.

18. WMW means Baird's division. Cozzens, *This Terrible Sound*, 136–37, 146–48.

19. WMW is confused. John H. King's 3rd Brigade of Baird's division, composed entirely of regulars, did break, but not in the face of Longstreet's "eastern troops." Cozzens, *This Terrible Sound*, 136–37, 146–48.

20. This was the western slope of the hill located just north of the western end of Dyer Road.

21. Van Cleve reported: "My division took position on the left of the First Division, General Wood, on the eastern slope of Missionary Ridge, and on the west side of the road running from Crawfish Springs to Rossville." OR, ser. 1, vol. 30, pt. 1, p. 803.

22. Only 71 members of the 17th Tennessee were captured on Brotherton Ridge. The others escaped. Cozzens, *This Terrible Sound*, 261.

23. Van Cleve wrote: "With the First and Second Brigades I was ordered to the front and left. . . . The eastern slope of this hill was a clear field, at its foot a strip of timber, beyond which was a large cornfield bordered by timber." The cornfield was Dyer Field. OR, ser. 1, vol. 30, pt. 1, p. 803.

24. At 9:30 A.M., Breckinridge attacked the Federal left in the area of Kelly Field. Cozzens, *This Terrible Sound*, 319–26.

25. Around 10:15 A.M., Rosecrans ordered his reserves to the left. Beatty's brigade initially moved to the rear of Wood. OR, ser. 1, vol. 30, pt. 1, pp. 812, 814; Van Horne, 1:346.

26. The brigade was ordered just to the left to support Brannan in the western part of Poe Field.

27. At 11:10 A.M., the Confederate left wing, under the command of Longstreet, advanced toward the Brotherton House and the fatal breach in the Federal lines. OR, ser. 1, vol. 30, pt. 1, pp. 813, 816; Cozzens, *This Terrible Sound*, 369.

28. Col. John M. Connell's 1st Brigade of Brannan's division. OR, ser. 1, vol. 30, pt. 1, pp. 409, 809; Cozzens, *This Terrible Sound*, 372–73.

29. The 19th Ohio and the 79th Indiana. OR, ser. 1, vol. 30, pt. 1, p. 814.

30. Almost certainly Battery D of the 1st Michigan Light Artillery, assigned to Connell's brigade. Its commander, Capt. Josiah Church, wrote: "My caissons had already been taken away by Sergt. S. S. Lawrence." OR, ser. 1, vol. 30, pt. 1, pp. 414, 809; Van Horne, 1:347, 1:381.

31. Lt. Philip Reefy. *Official Roster of the State of Ohio in the War of the Rebellion, 1861–1866* (Cincinnati, Ohio: Wilstach, Baldwin, 1886), 2:639.

32. According to Cram, this "rude breastwork of logs," located south of the Poe House, had been "thrown up during the night by General Davis' division." In fact, it had been constructed that morning by the 17th Ohio Infantry of Connell's division. OR, ser. 1, vol. 30, pt. 1, pp. 409, 413, 814; Cozzens, *This Terrible Sound*, 345.

33. Apparently Battery C, 1st Ohio Light Artillery. Cozzens, *This Terrible Sound*, 374.

34. Apparently Lumsden's Alabama Battery.

35. They in fact escaped. Cozzens, *This Terrible Sound*, 374.

36. Battery M, 1st Ohio Light Artillery, on the extension of Horseshoe Ridge where the South Carolina Monument now stands. The attackers were Brig. Gen. Jerome B. Robertson's Texas Brigade of Longstreet's corps. Cozzens, *This Terrible Sound*, 407–9.

37. Brannan and Harker's brigades. Brannan reported: "Finding that this . . . point was the key . . . I made every preparation to defend it to the last, my command being somewhat increased by the arrival of Palmer's [Van Cleve's?] and Negley's Divisions, and most opportunely re-enforced by Colonel Ferdinand Van Derveer's brigade." OR, ser. 1, vol. 30, pt. 1, p. 402.

38. Joseph Kershaw's brigade of South Carolinians, incredibly outfitted *en route* in dark blue shell jackets and light blue trousers. Cozzens, *This Terrible Sound*, 407, 411–12, 424–25.

39. Although both Harker and Wood admitted being fooled by the Confederates' blue uniforms, no lieutenant colonel made a similar admission in after-action reports. WMW may well mean Harker. OR, ser. 1, vol. 30, pt. 1, pp. 637, 664–65, 694–95, 700–01.

40. This "blue flag" is a mystery, as these Army of Northern Virginia veterans would not have been carrying the blue Hardee flags common in

the Army of Tennessee. Indeed, Lt. Col. James T. Embree of the 58th Indiana reported that the blue-clad Rebels carried "dark-red flags," presumably the Confederate battle flag. WMW may have confused this with subsequent assaults carried out by units carrying Hardee flags, or perhaps the 54th or 63rd Virginia regiments, which carried the Virginia state flag. OR, ser. 1, vol. 30, pt. 1, p. 664.

41. OR, ser. 1, vol. 30, pt. 1, p. 810.
42. Brig. Gen. James Blair Steedman commanded the 1st Division of Granger's Reserve Corps. He despised the common misspelling of his name used by WMW. Boatner, 794.
43. WMW apparently attached himself to Brig. Gen. Walter C. Whitaker's 2nd Brigade just before it attacked Brig. Gen. Patton Anderson's brigade of Mississippians. Cozzens, *This Terrible Sound*, 444–46.
44. Kershaw launched a counterattack to cover Anderson's retreat. Cozzens, *This Terrible Sound*, 446.
45. Apparently Garrity's Alabama Battery. Cozzens, *This Terrible Sound*, 445.
46. The Mullis-Vittoe Road.
47. The McFarland Gap Road was the main escape route to Chattanooga. Cozzens, *This Terrible Sound*, 403, 424, 466.
48. AGR, 795.
49. The remnants of Beatty's brigade rallied on Snodgrass Hill just to the west of the house and actually not far from WMW.
50. *History of 79th Indiana*, 1.
51. Thomas was at Rossville Gap. Faust, 137.
52. Maj. Gen. Ambrose Burnside commanded the Army of the Ohio in East Tennessee. Boatner, 107.

Chapter 9. The Storming of Mission Ridge Was a Fearful Undertaking

1. McPherson, *Battle Cry of Freedom*, 674–81; James Lee McDonough, *Chattanooga: A Death Grip on the Confederacy* (Knoxville: Univ. of Tennessee Press, 1984). Peter Cozzens, *The Shipwreck of Their Hopes: The Battles for Chattanooga* (Urbana: Univ. of Illinois Press, 1994), appeared just as this volume was completed.
2. George W. Butram, Elijah D. Dixon, and Alexander W. Short. Short was a member of WMW's company. AGR, 791, 799, 803.
3. The YMCA organized the U.S. Christian Commission in 1861 to provide aid and relief to soldiers. Christian Commission agents furnished reading material, writing paper, and food. Faust, 140.
4. WMW means 30-pounder Parrott guns. *History of 79th Indiana*, 95.

5. Hooker's men actually started arriving on Sept. 30. Boatner, 142.
6. The Reserve Corps actually was attached to the XIV Corps. Van Horne, 1:395.
7. Boatner, 189–90, 195, 239, 390–91, 929–30.
8. Rosecrans relieved Crittenden after Chickamauga. The latter demanded a court of inquiry, which acquitted him. He then served briefly in Virginia and resigned. Faust, 192–93.
9. The rumor was true. Boatner, 526–27.
10. Warner, *Generals in Blue*, 522, implies that Van Cleve was relieved because of his division's collapse at Chickamauga.
11. Formerly an Ohio congressman, Vallandigham was the best known northern Copperhead. He ran for governor despite Lincoln's order exiling him from the United States, but lost by a two-to-one margin. Faust, 775.
12. WMW crossed out "this evening."
13. Having quietly floated downstream past Confederate defenses during the night, 1,500 hand-picked men from Hazen's brigade established a foothold at Brown's Ferry, where they were joined by the remainder of their brigade as well as Willich's. They then threw up a pontoon bridge across the river. Hooker meanwhile moved from Bridgeport, Ala., to join them. Van Horne, 1:395–98.
14. Longstreet attacked Brig. Gen. John W. Geary's division but failed to dislodge it. Van Horne, 1:398–401.
15. The shelling killed only a few and did little damage. Fairfax Downey, *Storming of the Gateway: Chattanooga, 1863* (New York: David McKay, 1960), 148–49.
16. Citico Creek. *History of 79th Indiana*, 101.
17. "Ordered to stand firm and aim low. Not a man to leave rank to care for the wounded. If any man left rank to be considered a deserter in front of the enemy and treated as such." *History of 79th Indiana*, 101.
18. Grant had planned to launch the attack on the 21st, but Sherman could not get into position in time. The continuing rain then forced Grant to delay again. McDonough, *Chattanooga*, 109.
19. Sherman had arrived in Bridgeport on Nov. 15 and at Browns Ferry on Nov. 20. Bragg had ordered Longstreet to East Tennessee on Nov. 4. Boatner, 142–44, 466–68.
20. In order to deceive the Confederates, the men had dressed in full uniform, as if participating in a formal review of troops. Curious Johnny Rebs even emerged from their rifle pits to watch the show. Faust, 547.
21. The 42nd Alabama Infantry. OR, ser. 1, vol. 31, pt. 2, p. 266.
22. Grant had ordered Sheridan's and Wood's divisions forward toward Orchard Knob as a reconnaissance-in-force. Beatty's brigade was to support Willich. Beatty first ordered the 9th Kentucky to the reserve station to support the 19th Ohio. As Cram reported, the regiment

then deployed as skirmishers "and moved by the right flank across the Western and Atlantic Railroad and some 200 yards, then forward toward the East Tennessee railroad. . . . I now received an order from General Beatty to move along the road to the right about 200 yards to a house, cross the road, and advance into the woods with the skirmish line." OR, ser. 1, vol. 31, pt. 2, pp. 300, 308; Boatner, 144.

23. Three Robinsons were members of the company; I was unable to identify the wounded man. Wood's casualties totaled 125. AGR, 793–94; Van Horne, 1:415.

24. The *Dunbar* had been used to ferry troops across the river. McDonough, *Chattanooga*, 120.

25. Sherman had moved forward the day before, only to discover that Tunnel Hill, his target, actually was not part of Missionary Ridge. He launched his attack against the Confederate right at 11 A.M. the following morning, without success. It is noteworthy that WMW was looking east instead of toward Lookout Mountain and the 8th Kentucky's celebrated planting of the Stars and Stripes, an event he does not mention. Faust, 499.

26. Baird commanded the 3rd Division, XIV Corps. Boatner, 38–39, 146.

27. Again, the 9th Kentucky was deployed as skirmishers on the front left of the brigade, "covering a front of nearly half a mile to the left of [Beatty's] immediate front." This placed the unit next to Baird's division and 800 yards from the Rebel works. OR, ser. 1, vol. 31, pt. 2, pp. 301, 303, 308.

28. Patton Anderson's brigade, commanded that day by Col. William F. Tucker. McDonough, *Chattanooga*, 170, 174, 194, 270.

29. Apparently the 22nd Alabama Infantry. OR, ser. 1, vol. 31, pt. 2, pp. 308–9.

30. Simmons commanded Co. G. AGR, 798.

31. Actually Capt. John L. Watson of the 59th Ohio. OR, ser. 1, vol. 31, pt. 2, pp. 268, 302–3.

32. Apparently elements of Cheatham's division. McDonough, *Chattanooga*, 207–8.

33. Casualties were never broken down on a day-by-day basis. The Confederates lost 6,667 men (14% of effectives) over the three days, compared to 5,824 Federals (10%). Boatner, 147.

34. William T. Spann of Co. F. AGR, 798.

35. AGR, 794.

36. Pope served in Co. C. AGR, 791.

Chapter 10. The Famous City of Knoxville

1. Van Horne, 2:1–4, 2:13, 2:15, 2:22–26; Castel, *Decision in the West*, 1–120.

2. Brig. Gen. Jefferson C. Davis's 2nd Division, XIV Corps, attacked Bragg's rear guard at Chickamauga Station. OR, ser. 1, vol. 31, pt. 2, pp. 490–93.

3. On Nov. 29, Longstreet assaulted Fort Sanders, a salient in the city's fieldworks, and was repulsed. When he learned that Sherman and Granger were approaching, Longstreet raised the siege and moved deeper into East Tennessee, taking up winter quarters at Bull's Gap, near Greenville. Van Horne, 2:3; Boatner, 468.

4. WMW's footnote: "They were sent back to Little River to guard a mill."

5. The Veteran Volunteer Act encouraged men to re-enlist by providing a distinctive insignia, a bounty, a month-long furlough, and free transportation home. Units with a 75% majority of veterans could maintain their organization. The men of 88 infantry regiments in the Army of the Cumberland did enlist as veterans, but only 106 of the 9th Kentucky's 417 eligible soldiers chose to re-up. Most ended up in the 23rd Kentucky Veteran Volunteer Infantry or the Veteran Reserve Corps. Van Horne, 2:28–30; McPherson, *Battle Cry of Freedom*, 719–20; *Journal Junior* 1 (Mar. 1992): 7–10.

6. WMW actually received his leave on the 4th; WC.

7. These men served in Cos. D and K respectively. AGR, 793, 803.

8. On Dec. 28, 1863, Wheeler and 1,500 cavalrymen attacked a supply train commanded by Col. Bernard Laiboldt of the 2nd Missouri Infantry. As it turned out, the train was defended by 3,000 Federals, most of whom were convalescents or men returning from furloughs. The defenders drove off Wheeler's horsemen and captured 132 of them. In contrast, the Federals suffered only 15 casualties. OR, ser. 1, vol. 31, pt. 1, pp. 642–44.

9. WMW identifies this officer in his Journal, no. 5, 1st ser., as "Lt. Erdman." Adolphus Erdman was quartermaster of the 15th Missouri, according to *Annual Report of the Adjutant General of Missouri For the Year Ending Dec. 31, 1865* (Jefferson City, Mo.: Emory S. Foster, 1866), 162.

10. Possibly Lt. Henry M. Miller, assistant commissary of musters on Maj. Gen. Edward McCook's staff. OR, ser. 1, vol. 31, pt. 1, p. 656.

11. Lt. Norman R. Christie, Co. A, 3rd Kentucky. URK, 206.

12. Boatner, 665.

13. URK, 497.

14. Manuscript Census, Kentucky, Allen County, Schedule I, 1860, NA.

15. The leave was extended on Jan. 30, Feb. 19, and Mar. 10, 1864; WC.

16. Cram returned to the regiment late in Apr. *Journal Junior* 2 (Fall-Winter 1993): 3.

17. The 9th Kentucky had served as provost guards in Maryville, Tenn., in Jan. and Feb. *History of 79th Indiana*, 118–19.

18. WMW means the 1st and 2nd Divisions, commanded by Maj. Gen. David S. Stanley and Brig. Gen. John Newton, respectively. Boatner, 593, 791.

19. AGR, 796.

20. By "Nelson," WMW means John Newton. Sherman intended this reorganization both to reduce dissension within his command and to get rid of, or at least subordinate, troublesome personalities such as Hooker and Granger. He also hoped to replace Palmer with Buell but failed to accomplish that. Boatner, 593; Castel, *Decision in the West*, 94–98.

21. Each man fired three rounds. *History of 79th Indiana*, 129.

22. At this point in time, George B. McClellan already had emerged as the leading Democratic contender. Meanwhile, many Radical Republicans, unhappy with Lincoln, were floating trial balloons for Salmon P. Chase and John C. Frémont. McPherson, *Battle Cry of Freedom*, 713–17, 771–73.

Chapter 11. Our Destination Was Atlanta

1. In addition to McPherson, *Battle Cry of Freedom*, 718–22, 743–50, I consulted Castel's excellent *Decision in the West*, esp. 90–254, throughout the chapter.

2. The Confederate Army of Tennessee had occupied Dalton since the fall of Chattanooga. Castel, *Decision in the West*, 30, 47.

3. "*Catoosa Springs* are some 2 mi. N of Ringold . . . the buildings are elegant, the mountain scenery . . . is the most romantic and delightful. About 50 springs are in this valley, all of a mineral character." Sherwood, *Gazetteer of Georgia*, 170.

4. Palmer's XIV Corps had driven the Confederates from Tunnel Hill and pushed them back to Buzzard's Roost, also known as Mill Creek Gap. Boatner, 705.

5. Johnston's army had made Rocky Face Ridge an imposing barrier to Sherman's advance, "a terrible door of death" as the latter referred to it. Refusing to play Johnston's game and attack the formidable positions head on, Sherman sent Maj. Gen. James B. McPherson's Army of the Tennessee to the right and toward Snake Creek Gap, from which it could flank the Confederates and cut Johnston's supply line at Resaca. Thomas, as well as Maj. Gen. John M. Schofield's Army of the Ohio, would demonstrate against Johnston's front in order to divert him. Van Horne, 2:47; Castel, *Decision in the West*, 90–91, 98, 121–29.

6. Lt. Col. Chesley D. Bailey of the 9th Kentucky. AGR, 786–87; OR, ser. 1, vol. 38, pt. 1, pp. 458–61.

7. OR, ser. 1, vol. 38, pt. 1, pp. 445, 459.
8. The Army of the Cumberland's mission was to feint against the ridge during the day, while McPherson passed through Snake Creek Gap. Van Horne, 2:49.
9. Van Horne, 2:48–49.
10. AGR, 793. Many Confederate sharpshooters atop Rocky Face were equipped with Whitworth or Kerr rifles, the former with a range of 1.5 miles. Castel, *Decision in the West*, 109; Faust, 823.
11. Rhoten died on June 23. AGR, 799.
12. On the morning of May 10, Sherman learned that McPherson had failed to destroy the railroad at Resaca. Sherman then determined to push most of the Army of the Cumberland through Snake Creek Gap, but left Howard's IV Corps to continue putting pressure on Buzzard's Roost. Castel, *Decision in the West*, 142–46.
13. George Stoneman commanded the Cavalry Division of the Army of the Ohio. Boatner, 801.
14. It is interesting that WMW fails to note a fascinating encounter while on picket. William Hutsinger of the 79th Indiana wrote: "Regiment relieved at 8 P.M. by the 9th Kentucky. The rebels asked 'What regiment is that down there?' Our men answered 'The 9th Kentucky.' 'You lie,' said the rebs, 'the 9th Kentucky is up here.' One 9th Kentucky asked the rebs, 'Is Bill So-and-so, Jim So-and-so and Dick So-and-so up there?' 'Yes,' said the rebs. Then they, the rebs, asked about persons they knew also. The two regiments . . . had been raised in the same neighborhood. The conversation was kept up by the two regiments." *History of 79th Indiana*, 133–34.
15. AGR, 798.
16. Alarmed by McPherson's advance, Johnston began falling back to Resaca on May 12. Castel, *Decision in the West*, 147–50.
17. Sherman had ordered Howard to pursue Johnston from Dalton. The rumors WMW reports were more accurate than the opinions of his commanders; all, including Sherman, expected that Johnston would continue falling back across the Oostanaula River instead of making a stand north of the river at Resaca. Castel, *Decision in the West*, 147, 151.
18. The Cumberlanders came up to relieve Maj. Gen. Jacob D. Cox's division of the XXIII Corps, one of the four lead divisions in the failed assault. Castel, *Decision in the West*, 161.
19. WMW is wrong. Brig. Gen. Hugh Judson Kilpatrick had been wounded the previous day. Brig. Gen. John W. Geary was not injured. Boatner, 327–28, 459–60.
20. WMW refers to John B. Hood's late-afternoon attack on Stanley's division, repelled with the help of Hooker. Castel, *Decision in the West*, 163–66.
21. Most of the IV Corps attacked Maj. Gen. Thomas C. Hindman's divi-

sion of Hood's corps around 1 P.M. but were quickly thrown back. Castel, *Decision in the West*, 170–75.

22. Willich was German; WMW refers to his celebrated misuse of his second language. Willich had been wounded in the arm and side. Boatner, 929–30; Castel, *Decision in the West*, 173.

23. WMW refers to Geary's capture of Capt. Max Van Den Corput's "Cherokee Battery." Castel, *Decision in the West*, 174–75, 179–80.

24. Again flanked by McPherson, Johnston fell back after midnight, first to Calhoun and then Cassville. WMW sarcastically refers to the well-known southern boast of "fighting to the last ditch." McPherson, *Battle Cry of Freedom*, 745.

25. Artillerymen. Faust, 772.

26. WMW neglects to mention that Harker's men had a footbridge built on what was left of the railroad bridge by early afternoon. By evening, a pontoon bridge spanned the river as well. Castel, *Decision in the West*, 190.

27. WMW refers to skirmishing with Wheeler's cavalry, the latter acting as rear guard. Castel, *Decision in the West*, 190.

28. WMW apparently refers to Oothcaloga Creek. Burton J. Bell, ed., *Bicentennial History of Gordon County, Georgia* (Calhoun, Ga.: Gordon County Historical Society, 1976), 262.

29. I am grateful to Albert Castel for confirming that the 2nd Division was involved in this incident.

30. AGR, 789.

31. Bridges's battery, Illinois Light Artillery, was commanded by Lt. Lyman A. White and attached to Wood's division. OR, ser. 1, vol. 31, pt. 3, p. 551.

32. The Confederates were Johnston's rear guard, consisting of Wheeler's cavalry plus artillery and, at times, infantry. Van Horne, 2:71–72.

33. WMW apparently refers to Grant's move south after the fighting in the Wilderness. Boatner, 919–23.

34. Johnston wanted the Federals to think this, but in fact only Hardee's corps was there. Polk's and Hood's corps actually were on the Cassville Road, hoping that Sherman would divide his army and provide Johnston with an opportunity to destroy an isolated corps. Castel, *Decision in the West*, 194–98.

35. The boy was confused. The county originally was named for prominent Michigan Democrat Lewis Cass. After Cass expressed his support for the Union in 1861, the legislature renamed the county in honor of Col. Francis S. Bartow, a Georgian killed at the First Battle of Manassas. Lucy Josephine Cunyus, *The History of Bartow County, Formerly Cass* (Easley, S.C.: Georgia Genealogical Reprints, n.d.), 33–34.

36. Fort Pillow, Tenn., fell on Apr. 12, 1864, to Confederates under the command of Nathan Bedford Forrest. The North charged that

Forrest's men shot, burned, and even buried alive Federal prisoners. At least one captured Confederate was killed at Resaca for having "Fort Pillow" either tattooed on his arm or embroidered on his sleeve. Faust, 277–78.

37. Stanley's division led Howard's advance toward Cassville when it encountered elements of Hardee's corps. The Confederates had been ordered to demonstrate against Howard in order to buy time for Johnston's retreat to a position south of Cassville, a retreat occasioned by the failure of Johnston's trap north of town. After significant Confederate opposition developed, Wood moved up to support Stanley. Van Horne, 2:72–73; Castel, *Decision in the West*, 202–3.

38. WMW means Hooker's XX Corps. Van Horne, 2:72.

39. Johnston had fallen back south of the Etowah River to Allatoona Pass, a strong defensive position. Unwilling to attack head on, Sherman determined to rest his men for three days and then flank to the right, hoping either to turn the position or cut Confederate communications at Marietta. Van Horne, 2:74.

40. WMW was unaware that Dallas, Ga., was his army's goal. Van Horne, 2:74.

41. WMW describes the Battle of New Hope Church, which actually began at 5 P.M. The IV Corps moved up to support Hooker's left. Van Horne, 2:75–77; Castel, *Decision in the West*, 221–26.

42. WMW refers to Johnson's 1st Division. Boatner, 438.

43. Sherman had ordered Howard to move Wood's division to the far left and launch an attack on Johnston's right. Confused by the terrain, Howard faltered. Instead of flanking the Confederates, he stumbled into Pat Cleburne's strong position near Pickett's Mill, two miles from New Hope Church. He then ordered in Wood's division in column of brigades—Hazen first, then William H. Gibson, and finally Knefler. Hazen and esp. Gibson were mauled. Van Horne, 2:78–80; Castel, *Decision in the West*, 229–35.

44. No other authority places Sherman at the scene. WMW may mean Thomas, who was with the column earlier in the day. Van Horne, 2:78; Castel, *Decision in the West*, 229–30, 235, 239.

45. Howard had just received orders from Sherman calling off the attack. Thus Knefler went in largely to hold the position while the dead and wounded were carried out and a defensive line was established to the rear. Castel, *Decision in the West*, 239–40.

46. WMW expanded upon his wounding in WMW, *1911 Reminiscence*: "I . . . and 1st Lieut. Hestand were standing (like fools) close up to the company and watching and commenting upon the individual characteristics of the boys—when a spent ball struck me" (18–19).

47. Around 10 P.M., Brig. Gen. Hiram B. Granbury's night attack drove Knefler from the ravine. Castel, *Decision in the West*, 240–41.

48. Five members of the regiment died: William B. Carver (Co. A), Richard Freeman (Co. A), James F. Mayhew (Co. I), Alexander T. Pipkin (Co. I), and Andrew J. Star (Co. E). Knefler's brigade suffered 250 casualties, and Wood's entire division lost a total of 1,600 men, according to Castel, *Decision in the West*, 241.
49. WMW refers to the Battle of Dallas. Maj. Gen. William B. Bate's division attacked part of the Army of the Tennessee but was repulsed. Castel, *Decision in the West*, 243–47.
50. WMW means Gilbert H. Wakefield. AGR, 790.
51. No such regiment existed. WMW apparently means the 2nd Alabama Infantry, later the 110th Regiment U.S. Colored Troops. Dyer, *Compendium*, 3:997, 3:1739.

Epilogue

1. This and subsequent paragraphs are based on WMW, Journals, nos. 7 and 8, 1st ser., WC, as well as Castel, *Decision in the West*, 467–553.

Bibliography

Primary Sources

Books

Annual Report of the Adjutant General of Missouri for the Year Ending December 31, 1865. Jefferson City, Mo.: Emory S. Foster, 1866.

Dyer, Frederick. *A Compilation of the War of the Rebellion.* 3 vols. Des Moines, Iowa: Dyer, 1908. Reprint, New York: Thomas Yoseloff, 1959.

History of the Seventy-Ninth Regiment, Indiana Volunteer Infantry, in the Civil War of Eighteen Sixty-One in the United States. Indianapolis, Ind.: Hollenbeck, 1899.

Official Roster of the State of Ohio in the War of Rebellion, 1861–1866. 12 vols. Cincinnati, Ohio: Wilstach, Baldwin, 1886.

Report of the Adjutant General of the State of Kentucky. 2 vols. Frankfort, Ky.: John H. Harney, 1866.

Sherwood, Adiel. *A Gazetteer of Georgia, Containing a Particular Description of the State; Its Resources, Counties, Towns, Villages and Whatever Is Usual in Statistical Work.* 4th ed. Macon, Ga.: S. Boykin, 1860.

Speed, Thomas. *The Union Regiments of Kentucky, Published Under the Auspices of the Union Soldiers and Sailors Monument Association.* Louisville, Ky.: Courier-Journal, 1897.

Van Horne, Thomas B. *History of the Army of the Cumberland, Its Organizations, Campaigns, and Battles.* 2 vols. Cincinnati, Ohio: Ogden, Campbell, 1875.

The War of the Rebellion: A Compilation of the Official Records of the Union and Confederate Armies. 70 vols. Washington, D.C.: Government Printing Office, 1880–1901.

Interviews

Teschan, Martha. Interviews by Kenneth W. Noe. Notes, May 15, 1993, Mar. 26, 1994. Monteagle and Nashville, Tenn. Collection of Kenneth W. Noe, Carrollton, Ga.

Thomas, Betty Margaret. Interview by Kenneth W. Noe. Notes, May 15, 1993. Monteagle, Tenn. Collection of Kenneth W. Noe, Carrollton, Ga.

Woodcock, Wilson Wiley, Jr. Interview by Kenneth W. Noe. Notes, May 15, 1993.
    Monteagle, Tenn. Collection of Kenneth W. Noe, Carrollton, Ga.

Manuscript Collections

9th Kentucky Infantry, Combined Service Records. Record Group 94. National Ar-
    chives and Records Administration, Washington, D.C.
The Eldress Nancy. Diary. Kentucky Library, Western Kentucky University, Bowling
    Green, Ky.
Manuscript Censuses, Kentucky. Adair, Barren, Hart, and Metcalf Counties. Sched-
    ules I and II, 1850, 1860, 1900, 1910. National Archives and Records Admin-
    istration, Washington, D.C.
Manuscript Censuses, Tennessee. Davidson and Macon Counties. Schedules I and
    II, 1850, 1860, 1900, 1910. National Archives and Records Administration,
    Washington, D.C.
U.S. Army, 9th Kentucky Volunteer Infantry. Quartermaster Files. Kentucky Depart-
    ment of Military Affairs, Frankfort, Ky.
Woodcock, William Marcus. Collection. In Possession of Martha Teschan, Nash-
    ville, Tenn.

Periodicals

Baptist and Reflector (Nashville), 1914.
Journal Junior (Brentwood, Tenn.), 1992–94.
Knoxville (Tenn.) Whig, 1865–68.
Missionary Messenger (Nashville), 1910.

Secondary Sources

Adams, George Worthington. *Doctors in Blue: The Medical History of the Union Army
    in the Civil War.* New York: Henry Schuman, 1952.
Alexander, Thomas B. *Political Reconstruction in Tennessee.* Nashville, Tenn.:
    Vanderbilt University Press, 1950.
Andrews, J. Cutler. *The North Reports the Civil War.* Pittsburgh, Pa.: University of
    Pittsburgh Press, 1955.
Ash, Stephen V. *Middle Tennessee Society Transformed, 1860–1870: War and Peace in
    the Upper South.* Baton Rouge: Louisiana State University Press, 1988.
Bell, Burton J. *Bicentennial History of Gordon County, Georgia.* Calhoun, Ga.: Gordon
    County Historical Society, 1976.
Blankenship, Harold G. *History of Macon County, Tennessee.* Tompkinsville, Ky.:
    Monroe County Press, 1986.
Boatner, Mark M., III. *The Civil War Dictionary.* Rev. ed. New York: Vintage, 1991.
Brewer, James H. *The Confederate Negro: Virginia's Craftsmen and Military Laborers,
    1861–1865.* Durham, N.C.: Duke University Press, 1969.
Campbell, Mary Emily Robertson. *The Attitude of Tennesseeans Toward the Union,
    1847–1861.* New York: Vantage, 1961.
Castel, Albert. *Decision in the West: The Atlanta Campaign of 1864.* Lawrence: Univer-
    sity Press of Kansas, 1992.
Coggins, Jack. *Arms and Equipment of the Civil War.* New York: Fairfax, 1983.

Corlew, Robert E. *Tennessee: A Short History*. 2d ed. Knoxville: University of Tennessee Press, 1990.

Coulter, E. Merton. *The Civil War and Readjustment in Kentucky*. Chapel Hill: University of North Carolina Press, 1926.

Cozzens, Peter. *No Better Place to Die: The Battle of Stones River*. Urbana: University of Illinois Press, 1990.

————. *The Shipwreck of Their Hopes: The Battles for Chattanooga*. Urbana: University of Illinois Press, 1994.

————. *This Terrible Sound: The Battle of Chickamauga*. Urbana: University of Illinois Press, 1992.

Cunyus, Lucy Josephine. *The History of Bartow County, Formerly Cass*. Easley, S.C.: Georgia Genealogical Reprints, n.d.

Current, Richard Nelson. *Lincoln's Loyalists: Union Soldiers from the Confederacy*. Boston: Northeastern University Press, 1992.

Davis, William C. *The Orphan Brigade: The Kentucky Confederates Who Couldn't Go Home*. Baton Rouge: Louisiana State University Press, 1980.

Downey, Fairfax. *Storming of the Gateway: Chattanooga, 1863*. New York: David McKay, 1960.

Faust, Patricia L., ed. *Historical Times Illustrated Encyclopedia of the Civil War*. New York: Harper and Row, 1986.

Fertig, James Walter. *The Secession and Reconstruction of Tennessee*. Chicago: University of Chicago Press, 1898.

Gallagher, Gary W., ed. *Fighting for the Confederacy: The Personal Recollections of General Edward Porter Alexander*. Chapel Hill: University of North Carolina Press, 1989.

Gray's Manual of Botany. New York: Van Nostrand, 1970.

Harrison, Lowell H. *The Civil War in Kentucky*. Lexington: University Press of Kentucky, 1975.

Hattaway, Herman, and Archer Jones. *How the North Won: A Military History of the Civil War*. Urbana: University of Illinois Press, 1983.

Hessler, Gene. *The Comprehensive Catalog of U.S. Paper Money*. Chicago: Henry Regnery, 1977.

Kleber, John E., ed. *The Kentucky Encyclopedia*. Lexington: University Press of Kentucky, 1992.

Linderman, Gerald F. *Embattled Courage: The Experience of Combat in the American Civil War*. New York: Free Press, 1987.

McConnell, Stuart. *Glorious Contentment: The Grand Army of the Republic, 1865–1900*. Chapel Hill: University of North Carolina Press, 1992.

McDonough, James L. *Chattanooga: A Death Grip on the Confederacy*. Knoxville: University of Tennessee Press, 1984.

————. *Stones River—Bloody Winter in Tennessee*. Knoxville: University of Tennessee Press, 1980.

————. *War in Kentucky: From Shiloh to Perryville*. Knoxville: University of Tennessee Press, 1994.

McKinney, Francis F. *Education in Violence: The Life of George H. Thomas and the History of the Army of the Cumberland*. Detroit, Mich.: Wayne State University Press, 1961.

McPherson, James M. *Battle Cry of Freedom: The Civil War Era*. New York: Oxford University Press, 1988.

Montell, William Lynwood. *Monroe County History, 1820–1970.* Tompkinsville, Ky.: Tompkinsville Lions Club, 1970.

Tennesseans in the Civil War: A Military History of Confederate and Union Units with the Available Rosters of Personnel. 2 pts. Nashville: Civil War Centennial Commission, 1964.

Warner, Ezra J. *Generals in Blue: Lives of Union Commanders.* Baton Rouge: Louisiana State University Press, 1964.

Wilson, John. *Scenic Historic Lookout Mountain.* 2d ed. Chattanooga, Tenn.: Chattanooga News–Free Press, 1977.

Index

Southern boy in blue :